2016

China Grain Market
Development Report

# 中国粮食市场发展报告

李经谋 主编

刘文进 乔林选 副主编

中国财政经济出版社

# 雄关漫道从头越

（代　序）　李经谋

一元复始，万象更新。被誉为“中国世纪元年”的2015年已圆满收官，但围绕中国经济兴衰的论争却有增无已。据国外媒体报道，“在中国问题上的歇斯底里已经到了集体疯狂的地步”，就连金融巨鳄索罗斯也公然看空中国，伺机一雪18年前“香港金融保卫战”的耻辱。然而也有不少有识之士认为“担心中国经济崩溃是杞人忧天”、“中国经济正在成功转型”、“中国将继续成为全球经济增长引擎”。

2015年的确是值得回味的。在我国面临多重困难和严峻挑战的情况下，改革全面发轫，反腐深入进行，足见中国领导踔厉风发、攻坚克难的非凡勇气和一往无前、勇于担当的坚定信念。特别令人欣慰的是，由大众创业、万众创新所激发的新业态、新模式、新动能正在积聚，必将成为中国经济发展的内生动力和全新引擎，予人信心，催人奋进。

然而，步入深水区的中国经济体制改革面临诸多前所未有的新矛盾、新挑战。特别突出的当属粮食阶段性供过于求和粮价多重扭曲所面临的困境，即粮食的高产量、高进口量、高库存量“三量叠加”，粮食价格的产区与销区、原粮与成品粮、国内与国际市场“三价倒挂”，成为当前我国粮食安全可持续发展的新隐患，“我国农业面临千年未有之变局”。那么变局之下，路又在何方？

认真回顾艰难曲折的粮改历程，不难发现，历史总是惊人的相似。1993年国务院《关于加快粮食流通体制改革的通知》提出：“争取在二三年内全部放开粮食价格”，光阴荏苒，24年过去，粮食流通体制改革却在政策彷徨与市场收放间历经了两次轮回，现在又站到了一个关键的节点。

1993年到2003年，保护价收购主导市场。2004年至今，最低收购价收购主导市场。两轮粮改的出发点都是推进粮食市场化，由于种种原因，最终都未能突破价格屏障，或多或少打上了统购的烙印。

无论是保护价收购，抑或是最低收购价收购，在提高农民收益、稳定市场粮价、保障国家粮食安全等方面都曾有明显的成效。但不可否认，两大政策具有与生俱来的缺陷，且边际效应递减，市场机制扭曲，产业陷于困局，财政压力过大等负效应终究显现。实践证明，长期实行政府主导价格的政策，必然颠覆市场形成价格的机制，与市场在资源配置中起决定性作用的理念相悖。

保护价收购阶段，由于客观上顺价难销售，敞开收购因此也打了折扣。“顺价不销售，敞开不收购”透出一些基层企业的消极情绪及政策落地变形。其结果，非但没有完全落实“三项政策”，反而出现一些负面现象，国有粮食购销企业又吃上政策“大锅饭”，金融部门有稳定的利息收入，粮食能否顺价销售出去并没有太多的紧迫感，由此形成了建国以来的第二次、第三次财务挂账，国家财政为此付出巨额成本。

托市价收购阶段，收储企业不再对销售负责，没有经营风险，只要多收购、多储存，就能增加收益。地方政府积极支持，相关部门乐见其成，于是乎，超量收储成常态，有些年份，一些主产省托市收购量超过商品量的60%以上，导致储备粮库存远超正常规模，背离了“托底收购”的政策初衷，阻碍了多元市场主体的发育和产业健康发展。稻强米弱，麦强面弱，加工业开工率不足，利润下降，经营持续低迷，整个行业举步维艰。

大幅度提高临时收储价格和最低收购价造成市场扭曲，有的品种早已供大于求，但政策性收储仍然频频启动，供给侧产能的扩张“涛声依旧”，导致增产的未必是需要的，减产的可能是必需的。

更为严重的是，2011 年以后，国际粮价下跌了 40% ~50%，而国内收储价格却持续提高，加之美元升值、海运价格暴跌，致使国内外粮价差距不断拉大，粮食进口大幅攀升，供求矛盾进一步加剧。财政包袱沉重，明亏与潜亏触目惊心，更有粮食品质陈化劣变的风险。

盘点两轮粮改的得与失不难发现，问题的症结集中在粮价政策上。“价格国家定、资金银行贷、储备财政补、亏损给挂账”，渐致市场主体单一化，政策性职能和经营性职能混淆不清，扭曲了粮食购销市场机制，抑制了市场创新活力及多元主体的经营空间，加之近年来国内外市场深度融合，使得宏观调控的政策效能不断降低。面对粮食特别是粮食供给侧的诸多矛盾，面对全世界最庞大的粮食库存，在经济新常态下，粮改的“硬骨头”再次进入人们的视野。正如一首老歌所唱：“无助的我，已经疏远那份情感，许多年以后才发觉，又回到你面前。”

2016 年中央 1 号文件《关于落实发展新理念 加快农业现代化 实现全面小康目标的若干意见》（以下简称“1 号文件”）用“创新、协调、绿色、开放、共享”的全新理念提出了一系列破解“三农”和粮食难题的新观点、新政策、新举措，是对近年来涉农、涉粮改革的集中表述和“系统升级”。文中首次提出的“供给侧结构性改革”，其核心就是市场和价格问题，即农业生产要符合市场需要，市场形成价格引导农业生产，让市场在资源配置中起决定性作用，这正是“三农”问题的症结所在，可谓一语中的、茅塞顿开。作为一个完整的现代农业发展蓝图，多项有关粮食流通和消费的新政策、新举措引人注目，如“去库存、降成本、补短板”、“改革完善粮食等重要农产品价格形成机制和收储政策”、“强化农产品质量和食品安全责任制”、“健全现代农产品市场体系”、“加快农产品批发市场升级改造”、“支持企业开展多种形式的跨国经营”等，成为今后一个相当长时期内深化粮食体制机制改革的基本指导思想和行动指南。

2016 年是全面建成小康社会决胜阶段的开局之年，也是推进农业结构性改革的攻坚之年。中央 1 号文件解开了“三农”问题积聚多年的绀结，为粮食安全的持续稳定打开了希望之门。进一步更新观念，深化改革，建立与现代农业相适应的粮食流通体系，健全促进粮食供求平衡的长效机制，是粮食经济持续健康发展的要旨和关键。

**重视有效供给，加快农业供给侧结构改革**。“三量叠加”、“三价倒挂”，暴露出我国粮食品种结构失衡、价格竞争力不足两大软肋和短板，破解之道在于把准“市场脉”，打好“调整牌”，做好“加减法”，坚定不移地推进“供给侧结构性改革”，矢志不渝地提高农业供给体系的质量和效率，进而全面提高农业效益和竞争力。

长久以来，我们一直强调粮食增产，短缺经济下的单向思维左右着主流的价值判断。实际上，我们曾经数次有过这样的感受与体验：大幅提高粮价刺激粮食增产，却走进了“多了少了，少了多了”的历史怪圈。增产偏好尚未真正扭转，导致某些品种产大于需，却还在吃政策“偏饭”；某些品种产不足需，却因为产量、比价劣势，无从得到眷顾与垂怜；某些品种产滞于需，因为质量、安全性等方面的“瑕疵”，不得不舍近求远，为进口粮食让出市场空间。这种扭曲的供求关系，很难同“有效供给”相提并论。

“往者已不及，尚可以为来者之戒。”对于粮食经济而言，站在第三次粮改的节点，要认真领会1号文件关于“供给侧结构性改革”的精神实质，深刻反思结构性失衡的深层原因。“粮食产量并非越多越好”，而是要以市场需求为导向，调整种植结构，优化资源配置，“减少无效和低端供给，扩大有效和中高端供给”，摆脱“销不掉”与“买不到”并存的尴尬局面。同时，更加注重农业科技创新、组织创新，大力支持精深加工，延伸产业链条，降低农业成本，提高农业效率，提升粮食的国际价格竞争力。唯有做到生产与需求匹配、质量与效益并重、稳定性与灵活性兼容，粮食生产和流通才会真正走上良性循环的轨道。

去库存、去不良产能成为供给侧改革必须完成的硬任务。不讲成本、不计后果的过度生产，不仅透支资源环境，还会触及生态红线，危及可持续发展。积极稳妥地去边际产能、不健康产能，让超负荷、甚至是带病作业的土地休养生息，既是纾困当下，更是谋划长远。今年国家将适当调减玉米种植面积，制订退耕还林还草方案，探索耕地轮作休耕制度试点。对于玉米等品种的巨量库存，要权衡利弊，适时降价促销，以刺激国内消费需求。

**补短板，强基础，“三藏”并举，厚植发展优势，走内涵式现代农业发展道路**。藏粮于地，确保产能，高标准建设“口粮田”，保住子孙“饭碗田”；藏粮于技，加强农业科技创新与推广，让科技成果落地生根，开花结果；藏粮于民，积极发展多种形式农业适度规模经营，培育扶持新型经营主体，寻觅发现新农人，解农业后继乏人之忧。只要沃土常在，科技先进，农人欢愉，潜在产能就能及时转化为现实的有效供给。

**实行目标价格制度，逐步完善粮食价格形成机制**。粮价改革的基本主导思想是“市场定价、价补分离”，价格形成由市场决定，农民利益由政府保障。目标价格补贴是价格改革的重要选择，即由政府对多种价格因素进行综合考量，确定目标价格，并通过行政手段对受损者进行补贴。目标价格补贴试点两年来，成效较为明显，得到试点区群众的理解和支持。但由于多种原因，如补贴发放操作复杂、成本较高，产量、面积计算较难，基期数据采纳时限尚需研讨等，这些问题还需要在实践中不断完善和提高。

目标价格保险是价格改革的另外一种选择，即由保险公司设计出应对粮食价格风险的保险产品，由生产者与保险公司签订合同，并由保险公司负责定损与理赔，政府给予一定保费补贴。该种方式能够较好地防范虚报面积等投机行为，其多种产品形态可给投保者较大的选择余地，如果能走出“保险+期货”的路子，发展前景将更加广阔。目前已有近20个省市开展试点工作。未来目标价格补贴与目标价格保险或共同构成保障农民基本收益的安全网。

**改革完善粮食收储制度，发展多元化市场购销主体**。国家粮食收储制度改革主要包括粮食购销主体多元化和粮食储备管理体制改革。购销主体多元化虽已实施多年，但由于政策粮的不断扩大，国有收储企业“一业独大”的状况并没有真正改变，随着粮价改革的逐步推进，其状况当会大大改观。政策性职能和经营性职能的分离则是中央储备粮管理体制的一项重大改革，不仅有利于提高储备粮管理水平、消除滋生腐败的温床，更有利于发挥其国家粮食安全保障的功能。“储备粮并非越多越好”，要根据中国国情并参照国际惯例（库存与消费量的比例为17%~18%），科学合理地确定国家粮食储备规模。

**运用互联网思维，刷新营销理念，提振粮食经济**。没有人可以忽视“互联网⁺”的颠覆效应、倍增效应，谁先搭上“互联网⁺”快车，谁就能拓宽生产经营的边界，抢占市场竞争的高点。农业的个性化、品牌化生产，契合民众求新求异、品质优先的消费诉求，“互联网+”更像是为特色农产品量身打造的营销方案。当“互联网+农业品牌”成为主流选择，当独特的产品品质与深蕴的人文气质相融相映，这样的魅力组合怎会不推动农业的华丽蝶变？然而，大宗粮油商品如何进入“互联网俱乐部”，尚需认真探索。

**促进内外市场深度融合，适度进口，加快农业“走出去”步伐**。统筹利用国际国内两个市场、两种资源，实现内外市场的深度融合，是构建开放型经济体制的必然要求，更是需要长期坚持的一项基本政策。适度进口不是权宜之计，作为一个人多、地少、水缺的发展中大国，利用国际市场和国外资源，补充国内市场需求，是大势所趋，也是理性选择。要建立多元、稳定的农产品国际贸易体系，大力支持农产品出口和开展农产品加工、储运、贸易等多种形式的跨国经营。加快农业“走出去”步伐，以改变中国农产品大而不强、多而不优、竞争力薄弱的问题，培育具有国际竞争力的粮商和农业企业集团，赢得国际竞争的主动权。同时，打好国际粮援牌，用好粮食新“调控阀”，挖掘远洋物流运输等附加值。中国已与世界五大洲的多个国家建立了农业投资合作关系，亚非拉广袤的未开垦的处女地正在向中国的粮食人敞开博大的胸怀。

**健全现代粮食市场体系，加快粮食批发市场升级改造**。现代粮食市场体系是社会主义市场经济的重要组成部分，只有借助于统一开放、布局合理、竞争有序的现代粮食市场体系，才能有效地配置粮食资源。我国现代粮食市场体系建设始于20世纪90年代初，二十多年来，由粮食批发市场、粮食期货市场和粮食电子商务所构建的现代粮食市场体系的主体框架已基本形成，其功能和作用也得到初步发挥。然而，分散化的粮食生产和政策性的价格屏障成为现代粮食市场体系建设最大的制约因素。1号文件多条政策举措为健全完善现代农产品市场体系清障除弊，同时也对市场建设提出更高的要求：粮食期货市场要“创设农产品期货品种，开展农产品期权试点”、“稳步扩大‘保险+期货’试点”；农产品批发市场要“加快升级改造”等，这无疑对粮食期货和粮食批发市场是一个利好消息。但由于各级各类粮食批发市场在管理体制、交易机制、品种结构、发展方式等方面均存在较大的不平衡性，如何“升级改造”，尚需根据市场功能定位，认真进行探索。

中国的特殊国情和粮食的准公共物品属性，决定了无论粮食供求关系发生何种变化，粮食安全的战略地位都不会改变。然而，改革开放以来，粮食生产流通经历了数次迂回徘徊。当粮食供不应求时，粮食安全备受关注；粮食阶段性供过于求时，则遭受冷落非议，这是对粮食安全认知失之偏颇的重要表现。在粮食质量和食品安全危机与日俱增的情况下，坚持新时期的国家粮食安全战略，更加不能有丝毫的动摇和懈怠。我们必须明确粮食安全的战略稳定与战术调整之间的区别，诚如国家权威部门负责人所说："现在粮食多了一点，补贴多了一点，仓容紧张了一点，这只是技术性问题，通过深化改革、完善体制机制，能够很好地解决。但是粮食安全却是战略性问题，千万不能因为'十二连增'而在粮食安全问题上掉以轻心。"

在新形势下，我们要秉持"坚守战略、稳中有变、激活市场"的原则，正确处理好短期策略与长期战略、国内生产与国外供给、数量安全与质量安全、总量平衡与结构平衡、价格竞争与价值竞争、政府干预与市场配置、农民增收与粮价改革之间的关系。为了防止顾此失彼，针对我国粮食管理存在的部门分割、职能分散的现状，强化顶层设计，建立权威的、专家型的国家粮食安全委员会和国家粮食宏观调控中心，势在必行。其职能是：协调相关部门的政策，建立权威的监测预警体系，对粮食供求、粮食价格等实施监测和预测，对粮食及食品安全形势进行评估和预警；向国务院提出涉及粮食生产、流通、消费、进出口管控、储备粮调节以及财政、税收、信贷等方面的宏观调控建议，增强重大决策的时效性、准确性和权威性，减少部门间的推诿扯皮。

从当前最紧迫的改革任务来看，政策性收储经年累月，渐成常态，一些问题积重难返，加之行政惯性和部门利益与市场配置资源的矛盾较难调和，为了确保改革顺利推进，客观上也亟须建立超越部门、地方利益的权威机构，以国家的名义，保障粮食安全的长治久安。

对于微观经营层面而言，粮食的一般商品属性应得到尊重和体现。随着粮食去库存与国家粮食收储制度改革的推进，粮食流通将逐步回归市场化收购主导的格局。习惯了执行政策收储任务的粮食企业可能面临业务逐渐萎缩、经营后续乏力的考验与挑战，"收原粮、管原粮、卖原粮"的经营模式将难以为继。农业产加销紧密衔接、一二三产业深度融合，新型农业经营主体、新型农业服务主体、多元化市场购销主体的兴起，跨界跨域整合的快速蜕变，方兴未艾的电子商务风起云涌，均向传统粮食流通体制发起挑战。国有粮食企业必须培育新的经济增长点，开辟新路径，进而优化发展模式，激发内生动力，实现转型升级。

形势逼人，“不革旧无以图新，不变法无以图存”。数十年如一日，朝乾夕惕、克尽厥职、扶困济贫、保障供给，为国家粮食安全和人民生产生活做出重大贡献的粮食人，要与时俱进、革故鼎新、攻坚克难、未雨绸缪，用全新理念引领粮食流通新发展，用深化改革破解粮食工作新难题，用奋力拼搏再造粮食工作新辉煌。

“雄关漫道真如铁，而今迈步从头越。”以一代伟人毛泽东的壮丽诗篇况味本轮粮改的昨天、今天、明天，似乎再妥帖不过。

2016年3月10日

# Fear Not the Strong Pass Iron-clad on All Sides

## ( Preface )

Li Jingmou

Everything is updating as another new year begins. Although the year of 2015, known as "the first year of the China Century", has come to an end satisfactorily, the arguments on rise or fall of China's economy are still on the increase. According to some foreign media reports, "the hysteria on China has come to the point of collective craziness". Even Soros, a famous financial giant, openly expressed his bearish outlook for China's economy, wanting to get rid of his shame during "the Hongkong Financial Defense Battle" 18 years ago. However, many people of insight think that "it makes no sense to worry about possible collapse of China's economy", "China's economy is transforming itself successfully", and "China will continue to be the engine of global economic growth".

The year of 2015 is memorable. In the face of so many difficulties and challenges, China's reforms started in all fields, and anti-corruption activities got underway effectively, clearly reflecting the Chinese leaders' extraordinary courage and firm confidence to make every effort to overcome hardships and difficulties vigorously and responsibly. What is especially exciting is that the new format, the new mode and the new kinetic energy stimulated by popular entrepreneurship and massive innovation, are in accumulation and will become an endogenous driving force and a completely new engine for the development of China's economy. That is really encouraging.

Yet the reforms of China's economic system are now in deep-water zone, facing numerous unprecedented new contradictions and challenges, especially the dilemma of the current periodic excess of grain supply over demand and the multiple distortions of grain prices. The "three-amount overlap" of high production, high import and high reserve, and the "three-price inversion" in grain production areas and sale areas, for raw grain and processed grain, and in domestic markets and international markets, have now become new hidden dangers to the sustainable development of China's food security. "China's agriculture is facing a fast changing situation that has never appeared in the past millennium." In this fast changing situation, what direction should we take?

Looking back at the difficult and tortuous course of China's grain industry reforms, it is easy to find that histories are always amazingly similar. *Notice on Speeding up Reform of the Grain Circulation System* issued by the State Council in 1993 pointed out: "We shall try our best to open up all the grain prices within 2 to 3 years." Since then, 24 years has passed in a blink, there have been 2 rounds of reforms of China's grain circulation system between the policy hesitation and the market regulation and deregulation, and now the reform is again at a critical point.

From 1993 to 2003, purchasing at protective prices dominated the market. Since 2004, purchasing at minimum prices has dominated the market. The purpose of both the rounds of reforms is to achieve grain marketization, but due to various reasons the reform has not broken through price barriers and has been branded more or less with unified purchasing.

Both purchasing at protective prices and purchasing at minimum prices did effectively increase farmers' income, stabilize grain market prices and ensure-national food security. Yet it is undeniable that the 2 policies had innate defects with their marginal effects gradually decreasing, which have eventually caused negative results of distortion of market mechanisms, great troubles for the grain industry, overpressure on government finance, etc. The practice has proved that longtimeimplementation of the policy of government-dominated prices will certainly overturn the mechanism for market-formed prices, and it is not in line with the concept for the market to play the decisive role in allocation of resources.

During the period of purchasing at protective prices, purchasing without any restriction was rebated as in fact it was hard to sell at profitable prices. "No selling at profitable prices and no purchasing without any restriction" reflected the negative emotions of some basic-level enterprises and the distortion of policies when they were implemented. As a result, the "3 policies" were not implemented fully and some negative effects appeared instead. The state-owned grain purchasing and selling enterprises lived off the "Big Pot Rice" of policies again. The financial institutions had stable income from interest, so they had no urgent worry about whether grain could be sold at profitable prices. Therefore, there appeared the second and the third financial losses since the foundation of New China at the great cost of the state finance.

During the period of purchasing at minimum prices, grain purchasing and reserving enterprises have been no longer responsible for grain sale, so they have had no operation risks and they can gain benefits as long as they can purchase and reserve more grain, which is supported actively by the local governments and appreciated by the related departments. Therefore, over-purchase and over-reserve have become a normal, and in some major production provinces the amount of grain purchased at minimum prices in some years were more than 60% greater than the amount sold, causing grain reserve exceeding by far the normal scale, deviating from the original purpose of the policy of "purchasing to support the bottom line", and hindering the nurturing of diversified market main bodies and the healthy development of the grain industry. The whole industry is now struggling to deal with the severe situation of high paddy rice production and low milled rice production, high wheat production and low flour production, low utilization of processing capacity, decrease of profits, and continuously depressed operation.

Sharp increase of the temporary purchasing and reserving prices and the minimum purchasing prices has caused market distortions and excess of supply over demand for some varieties of grain. However, policy-oriented purchasing and reserving still get underway again and again, and capacity expansion on the supply side is still going on. Need is not necessarily causing production increase, and maybe it is necessary that we reduce production.

What's worse, since 2011 international grain prices have fallen by 40% ~

50% , the US dollar has appreciated, and the freight rates have dropped sharply, but domestic purchasing prices have continuously risen, widening the gap between domestic and international prices, rapidly increasing grain import, and worsening the contradiction of supply and demand. The government financial burden is heavier, explicit and implicit losses are surprisingly high, and there is also the danger of grain aging and quality worsening.

Looking back at the gains and losses of the 2 rounds of reforms of the grain industry, it is easy to find that the problem is attributed to our policies on grain prices. "Prices are set by the government, money is borrowed from the bank, reserve is subsidized by the finance, and losses are on credit". That is why the market main bodies are unitized gradually, the policy-oriented functions and operation-oriented functions are confused, the market mechanisms for grain purchase and sale are distorted, and the energy for market innovation and the operation space for diversified main bodies are restrained. In addition, the deeper integration of domestic and international markets in recent years is also decreasing the effects of China's policies on macroeconomic regulation. Under the new economic normal, along with so many contradictions in the grain industry, especially on the grain supply side, as well as the biggest grain stock in the world, the "hardest bone" of the reform of the grain industry is again in sight. Just as an old song reads, "Helpless, I became estranged from that emotion only to find myself in front of you again after so many years."

*Several Opinions about the Implementation of the New Development Concepts to Speed up Agricultural Modernization And to Realize the Goal of All-round Well-off Society*, the No. 1 Document of the Central Committee of the Communist Party of China in 2016 (hereinafter simplified as the No. 1 Document), adopts the brand-new concept of "innovation, coordination, green, opening-up, and sharing", and puts forward a series of new ideas, policies and measures to solve the problems with "agriculture, farmers, and rural areas" as well as the grain industry, which is a concentrated statement and a systematic upgrade of the reforms related to agriculture and grain industry in recent years. The document calls for the "supply-side structural reform" for the first time, the core of which is market and price. That is to say, agricultural production should meet market demand, market should form prices in order to guide agricultural production, and market should play the decisive role in allocation of resources. That is the only solution to all the problems with "agriculture, farmers, and rural areas", and it is so enlightening that we see the light suddenly. As a comprehensive blueprint for modern agricultural development, the new policies and new measures on grain circulation and consumption are very attractive. For example, "we shall reduce inventory, cut costs, and make up for short boards", "we shall reform and perfect the price forming mechanisms and the purchasing and reserving policies for grain and other major agricultural products", "we shall strengthen responsibilities for agricultural products' quality and food safety", "we shall perfect the modern agricultural product market system", "we shall expedite the upgrade and transformation of agricultural product wholesale markets", and "we shall support enterprises in doing international business in various forms". They will be the basic guideline and the course of action for further reforms of the grain system and mechanisms for quite a long time in the future.

2016 is the first year of the decisive phase to achieve the all-round well-off society, and a tough year as well to speed up the agricultural structure reform. The No. 1 Document points out the causes of the problems with "agriculture, farmers, and rural areas" that have been in accumulation for so many years, and opens up a door of hope for sustainable development of China's food security. It is the gist of and the key to sustainable and healthy development of the grain economy to further update the concepts, deepen the reforms, set up a grain circulation system in alignment with the modern agriculture, and perfect the long-term effective mechanism for improvement of grain supply and demand balance.

**We should give importance to effective supply, and speed up reforms of the agricultural supply-side structure.** The "three-amount overlap" and the "three-price inversion" reveal 2 soft ribs or short boards of China's grain industry, that is, structural imbalance among grain varieties and lack of competitiveness in prices. The solution is to feel the "market pulse" correctly, play the "adjustment cards" well, do the right "additions and subtractions", push forward the "supply-side structural reforms" persistently, and firmly improve the quality and effectiveness of the agricultural supply system, so as to enhance China's agricultural effectiveness and competitiveness comprehensively.

For a long time, we have always been focusing on increasing grain production due to the one-way thinking mode originated from the shortage economy that once dominated the mainstream value assessment. In reality, we have been through such feelings and experiences many times. We sharply raised grain prices to stimulate grain production only to end up in the strange historical circle of "too much and then too little and again too much". The bias for increasing production has not been really corrected. Therefore, some varieties of grain are in excess of supply over demand, and they live off the "biased meal" of policies; some varieties of grain can't meet the demand, and due to their disadvantages in production and prices, they can't get any support or pity; some varieties of grain can't catch up with the demand, and due to their "defects" in quality and safety, they make room for imports from far away in the market. This kind of distorted relationship between supply and demand is certainly not in agreement with "effective supply".

"The history can't be rewritten but can be a lesson for the future." China's grain economy is now at the point of the third round of reforms of the grain industry. We must carefully understand the essence of "supply-side structural reforms" called for by the No. 1 Document, and thoroughly explore the deep causes of structural imbalance. "It is not necessarily good to have more and more production." We should take market demands as the orientation, adjust planting structures, optimize allocation of resources, "reduce ineffective and low-end supply, expand effective and medium and high-end supply", and get away from the awkward situation in which "unable to sell" and "unable to buy" coexist. Meanwhile we should pay more attention to innovation of agricultural science and technology and innovation of organization, support intensive processing, extend industry chains, cut down agricultural costs, improve agricultural effectiveness, and enhance international competitiveness of China's grain prices. If only production and demand are in line with each other, quality and quantity are both in focus, and stability and flexibility are both taken into account, China's grain production and circulation will really take the road of virtuous cycle.

Reducing inventory and bad capacity is a tough task that the supply-side reform must finish. Overproduction without taking costs and results into account would not only overdraw from China's resources and environment, but also touch the red line of ecology and endanger China's sustainable development. Actively and properly reducing marginal and unhealthy capacity and allowing the overplanted or even ill-planted farmland to rest, will not only help overcome the current difficulties, but also benefit long-term plans for the future. This year China's government plans to properly reduce corn planting area, work out programs for returning land from planting to forestry and pasture, and explore pilot test of cropland rotation and fallow system. As to the giant stock of corn and other varieties, we should weigh all the advantages and disadvantages, lower the prices at proper time to increase sales so as to stimulate domestic consumption demands.

**We should make up for short boards, strengthen infrastructure, focus equally on the "3 hidings", improve development advantages, and take the road for connotative modern agricultural development.** Hiding grain in land means that we should ensure our production capacity, build "ration land" with high standards, and maintain the "bowl land" for future generations; Hiding grain in technology means that we should improve innovation and extension of agricultural technologies and make full use of technological achievements; Hiding grain in farmers means that we should actively develop various modes of proper-scale agricultural operations, nurture and support new types of operational main bodies, search for new types of farmers, and help get rid of worries on lack of agricultural successors in the future. As long as fertile land exists, science and technology is advanced, and farmers are happy, the potential will surely be transferred into real effective supply.

**We should achieve the target price system, and gradually perfect the grain price forming mechanisms.** The basic guideline for reform of the grain industry is "market forms prices, and prices and subsidies are separated", that is, prices should be determined by the market and farmers' interests should be guaranteed by the government. Target price subsidy is an important option for price reform. It means that the government takes various pricing factors into account, sets a target price, and pays subsidy through administrative means to anyone who suffers losses. Pilot test of target price subsidy in the past 2 years has achieved positive effects, and has won understanding and support from farmers in the test zones. However, due to many reasons, there are still many problems, such as complexity in subsidy payment, high cost, difficulty in calculating output and area, time limit on collection of base-period data, etc. We need to solve all the above problems through practices.

Target price insurance is another option for price reform. It means that insurance companies work out insurance products against risks in grain prices, producers sign contracts with insurance companies, insurance companies are responsible for damage assessment and compensation, and the government provides certain amount of premium subsidy. This mode can very well prevent speculations such as false area reports, and policyholders are able to have many choices among various insurance products. If there appears the mode of "insurance + futures", we would have a broader development outlook. Right now, pilot tests are already underway in nearly 20 provinces and cities. Target price subsidy and target price insurance are likely to form a safety network to ensure farmers' basic income in the future.

**We should reform and perfect the grain purchasing and reserving system, and develop diversified market main bodies.** The reform of the state grain purchasing and reserving system mainly includes the diversification of main bodies in grain purchasing and reserving and the reform of the grain reserve management system. Diversification of main bodies in grain purchasing and reserving has been underway for many years, but due to the gradual increase of policy grain, the state-owned enterprises' domination has not changed really. However, along with the implementation of grain price reforms, this situation would be improved to a great extent. The separation of policy-oriented functions and operation-oriented functions is another major step to reform the central grain reserve management system. It will not only help improve the level of grain reserve management and remove the hotbed of corruptions, but also help bring into full role its function of guaranteeing China's food security. "It is not necessarily good to have more and more grain reserve." We should scientifically and reasonably determine the scale of national grain reserve in accordance with China's actual conditions and international practices (the stock/consumption ratio of 17% ~ 18%).

**We should adopt the internet thinking modes, update the marketing concepts, and revive China's grain economy.** No one should neglect the subverting and multiplying effects of "internet +". Whoever board the fast train of "internet +" will be able to broaden their borders for production and operation, and grab the commanding heights in market competition. "Internet +" can help create personalized and branded agricultural production, and meet consumers' appeal for new and exotic quality products, so it is more like a marketing program uniquely designed for special agricultural products. When "internet + agricultural brands" becomes a mainstream choice, and when unique product quality is integrated with profound human quality, such a charming combination will surely boost the evolution of agriculture. However, we need first to seriously explore how staple grain and oil could join the "internet club".

**We should expedite the deep integration of domestic and international markets, import properly and speed up "going abroad" of China's agriculture.** We should make an overall plan to make full use of both international and domestic markets and resources, and to achieve deep integration of domestic and international markets. It is not only a necessary requirement for establishing an open economic system, but also a basic long-term policy that we should stick to. Proper import is not just a temporary strategy. As a big developing country with so large a population and in great lack of land and water, it is an irresistible trend and a reasonable choice for China to make full use of international markets and resources to supplement its domestic supply. We should set up a diversified and stable international agricultural products trading system, make great efforts to support agricultural export and various types of international operations, such as agricultural product processing, reserving and transportation, trade, etc. We should speed up "going abroad" of China's agriculture in order to solve its problem of having large amounts of agricultural products with not so good quality and poor competitiveness, nurture grain traders and agribusinesses with strong international competitiveness, and win initiative in international competition. In the meantime, we should play well the card of international grain aid, use well the new "regulating valve" for the grain industry, and maximize added values of maritime logistics and transportation. China has established agricultural investment cooperation relationships with many countries throughout the world, and the vast uncultivated virgin land in Asia, Africa and Latin America is waiting for China's grain workers.

**We should perfect the modern grain market system, and speed up upgrade and transformation of the grain wholesale markets.** The modern grain market system is an important part of the socialist market economy, and we can't effectively allocate grain resources without an integrated, open, reasonably composed, competitive and orderly modern grain market system. The building of China's modern grain market system began in early 90s. After more than 20 years, its framework, made up of the grain wholesale market, the grain futures market and the electric grain business firm, has basically come into being, and its functions and roles are basically brought into play. However, dispersed grain production and policy-oriented price barriers have become the biggest limiting factor to the building of China's modern grain market system. The policies and measures put forward by the No. 1 Document not only remove the barriers but also make higher requirements for building and perfecting the modern agricultural product market system: the grain futures market shall "work out more agricultural varieties for futures, carry out pilot test of agricultural product options", "and smoothly expand pilot test of 'insurance + futures'"; the agricultural product wholesale market shall "speed up upgrade and transformation", etc. This is certainly good news to the grain futures market and the grain wholesale market. However, due to the serious unbalance in management systems, trading mechanisms, variety structures and development modes of all levels and kinds of grain wholesale markets, we need to carefully explore how to "upgrade and transform" in accordance with the positioning of their market functions.

China's special conditions and grain's attribute of quasi-public goods determine that no matter how the relationship between grain supply and demand changes, the strategic position of food security will never change. However, since the reform and opening-up, China's grain production and circulation have gone through several ups and downs. When grain supply is less than demand, food security is a top priority; when grain supply is in excess over demand, food security is seldom discussed, which reflects some people's biased attitudes to food security. Faced with deteriorating grain quality and food safety crisis, we should stick to the national food security strategy in the new period without any doubt or negligence. We must clearly define the difference between strategic stability and tactical adjustments for food security. Just as one chief official of a governmental department said, "Although we now have to purchase too much grain and pay too much subsidies, and we lack stock houses, this is just a technical problem, which can be well solved through further reforms and perfection of mechanisms and systems. Anyhow, food security is of strategic importance. We must never neglect it just because of the grain production increases for 12 consecutive years.

Under the new situation, we should adhere to the principle of "holding to strategy, changing in stability, and activating markets", correctly handle the relationships between short-term policies and long-term strategies, domestic production and foreign supply, quantity security and quality security, overall balance and structural balance, price competition and value competition, government intervention and market allocation, and farmers' income increase and grain price reform. Faced with the current situation of departmental segmentation and functional dispersion in China's grain management, in order to prevent neglecting one priority while focusing on another, it is very urgent that we should strengthen the top level design and set up an authoritative and expert national food security committee and a national grain macro-regulation center. Their functions are to coordinate policies of related departments, set up an authoritative monitoring and alarming system on grain supply and demand as well as grain prices, make microeconomic suggestions to the state council on grain production, circulation, consumption, import and export control, grain reserve adjustment, finances, taxes, credits, etc., enhance important decisions' timeliness, accuracy and authority, and prevent shifting of responsibilities among different departments.

From the viewpoint of the most urgent reform tasks at present, the policy-oriented grain purchase and reserve has gradually become a normal after so many years, some problems are deeply rooted, and it is very hard to ease the contradiction between the administrative inertia and departmental interests and the allocation of resources by the market. Therefore, in order to ensure successful implementation of reforms, there is an urgent need objectively to set up an authoritative agency that transcends departmental or local interests to guarantee China's food security for the long future in the name of the country.

To the microeconomic operation level, grain's attribute of general commodity should be respected and reflected. Along with the implementation of reduction of grain reserve and reforms of the national grain purchasing and reserving system, grain circulation will gradually return to the situation in which marketized purchasing will dominate. Those enterprises accustomed to implementing policy-oriented purchasing and reserving tasks may face ordeals and challenges of dwindling business and slackening operation, and their operation mode of "purchasing, reserving and selling raw grain" will hardly go on. The traditional grain circulation system will be challenged jointly by the close connection of agricultural production, processing and sale, the deep integration of the first, second and third industries, the new type of main bodies in agricultural operation and services, the rise-up of diversified market purchasing and selling main bodies, the rapid changes of trans-border and trans-region mergers, and the rapidly emerging electric business. State-owned grain enterprises must develop new economic growth points, open up new roads, optimize their development modes, activate their intrinsic potentials, and achieve transformation and upgrade.

The current situation demands immediate actions. "We can't make any new achievements without getting rid of the old practices, and we can't survive without reforms." All of us—the grain workers who have been working hard day and night for decades to finish their duties to support the poor and those in need, and to guarantee supply, making great contributions to China's food security and people's production and lives, should keep up with the times, keep improving through reforms, overcome various hardships and difficulties, take precautions before it is too late, guide the new development of grain circulation with wholly new concepts, solve new problems through deepening reforms, and create new brilliance for the grain industry through great diligence.

"Fear not the strong pass iron-clad on all sides! The summit's now surmounted with big strides." It seems most suitable to review the past, to analyze the present and to foresee the future of this round of reforms with the splendid poem by Mao Zedong, a great man in history.

March 10, 2016

# 目录

# Content

# 第一部分

## 2015年

## 粮食市场概述

# 一、中国粮食市场

【内容提要】

2015 年，面对错综复杂的国际形势和不断加大的经济下行压力，党中央、国务院加强战略定力，统筹谋划国际国内两个大局，坚持稳中求进工作总基调，主动适应引领新常态，以新理念指导新实践，以新战略谋求新发展，不断创新宏观调控，深入推进结构性改革，扎实推动“大众创业、万众创新”。2015 年我国“三农”工作获得稳步推进，粮食产量实现“十二连增”，农民增收实现“十二连快”，农村基础设施和公共服务明显改善，农村社会和谐稳定，社会主义新农村建设稳步推进。

2015 年，我国国民经济保持了总体平稳、稳中有进、稳中有好的发展态势。国家统计局数据显示，2015 年全年国内生产总值 676 708 亿元，按可比价格计算，比上年增长 6.9%；农村居民人均可支配收入 11 422 元，比上年增长 8.9%，扣除价格因素实际增长 7.5%，实现连续 12 年较快增长，增幅连续第 6 年超过城镇居民收入增幅；城乡居民人均收入倍差 2.73，比上年缩小 0.02，农民生活显著改善。2015 年全国粮食总产量 62 143.5 万吨（12 428.7 亿斤），比 2014 年增加 1 440.8 万吨（288.2 亿斤），增长 2.4%，粮食总产量连续 3 年稳定在 12 000 亿斤以上，标志着我国农业综合生产能力显著提升。

2015 年全国粮食总产量再创新高，主要得益于粮食种植面积和单产的同步提升。按季节性因素来看，主要是夏粮和秋粮产量增加。其中，夏粮产量 14 112 万吨，比上年增长 3.3%；早稻产量 3 369 万吨，比上年下降 0.9%；秋粮产量 44 662 万吨，比上年增长 2.3%；谷物产量 57 225 万吨，比上年增长 2.7%（见图 1－1－1、表 1－1－1）。

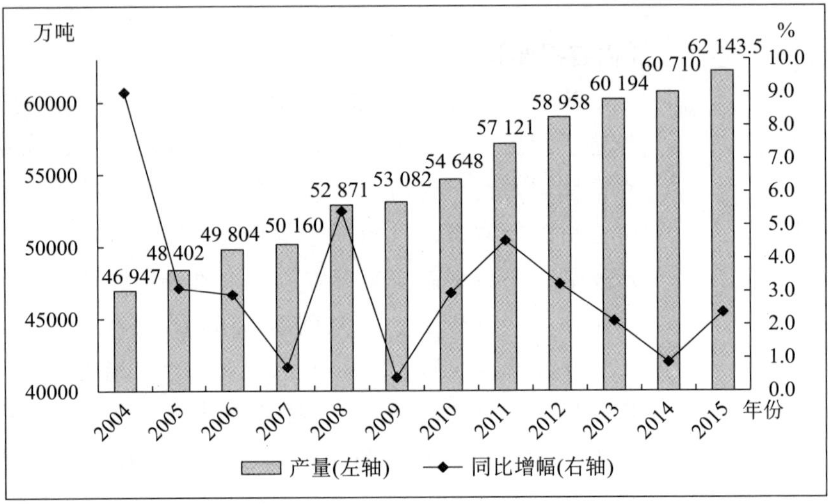


资料来源：国家统计局：《2015 中国统计年鉴》，中国统计出版社 2016 年版；《2015 年国民经济和社会发展统计公报》。

**图 1－1－1　2004—2015 年全国粮食产量及增幅**

**表 1－1－1　　2014 年和 2015 年我国粮食产量情况**　　单位：万吨

| | 2014 年 | 2015 年 | | |
|---|---|---|---|---|
| | 产量 | 产量 | 比上年增减 | 增减幅度 |
| 粮食总产量 | 60 710 | 62 143.5 | 1 434 | 2.4% |
| 其中：夏粮 | 13 659.6 | 14 112 | 452 | 3.4% |
| 早稻 | 3 401 | 3 369.1 | －32 | －0.9% |
| 秋粮 | 43 649.3 | 44 662.4 | 1 013 | 2.3% |

资料来源：国家统计局：《2014 年国民经济和社会发展统计公报》、《2015 年国民经济和社会发展统计公报》。

## （一）粮食生产“十二连增”，粮食市场有序运行

2015 年，我国粮食安全形势总体较好，但粮食高产量、高价格、高库存、高进口的“四高”特征更加明显，农民增收、农业增效、农村发展也都面临着新的挑战。面对机遇与挑战，2015 年中央发布了第 12 个涉农中央 1 号文件，财政预算“三农”支出持续增长，粮食收储政策稳中有变，保障了粮食市场的有序运行。

### 1. 继续出台第 12 个涉农中央 1 号文件

2015 年 2 月，中央发布了《关于加大改革创新力度 加快农业现代化建设的若干意见》（以下简称《意见》），这是自 2004 年以来连续出台的第 12 个关于“三农”问题的中央 1 号文件。2015 年的 1 号文件聚焦改革和农业现代化，与 2014 年发布的《关于全面深化农村改革 加快推进农业现代化的若干意见》一脉相承。《意见》分为 5 个部分 32 条，包括：围绕建设现代农业，加快转变农业发展方式；围绕促进农民增收，加大惠农政策力度；围绕城乡发展一体化，深入推进新农村建设；围绕增添农村发展活力，全面深化农村改革；围绕做好“三农”工作，加强农村法治建设。《意见》提出，加快转变农业发展方式，要强化农业科技创新驱动作用，创新农产品流通方式，提高统筹利用国际国内两个市场、两种资源的能力；要加快全国农产品市场体系转型升级，着力加强设施建设和配套服务，健全交易制度；在完善农产品价格形成机制方面，要增加农民收入，必须保持农产品价格合理水平，继续执行稻谷、小麦最低收购价政策，完善重要农产品临时收储政策，积极开展农产品价格保险试点。

### 2. 财政“三农”支出保持增长

2015 年，中央财政继续加大强农惠农支持力度，及时下拨 2015 年粮食直补、良种补贴等各种补贴资金。在财政收入增长速度放缓的背景下，中央财政年初预算安排用于“三农”的支出继续保持同比增长。2015 年，中央财政年初预算安排用于“三农”的支出 12 286. 6 亿元，比上年增长

17.9%。在中央财政已拨付的2015年“三农”相关支出中，拨付农业消费支出和“四项补贴”3 714.18亿元，占年初预算的58.5%。2015年，中央财政在先期下达的地方粮食直补、农资综合补贴、良种补贴、农机购置补贴四项补贴1 315亿元的基础上，考虑到油价上涨以及其他农用消费资料价格变化因素，于3月份再次增拨各省农资综合补贴资金243亿元，其中，安排种粮农民直接补贴资金140.5亿元；安排农作物良种补贴资金203.5亿元，对水稻、小麦、玉米、棉花，东北和内蒙古的大豆，长江流域10个省（市）、河南信阳、陕西汉中和安康地区的冬油菜，藏区青稞实行全覆盖，并对马铃薯和花生在主产区开展补贴试点。财政“三农”支出继续增加，降低了农民的种粮成本，稳定了农民的种粮收入预期。

**3. 收储政策稳中有变**

2015年，国家继续在小麦、稻谷主产区实行最低收购价政策，保持小麦和稻谷的最低收购价格水平与上年持平；继续对玉米实行临时收储政策，但将玉米临储收购价格由1.11～1.13元/斤统一调降至1元/斤，调降幅度达9.91%～11.50%；将油菜籽临时收储政策改为由省级政府自行组织收购。根据2015年中央1号文件关于总结东北和内蒙古大豆目标价格改革试点经验的要求，继续实施东北三省一区大豆目标价格改革试点，2015年大豆目标价格定为2.4元/斤，与2014年大豆目标价格持平。继续在2015年秋冬播种之前公布2015年小麦最低收购价格，2015年生产的小麦（三等）最低收购价为1.18元/斤，与2014年持平，稳定农民对小麦种植的收益预期。总体看来，2015年粮食收储政策稳中有变，对小麦、稻谷这两大口粮品种收储政策继续保持稳定；对于国内出现阶段性供大于求的玉米适当下调临储收购价格；对大豆和油菜籽等对外依存度较大的品种采取了更加市场化的政策取向。

国家统计局数据显示，2015年全国粮食播种面积113 340.5千公顷（170 010.7万亩），比上年增加617.9千公顷（926.9万亩），增长0.5%。从农业种植结构调整来看，2015年耕地面积继续向粮食品种集中，玉米播种面积增长势头明显。由于种植棉花、油菜籽等费工费时，比较效益较低，一些地区调减棉花和夏收油菜籽种植面积，扩大了冬小麦、玉米等粮食种植面积，如江淮部分地区棉花播种面积减幅接近30%。因粮食播种面积扩大而增产粮食约 67 亿斤，对粮食增产的贡献率为 23.1%。其中，2015 年全国玉米播种面积比上年增加 993.2 千公顷（1 489.8 万亩），增长 2.7%，拉动全国粮食单产提高 1.3 个百分点（见图 1－1－2）。

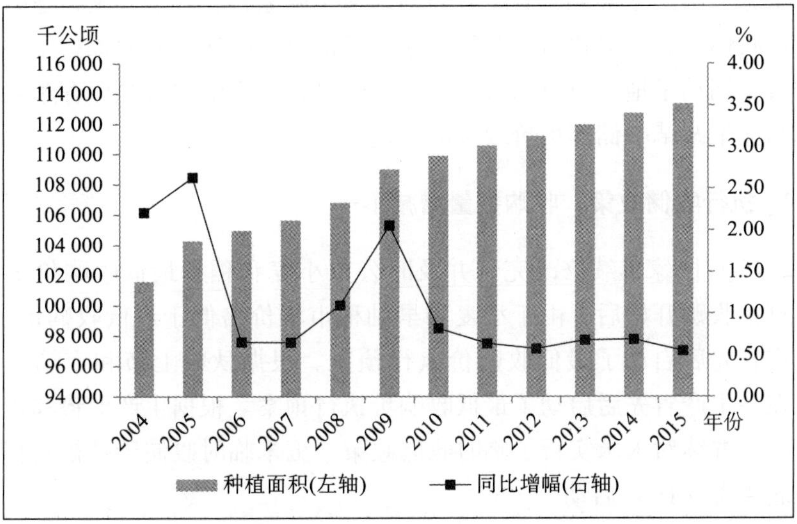


资料来源：国家统计局《2015 年中国统计年鉴》、《2015 年国民经济和社会发展统计公报》。

**图 1－1－2　2004—2015 年全国粮食种植面积及增幅**

统计数据显示，截至 2015 年底，全国各类企业玉米库存超过 4 000 亿斤，大大超出了合理水平，阶段性供大于求特征明显。一部分主产区出现了收不了、储不下、销不掉的尴尬局面，更有财政补不起的“丰收后的烦恼”。面对困局，国家按照“市场定价、价补分离”原则，积极稳妥推进玉米收储制度改革。

## （二）现有机制难以为继　政策改革迫在眉睫

2015 年我国粮食生产连续 12 年丰收，国内粮食供需总体平衡有余，库存充裕，但结构性矛盾突出。一是库存迅速增加。2012 年以来，由于实施最低收购价和临时收储政策，我国粮食临储库存迅速累积，目前已处于历史最高水平。截至 2015 年底，玉米临储库存超过 2 亿吨，稻谷最低收购价库存超过 6 000 万吨。二是替代性进口迅速增加，玉米替代品大量进口，导致国内玉米供需矛盾进一步恶化。面对我国粮食连年丰收、收储矛盾十分突出的新形势，有关方面认真落实国家粮食收购政策，适时启动政策性收储，着力强化市场监管，切实规范收购秩序，有效保护了种粮农民利益，调动了地方政府抓粮积极性；但日益严重的粮食高库存和高进口问题凸显了改革临储等粮价政策的紧迫性。

**1. 执行收储政策，收购数量增减不一**

2015 年国家继续修改完善并及时公布小麦和稻谷最低收购价执行预案。夏粮收购开始后，由于小麦和早籼稻市场价格低于最低收购价水平，在主产省先后启动了最低收购价执行预案。根据秋粮上市和市场价格情况，在各主产省先后启动了最低收购价执行预案。根据生产形势和市场价格情况，继续对玉米实行了临时收储政策。玉米临时收储于秋粮收获季节在东北 4 省（区）启动。

国家粮食局数据显示，2015 年全年各类粮食企业的粮食收购量首次突破 8 000 亿斤，总量达 8 465 亿斤（4.2325 亿吨），同比增加 409 亿斤，增量主要以玉米为主。分品种来看，除玉米收购量明显增加外，其他品种收购量均出现不同程度下降。由于临时收储政策被取消，油菜籽、大豆收购数量均出现明显下降；小麦、粳稻、早籼稻和中晚籼稻收购数量略有下降；玉米收购数量则大幅上升。据国家粮食局统计，截至 9 月 30 日，河南、江苏等 9 个主产区各类粮食企业收购新产小麦 6 631 万吨，比上年同期减少 732 万吨；江西、湖南等 8 个主产区各类粮食企业收购新产早籼稻 793 万吨，比上年同期减少 53 万吨；四川、湖北等 9 个主产区各类粮食企业收购新产油菜籽 160 万吨，比上年同期减少 188 万吨。截至 11 月 25 日，主产区各类粮食企业累计收购中晚籼稻、玉米和大豆 6 438 万吨，比上年同期增加 917 万吨；其中，湖北、安徽等 14 个主产区各类粮食企业累计收购新产中晚籼稻 1 622 万吨，同比减少 50 万吨；黑龙江等 7 个主产区各类粮食企业累计收购新产粳稻 1 769 万吨，同比减少 53 万吨；黑龙江、山东等 11 个主产区各类粮食企业累计收购新产玉米 3 016 万吨，同比增加 1 047 万吨；黑龙江等 5 个主产区各类粮食企业累计收购新产大豆 31 万吨，同比减少 27 万吨（见表 1－1－2）。

**表 1－1－2　2014—2015 年各类粮食企业分品种累计收购量**　单位：万吨

| | 总计收购量 | 小麦 | 玉米 | 粳稻 | 中晚籼稻 | 油菜籽 | 早籼稻 | 大豆 |
|---|---|---|---|---|---|---|---|---|
| 2014 年 | 36 490 | 7 363 | 4 714 | 3 096 | 2 538 | 349 | 846 | 136 |
| 2015 年 | 14 022 | 6 631 | 3 016 | 1 769 | 1 622 | 160 | 793 | 31 |
| 同比增减幅度（%） | | －9. 94 | 53. 17 | －2. 91 | －2. 99 | －54. 02 | －6. 26 | －46. 55 |

数据来源：国家粮食局（2015 年数据截至 2015 年 11 月 25 日）。

### 2. 市场供应充足，政策性拍卖遇冷

尽管市场粮源充裕，2015 年国家有关部门仍通过定期适量的国家政策性粮油竞价销售保障了国内粮油市场的正常供应，促进了产销区市场的有效衔接。积极推动产销合作，2015 年粮食跨省流通量达到 17 万吨，高效完成 300 万吨跨省移库任务，全年累计拍卖政策性粮食 1 850 万吨，保持了产销区市场的供需平衡和粮食价格基本稳定。整体来看，2015 年国内政策性粮油竞价销售成交量同比降幅达 64. 86%，说明政策性粮油拍卖底价与市场价格或存在一定程度的脱节。

## （三）CPI 重回 1 时代　粮价涨幅缩小

2015 年物价总体运行平稳，处于温和上涨的水平。根据国家统计局的数据，2015 年全年居民消费价格比上年上涨 1. 4%，完成了全年 3% 的物价调控目标，涨幅创 2009 年 CPI 负增长以来的新低，国内通胀压力显著低于预期。分类别看，食品价格同比上涨 2. 3%，在食品价格中，粮食价格上涨 2. 0%，油脂价格下降 3. 2%。2015 年粮食价格涨幅较 2014 年继续缩窄，与 2010—2011 年两位数的涨幅相比，2012—2015 年粮食价格涨幅回落态势明显（见表 1－1－3）。从 2015 年粮食价格指数的月度走势来

看，基本在2.0%～2.9%窄幅区间震荡，且呈现前高后低、逐月走低的趋势，与月度CPI走势基本一致。

表1－1－3　　2010—2015年粮食类居民消费价格指数与CPI

| 年份 | 1月 | 2月 | 3月 | 4月 | 5月 | 6月 | 7月 | 8月 | 9月 | 10月 | 11月 | 12月 | 年度CPI |
|---|---|---|---|---|---|---|---|---|---|---|---|---|---|
| 2010 | 109.8 | 109.7 | 109.5 | 109.8 | 110.2 | 110.4 | 110.6 | 110.8 | 110.9 | 111.1 | 111.4 | 111.8 | 103.3 |
| 2011 | 115.1 | 114.8 | 114.9 | 114.6 | 114.3 | 113.9 | 113.7 | 113.5 | 113.3 | 113.2 | 112.7 | 112.2 | 105.4 |
| 2012 | 106.1 | 105.7 | 105.2 | 104.8 | 104.6 | 104.3 | 104.1 | 104.0 | 104.0 | 104.0 | 103.9 | 104.1 | 102.6 |
| 2013 | 104.7 | 104.9 | 105.0 | 105.0 | 105.1 | 105.1 | 105.1 | 105.0 | 104.9 | 104.8 | 104.7 | 104.6 | 102.6 |
| 2014 | 103.1 | 102.8 | 102.7 | 102.8 | 103.0 | 103.2 | 103.3 | 103.4 | 103.4 | 103.5 | 103.2 | 103.1 | 102.0 |
| 2015 | 102.9 | 102.9 | 102.8 | 102.8 | 102.7 | 102.6 | 102.5 | 102.4 | 102.3 | 102.2 | 102.1 | 102.0 | 101.4 |

资料来源：根据国家统计局公布的数据整理。

说明：

（1）粮食是指人们用作主食的各种成品粮及其加工品，包括大米、面粉、粗杂粮以及各种粗、细粮制品，不包括薯类、豆类及糕点食品。

（2）以上年同期价格指数为100。

从2015年全国主要粮油批发市场主要粮食品种的年度个体价格指数看，除晚籼米价格指数同比小幅上涨外，其他粮食品种价格指数均有不同程度的下跌，其中，大豆、黄玉米和白小麦位居跌幅前三甲，早籼米和粳米仅小幅下跌。2015年大豆目标价格补贴政策继续实施，大豆价格由市场供需决定，受到国际市场大豆价格持续下跌的影响，大豆价格指数跌幅位居榜首。2015年国家大幅调降玉米临储收购底价，而国内外价格差过大使得进口替代品迅速增加，共同导致国内玉米供过于求局面的恶化，玉米价格同比明显下跌。小麦、晚籼米、早籼米和粳米价格指数均受到最低收购价底价的有力支撑，但由于2015年小麦政策收储数量较2014年明显下降，2015年小麦价格指数跌幅较大。大米市场继续受到进口低价大米冲击，市场“优质优价”的格局愈发明显，晚籼米价格小幅上涨，粳米价格基本持平，而早籼米价格小幅下跌，消费者更加青睐优质优价的晚籼米和粳米（见表1－1－4）。

表 1－1－4　2013～2015 年全国主要粮油批发市场价格指数（年度个体指数）

| 年　度 | 2013 年 | 2014 年 | 2015 年 |
|---|---|---|---|
| 白小麦（普通） | 214.78 | 219.77 | 211.16（－3.92%） |
| 黄玉米 | 227.02 | 233.66 | 219.36（－6.12%） |
| 粳米 | 242.06 | 244.48 | 244.14（－0.14%） |
| 早籼米 | 225.54 | 227.04 | 225.46（－0.70%） |
| 晚籼米 | 238.25 | 243.77 | 245.69（0.79%） |
| 大豆（油脂业） | 216.82 | 209.86 | 194.93（－7.11%） |

资料来源：中华粮网。

说明：基期：1994 年 6 月＝100。括号中为同比涨幅。

## （四）粮油进口迅速增加　加剧国内结构性矛盾

2015 年我国粮食产量和库存继续增加，国内粮食整体供应增加，国内粮食消费量也继续快速增长，全年粮食整体供需继续保持紧平衡状态，但结构性矛盾突出，尤其是国内供应过剩的粮食品种及替代品的大量进口，导致“国货入库，洋货入市”的情况，国内玉米、稻谷供需矛盾迅速激化。

从年度数据来看，粮油进口量整体保持迅速增长的势头。据海关统计，我国 2015 年全年累计进口谷物及谷物粉 3 270 万吨，上年同期为 1 951 万吨，同比增长 67.6%；2015 年大豆进口量 8 174 万吨，同比增加 14.48%。粗略统计，2015 年谷物和大豆进口量合计为 11 444 万吨，较 2014 年同比增加 25.89%，首次突破 1 亿吨关口。其中，传统三大谷物品种进口量均呈增加趋势，与上年相比，2015 年玉米进口增幅最大，达到 85.02%，大米进口也明显增加，小麦进口仅微幅增加。此外，近两年来我国高粱和大麦进口量增幅明显，2015 年进口量均超过 1 000 万吨。2009 年至今，我国已经连续 7 年成为谷物净进口国，2012 年及 2013 年五大谷物净进口量均超过 1 300 万吨，2014 年净进口量超过 1 800 万吨，2015 年则创下 3 200 万吨的纪录新高（见图 1－1－3、表 1－1－5）。

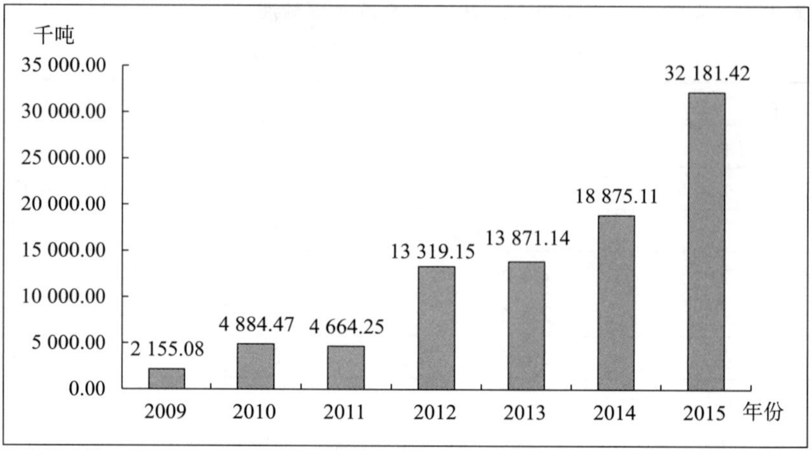


数据来源：中国国家海关总署。

说明：五大谷物指小麦、大米、玉米、高粱和大麦。

**图1-1-3 2009—2015年我国五大谷物净进口情况**

**表1-1-5 2010—2015年我国粮油产品年度进出口数据** 单位：千吨

| 项　目 | 2010年 | 2011年 | 2012年 | 2013年 | 2014年 | 2015年 | 同比（%） |
|---|---|---|---|---|---|---|---|
| 进　口 | | | | | | | |
| 小　麦 | 1 218.72 | 1 248.82 | 3 688.62 | 5 507.05 | 2 971.39 | 2 972.74 | 0.05 |
| 大　米 | 366.17 | 578.38 | 2 344.62 | 2 244.32 | 2 598.04 | 3 349.98 | 28.94 |
| 玉　米 | 1 572.14 | 1 752.74 | 5 207.38 | 3 264.88 | 2 556.55 | 4 730.04 | 85.02 |
| 高　粱 | 83.26 | 0.05 | 86.60 | 1 078.00 | 5 775.70 | 10 699.69 | 85.25 |
| 大　麦 | 2 367.53 | 1 775.55 | 2 528.28 | 2 335.44 | 5 413.47 | 10 731.27 | 98.23 |
| 大　豆 | 54 796.82 | 52 639.55 | 58 383.82 | 63 375.15 | 71 398.98 | 81 740.34 | 14.48 |
| 豆　油 | 1 340.91 | 1 143.19 | 1 826.11 | 1 157.59 | 1 135.47 | 817.88 | -27.97 |
| 油菜籽 | 1 599.85 | 1 262.27 | 2 929.59 | 3 662.41 | 5 081.04 | 4 469.66 | -12.03 |
| 菜籽油 | 985.32 | 550.90 | 1 175.82 | 1 526.83 | 809.96 | 815.06 | 0.63 |
| 棕榈油 | 5 696.11 | 5 912.23 | 6 341.16 | 5 979.07 | 5 323.89 | 5 909.66 | 11.00 |
| 出　口 | | | | | | | |

续表

| 项　目 | 2010 年 | 2011 年 | 2012 年 | 2013 年 | 2014 年 | 2015 年 | 同比（%） |
|---|---|---|---|---|---|---|---|
| 小　麦 | 0. 00 | 39. 79 | 0. 00 | 2. 52 | 0. 96 | 5. 30 | 451. 70 |
| 大　米 | 596. 19 | 515. 50 | 279. 09 | 478. 40 | 419. 07 | 285. 94 | -31. 77 |
| 玉　米 | 127. 16 | 136. 00 | 257. 26 | 77. 63 | 20. 01 | 11. 07 | -44. 69 |
| 大　豆 | 163. 60 | 208. 30 | 320. 10 | 208. 97 | 207. 07 | 133. 60 | -35. 48 |
| 豆　粕 | 1 016. 01 | 406. 32 | 1 232. 67 | 1 070. 11 | 2 090. 95 | 1 695. 71 | -18. 90 |

资料来源：中国国家海关总署。

说明：0. 00 表示不够一个统计单位。

2015 年国内外粮食价格差继续扩大，巨大的价差是粮食进口猛增的主要原因。尽管国内粮食价格因收储政策调整而下降，但国际市场粮食价格跌幅更大。2015 年全球粮食产量连续第三年丰产，全球农产品供应充足而需求低迷，同时美元不断升值，受此影响，国际粮价持续下行，全年跌幅巨大。根据联合国粮农组织 2016 年 1 月 7 日发布的粮农组织食品价格指数和农产品价格指数显示，2015 年粮农组织谷物价格指数年度均值为 162. 4，较 2014 年下跌 29 点，跌幅为 15. 4%；2015 年粮农组织植物油价格指数年度均值为 147，比 2014 年下降 19%，均创下 9 年以来的最低点（见图 1 -1 -4）。

数据来源：联合国粮农组织（FAO）。

**图 1 -1 -4　1990—2015 年联合国粮农组织谷物和植物油价格指数**

预计未来我国粮油进口增长将会出现分化，国内收储政策转变将对进口产生巨大影响。一是在国内外粮食价差的巨大利益驱动下，国内企业将继续加大进口力度，传统三大谷物将继续受到配额内低价进口谷物的冲击。二是随着我国城镇化水平提高以及城乡居民收入增加，食品消费结构中肉禽蛋奶和食用植物油的需求将继续保持增长，我国饲用原粮和油脂油料需求增长较快，传统的短缺品种如大豆、油菜籽等进口将维持较高的增速。三是玉米临时收储政策转变将对玉米及玉米替代品进口产生巨大影响。如果玉米临储政策取消或收储底价大幅下调，导致国内玉米价格与国际市场玉米价格接轨，将会堵住国内市场对国外玉米、大麦、高粱等品种的进口需求，玉米及玉米替代品进口量将会大幅下降。

（郑州粮食批发市场　　杨京）

# 二、世界粮食市场

**【内容提要】**

2015年，世界粮食总产量为25.31亿吨，仅次于创历史最高纪录水平的2014年，减少1.18%，其中，小麦增产，粗粮、大米减产。2015/2016年度，世界粮食总消费量25.27亿吨，比2014/2015年度略增0.8%，其中，小麦、大米消费增加，粗粮基本持平。2015/2016年度粮食产大于消，期末库存略微增长，为6.42亿吨，比期初水平略增0.38%，其中，小麦、粗粮库存增加，大米库存减少。2015年世界粮食供求安全系数为24.94%，比2014年减少0.39个百分点，其中，小麦为29.47%，粗粮为19.85%，大米为32.78%。2015/2016年度，世界粮食总贸易量3.68亿吨，比2014/2015年度减少2.2%，其中，小麦、粗粮减少，大米增加。2015年，世界市场小麦年度平均价格比2014年下降21.4%，玉米下降11.8%，大米下降2.2%。

2015/2016年度，世界大豆产量略增0.5%，消费量增长4.7%，2015/2016年度仍然产大于消，期末库存增长4.3%，贸易量增长3.2%。2015年，世界市场大豆年度平均价格比2014年下降24.1%。

据联合国粮农组织（FAO）2016年2月《粮食供需概要》、2015年12月《作物前景与粮食形势》、2015年10月《粮食展望》，美国农业部（USDA）2016年2月《世界农产品供需预测报告》等机构有关信息资料，现对2015/2016年度世界粮食市场形势作如下综合分析：

## （一）世界粮食生产

2015年，世界粮食（包括小麦、粗粮和大米三种主要谷物，其中，大米为碾米，由稻谷折算，下同）总产量预计为25.3092亿吨，与创历史最高纪录水平的2014年相比，减产3 013万吨，减少1.18%。三种主要粮食品种中，小麦小幅增产，粗粮、大米减产。发达国家粮食产量比2014年减少3.5%，发展中国家略增0.3%。

2015年，世界粮食总产量构成比例是：小麦占29.11%，比2014年提高0.49个百分点；粗粮占51.45%，比2014年下降0.62个百分点；大米占19.43%，比2014年提高0.13个百分点。

2015年，三种主要粮食品种的具体生产情况为：小麦产量为7.3685亿吨，比2014年增产385万吨，增长0.53%；粗粮产量为13.0228亿吨，比2014年减产3 152万吨，减少2.36%，其中，玉米产量为9.7008亿吨，占粗粮产量的74.49%，比2014年减产3 891万吨，减少3.86%；大米产量为4.918亿吨，比2014年减产246万吨，减少0.5%（见表1－2－1）。

**表1－2－1　　2013—2015年世界粮食生产情况**　　单位：百万吨

| 品　　种 | 2013年 | 2014年 | 2015年 | 2015年比2014年增减（%） |
|---|---|---|---|---|
| 粮食合计 | 2 525.16 | 2 561.05 | 2 530.92 | －1.18 |
| 其中：小麦 | 715.59 | 733.00 | 736.85 | 0.53 |
| 粗粮 | 1 315.11 | 1 333.80 | 1 302.28 | －2.36 |
| 大米 | 494.47 | 494.26 | 491.80 | －0.50 |

资料来源：联合国粮农组织（FAO）。

近10年来，世界粮食产量变化的特点是：总体上呈小幅增长趋势，但年度间增减互现，个别年份波动较大，如2013年增长幅度高达9.8%。其中，低收入缺粮国粮食产量除个别年份外，基本上呈增长趋势，且年增长率略高于世界平均水平（见表1－2－2）。

表 1-2-2　　近年来世界粮食生产变化情况　　单位：%

| 指　标 | 年增长率趋势 | 与 2014 年相比的产量增长率 | | | | |
|---|---|---|---|---|---|---|
| 时　间 | 2005—2014 年 | 2011 年 | 2012 年 | 2013 年 | 2014 年 | 2015 年 |
| 世界粮食产量变化情况 | 2.5 | 4.2 | -2.1 | 9.8 | 1.5 | -1.2 |
| 低收入缺粮国粮食产量变化情况 | 3.6 | 2.0 | 3.8 | 1.2 | 1.8 | -4.4 |
| 除印度外其他低收入缺粮国粮食产量变化情况 | 5.2 | -3.5 | 5.6 | 1.1 | 4.5 | -4.8 |

资料来源：联合国粮农组织（FAO）。

## （二）世界粮食消费

2015/2016 年度，世界粮食总消费量为 25.2658 亿吨，比 2014/2015 年度增加 2 000 万吨，增长 0.8%，与当年粮食总产量 25.3092 亿吨相比，产大于消，产消过剩 434 万吨，这意味着可以继续对库存予以一定补充，粮食供求形势持续维持良好状态。

近 16 年来，世界粮食产消形势可以分为三个阶段来分析：第一阶段，即 2000/2001 年度至 2003/2004 年度，世界粮食连续 4 年产不足消，4 年累计粮食短缺量为 2.1541 亿吨，均是靠挖库存弥补产消缺口，致使粮食供求形势持续偏紧；第二阶段，即 2004/2005 年度至 2007/2008 年度，产大于消年度 3 个，产不足消年度 1 个，4 年累计粮食产消剩余量为 1 880 万吨。即便这 4 个年度产消相抵有剩余，但因第一阶段产消缺口巨大，致使库存量与消费量之比在 2006/2007 年度、2007/2008 年度处于近 10 年来的最低水平，粮食供求形势处于偏紧甚至严峻状态；第三阶段，即 2008/2009 年度至 2015/2016 年度，产大于消年度 6 个，产不足消年度 2 个，8 年累计粮食产消剩余量为 2.7101 亿吨，对库存有较大程度弥补，缓解了持续多年的粮食供求形势偏紧的状态。从第一至第三阶段的 16 年中，累计粮食产消剩余量为 7 440 万吨，粮食供求形势整体呈供大于求格局（见表 1-2-3）。

表1-2-3　　近年来世界粮食产消形势变化情况　　单位：万吨

| 第一阶段 | 2000/2001年度 | 2001/2002年度 | 2002/2003年度 | 2003/2004年度 | 4年累计 |
|---|---|---|---|---|---|
| 产量—消费量 | -3 280 | -1 970 | -9 610 | -6 681 | -21 541 |
| 第二阶段 | 2004/2005年度 | 2005/2006年度 | 2006/2007年度 | 2007/2008年度 | 4年累计 |
| 产量—消费量 | 4 941 | 1 340 | -4 656 | 255 | 1 880 |
| 第三阶段 | 2008/2009年度 | 2009/2010年度 | 2010/2011年度 | 2011/2012年度 | 2012/2013年度 |
| 产量—消费量 | 9 901 | 4 182 | -2 531 | 3 271 | -2 810 |
| 第三阶段 | 2013/2014年度 | 2014/2015年度 | 2015/2016年度 | 8年累计 | 16年累计 |
| 产量—消费量 | 9 208 | 5 446 | 434 | 27 101 | 7 440 |

资料来源：根据联合国粮农组织（FAO）有关资料测算。

2015/2016年度，世界粮食食用消费量占粮食总消费量的43.4%，为10.96亿吨，比2014/2015年度增长1.2%，与世界人口增长率基本相当，因此世界整体人均食用消费量稳定在每年150千克的水平；世界粮食饲料消费量占粮食总消费量的35.8%，为9.06亿吨，比2014/2015年度增长1.3%；世界粮食其他用途消费量（主要是工业用途）占粮食总消费量的20.93%，为5.287亿吨，比2014/2015年度增长0.5%。

2015/2016年度，世界粮食总消费量的构成比例是：小麦占28.84%，比2014/2015年度增加0.34个百分点；粗粮占51.44%，比2014/2015年度减少0.41个百分点；大米占19.73%，比2014/2015年度增加0.07个百分点。

2015/2016年度，预计三种主要粮食品种的具体消费情况为：小麦消费量为7.2856亿吨，比2014/2015年度增加1 439万吨，增长2.01%；粗粮消费量为12.9961亿吨，比2014/2015年度减少5万吨，基本持平。其中，玉米消费量9.6745亿吨，占粗粮消费量的74.44%，比2014/2015年度减少1 016万吨，下降1.04%；大米消费量为4.9841亿吨，比2014/2015年度增加565万吨，增长1.15%（见表1-2-4）。

表1-2-4　2013/2014—2015/2016年度世界粮食消费情况　单位：百万吨

| 年度<br>品种 | 2013/2014 | 2014/2015 | 2015/2016 | 2015/2016年度比2014/2015年度增减（%） |
| --- | --- | --- | --- | --- |
| 粮食合计 | 2 433.08 | 2 506.59 | 2 526.58 | 0.80 |
| 其中：小麦 | 695.04 | 714.17 | 728.56 | 2.01 |
| 粗粮 | 1 254.89 | 1 299.66 | 1 299.61 | -0.003 |
| 大米 | 483.15 | 492.76 | 498.41 | 1.15 |

资料来源：联合国粮农组织（FAO）。

## （三）世界粮食贸易

2015/2016年度，世界粮食总贸易量为3.6787亿吨，比2014/2015年度减少827万吨，下降2.2%。三种主要粮食品种中，小麦、粗粮贸易量减少，大米贸易量增加。

2015/2016年度，世界粮食总贸易量的构成比例是：小麦占41.19%，比2014/2015年度减少0.2个百分点；粗粮占46.47%，比2014/2015年度减少0.23个百分点；大米占12.33%，比2014/2015年度增加0.43个百分点。

2015/2016年度，三种主要粮食品种的具体贸易情况为：小麦贸易量为1.5154亿吨，比2014/2015年度减少416万吨，下降2.67%；粗粮贸易量为1.7096亿吨，比2014/2015年度减少472万吨，下降2.69%；大米贸易量预计在2 016日历年为4 537万吨，比2014年增加61万吨，增长1.37%（见表1-2-5）。

表1-2-5　2013/2014—2015/2016年度世界粮食贸易情况　单位：百万吨

| 年度<br>品种 | 2013/2014 | 2014/2015 | 2015/2016 | 2015/2016年度比2014/2015年度增减（%） |
| --- | --- | --- | --- | --- |
| 粮食合计 | 361.95 | 376.14 | 367.87 | -2.20 |
| 其中：小麦 | 156.48 | 155.71 | 151.54 | -2.67 |
| 粗粮 | 159.95 | 175.68 | 170.96 | -2.69 |
| 大米 | 45.52 | 44.76 | 45.37 | 1.37 |

资料来源：联合国粮农组织（FAO）。

## （四）世界粮食库存

根据对 2015 年世界粮食总产量和 2015/2016 年度世界粮食总消费量的最新预测，2015/2016 年度世界粮食产量略高于消费量，世界粮食期末库存量将增加至 6.4238 亿吨，与本年度期初水平相比增加 246 万吨，略微增长 0.38%。

2015/2016 年度，世界粮食库存的构成比例是：小麦占 32.8%，比 2014/2015 年度增加 0.62 个百分点；粗粮占 41.27%，比 2014/2015 年度增加 0.34 个百分点；大米占 25.93%，比 2014/2015 年度减少 0.96 个百分点。

2015/2016 年度，世界三大粮食品种期末库存量具体情况是：小麦库存量为 2.1071 亿吨，比 2014/2015 年度增加 478 万吨，增长 2.32%；粗粮库存量为 2.651 亿吨，比 2014/2015 年度增加 321 万吨，增长 1.22%；大米库存量为 1.6657 亿吨，比 2014/2015 年度减少 553 万吨，下降 3.21%（见表 1－2－6）。

**表 1－2－6　2013/2014—2015/2016 年度世界粮食库存情况**　　单位：百万吨

| 年度<br>品种 | 2013/2014 | 2014/2015 | 2015/2016 | 2015/2016 年度比 2014/2015 年度增减（%） |
|---|---|---|---|---|
| 粮食合计 | 591.76 | 639.91 | 642.38 | 0.38 |
| 其中：小麦 | 189.06 | 205.93 | 210.71 | 2.32 |
| 粗粮 | 231.16 | 261.89 | 265.10 | 1.22 |
| 大米 | 171.54 | 172.10 | 166.57 | -3.21 |

资料来源：联合国粮农组织（FAO）。

在世界小麦库存量中，主要出口国和地区（阿根廷、澳大利亚、加拿大、欧盟、哈萨克斯坦、俄罗斯、乌克兰和美国）拥有的库存量为 5 390 万吨，比 2014/2015 年度增加 580 万吨，增长 12.06%。

在世界粗粮库存量中，主要出口国和地区（阿根廷、澳大利亚、巴西、加拿大、欧盟、俄罗斯、乌克兰和美国）拥有的库存量为 8 530 万吨，比 2014/2015 年度减少 110 万吨，下降 1.27%。

在世界大米库存量中，主要出口国（印度、巴基斯坦、泰国、美国和越南）拥有的库存量为 3 070 万吨，比 2014/2015 年度减少 1 150 万吨，下降 27. 25%。

2015/2016 年度，世界粮食供求安全系数（本年度期末库存量与下年度消费量的比率）为 24. 94%，比近 10 年最高水平的 2014/2015 年度减少 0. 39 个百分点，比近 10 年最低水平的 2007/2008 年度高出 4. 8 个百分点，远高于世界粮食供求安全指标 17% ~18% 的警戒线水平。近 10 多年来，世界粮食供求安全系数最高的年度是 1998/1999 年度和 1999/2000 年度，均为 33%。随后，世界粮食供求安全系数基本上一路下降，2004/2005 年度止降回升，2005/2006 年度继续有所回升，2006/2007 年度又比 2005/2006 年度急剧下降，2007/2008 年度又比 2006/2007 年度下降，为历史的谷底水平。2008/2009 年度反弹至 23. 77%，比 2007/2008 年度增加 3. 63 个百分点，扭转了粮食欠安全的状态。随后几年，基本上维持该水平，呈小幅度波动态势。2015/2016 年度，主要出口国粮食供求安全系数为 15. 74%，比 2014/2015 年度减少 1. 8 个百分点。

2015/2016 年度，世界主要粮食品种的供求安全系数：小麦为 29. 47%，比 2014/2015 年度增加 1. 2 个百分点；粗粮为 19. 85%，比 2014/2015 年度减少 0. 3 个百分点；大米为 32. 78%，比 2014/2015 年度减少 1. 75 个百分点。

## （五）世界粮食价格

2015 年，三大粮食品种价格走势具体如下：

### 1. 小麦价格

2015 年，国际市场小麦年度平均价格（美国 1 号硬红冬麦，西北太平洋港口交货价）为 226. 3 美元/吨，比 2014 年下降 21. 4%。从分月份走势看，1—8 月价格总体呈下降态势，8 月到达年度最低价 207. 2 美元/吨，9—10 月价格略涨，11—12 月价格小幅回落。12 月价格为 208. 1 美元/吨，比 11 月下降 2. 3%，比 2014 年同期大幅下降 24. 9%。1—12 月，各月价格均明显低于2014 年同期水平，1 月价格为全年最高价（见图1 –2 –1）。

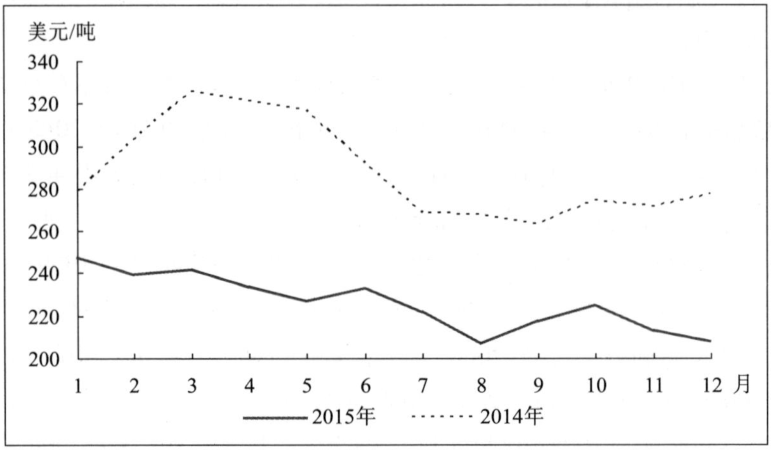


**图1 –2 –1　国际市场小麦价格走势图**

**2. 玉米价格**

2015 年，国际市场玉米年度平均价格（美国2 号黄玉米，海湾地区交货价）为169. 8 美元/吨，比2014 年下降11. 8%。从分月份走势看，1—5 月价格总体呈微幅缓慢下降态势，6—10 月价格呈小幅波动，7 月到达年度最高价179. 3 美元/吨，8 月到达年度最低价162. 7 美元/吨，11—12 月价格持续小幅下降。12 月价格为163. 8 美元/吨，比上月略降1. 3%，比2014 年同期下跌8. 3%。1—12 月中，9 月、10 月价格略高于2014 年同期水平，其他月价格均低于2014 年同期水平，尤其是在前6 个月（见图1 –2 –2）。

**3. 大米价格**

2015 年，国际市场大米年度平均价格（泰国曼谷大米离岸价，破碎率25%）为373 美元/吨，比2014 年下跌2. 2%。从分月份走势看，全年呈波动下行态势，2—6 月价格持续下跌，随后基本呈波动下降走势，2 月为年度最高价401. 1 美元/吨，9 月降至年度最低价347. 7 美元/吨。12 月价格为356. 2 美元/吨，与11 月持平略降，比2014 年同期下跌10. 6%。1—12 月，上半年各月价格均高于2014 年同期水平，下半年各月价格均

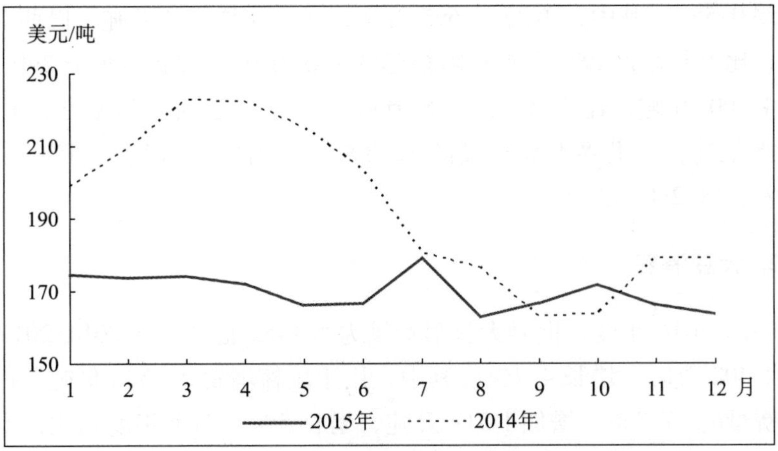


**图 1－2－2　国际市场玉米价格走势**

低于 2014 年同期水平（见图 1－2－3）。

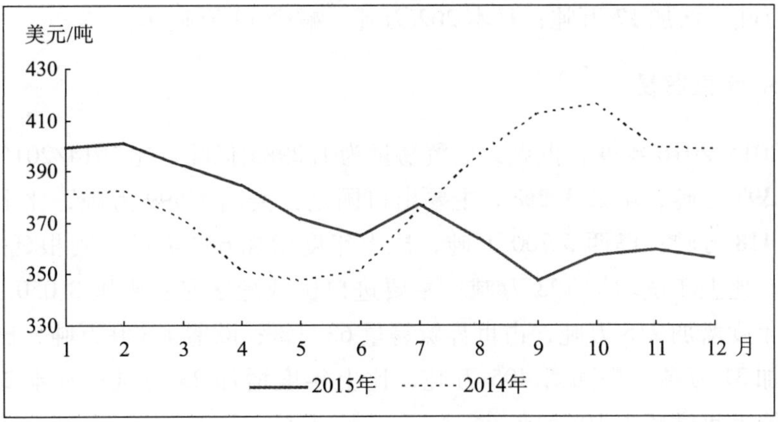


**图 1－2－3　国际市场大米价格走势**

## （六）世界大豆市场

### 1. 大豆生产

2015 年，世界大豆产量为 3.2051 亿吨，比上年增产 171 万吨，比上年略增 0.5%。其中，美国 10 695 万吨，比上年增产 7 万吨；巴西 10 000 万吨，比上年增产 380 万吨；阿根廷 5 850 万吨，比上年减产 290 万吨；中国 1 200 万吨，比上年减产 15 万吨。美国、巴西、阿根廷产量合计 2.6545 亿吨，占世界大豆产量的 82.8%，三国所占份额分别为 33.4%、31.2%、18.2%。

### 2. 大豆消费

2015/2016 年度，世界大豆消费量为 3.1452 亿吨，比 2014/2015 年度增加 1 402 万吨，增长 4.7%。其中，用于压榨消费 2.7586 亿吨，占大豆总消费量的 87.7%，增加 1 319 万吨，增长 5%。与上年度相比，本年度大豆压榨量居世界前几位的国家和地区是：中国 8 070 万吨，增加 620 万吨；美国 5 117 万吨，增加 19 万吨；阿根廷 4 350 万吨，增加 326 万吨；巴西 4 000 万吨，增加 7 万吨；欧盟 1 480 万吨，增加 60 万吨；墨西哥 435 万吨，增加 17 万吨；日本 202 万吨，减少 13 万吨。

### 3. 大豆贸易

2015/2016 年度，世界大豆贸易量为 1.2985 亿吨，比 2014/2015 年度增加 397 万吨，增长 3.2%。主要出口国是：美国 4 599 万吨，比上年度减少 418 万吨；巴西 5 700 万吨，比上年度增加 639 万吨；阿根廷 1 180 万吨，比上年度增加 123 万吨。主要进口国或地区是：中国 8 050 万吨，比上年度增加 215 万吨，占世界贸易量 63.3%；欧盟 1 370 万吨，比上年度增加 31 万吨；墨西哥 405 万吨，比上年度增加 23 万吨；日本 290 万吨，比上年度减少 10 万吨。

### 4. 大豆库存

2015/2016 年度，世界大豆产量略增 0.5%，消费量增长 4.7%，但仍然产大于消，期末库存小幅增加。世界大豆期末库存为 8 042 万吨，比 2014/2015 年度期末库存（也即本年度期初库存）增加 334 万吨，增长 4.3%。其中主产国中，阿根廷 2 980 万吨，比期初库存减少 186 万吨；巴西 1 931 万吨，比期初库存增加 30 万吨；美国 1 223 万吨，比期初库存增加 704 万吨。

### 5. 大豆价格

2015 年，国际市场大豆年度平均价格（美国 1 号黄豆，海湾地区交货价）为 374. 8 美元/吨，比 2014 年大跌 24. 1%。从分月份走势看，1—5 月价格总体呈微幅缓慢下降态势，6—7 月价格连续上升，7 月到达年度最高价 401. 2 美元/吨，8—11 月价格持续下跌，11 月降至年度最低价 343. 4 美元/吨，12 月价格略涨。12 月价格为 347. 2 美元/吨，比上月略涨 1. 1%，比 2014 年同期下跌 15. 8%。1—12 月，各月价格均远低于 2014 年同期水平，尤其是在前 6 个月（见图 1 -2 -4）。

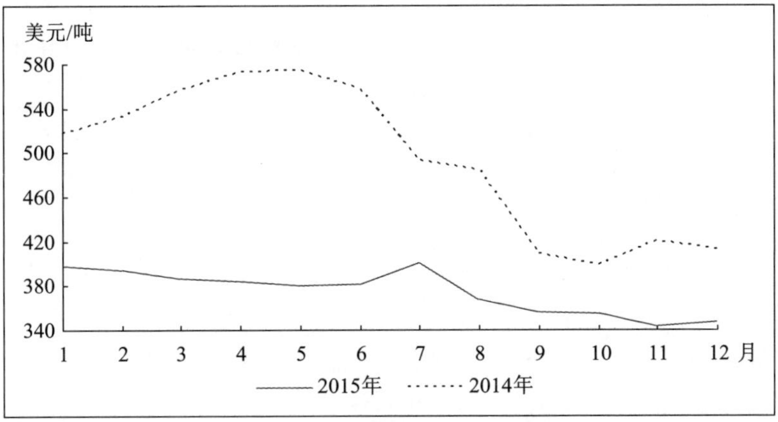


**图 1 -2 -4 国际市场大豆价格走势**

**说明：**

（1）本报告的粮食口径为：谷物即小麦、粗粮和大米，不包括豆类和薯类；粗粮口径为除小麦、大米以外的谷物；大米口径为碾米，由稻谷折算。

（2）由于各国（地区）粮食生产的季节差异，世界粮食产量、消费量与期末库存数据均以各国（地区）的粮食市场年度为准。各国（地区）的粮食市场年度与其不同品种的市场年度并不完全一致，但分国别（地区）的粮食市场年度基本保持稳定，因而年度汇总数据具有可比性。

产量数据系指市场年度所列第一个年份日历年（1—12 月）的产量。例如，市场年度 2015/2016 年度的产量，系指 2015 年日历年的产量。

期末库存数据得自各国（地区）市场年度期末结转库存总量，因此不反映某时间点世界库存水平。由于各国（地区）的市场年度不完全相同，期末库存可能不完全等于供给量（产量 + 期初库存）与消费量之差。

小麦和粗粮贸易量系指市场年度所列第一个年份 7 月/第二个年份 6 月的销售年度的出口量，大米贸易量系指市场年度所列第二个年份日历年（1—12 月）的销售年度的出口量。大豆市场年度系指所列第一个年份 10 月/第二个年份 9 月。

（3）由于有关国际组织、机构和国家及地区根据掌握的最新信息情况，一直在对世界粮食产量、消费量、贸易量与期末库存数据等进行动态调整，所以本书中的历史数据与往年书中的数据可能并不完全相同。

（4）低收入缺粮国系指人均收入水平低于世界银行用于确定接受国际开发协会援助资格水平（即 2011 年为 1 945 美元）的缺粮国。根据粮食援助政策及计划委员会商定的准则和标准，在分配粮食援助时应优先考虑这些国家。

（农业部信息中心　　刘桂才）

# 第二部分

## 中国粮食市场
## 主要品种供求形势

# 一、小麦市场分析

**【内容提要】**

回顾2015年，我国小麦产量突破1.3亿吨关口，实现“十二连增”，但受收获期降水影响，黄淮、江淮多地小麦的不完善粒所占比例大幅增加；我国小麦消费总量明显下降，主要体现在制粉消费及工业消费方面，饲用消费在2015年下半年也呈显著减少态势；全年小麦进口总量与2014年持平略增，其中加麦占比显著提升，美麦和澳麦占比下降。2015年，我国小麦价格出现近10年来罕见的持续下跌，终端消费极度不振、流通小麦质量偏差是导致行情走低的主要原因；国家先后在苏鄂皖豫鲁冀启动小麦托市收购，并继续在2016年实施小麦最低收购价政策，收购价格维持不变。

展望2016年，中国小麦产量或维持较高水平；在国家经济增速下滑、全力推进供给侧结构性改革的环境下，终端消费状况或依旧不容乐观；收购期大范围启动托市的可能性较大，同时也存在下调临储小麦竞价交易底价及下调2017年小麦托市价格水平的可能；2016年，在基础消费的支撑下，宽松的供需格局或让小麦价格行情维持在窄幅区间内小幅波动。

## （一）2015年我国小麦供需形势回顾

### 1. 小麦产量再增，收益质量下滑

据国家统计局数据，2015年小麦产量达到13 019

万吨，较2014年增产401.6万吨。“十二连增”的佳绩继续改写中国粮食生产纪录。小麦播种面积24 141千公顷，较2014年增加77.4千公顷（见图2－1－1）。

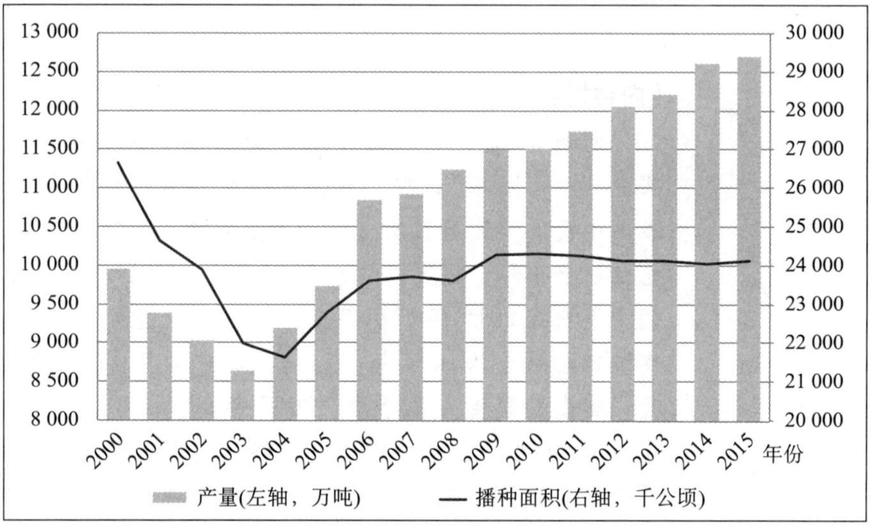


数据来源：中国统计局历年《中国统计年鉴》，中国统计出版社出版。

**图2－1－1 2000—2015年我国小麦产量与播种面积图**

尽管小麦产量连增，但质量分化却比2014年严重。华北地区冬小麦质量保持稳定，容重基本在二等以上水平，不完善粒占比多在3%以下。但南方冬麦区由于在收获时期遭遇较大范围降水，江淮、黄淮流域冬小麦大面积出现芽麦和萌动粒情况，个别地区的不完善粒占比达50%甚至更高。

据综合测算，如不计土地及人工成本，2015年主产区小麦种植收益较2014年有所下降。其中，亩均种植投入略减，因为农资支出减少；但市场收购价格明显降低，导致亩均毛收入降低。综合亩均收益384元，较上年降低66元。

**2. 小麦年度消费总量减少**

据机构数据，2014/2015年度我国小麦总消费量12 020.4万吨，较2013/2014年度减5.7%。其中，2014/2015年度，制粉消费同比减

4.5%；饲用消费及消耗同比增3.7%；工业消费同比减26.9%；种用消费同比持平（见表2－1－1）。

**表2－1－1**　　**小麦供需平衡表**　　单位：千公顷，吨/公顷，千吨

| 项　目 | 2012/2013年度 | 2013/2014年度 | 2014/2015年度<br>12月份估计值 | 2015/2016年度<br>12月份预测值 |
|---|---|---|---|---|
| 播种面积 | 24 268 | 24 117 | 24 064 | 24 136 |
| **生产量** | **120 843** | **121 926** | **126 208** | **130 187** |
| 进口量 | 2 895 | 6 772 | 1 495 | 2 000 |
| **新增供给** | **123 738** | **128 698** | **127 703** | **132 187** |
| 制粉消费 | 97 100 | 96 300 | 92 000 | 90 000 |
| 其中：面粉 | 72 825 | 72 225 | 69 000 | 67 500 |
| 次粉 | 4 855 | 4 815 | 4 600 | 4 500 |
| 麸皮 | 19 420 | 19 260 | 18 400 | 18 000 |
| **饲用及损耗** | **21 000** | **13 500** | **14 000** | **10 500** |
| 工业消费 | 12 000 | 13 000 | 9 500 | 9 000 |
| 种用量 | 4 700 | 4 700 | 4 700 | 4 700 |
| 年度国内消费 | 134 800 | 127 500 | 120 200 | 114 200 |
| 出口量 | 0 | 0 | 4 | 0 |
| **年度总消费** | **134 800** | **127 500** | **120 204** | **114 200** |
| **年度结余量** | **−11 062** | **1 198** | **7 499** | **17 987** |

数据来源：国家粮油信息中心（2015年12月数据）。

分析来看，2014/2015年度制粉消费减少的主因是国内总体消费不振，企业开机率降低；饲料及损耗数量较上年度略有增加的主因是2014年下半年及2015年上半年玉米价格较高，小麦用作饲料消费量增加；小麦工业消费大幅减少的主因是宏观形势不景气，粮食深加工业普遍亏损而降低了用量。

### 3. 小麦进口总量持平略增

2015年我国小麦累计进口297.4万吨，较2014年略增。其中，自澳大利亚进口125.5万吨，占比为42.2%；自加拿大进口99.2万吨，占比为33.4%；自美国进口60.3万吨，占比为20.3%；自哈萨克斯坦进口

11.8 万吨，占比为 4%。全年小麦进口均价 299.09 美元/吨，较 2014 年降低 24.78 美元/吨。国内需求稳定、国际小麦价格持续下跌是导致小麦进口量平稳，进口均价降低的主要原因。

2015 年，我国累计出口小麦 0.53 万吨，较 2014 年增加 0.434 万吨；面粉出口 11.65 万吨，较 2014 年减少 7.22 万吨（见图 2-1-2）。

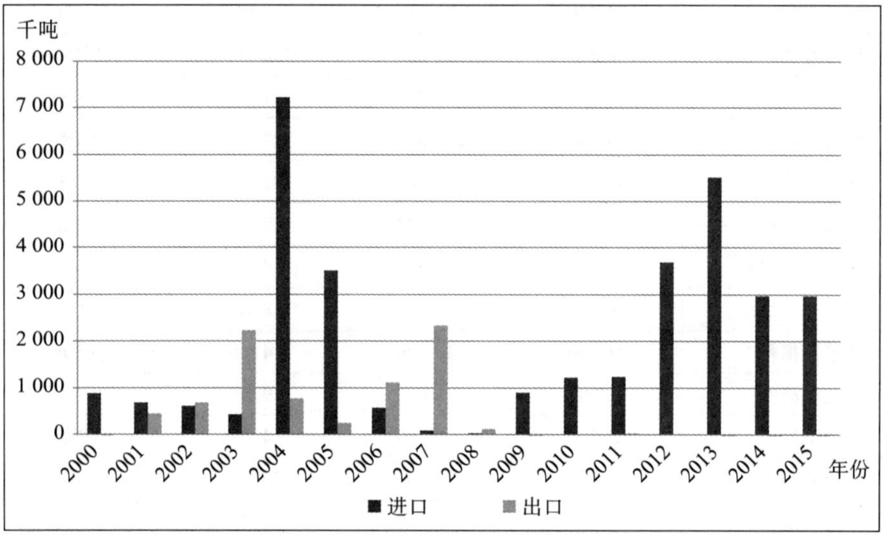


数据来源：中国海关总署。

**图 2-1-2　2000—2015 年中国小麦进口和出口情况**

## （二）2015 年我国小麦市场行情回顾

### 1. 价格跌至三年前水平

2015 年，国际形势错综复杂，全球大宗商品步入漫漫"熊途"，中国经济承压前行，多种因素让国内小麦行情出现近 10 年来罕见的持续下跌。

第一阶段，2015 年元旦至 5 月下旬，接新前行情稳中偏弱。1 月份，黄河以北地区小麦价格多在 1.27～1.3 元/斤，黄河以南大部地区小麦在 1.25～1.28 元/斤。至接新前，黄河以北地区陈麦收购价基本维持在 1.26～1.29 元/斤，黄河以南陈麦价格在 1.24～1.27 元/斤。价格虽然只是略下滑，但企业开机率降低、采购意愿消极都反映出市场后劲严重不足。

分析来看：一方面，市场供应充裕，消费不振，企业并不急于建立库存。在供应端，年初的专场交易、后期的储备轮换、临储小麦投放、贸易流通等让企业采购无忧。在消费端，面粉消费环节无亮点，企业开机率一度降至 50% 以下。饲料粮消费也随生猪行情降至低点，尽管 3 月份猪肉价逐步回升，但饲料消费的滞后性让小麦饲用需求显著降低。另一方面，面粉价格难以上调，但麸皮价格却从 2 月份的 0.85 元/斤之上跌至 5 月中下旬的 0.58 元/斤，让企业陷入“保生产还是保利润”的两难境地。

第二阶段，5 月下旬至 9 月底新麦收购阶段，南方小麦质量较差拖累行情。新麦初上市价格相对混乱，由南至北收购价从每斤 1 元出头到每斤 1.15 元都有。随着托市启动，价格逐步向托市价格水平靠拢，但在收购过程中出现价格不升反降的现象，特别是河北、山东东北部等传统的“高价区域”，市场价格已经低于托市价格水平，在全面启动托市后才止住麦价下行的趋势。

究其原因：一是企业对后期行情持谨慎态度导致收购动力不足；二是南方大量难以入库的低质小麦流入华北市场；三是农村经纪人加快售粮进度；四是执行收购任务的粮库严格管控，导致超标小麦只能通过地方政府出台相应办法缓解，而对于华北地区质量标准的小麦，仓容问题又成为收储的“瓶颈”。

第三阶段，10 月份至年底，购销趋于平稳，行情缓步运行并小幅回升。由于托市结束，较大数量未被收购的小麦遭抛售，导致国庆期间主产区小麦价格“断崖式”下跌。华北地区小麦价格从 9 月底的 1.19 元/斤附近跌至国庆期间的 1.13 元/斤以下；南方产区的小麦价格也从 1.12 元/斤跌至 1.02 元/斤左右。

国家维持 2016 年托市价格不变、超跌导致惜售，让小麦行情出现些许修复性回升，但整个 10 月价格行情表现依旧疲软。11 月中下旬开始市场价格止稳回升。至 12 月初，华北地区小麦入厂价多涨至 1.24～1.27 元/斤，基本触及年初时的最高点，其他地区小麦收购价也有不同程度回升。

华北地区大到暴雪阻碍交通，企业扩大原粮储备，麸皮从之前的0.53元/斤涨至0.65元/斤左右，提振了面粉企业的加工积极性，是推动这一轮上涨的主要原因。但行情走高不仅刺激了贸易商出库的积极性，加工量的快速扩大也导致市场上面粉及麸皮供应再度承压。麸皮再度回落至0.52元/斤左右。至12月底，黄河以北地区小麦价格降至1.19元/斤左右，其他地区标准品小麦降至1.16元/斤左右（见图2-1-3）。

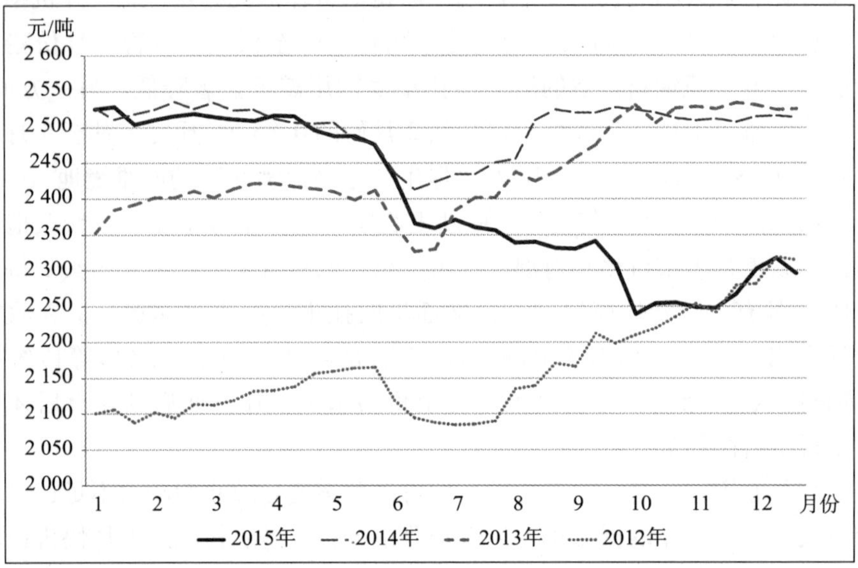


数据来源：郑州粮食批发市场。

**图2-1-3 郑州粮食批发市场白小麦（三等）价格走势图**

**2. 政策性收购高位徘徊**

2015年收购期内，各主产区累计收购新产小麦6 631万吨，比2014年减少732万吨。其中，托市收购2 079万吨，较2014年减少456万吨。企业收购态度谨慎、南部区域小麦质量偏差、宏观经济低迷压制市场预期、打击不合规收购等因素是2015年收购量降低的主要原因（见图2-1-4）。

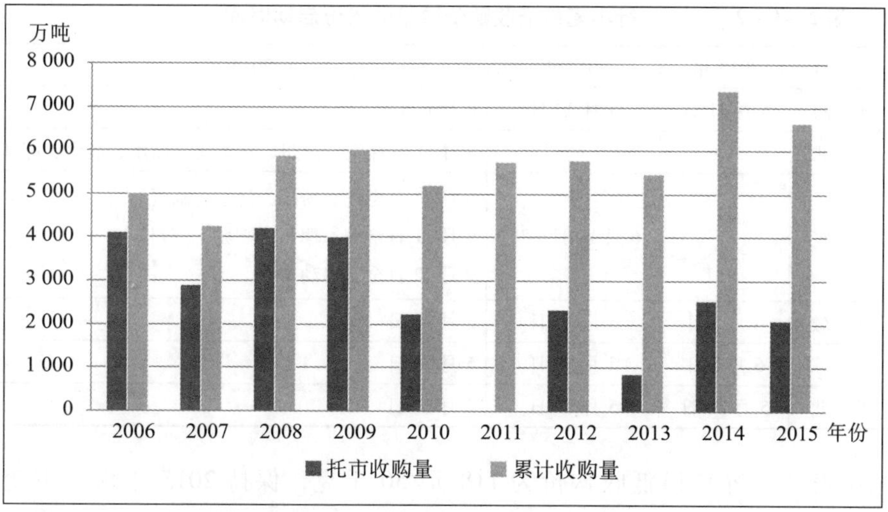


数据来源：国家粮食局网站、中华粮网。

**图 2-1-4　小麦托市收购量与累计收购量对比图**

回顾来看，2015 年的小麦收购有三个特点较为突出：一是“抢收、惜售”的现象不复存在。由于国家在政策执行层面的严格把关，加之市场购销低迷，往年经常会发生的企业抢收、农民及经纪人惜售的现象在 2015 年鲜有发生。二是针对质量未达标小麦的收购意见由地方政府出台。为保护种粮农民利益，安徽省、湖北省针对质量未达标小麦先后启动省级小麦临时收储政策，河南省也安排 1 500 万元用于不完善粒小麦超标的补贴。改由地方政府出台政策，更有助于所收问题小麦的监管，提高专项资金运作效率，减少操作中的违规现象。三是河北启动托市收购，山东托市收购全面开展。由于在收购期后期主产区小麦价格持续弱势下行，为增加农民收入、调动种粮积极性、维持粮食价格在合理区间，河北、山东相继适时扩大托市收购启动范围（见表 2-1-2）。

### 3. 托市价格维持不变

2015 年国庆过后，国家正式发布 2016 年小麦托市收购价格。据国家发改委网站，为保护农民利益，防止“谷贱伤农”，2016 年国家继续在小麦主产区实行最低收购价政策。综合考虑粮食生产成本、市场供求、国内外市场价格和粮食产业发展等各方面因素，经国务院批准，2016 年生产

**表 2-1-2　　执行小麦最低收购价政策的省份启动时间**

| 省　份 | 2013 年 | 2014 年 | 2015 年 |
|---|---|---|---|
| 河　南 | 5 月 31 日 | 5 月 30 日 | 6 月 1 日 |
| 河　北 | — | — | 9 月 11 日保定、沧州、石家庄、衡水、邢台、邯郸 |
| 山　东 | — | 6 月 14 日枣庄 | 6 月 17 日枣庄、荷泽、济宁、临沂<br>9 月 11 日泰安、德州、聊城、滨州<br>9 月 22 日全省启动 |
| 安　徽 | 6 月 5 日 | 5 月 30 日 | 5 月 28 日 |
| 江　苏 | 6 月 6 日 | 5 月 30 日 | 5 月 26 日 |
| 湖　北 | 5 月 30 日 | 5 月 27 日 | 5 月 27 日 |

的小麦（三等）最低收购价为 118 元/50 千克，保持 2015 年水平不变，以稳定粮食生产，促进粮食产业健康发展（见图 2-1-5）。

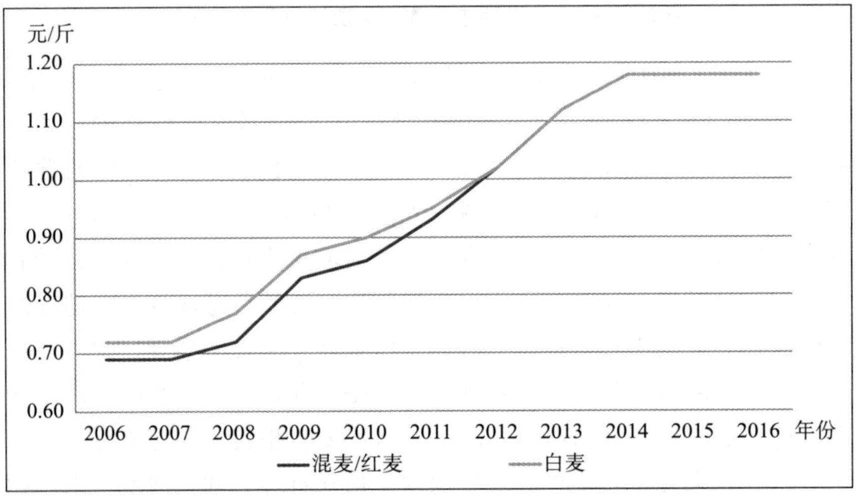


数据来源：国家发改委网站。

**图 2-1-5　历年小麦最低收购价变化情况**

在粮价弱势下行、需求极度不振、玉米临储收购价格大幅下调的背景下，维持 2016 年小麦托市收购价格不变，无疑是给农民及市场各吃了一颗“定心丸”，一方面稳定了农民种粮的心态，在正常的种植投入情况下不至于赔钱；另一方面也算是稳定市场预期，防止因粮价过度下滑而对各产业环节造成打击。同时，相对平稳的政策价格预期，可以给国家提供更多的时间和更大的空间来进行未来的粮食价格政策和补贴政策的设计与改革。

### 4. 政策粮成交跌至谷底

受政策价格调整、消费不振以及市场供应过剩等因素综合影响，2015年国家临储小麦交易情况持续低迷。

2015 年，临储小麦投放共 47 次（不含 2015 年首周的专场小麦交易，下同），周均投放 109 万吨，较 2014 年增加 17 万吨。全年投放数量相对均匀，说明临储小麦供应保障性较强。2014 年托市收购小麦分别于 1 月、2 月和 4 月在安徽、湖北和河南投放。

临储小麦周均成交 10 万吨，较 2014 年减少 19 万吨。其中，6 月份以后的成交量降为个位数，更有一周是零成交，创下临储小麦交易 9 年来的最低。交易底价明显高于市场价格、加工消费需求极度不振是导致交易低迷的主要原因。

临储小麦交易底价提高导致 2015 年的成交均价较 2014 年提高 73 元/吨，达 2 461 元/吨，也正因如此，导致临储交易几乎被市场“孤立”。

2015 年第一周举行的专场交易会投放 201 万吨，由于是按成交量来分配小麦的进口配额，最终成交 168 万吨，创两年来新高。所投放 2012—2014 年托市小麦的交易底价在原基础上增加 140 元/吨，分别至 2 450 元/吨、2 500 元/吨、2 550 元/吨。其中，河南托市麦最高拍到 2 790 元/吨。专场交易对后期市场造成持续影响，如短期集中出库造成的供给压力、就地低价转卖造成的价格压力、交易成本加入后期进口小麦售价中造成的企业压力等（见图 2－1－6）。

### 5. 郑麦期货价格震荡攀升

2015 年郑州商品交易所郑麦期货价格震荡攀升，年内郑麦指数最低 2 533 点，最高 2 928 点，累计涨幅 15.6%。分阶段看，郑麦期货价格走势如下：

1 月初，1501 合约跌至年内最低的 2 500 元/吨后，主力转为 1 505 合约并在短期冲至阶段高点 2 720 元/吨，随后一路弱势下行至 5 月份。强麦现货低迷及仓单质量不稳定，导致期盘走低。

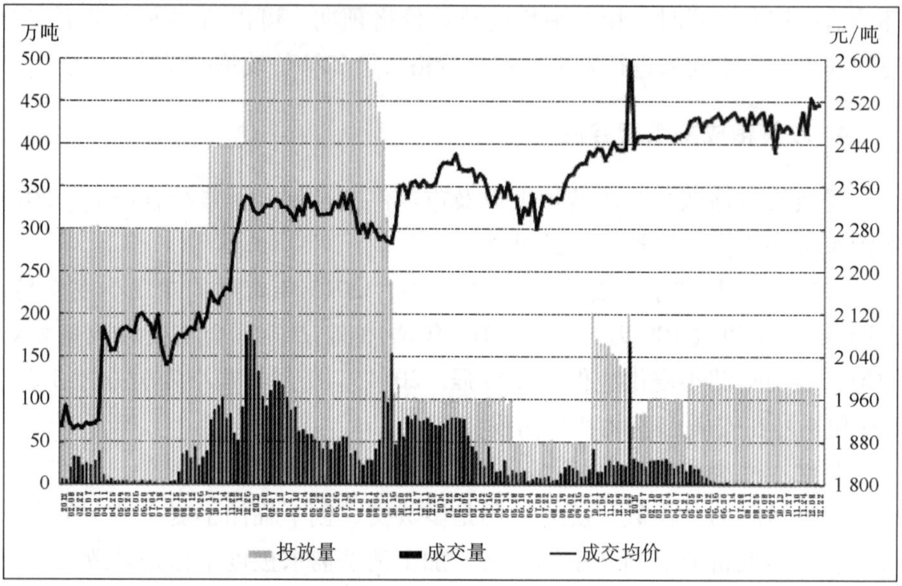


数据来源：郑州粮食批发市场、中华粮网。

**图2-1-6 2012—2015年政策性小麦竞价销售交易情况**

6月份开始，新合约生效，严加监管及升贴水调整，1601合约在中旬达到阶段高点2 840元/吨。由于强麦现货收购价从6月初开秤时的2 640元/吨快速涨至2 940元/吨，8月现货止涨并逐步回落，拖累了期货行情。1601合约在8月底降至2 660元/吨，后在9月围绕2 730元/吨一线小幅波动。

10月份后，郑麦主力转为1605合约，期货盘面开始逐步攀升，年内最高达到2 900元/吨。这一时期尽管现货市场强筋优质麦的价格基本稳定，但由于市场上能用于注册仓单的强麦数量相对较少，加之进口小麦配额在市场上已经炒到近800元/吨，期货行情随之走高（见图2-1-7）。

## （三）2015年国际小麦走势及2016年国际小麦行情展望

2015年，国际小麦走势相对平稳。回顾来看，1月全球小麦受产量预增、美元走强、大宗农产品下跌等因素影响，从2014年末的高位大幅下

数据来源：文化财经。

**图 2-1-7　2015 年郑麦期货指数走势图**

跌，并维持低位震荡达半年之久。6 月下旬，因炒作主产国小麦减产，全球小麦出现了一波急涨行情，美麦指数在 10 天时间从 496.2 点快速冲至 620.2 点。随之在机构报告利空、美元创阶段新高、能源及贵金属走弱以及技术层面卖盘压力等因素影响下大幅回落，至 9 月初跌至 467.4 点，创 2010 年 6 月来新低。尽管随后机构空头回补及炒作局部地区干旱，行情有所回升，但全球经济总体不景气、原油及其他大宗商品持续下跌，加之全球小麦增产预期强烈，美麦指数在 500 点整数关口下低位承压运行（见图 2-1-8）。

展望 2016 年，国际小麦价格走势将面临更为复杂的局面，利空因素强于利多，全球小麦价格回升空间有限。一方面，全球供需基本面维持宽松格局。美国农业部和联合国粮农组织的 12 月份报告均预测，2015/2016 年度全球小麦产量达 7.35 亿吨，创历史新高；而期末库存分别为 2.3 亿吨和 2.07 亿吨，均高于上年。另一方面，宏观经济及金融环境也在拖累国际小麦行情。美元对主要货币汇率保持升值状态，大宗商品价格已经连续 3 年下跌，美联储进入新一轮的加息周期等因素，均将导致全球消费需求减弱。

展望 2016 年，全球小麦走势或在 2015 年的基础上震荡回升。基于对 2015/2016 年度全球小麦产销预期和能源价格继续下跌空间有限的预测，

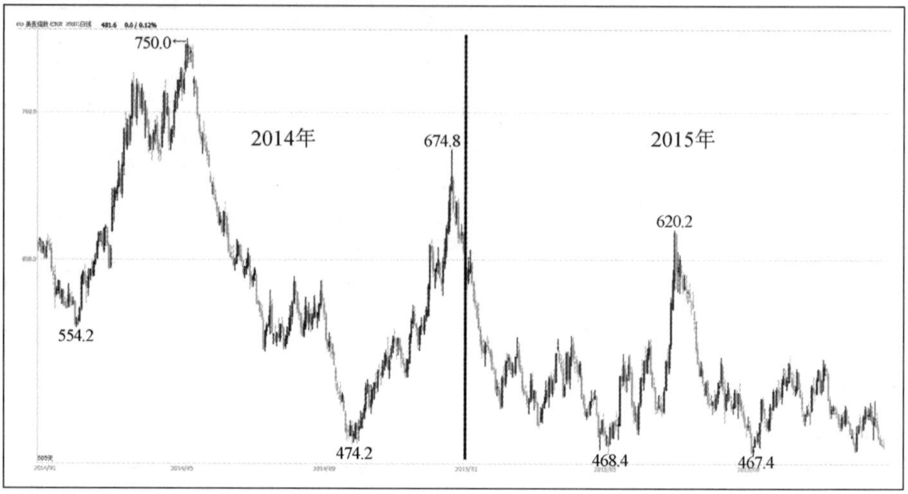


数据来源：文化财经。

**图2-1-8 2014—2015年芝加哥期货交易所美麦期货指数走势图**

加上以中国为首的新兴经济体国家的增长前景逐步向好，预计2016年芝加哥期货交易所美麦指数将在450~650点范围内运行。

## （四）2016年我国小麦市场展望

### 1. 播种面积稳中略增，产量或维持高位

据农业部农情调度信息，2015年秋冬播种进展顺利，冬小麦播种面积增加60多万亩。种植面积扩大将奠定2016年丰收的基础。据中央气象台网站信息，2015年秋冬播种后，大部地区墒情适宜，利于冬小麦播种出苗和分蘖生长。

综合来看，由于小麦生长期较长，可逆性较好，加之田间管理配套较为成熟，如果在后期的关键生长期不出现极端灾害性气候和爆发性病害，在“保证面积、促进单产”措施的引导下，2016年全国小麦产量依旧会维持一个较高水平，预计产量在1.28亿~1.32亿吨之间。

### 2. 消费低迷状况难改

宏观经济运行形势低迷，加之小麦在饲料消费领域的价格劣势，使小麦在2016年的消费状况不容乐观。

从制粉消费来看，近三个年度呈逐年递减的趋势，而企业开机率下降是导致制粉消费减少的直接原因。据监测，2014年我国面粉加工业的平均开机率已经从往年的75%降到60%左右，2015年降至55%左右。分析来看，社会发展带来的消费结构改善、产业结构调整带来的群体性集中消费减少、面粉及麸皮价格难以上调导致的加工积极性降低，或导致2016年加工企业开机率进一步降低。

从饲用消费来看，饲料养殖行业低迷、玉米价格大跌限制了小麦在饲用消费领域的用量。机构测算，2015/2016年度的小麦饲料消费为1 050万吨，较2014/2015年度减少25%。其中，饲料方面，农业部数据显示，2015年12月份生猪存栏3.84亿头，同比降9%，创有统计数据以来新低，能繁母猪存栏3 798万头，同比下降11.4%。存栏大幅下降势必影响到后期饲料的消费数量。玉米替代方面，在巨量玉米临储去库存的压力、玉米政策性价格下调的预期、其他低价饲料粮大量进口等因素影响下，玉米与小麦的价差或将进一步扩大（见图2－1－9、图2－1－10）。

### 3. 供应渠道多样　供应量不减

在消费低迷时期，市场的供应会显得格外充裕。从渠道上看：主渠道是临储小麦投放，约4 000万吨的各年托市小麦完全有能力保障市场的用粮需要。辅助渠道是企业贸易粮，出于降成本、还贷款目的，预计在2016年上半年将集中出库，在下半年为规避风险也将加快原粮和资金周转。其他渠道，如各级储备轮换、农户及农村经纪人手中存粮，也会支撑相应地区消费需求。同时，预计大范围启动托市的可能性较大，但严格的收购标准或让“被拒之门外”的低质量小麦拖累市场行情。由此预计2016年全年将保持较为宽松的供应环境，不会出现明显的供应紧张时期。

### 4. 政策性价格调整可能性较大

2016年收购方面，首先，湖北、安徽、江苏、河南及早启动托市的

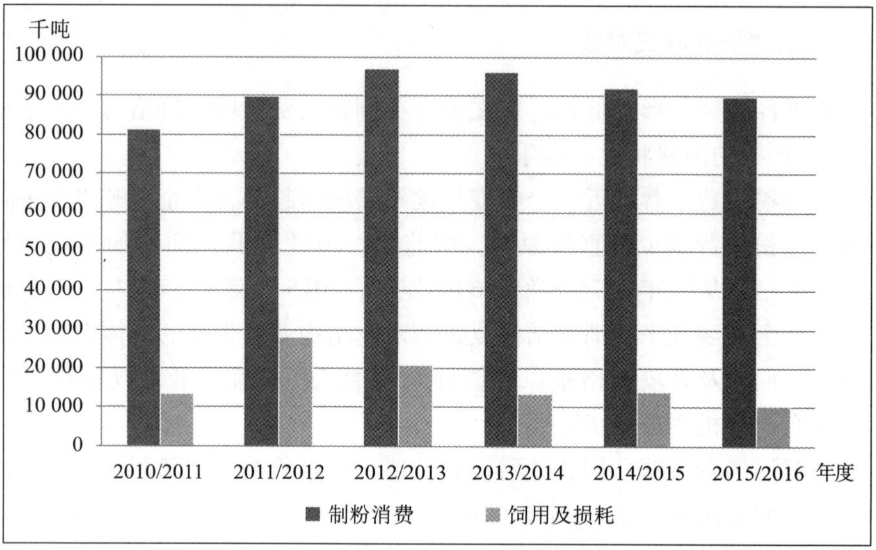


数据来源：国家粮油信息中心。

**图2－1－9　小麦制粉及饲用消费情况对比**

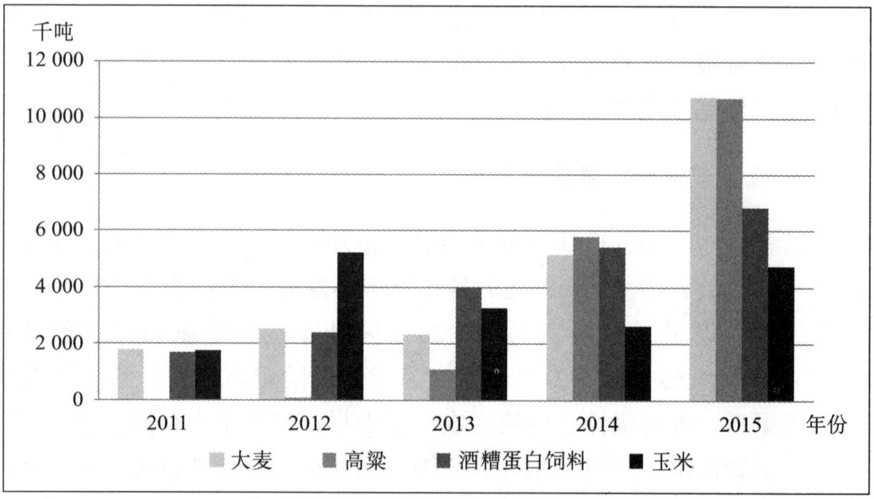


数据来源：中国海关总署。

**图2－1－10　玉米、高粱、大麦、酒糟蛋白饲料进口情况对比**

可能性较大，山东、河北也存在部分区域启动的可能性。其次，如果收购期天气正常，在严格监管之下，预计2016年托市收购量或在2 000万～

2 200 万吨之间。最后，综合估算 2016 年的全社会收购总量或在 6 600 万吨左右。

2016 年临储交易方面，首先，是否会在 2016 年投放 2015 年托市小麦，需要综合考虑托市小麦的交易底价的调整情况，以及各临储投放省份的成交情况。其次，考虑到回笼财政资金、减轻库存压力、提高供给效率等多方面原因，2016 年下调交易底价的可能性较大，预计下调幅度在 0. 03 ~0. 05 元/斤范围。

尽管国家明确提出“价补分离”的政策思路，但基于“分品种施策、渐进式推进”的原则，2016 年 10 月份或继续发布 2017 年小麦最低收购价格，但托市价格水平或有所下调。

### 5. 下行压力不减　基本面向好

2016 年作为“十三五”的开局之年，中国经济运行仍面临较大的下行压力。美元进入加息周期、资本外流势头不减、原油及大宗商品“熊途漫漫”以及结构性改革滞后等因素，都让中国经济在未来一段时期难以保持乐观。一方面，2016 年 GDP 同比增长下降到 6.5%，显示出让经济发展继续减速，以给予结构性改革更多空间；另一方面，PPI 持续负增长、CPI 涨幅低位运行，对经济的负面作用将进一步显现（见图 2 –1 –11）。但应该看到，当前中国经济企稳回升的因素正在逐步积累，发展长期向好的基本面没有变，只要采取积极有力的宏观政策，把握好稳增长、调结构和防风险的平衡，从供需两侧发力，中国经济仍旧能够保持在合理区间运行。

### 6. 行情维持窄幅区间波动

2016 年我国小麦行情难有大的涨跌空间，市场上的基础消费将在很大程度上支撑着小麦的价格底部，而常时常量定期投放的托市小麦也限制了小麦的价格顶部。预计全年主产区小麦价格将维持在窄幅区间内波动的运行态势。

以标准品质二等白小麦为例，预计 2016 年接新前，主产区加工企业到厂平均采购价将在 1. 16 ~1. 2 元/斤；如果 2016 年新产小麦平均质量正常，市场价格将主要围绕托市价格范围运行；收购期结束后至年底，主产

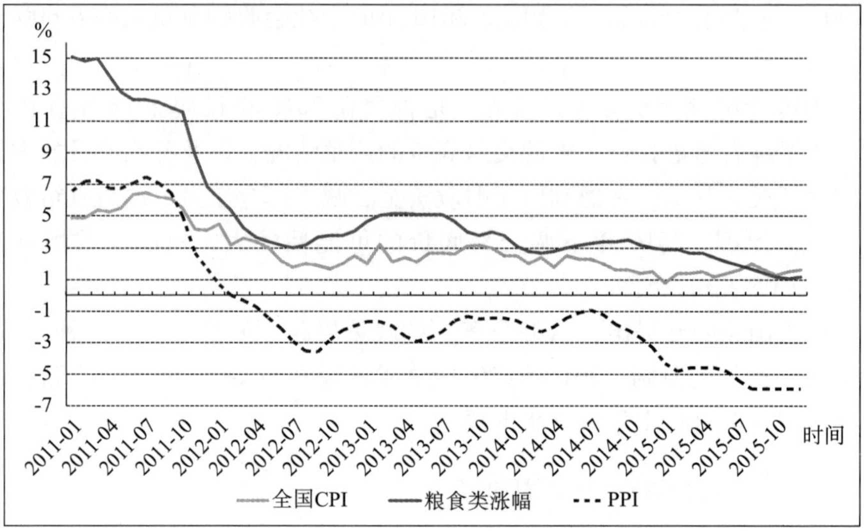


数据来源：国家统计局网站。

**图2－1－11　全国CPI、粮食、PPI同比涨幅**

区加工企业到厂平均收购价或增至1.18～1.22元/斤。其中，黄河以北地区小麦价格将基本维持在1.2～1.24元/斤区间运行，黄淮、江淮地区小麦价格将基本维持在1.16～1.2元/斤区间运行。

（郑州粮食批发市场　　申洪源）

# 二、稻米市场分析

【内容提要】

2015年国内稻谷产量继续稳居在2亿多吨的水平，消费保持小幅增长态势，产需略有缺口，进口大增，期末库存高位稳定，大米市场价格整体平稳。分品种看，早籼稻连续2年减产，市场供需不断萎缩；中晚籼稻供需稳定；粳稻在政策力度支持减弱的情况下，面临艰难的调整，价格波动也较大；进口大米以其价格优势大举进入中国，给国内的大米市场以很大的冲击。托市稻的销售仍然非常低迷，库存居高不下。展望未来，在“确保口粮自给”的粮食安全大目标下，国内稻米市场仍然会受到政策的重点照顾，市场整体仍然在“上有顶、下有底”的区间运行，不会有大的波动。

## （一）供需分析

### 1. 稻谷总产连续5年超2亿吨，早稻连续2年减产

根据国家统计局的数字，2015年全国稻谷总产20 824.5万吨，比2014年增产173.76万吨，增幅为0.8%。稻谷总产曾在1997年首次突破2亿吨，此后一路下滑，直到2011年才再次站在2亿吨之上，不过这次站稳了脚跟，截至2015年，中国稻谷总产已经是连续5年稳定在2亿多吨的水平。产量稳定的背后是播种面积的稳定，2011—2015年，稻谷播种面积连续5年稳定在3 000多万公顷（见图2-2-1）。

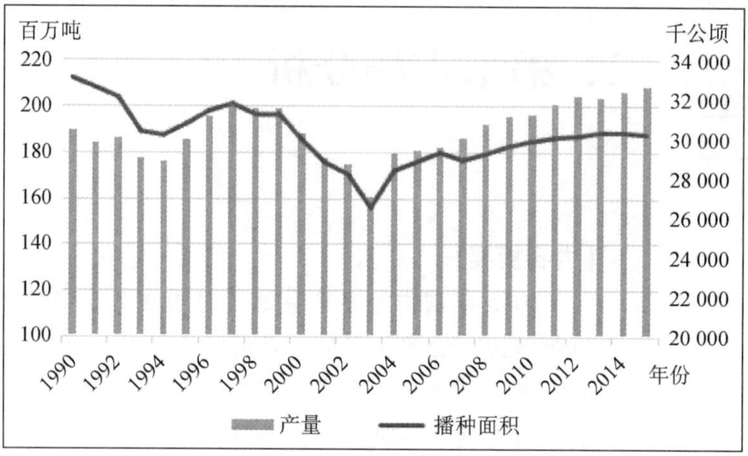


数据来源：WIND咨询，国家统计局。

**图2－2－1　稻谷总产与播种面积（1990—2015年）**

2015年早稻总产3 369.1万吨，比2014年减产31.9万吨，减幅为0.9%。这已经是连续2年减产，不过幅度很小。过去十多年，稻谷总播种面积呈上升趋势，但是早稻播种面积呈下降趋势。10年前，早稻播种面积还有600多万公顷，2015年只有571万公顷，下降了5%。这10来年，早稻的产量在3 200万吨左右徘徊（见图2－2－2）。

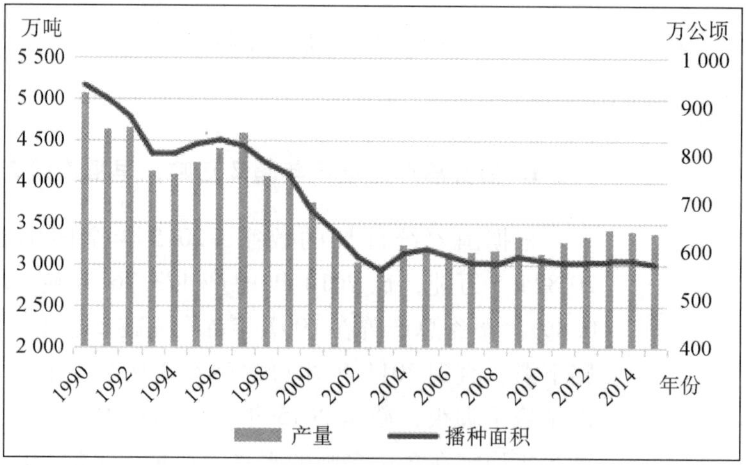


数据来源：WIND咨询，国家统计局。

**图2－2－2　早稻总产与播种面积（1990—2015年）**

### 2. 大米连续4年产不足需，进口猛增，库存稳定

根据美国农业部的数据，2015年中国大米产量14 577万吨，消费量15 000万吨，产消缺口423万吨，已经是连续4年产不足需。2007—2011年，连续5年是产大于需；2000—2005年，连续6年产不足需；1996—1999年，连续4年产大于需。过去20年，中国大米产需的一个基本规律是每隔5年左右，要么是持续产不足需，要么是持续产大于需。当然，除了新世纪头3年存在严重的产不足需情况（累计4 500万吨的供需缺口），其他年份产需之间的差距不大。

中国过去4年虽然都存在产需缺口，但是粮食库存却没有减少，反而略有增加，2015年末库存4 768万吨，库存消费比31.8%，仍然保持在高位，其原因在于进口。中国长期以来是大米净出口国，但从2010年开始，连续成为大米净进口国，并且净进口量越来越大。2015年大米净进口425万吨，创历史新高。6年时间净进口1 609万吨。近年来中国大量进口大米不是因为国内的大米供给出了问题，虽然连年有少量产需缺口，但是我们庞大的大米库存足以补充，然而进口大米有价格优势，国内的库存并不能形成有效的市场供给（见表2－2－1）。

**表2－2－1　　中国大米供需平衡表**　　单位：百万吨

| 年　份 | 期初库存 | 产　量 | 消　费 | 出　口 | 进　口 | 期末库存 |
|---|---|---|---|---|---|---|
| 1992 | 27.52 | 130.35 | 127.00 | 1.40 | 0.11 | 29.70 |
| 1993 | 29.70 | 124.39 | 128.00 | 1.52 | 0.70 | 25.20 |
| 1994 | 25.17 | 123.15 | 129.00 | 0.03 | 1.96 | 21.26 |
| 1995 | 21.54 | 129.65 | 130.00 | 0.27 | 0.83 | 21.76 |
| 1996 | 21.73 | 136.57 | 132.13 | 0.94 | 0.33 | 25.56 |
| 1997 | 25.56 | 140.49 | 135.85 | 3.75 | 0.26 | 26.72 |
| 1998 | 27.00 | 139.10 | 136.07 | 2.71 | 0.18 | 27.50 |
| 1999 | 96.00 | 138.94 | 133.76 | 2.96 | 0.28 | 98.50 |
| 2000 | 98.50 | 131.54 | 134.36 | 1.85 | 0.27 | 94.10 |
| 2001 | 94.10 | 124.31 | 134.58 | 1.96 | 0.31 | 82.17 |
| 2002 | 82.17 | 122.18 | 134.80 | 2.58 | 0.26 | 67.22 |

续表

| 年份 | 期初库存 | 产量 | 消费 | 出口 | 进口 | 期末库存 |
|---|---|---|---|---|---|---|
| 2003 | 67.22 | 112.46 | 135.00 | 0.88 | 1.12 | 44.93 |
| 2004 | 43.92 | 125.36 | 130.30 | 0.66 | 0.61 | 38.93 |
| 2005 | 38.93 | 126.41 | 128.00 | 1.22 | 0.65 | 36.78 |
| 2006 | 36.78 | 127.20 | 127.20 | 1.34 | 0.47 | 35.92 |
| 2007 | 35.92 | 130.22 | 127.45 | 0.97 | 0.30 | 38.02 |
| 2008 | 38.02 | 134.33 | 133.00 | 0.78 | 0.34 | 38.90 |
| 2009 | 38.55 | 136.57 | 134.32 | 0.65 | 0.39 | 40.53 |
| 2010 | 40.53 | 137.00 | 135.00 | 0.50 | 0.54 | 42.57 |
| 2011 | 42.57 | 140.70 | 139.60 | 0.44 | 1.79 | 45.02 |
| 2012 | 45.02 | 143.00 | 144.00 | 0.34 | 3.14 | 46.83 |
| 2013 | 46.83 | 142.53 | 146.30 | 0.26 | 4.02 | 46.81 |
| 2014 | 46.81 | 144.56 | 147.60 | 0.43 | 4.32 | 47.66 |
| 2015 | 47.66 | 145.77 | 150.00 | 0.45 | 4.70 | 47.68 |

资料来源：美国农业部。

## （二）价格分析

### 1. 零售价格：小幅上涨，速度放缓

2015年大米零售价格继续维持小幅上涨趋势。据国家统计局50个城市大米平均价格数据，2015年底大米平均零售价格为6.18元/千克，同比上涨2.66%。具体来看，前5个月价格持续上涨，由年初的6.02元/千克上涨到6.18元/千克，之后7个月，价格维持在6.18元/千克，上下波动不超过0.01元/千克。

2009—2010年，大米零售价格上涨速度很快，2011年之后，大米价格上涨速度明显放缓。最近3年，除了年底价格会有突然的小幅上涨外，大米年度间的零售价格都很稳定（见图2-2-3）。

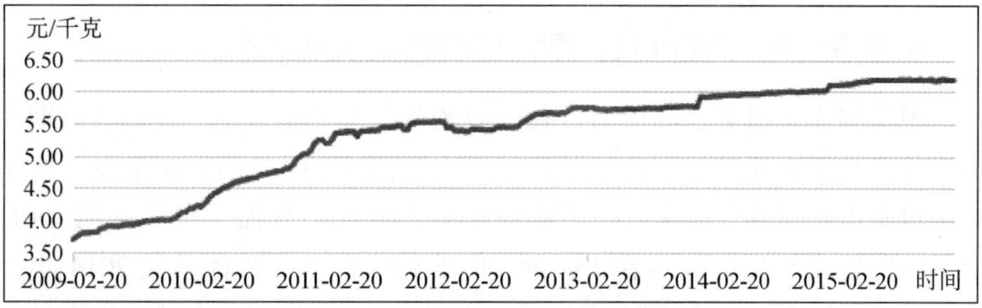


数据来源：WIND 咨询、国家统计局。

**图 2－2－3　50 个城市大米平均零售价格**

### 2. 稻谷生产价格指数：涨幅连续 4 年下降

2015 年，农民销售稻谷的价格仍高于上一年。根据国家统计局发布的农产品生产价格指数（该指数是农产品生产者出售农产品价格水平变动趋势及幅度的相对数），2015 年稻谷生产价格指数同比上涨 1.6%，但涨幅已经连续 4 年下降，这意味着农民稻谷销售收入增速在不断放缓（见图 2－2－4）。

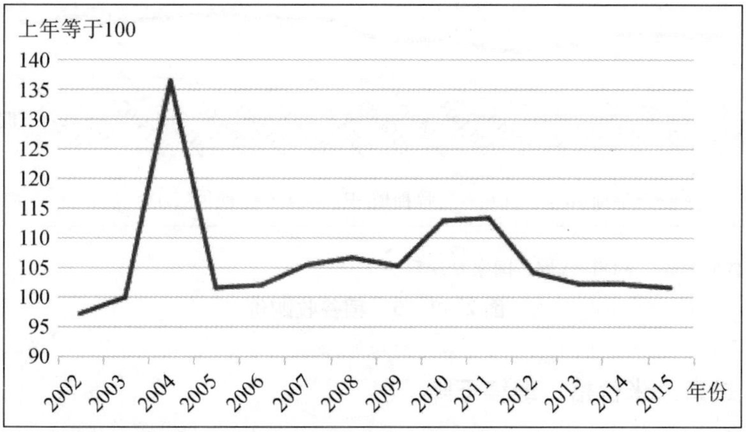


数据来源：WIND 咨询、国家统计局。

**图 2－2－4　稻谷生产价格指数（2002—2015 年）**

### 3. 收购价格：籼稻平稳，粳稻先高后低，波动略大

根据国家发改委公布的月度粮食收购价，早籼稻方面，收购高峰期的平均价格为 133 元/50 千克，比 2014 年同期微涨 1～2 元/50 千克，全年价格也基本稳定在 133 元/50 千克的水平。晚籼稻方面，与早籼稻类似，全年收购价很平稳，基本在 138 元/50 千克的水平，整体上比 2014 年微涨 1～2 元/50 千克。粳稻方面，价格波动稍微大些，1—4 月，价格呈小幅上涨趋势，由 154 元/50 千克涨到 158 元/50 千克，5—9 月，价格稳定在 158 元/50 千克的水平，此后价格持续回落，年底降到 152 元/50 千克。价格整体来说同比上涨 5 元/50 千克（见图 2－2－5）。

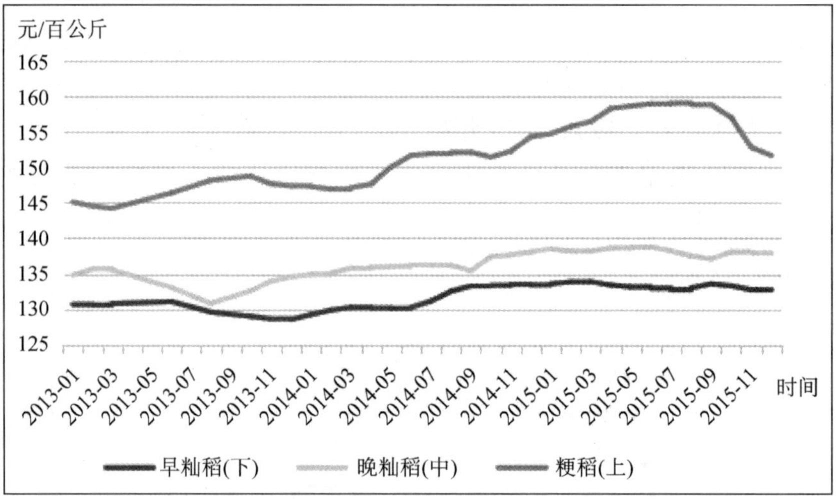


数据来源：WIND 咨询、国家发改委。

**图 2－2－5　稻谷收购价**

### 4. 进口大米价格：继续下降

根据国家粮油信息中心的数据，2015 年进口大米价格整体上仍处于下降通道，泰国大米 FOB 报价（5% 破碎）从年初的 418 美元/吨下降到 350 美元/吨（9 月），降幅达 16%，此后价格在 360 美元/吨左右震荡。越南大米 FOB 报价（5% 破碎）从 395 美元/吨一路下降到 9 下旬的 325 美元/吨，降幅为 18%，此后价格迅速反弹到 375 美元/吨，超过泰国大

米报价（见图 2－2－6）。

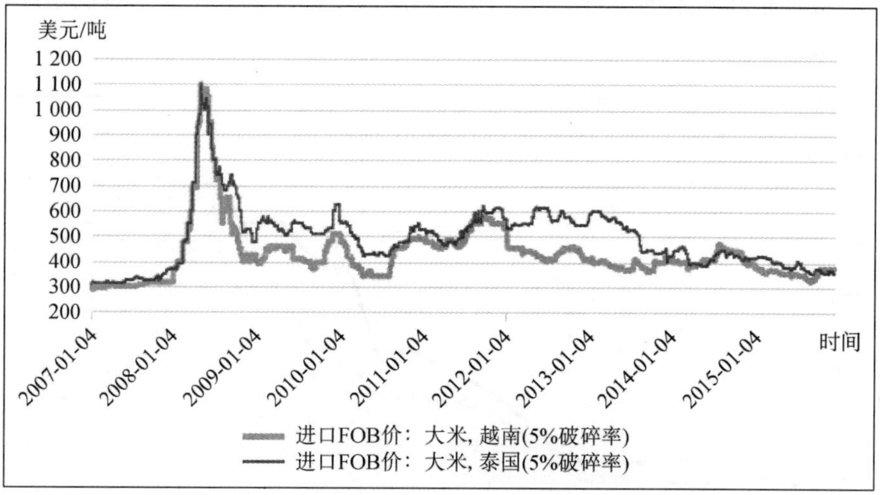


数据来源：WIND 咨询、国家粮油信息中心。

**图 2－2－6　泰国、越南大米（5%破碎）FOB 报价**

## （三）专题分析

### 1. 政策分析：政府不再一味鼓励稻谷增产

2015 年，稻谷最低收购价维持在 2014 年的水平，没有像往年一样继续提高。早籼稻、中晚籼稻和粳稻的最低收购价分别为 135 元/50 千克、138 元/50 千克、155 元/50 千克。

连年提高的稻谷最低收购价在 2015 年戛然而止，政府给出了明确的政策信号：当前稻谷库存规模过大，政府不再一味鼓励稻谷的生产。实际上，2015 年的玉米临时收储价格已经下调，如果不是为了确保口粮绝对安全的目的，稻谷的最低收购价也是可以下调的（见图 2－2－7）。

稻谷库存的主要压力在东北，因为这些年稻谷的增产主要在东北，而东北稻谷之所以增产迅猛，价格刺激是主因。2008 年之后，国家明显拉开了粳稻和籼稻的价格差。但是市场对东北粳稻的需求并没有那么强烈，这导致了东北稻谷库存居高不下。为此，国家几度推出粮食运费补贴政策，鼓励东北大米的消费。随着国家刺激力度的减弱，东北稻谷的增产势头会减缓。

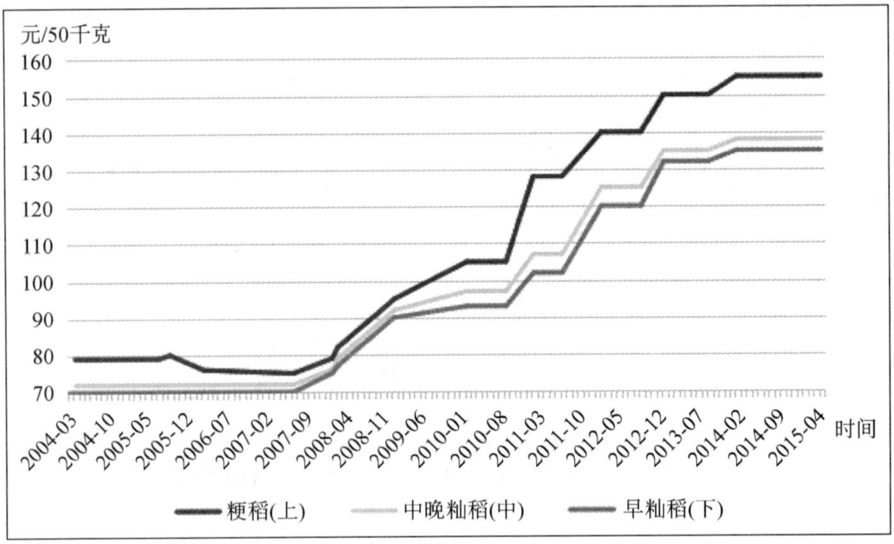


数据来源：WIND 咨询、国家发改委。

**图 2－2－7　历年稻谷最低收购价变化图**

### 2. 托市稻谷销售分析：定价过高，少人问津

根据 WIND 资讯的数据，2015 年政策性稻谷累计拍卖 9 002 万吨，实际成交 465 万吨，成交率为 5%，创下历史新低。其中，早稻累计拍卖量 1 945 万吨，实际成交 70 万吨，成交率为 4%；中晚籼稻累计拍卖量 3 731 万吨，实际成交 169 万吨，成交率为 5%；粳稻累计拍卖量 3 870 万吨，实际成交 246 万吨，成交率为 6%（见图 2－2－8 至图 2－2－11）。

个位数的成交率说明，托市稻谷进库容易出库难。供求规律告诉我们，没有卖不出去的商品，只有卖不出去的价格。托市稻谷之所以少人问津，主要原因还是定价过高，但是政府又不能降价，因为降价会直接冲击粮食市场，造成粮价下跌，对来年的托市造成更大的压力。如何处理托市稻谷是很考验智慧的一件事情。出于托市的考虑，政府不大可能调低稻谷的拍卖底价，要想提高拍卖的成交率恐怕只能寄希望于粮食价格走出当前的低迷行情，特别是国际大米价格能够上涨，这样的话，进口大米对国内市场的冲击减少，有利于托市稻的销售。

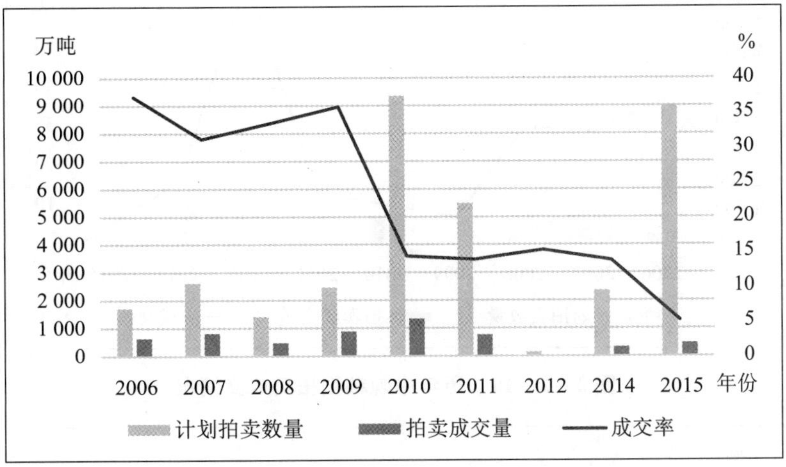


**图 2-2-8 历年稻谷拍卖成交情况**

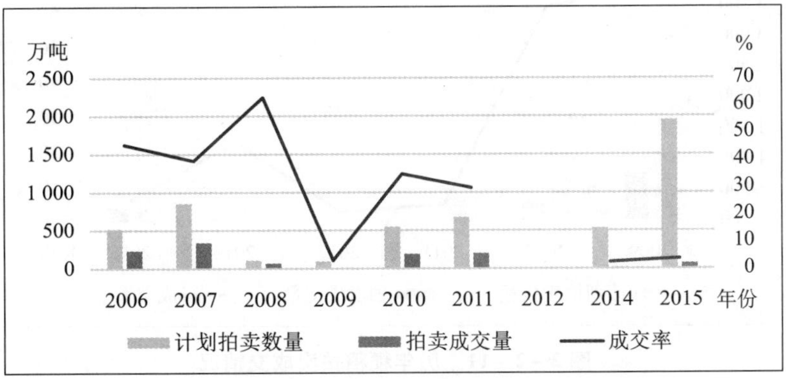


**图 2-2-9 历年早稻拍卖成交情况**

**3. 进口大米分析：有望长期成为全球最大大米进口国**

按照美国农业部的数据，2015 市场年度，中国大米进口量创历史新高，达到 470 万吨，已经是全球最大的大米进口国。目前东南亚主要大米生产国泰国、越南、柬埔寨、巴基斯坦、老挝等的大米均已进入中国。2016 年初，中美也已达成协议，很快美国大米也将进入中国市场。

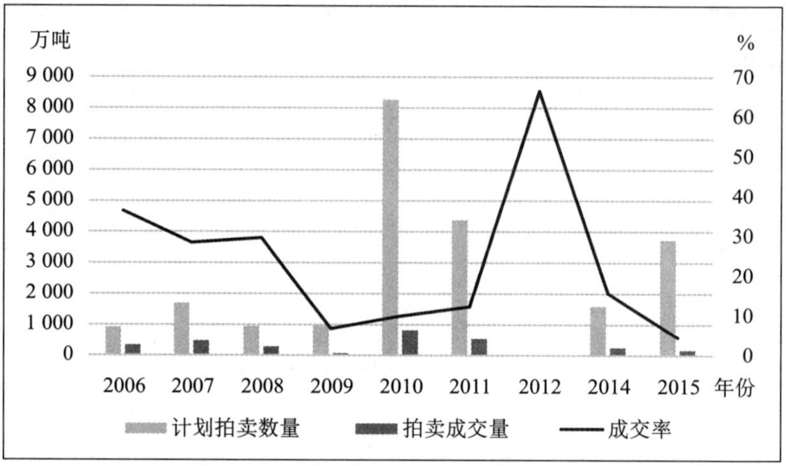


**图2-2-10 历年中晚籼稻拍卖成交情况**

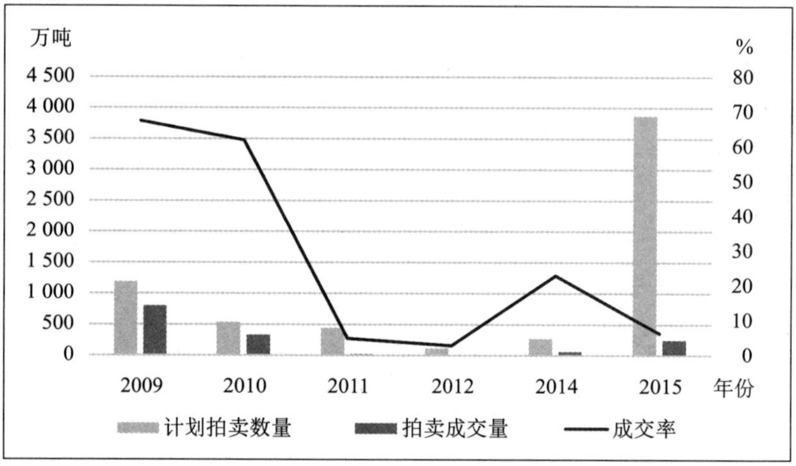


**图2-2-11 历年粳稻拍卖成交情况**

2015年泰国、越南大米FOB价格一直在400美元/吨下方弱势运行，年底在370美元/吨，折算成人民币为2 600元/吨，比国内大米价格便宜30%以上，加上运费及各种中间费用，在国内市场上的售价也比同等品质大米便宜20%，这是2015年中国进口大米创下历史新高的基础。只要这个价差不缩小，2016年进口大米数量不会低于2015年。

不过国际市场大米价格的持续下跌与泰国、印度等大米出口国去库存有关，特别是泰国英拉执政期间高价托市收购了大量大米，财政无以为继，这几年一直在向包括中国在内的国际市场“倾销”大米，直接压低了国际大米市场价格。随着去库存接近尾声（全球大米期末库存已经连降3年，库存消费比已经跌至金融危机期间水平），国际大米价格有望反弹（见图2－2－12）。

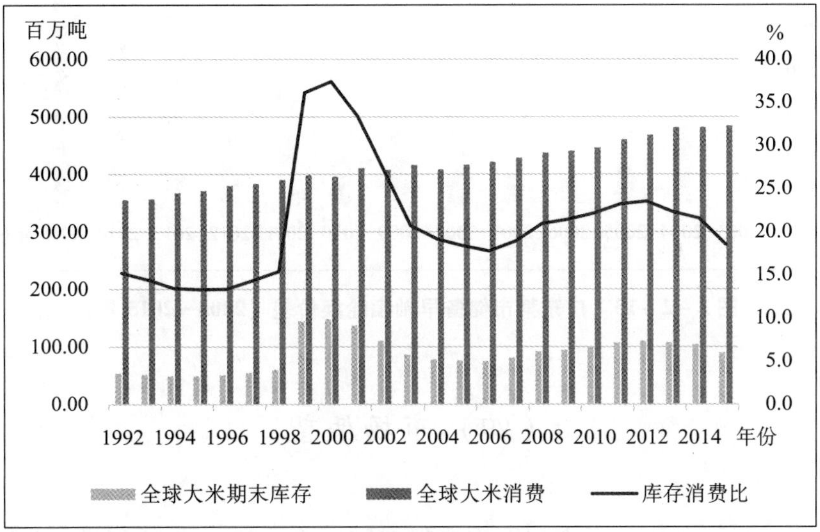


**图2－2－12　全球大米库存消费情况**

### 4. 储备早稻轮换分析：价差不断拉大，早稻正被市场抛弃

这几年储备稻谷特别是早籼稻轮换难是很普遍的情况。所谓难，就是采购的价格越来越高，而销售价格则相对越来越低，新旧早稻之间的价差越拉越大。图2－2－13是广东某市储备早稻历年早稻的轮换价差统计图。2010年以来，早稻价差不断拉大。6年前，早籼稻轮换价差还只是110元/吨，现在已经上升到600～700元/吨。

早籼稻轮换价差不断扩大的背后是早籼稻的终端需求越来越少，特别是口粮需求越来越弱，囤积一个终端需求越来越少的品种，自然亏损越来越大。当初，早籼稻作为优先储备的品种，主要是考虑到其存储成本低，但是考虑到不断跌价的现实，早稻的实际储备成本应该高于中晚籼稻。储备粮虽然是出于国家粮食安全的目的，但是也应该考虑以最经济的方式达成这样的目标。显然，储备早籼稻并非最佳的选择。

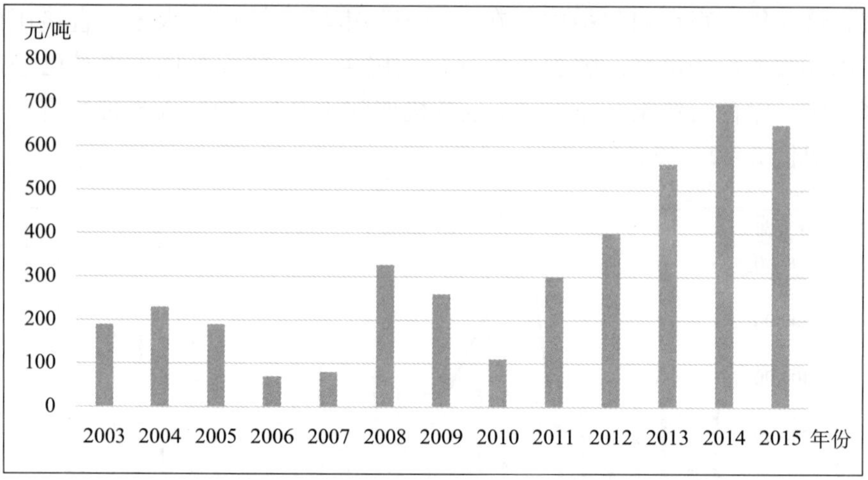


**图2-2-13 广东某市储备早籼稻轮换价差（2003—2015年）**

## （四）市场展望

第一，政策上，考虑到国家确保口粮安全，2016年稻谷最低收购价政策继续实行，但是早籼稻最低收购价已经有所下调。其中的几个原因是：一是国内外大米价差仍较大；二是托市稻谷库存仍然庞大；三是2016年CPI很大可能性依然维持低位。这三个方面的因素决定了在粮食政策上，国家依然是“维稳”。

第二，产量上，2016年稻谷总产仍然有望维持在2亿吨之上，可能略有减产，毕竟稻谷最低收购价连续2年没有提高，市场价格也有下行的趋势，农民继续扩大播种面积的可能性不大。

第三，消费上，2015年国内大米消费已经达到1.5亿吨，近5年，年均增长约300万吨。2016年在价格平稳的情况下，消费预期是继续稳步增长的态势。2016年，国内大米产需缺口仍然存在，而且有小幅拉大的趋势，因为消费刚性增长，而产量却踌躇不前。但是，考虑到国内外粮食的价差，产需缺口只会给国际大米进入中国市场的机会，政策性粮食难以弥补这个缺口。

第四，价格上，因为下有底（最低收购价）上有顶（庞大的政策性粮食等待出库），稻谷市场价格仍然会相对平稳，不会有大的波动。

（广东华南粮食交易中心　　胡锋）

# 三、玉米市场分析

**【内容提要】**

2015 年是中国玉米市场具有里程碑意义的一年，政策风向突变、临储收购价格下调、玉米市场由“牛”转“熊”、玉米品种市场化成为大势所趋。多年来政策主导市场的定式悄然生变，玉米价格涨跌规律已被打破，玉米价格走势判断与市场参与难度大大增加。随着玉米市场调整的不断深入，临储收购价格继续下调预期高企、临储陈粮去库存迫在眉睫、政策“组合拳”将全面发力，“后临储”时代已近在眼前。

## （一）2015 年玉米市场回顾

### 1. 中国玉米生产形势复杂

2015 年，全国玉米播种面积为 3 655 万公顷，同比增长 2.2%。其中，东北玉米播种面积为 1 462.02 万公顷，同比增长 3.7%；华北玉米播种面积为 941.21 万公顷，同比增长 0.1%；西北玉米播种面积为 650.8 万公顷，同比增长 0.9%；其他地区玉米播种面积为 600.99 万公顷，同比增长 3.2%。

2015 年，全国玉米平均单产为 5.7 吨/公顷，同比增长 1%。其中，东北玉米平均单产为 6.3 吨/公顷，同比下降 6.6%；华北玉米平均单产为 5.7 吨/公顷，同比增长 10.1%；西北玉米平均单产为 5.4 吨/公顷，同比增长 4.1%；其他地区玉米平均单产为 4.5 吨/公顷，同比增长7.7%。

2015年，全国玉米总产量为20 758.1万吨，同比增长3.2%。其中，东北玉米总产量为9 170万吨，同比下降3.2%；华北玉米总产量为5 349.9万吨，同比增长10.3%；西北玉米总产量为3 509.2万吨，同比增长5%；其他地区玉米总产量为2 729万吨，同比增长11.1%（见图2－3－1）。

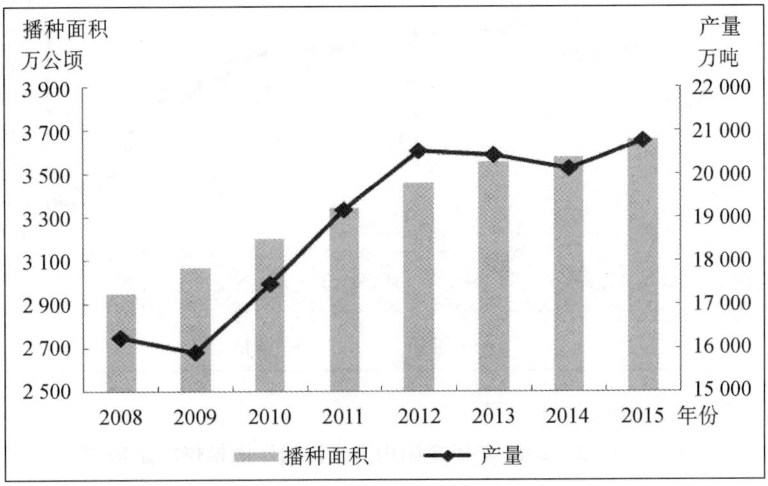


资料来源：中国玉米网。

**图2－3－1　2008年以来我国历年玉米播种面积和产量**

**2. 行业消费亮点匮缺**

受整体宏观经济疲弱及玉米供应压力过大等因素影响，玉米价格传统规律性走势被打破，深加工企业收购价格更多随行就市，2015年全年企业收购价高点出现在4月份，随后陆续转入持续下跌通道。新玉米上市后，因东北临储收购价格大幅下调，市场全面看空，深加工企业收购价下探新低。东北区第一季度，因临储收购“抢粮”致价格持续上涨；第二季度，深加工补贴政策促企业转向临储拍卖；第三季度，竞购临储玉米仍是企业首选；第四季度，临储降价影响企业新粮收购底价开秤。华北区第一季度，春节主导企业收购价格涨跌震荡；第二季度，供应压力带动企业收购价格由涨转跌；第三季度，粮源“滚滚”致使企业收购价格继续深跌；第四季度，天气因素主导企业收购价格止跌回涨。整体看影响因素，临储政策继续主导企业收购价格波动大趋势，深加工补贴政策定调东北企业收购方向，基本面供大于求主导华北企业收购价格波动，天气因素在企业价格波动中影响扩大，严重偏空心态直接作用企业收购节奏（见图2－3－2）。

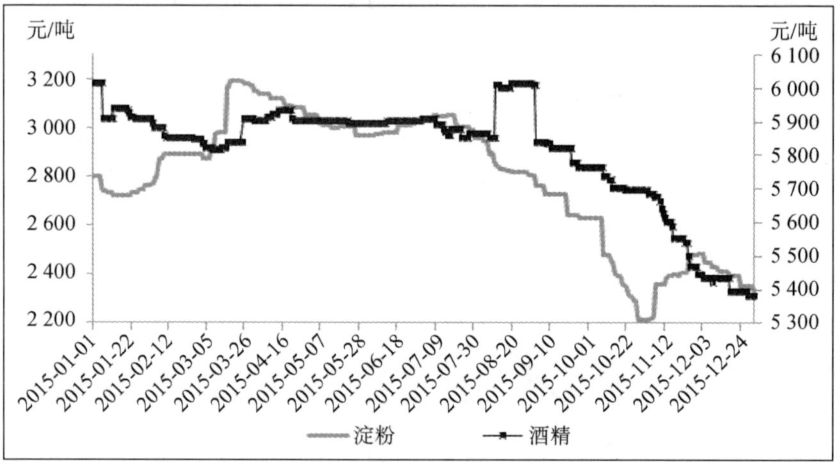


资料来源：中国玉米网。

**图 2－3－2　2015 年以来国内玉米淀粉和酒精价格走势图**

由于受到经济、成本、进口和消费等不同层面因素的制约，饲料养殖行业的产能萎缩远远大于需求萎缩，这种相对的萎缩也变相催生了另一种供小于求的市场格局。2015 年生猪存栏全年都运行在有历史数据以来的最低水平区间。与生猪供应市场不同，鸡蛋生产周期为 4 ~ 6 个月，肉鸡更短，在 40 天左右，2015 年禽蛋的行情整体处于消费乏力和供大于求的层面。市场上淘汰鸡价格较为坚挺，屠宰企业开工率维持较低水平，白条鸡价格较鸡蛋抗跌性更强，而鸡蛋价格在 9 月之前因阶段性需求刺激以及猪价上涨带动下才有了一波上冲，但随后又在供给宽松格局下迅速回调。2015 年全国平均生猪生产盈亏平衡点即猪粮比指标出现了一次新的调整，从点到区间的安全区间的增设，提升了市场和国家反应的弹性空间，同时新预案还完善了响应机制设置，适当提高了储备吞吐措施启动门槛，从单向调控到双向调控、从微观调控到宏观调控，政府干预猪价的频度降低，放手市场化意图明显（见图 2－3－3）。

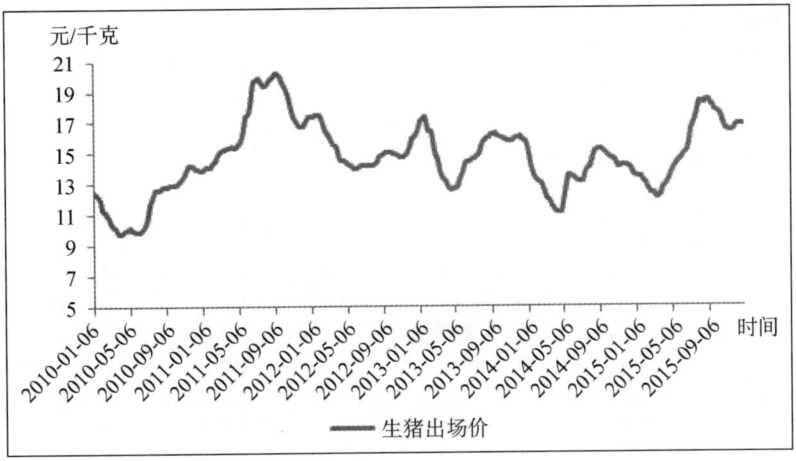


资料来源：中国玉米网。

**图 2－3－3　2010—2015 年国内生猪出厂价格走势图**

### 3. 2015 年中国玉米进口呈现新特点

2015 年中国进口玉米的国别结构一改 2014 年美国与乌克兰“两分天下”的特点，乌克兰一跃成为中国进口玉米的主要来源国，其次是进口量大量萎缩的美国玉米。2015 年全年，中国进口乌克兰玉米总量达 385.2 万吨，占总进口量的 81.44%；进口美玉米 44.1 万吨，占比降至 9.33%；保加利亚玉米进口量小幅增加至 16 万吨；此外，还从俄罗斯、老挝、缅甸等国进口玉米，其中美玉米进口量减少的原因之一是转基因事件令中国玉米进口由美国转向乌克兰（见图 2－3－4）。

### 4. 2015 年临储玉米拍卖

2015 年 1 月 6—8 日在安徽粮食批发交易市场及其联网市场举行的国家政策性粮食专场（玉米）竞价销售交易会是 2015 年的首次拍卖，4 月 9 日启动南方销区跨省移库拍卖，5 月 7—8 日增加东北三省一区拍卖。至 10 月 30 日当周，2015 年临储玉米竞价交易会结束。全年共计举行竞价交易会 29 次，总投放数量 1.27 亿吨，实际成交 572.71 万吨，总成交率 4.52%。截至 10 月 30 日临储玉米拍卖结束，临储玉米总库存为 1.53 亿吨（未考虑跨省移库和 2015/2016 年度临储收购），其中，2012 年玉米库

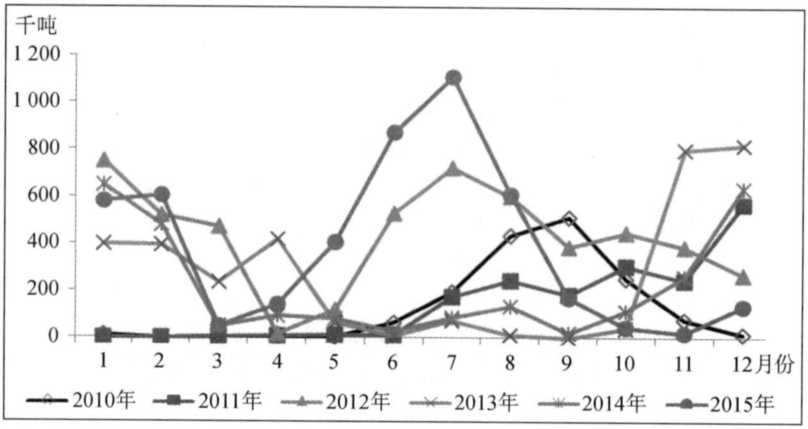


资料来源：中国玉米网。

**图2-3-4　2010—2015年中国玉米进口月度数量**

存为937.58万吨，占临储总库存的6.14%；2013年玉米库存为6 000.37万吨，占临储玉米总库存的39.30%；2014年玉米库存为8 328.76万吨（未参与拍卖投放），占临储玉米总库存的54.55%。

**5. 2015年国内玉米期货行情分析**

第一阶段（2015年1—3月），由于临储收购价较市场价优势明显，玉米销售利润颇丰，产区农户将手中粮源积极转入相关临储代收库点。随着收购进度的不断加速，优质粮源已主要集中在临储库和贸易商处，市场预期后期价格走势或重演2014年疯狂，涨价预期推升了期价走高。

第二阶段（2015年4—9月），由于市场关注焦点及基本面情况不同，从2015年4—9月，国内玉米期价不断下跌，走出一波近年来罕见的空头行情。4月初至6月初，临储提前拍卖及麦收前腾库挤压。6月中下旬至7月中旬，进口谷物冲击及下游需求疲软。7月下旬至9月底，轮换粮出库、南方春玉米上市以及临储政策预期不利。9月底临储政策较上年提前出台，2 000元/吨的收购价及“四省一价”政策坐实，市场心态悲观，期价创下近5年来最低。

第三阶段（2015年10月至今），新玉米粮食年度开启，虽然期价中止下跌并出现反弹上涨，但市场分歧加大，持仓持续走高，各项政策传言也甚嚣尘上。在诸多传言中，仅吉林省提高深加工补贴标准的政策予以落实，其对本省采购新粮的企业给予250元/吨的补贴，有利于新粮采购需求的提升，一定程度上利好玉米价格。但11月中下旬，东北、华北主产区频繁的雨雪天气打乱了价格节奏，一方面令交通运输出现延迟，导致企业到货量下降，而前期市场主体因价格大幅走低普遍保持观望心态，厂内库存水平偏低，到货减少令市场措手不及，价格应声走高；另一方面，阴雨天气不利玉米水分下降，市场干粮缺乏，导致干潮粮价格分化加大。再结合临储收购进度的加快，基层粮价也配合期货出现上涨。然而12月期价却暂停反弹之势，走出区间震荡行情，持仓也持续下降。虽然远期供大于求的市场结构长期内将压制价格走高，但短期临储收购规模较大及年前企业备库等因素使期价有一定抗跌性，总体上判断来年玉米期价仍面临较大下行压力（见图2－3－5）。

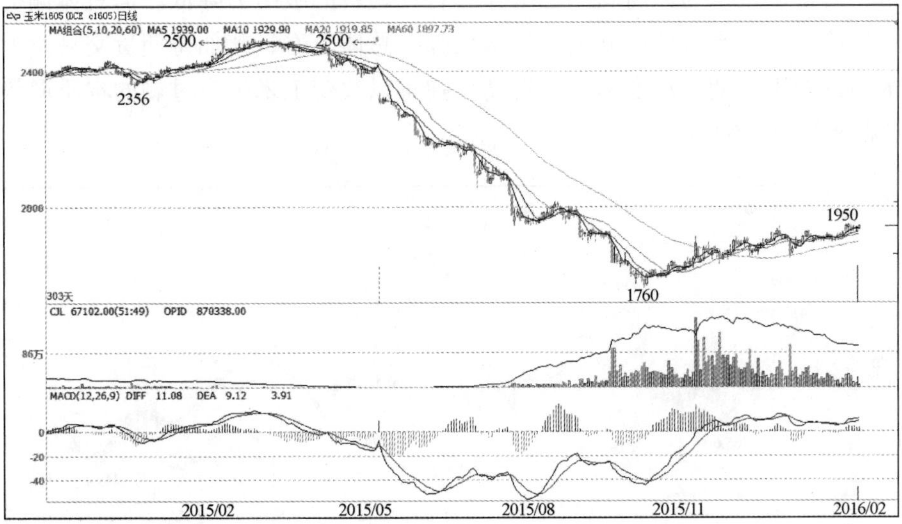


资料来源：文华财经。

**图2－3－5　2015年国内玉米期货行情走势图**

#### 6. 2015年国际玉米期、现货行情分析

第一阶段（2015年1—6月），2015年初，美国玉米期货结束自2014年10月以来的反弹上涨走势，再次步入下跌通道，主要受美玉米产量创纪录以及玉米库存充裕压制。同时，美乙醇库存已涨至两年最高，因担心

乙醇库存膨胀将导致玉米需求下降，玉米期价应声下挫。

第二阶段（2015 年 7—8 月），6 月下旬至 7 月中旬，美玉米期货出现一波急速拉升。虽然期价急升，但成交激增的同时持仓却大幅走低，显示多空双方对当前行情已基本确认，资金迅速流出，上涨不具有持续性。进入玉米扬花授粉关键期后，期货市场风云突变。种植区降雨减少，气温升高，田间积水逐渐消散，前期偏高的水分结合快速改善的积温条件反而有利玉米生长，市场预期 2015/2016 年度玉米生长形势将保持优良状态。与此同时，美元指数上涨、小麦价格下跌和以玉米为基础的乙醇产量下降也令玉米期货承压，随后行情走势以底部震荡整理为主。

第三阶段（2015 年 9 月至今），进入收割季后，市场供应总体宽松，美国农业部多次上调美国玉米产量预估，而由于原油价格暴跌压低汽油价格，使得以玉米为原材料的乙醇作为替代燃料的吸引力降低。但总体偏空的环境下，又有短期因素助推玉米反弹。总体上看，芝加哥期货交易所玉米期价处于长期下跌通道中，短期反弹难以改变玉米供应过剩的本质形势（见图 2－3－6）。

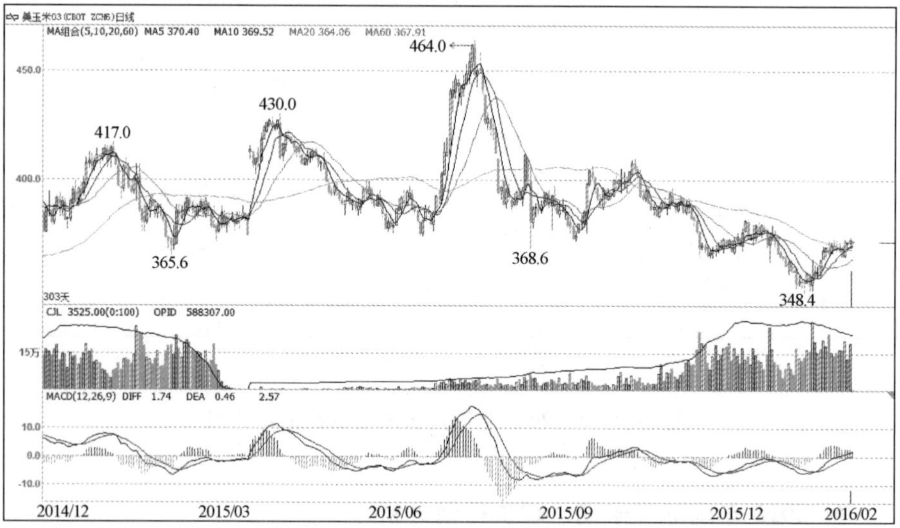


资料来源：文华财经。

**图 2－3－6　2015 年美国玉米期货行情走势图**

## 7. 美国玉米供需形势

1—3 月，美国农业部月度供需报告虽然基于出口需求的增长连续调低玉米库存，其中 2 月还调高了美乙醇行业以及食品、种子和工业行业的玉米需求量，但因产量提高和饲用需求的降低对期价仍然形成抑制。4 月因饲料和残渣使用下降，当月供需报告期末库存数据出现上调，之后在经历 5 月份的平稳之后，6 月供需报告的库存数据再次上调，加之小麦和乙醇期价大跌以及资金获利了结，报告发布当日芝加哥期货交易所期价创 3 月 31 日来最大单日跌幅。7 月开始，因为夏季乙醇消耗增多，同时结合饲用玉米的增加，期末库存数据下调，当时美国创纪录降雨对新作生长也产生不利影响，伴随种植面积和单产的下调，期价出现上扬。因生长季节的早期出现大雨导致玉米田被淹，一年一度的美国《职业农场主》杂志（*ProFarmer*）中西部作物巡查（8 月 17—20 日）的产量和单产数据均低于美国农业部的 8 月供需报告，但由于 8 月份产量和单产的数据又被修正上调、人民币的巨幅贬值等也令期价承压。虽然 9—10 月的产量数据有所下调，但基于美国玉米出口下降、玉米加工成乙醇的需求减少，加之中国饲料需求疲弱，造成全球供应上升，11 月、12 月的产量数据乃至出口需求的再次下调也是情理之中（见图 2－3－7）。

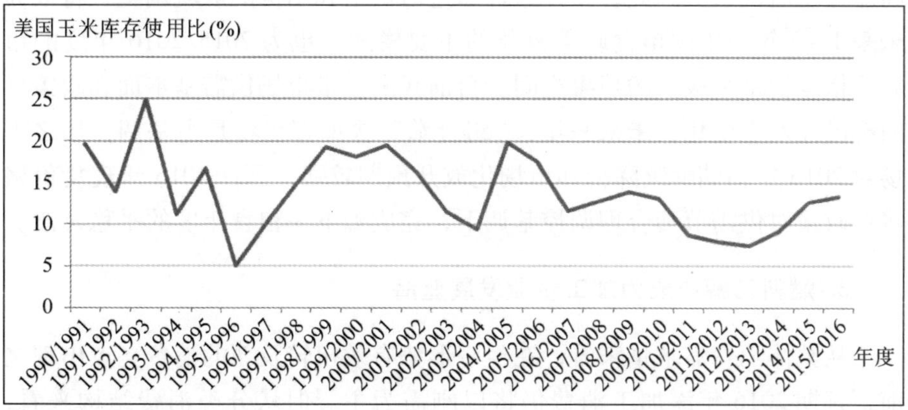


数据来源：美国农业部。

**图 2－3－7　1990/1991—2015/2016 年度美国玉米季度库存使用比**

## （二）2016 年玉米市场展望

### 1. 2016 年政策市色彩仍浓

对农业政策进行一次梳理不难发现，国家政策调控在 2015 年不但有方向上的调整，而且调控的思路更加立体，兼顾的层面更加多元。2015 年中国农业政策在推进和改革的过程中极具层次感和组织力，既能够兼顾粮食领域内传统量价关系的平衡，也能够统筹粮食行业从基层农户到出口环节、从种植生长到餐饮消费等各个领域。这种变化也并非一蹴而就。2008 年以来，中国政府对东北玉米实施临时收储政策，这项连年提价的政策一直持续到 2014 年。而由此带来的则是生产端成本的间接上涨，种植结构的集中和扭曲，原粮和产品库存大量堆积，全球粮价的制高点以及大量国际廉价谷物的涌入。基于此，2015 年中国农业政策的风向发生潜移默化的改变。从以往单纯的提高临时收储价格变为 2015 年不断降低价格、引导市场预期的降温，同时也注重对库存结构的改革和升级。当然，仅仅一年时间，对价格的调整和库存温和的调节不足以缓解当前中国玉米高库存矛盾现状。因此，预计这种通过对价格和结构的双轨调整，将成为未来 1 ~2 年内中国粮食政策改革的主要模式，也为 2015/2016 年度的市场价格运行带来极大的想象空间。目前我国玉米市场供需基本面和政策导向都已经发生变化，未来一年，“组合拳”去库存仍将是主基调，加之市场对 2016 年临储继续降价和市场化放开预期较强，预计 2016 年现货价格将在政策对供需节奏合理调控基调下，完成到下一粮食年度的平稳过渡。

### 2. 燃料乙醇或成为加工企业发展蓝海

从整体消费需求量来看，在经济形势有效扭转及新的消费亮点出现之前，预期 2016 年深加工消费仍将以刚需为主。但从分类消费结构来看，2016 年玉米淀粉、淀粉糖、酒糟蛋白饲料、燃料乙醇等需求有望回升，而原料玉米价格回落将是最大的推动因素。从 2015 年下半年实际情况来看，受玉米降价带动，国内玉米淀粉、淀粉糖、酒糟蛋白饲料价格均大幅回落，玉米淀粉与进口木薯淀粉比价优势回升；在白糖持续高价情况下，淀粉糖替代需求升温；中国已经在2016年1月启动对美国产进口酒糟蛋白饲料“双反”调查。2016年玉米价格继续下降预期较高，则玉米淀粉、淀粉糖、酒糟蛋白饲料替代使用均有望继续增加。此外，燃料乙醇消费量亦有增加预期，2015年部分省区油品升级已经实现，对燃料乙醇需求客观上有所提振。传闻国家已经部署新增160万吨燃料乙醇产能，未来增加燃料乙醇在汽油中的添加比例将是方向之举，也符合短期内玉米去库存需求。因此，2016年燃料乙醇消费有望成为拉升玉米深加工消费的一个亮点，但具体实施周期可能略长。

**3. 2016年饲料养殖行业有望温和复苏**

产能的萎缩大于需求的萎缩，其实也是另一种供小于求。2015年以来，生猪和能繁母猪存栏基数一直在最低值附近徘徊，这是一个新周期的开始。中国市场对于猪肉的需求仍然比较稳定，即便会受到一些冲击，也仍将保持在较高的水平。从阶段性影响因素上看，猪价反弹仍受到经济、进口和需求的制约。成本端的改善会带来业绩的弹性，较好的养殖利润仍将维持，这会进一步刺激生猪养殖产业产能的扩张。基于这样的考虑，预计2016年饲料玉米用量约有4%左右的增幅，即预计2015/2016年度的饲料消费玉米用量在1.17亿吨左右。对于行业发展前景来讲，2016年又不乏亮点。

**4. 慎重对待2016年进口前景**

尽管政策引导国内玉米现货价格市场化大方向不变，但在中国玉米产业发展现状下，与国际市场价格真正接轨仍需时间。目前面临的难题即为如何在保证国内粮食安全、保障农户种植积极性及种植收益的前提下，逐步通过政策引导及补贴刺激、种植结构调整、贸易物流优化及加工产业规划升级来实现国内中长期供需均衡，而国内玉米去库存是当前亟待解决的问题。在这个大前提下，尽管国际贸易趋向多样化、中国进口谷物或成常态，但在全球谷物市场供给整体宽松背景、国内外显著价差影响下，仍会刺激进口。政策层面的收紧也不容忽视：高粱、大麦、木薯、酒糟蛋白饲料自9月1日起纳入自动进口许可管理，并于2016年1月启动对美国产进口酒糟蛋白饲料“双反”调查，未来替代品进口风险增加。同时，复杂的国际政治经济环境及多变的气候因素也是影响进口到货的重要因素之一。加之国内玉米现货走势预期偏空且不排除各项补贴性政策出台，用粮企业在谨慎选择进口品种和进口国的同时，或将采购重心转移至购销易控的国内粮源，类似 2015 年春夏进口替代到货高峰景象难以再现。

（中国玉米网　　冯利臣）

# 四、大豆及豆油市场分析

【内容提要】

2015年我国大豆播种面积和产量继续减少，进口量继续增加并创历史新高，消费量继续稳步增长。国产大豆价格在国际和国内市场双重因素的影响下，经历了以下跌为主的行情。由于全球大豆产量增加，供给大于需求，国际市场价格大幅下跌；东北大豆主产区，由于国家实行直接补贴政策，失去临储收购价格的支撑，加之进口转基因大豆大量进入食品大豆市场，严重冲击了国产大豆销售，更使国产大豆雪上加霜。由于影响大豆市场的不利因素仍将持续，加之国家临储大豆2016年将拍卖销售出库，预计2016年国产大豆市场行情仍然难言乐观。2015年国内豆油市场利空因素有增无减，但因价格下跌幅度大，底部支撑较强，整体表现为“震荡筑底”的过程，豆油期、现货价格年内走势呈区间波浪式轨迹，方向上始终未能形成实质性上涨趋势。进入2016年，国内豆油市场仍将处在“多空交错、相互牵制”的局面中，预计豆油市场价格在2015年价位水平上有上移的空间和机会。

## （一）2015年我国大豆及豆油市场分析

### 1. 2015年大豆市场

（1）大豆生产情况。据博朗咨询·中国大豆网调查预计，2015年度全国大豆种植面积为8 164.9万亩，较 2014 年减少 14.9%，平均单产为 127.7 千克/亩，较 2014 年降低 1.6%，总产量为 1 043.0 万吨，较 2014 年减少 16.2%。种植大豆收益低是面积减少的主要原因。虽然国家在东北主产区实行了大豆目标价格补贴政策，但种植大豆收益仍低于玉米和水稻，加之补贴发放时间较晚，补贴额度低于农民预期，影响了农民种植大豆的积极性（见表 2－4－1）。

**表 2－4－1　　　　中国大豆种植面积及产量表**

单位：万亩，千克/亩，万吨

| 年　份 | 种植面积 | 单位面积产量 | 产量 |
|---|---|---|---|
| 2010 | 14 466.8 | 131.5 | 1 903.2 |
| 2011 | 12 431.3 | 126.0 | 1 566.0 |
| 2012 | 10 905.0 | 129.4 | 1 411.1 |
| 2013 | 10 523.2 | 119.3 | 1 255.8 |
| 2014 | 9 590.0 | 129.8 | 1 245.1 |
| 2015 | 8 164.9 | 127.7 | 1 043.0 |

数据来源：博朗咨询·中国大豆网。

（2）大豆进口情况。中国海关总署统计，2015 年我国大豆进口量破纪录达到 8 173.9 万吨，较 2014 年 7 139.9 万吨增加 1 034 万吨，增幅为 14.5%。按市场年度统计，2014/2015 年度我国大豆进口量为 7 835.1 万吨，较 2013/2014 年度 7 036.4 万吨增加 798.7 万吨，增幅为 11.4%。国内养殖业饲用蛋白粕需求稳步增加，菜籽粕、棉籽粕供给量减少，国际市场大豆价格大幅下跌导致进口成本降低，大豆压榨产能过剩并继续扩增等，是导致大豆进口量大幅增加的主要因素（见图 2－4－1）。

（3）大豆消费情况。2014/2015 年度中国大豆总消费量为 8 900 万吨，比 2013/2014 年度增加 6.9%。其中，大豆压榨量为 7 370 万吨，比 2013/2014 年度增加 7.2%；食用及食品工业消费量为 1 140 万吨，比 2013/2014 年度增加 1.9%；种用量略减，损耗量略增，出口量略减；期末结转库存量为 2 020 万吨，较 2013/2014 年度增加 9.8%（见表 2－4－2）。

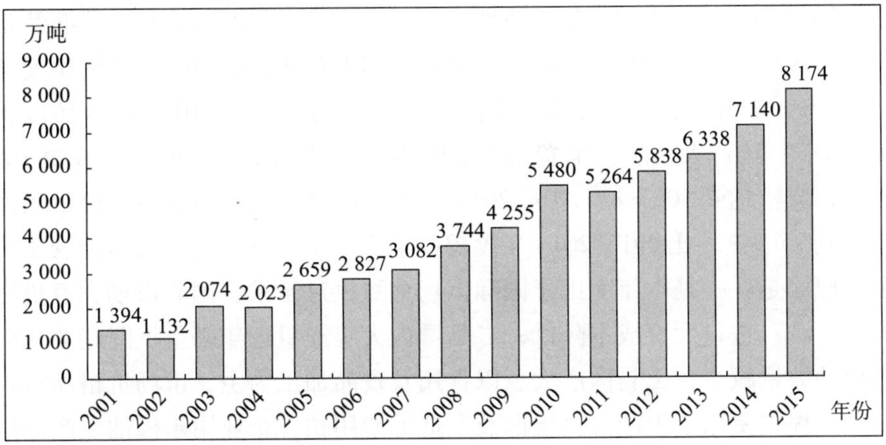


数据来源：博朗咨询·中国大豆网。

**图 2-4-1　2001~2015 年中国进口大豆数量统计**

**表 2-4-2　　2014/2015 年度中国大豆供需平衡表**　　单位：万吨

| 项　目 | 2013/2014 年度 | 2014/2015 年度 | 同比增减幅度（%） |
|---|---|---|---|
| 总供给量 | 10 164 | 10 920 | 7.4 |
| 期初库存 | 1 872 | 1 840 | -1.7 |
| 年度供给量 | 8 292 | 9 080 | 9.5 |
| 国内产量 | 1 256 | 1 245 | -0.9 |
| 进口总量 | 7 036 | 7 835 | 11.4 |
| 年度消耗量 | 8 324 | 8 900 | 6.9 |
| 压榨总量 | 6 875 | 7 370 | 7.2 |
| 国产大豆 | 330 | 230 | -30.3 |
| 进口大豆 | 6 545 | 7 140 | 9.1 |
| 食用及工业 | 1 120 | 1 140 | 1.8 |
| 饲料及其他 | 180 | 250 | 38.9 |
| 种用量 | 46 | 40 | -13.0 |
| 损耗量 | 82 | 85 | 3.7 |
| 出口量 | 21 | 15 | -28.6 |
| 期末库存 | 1 840 | 2 020 | 9.8 |

数据来源：博朗咨询·中国大豆网。

2014/2015 年度我国大豆消费量增加主要是因为大豆压榨量继续提高。2014/2015 年度我国大豆压榨量为 7 370 万吨，比 2013/2014 年度增加 7.1%。其中，进口大豆压榨消费量 7 140 万吨，比 2013/2014 年度提高 9.1%；国产大豆压榨消费量为 230 万吨，比 2013/2014 年度减少 100 万吨，减幅达到 30.3%。2014/2015 年度进口大豆占中国油用压榨市场份额达到 96.9%，比 2013/2014 年度提高了 2.3 个百分点。造成这种现象的主要原因是：一是本年度由于国际市场大豆供过于求，国际市场大豆价格大幅下跌，进口大豆成本降低；二是国内大豆产量近年来呈下降趋势，可供榨油数量减少；三是国产大豆以食用及食品加工为主，市场价格相对较高，压榨主要用于生产大豆蛋白及酿造等专用粕，企业用于榨油生产饲用豆粕无利可获，很多时间处于亏损状况。因此，国产大豆压榨量大幅减少，而进口大豆依存度继续提高。

2014/2015 年度我国食用及食品工业大豆消费量 1 140 万吨，比 2013/2014 年度增加 1.8%。按照国产大豆供需平衡分析，国产大豆食用及食品工业大豆消费量约为 950 万吨，进口大豆进入食品数量将达到 190 万吨，占食用及食品工业大豆消费总量的 16.7%。

（4）2014/2015 年大豆市场行情走势。2014/2015 年度国内大豆市场由持续下行⟶快速下跌⟶触底反弹⟶区间调整⟶快速上涨⟶高位回落几个阶段组成。2014/2015 年度东北产区大豆收购平均价波动幅度为 797 元/吨，高点发生在 2014 年 10 月初，收购平均价为 4 553 元/吨；低点出现在 2015 年 4 月 13 日，收购平均价为 3 756 元/吨，降幅达 17.5%。受芝加哥期货市场大豆期货价格和我国大豆进口成本下跌的影响，2014/2015 年度国内港口进口大豆分销价格也呈大幅下跌趋势，高点至低点下跌 855 元/吨，下跌幅度为 22.5%。

受美国及南美大豆大幅增产的影响，芝加哥期货市场大豆价格自 2014 年 4 月份开始大幅下跌，至 2014 年 9 月末跌至 912 美分/蒲式耳。2014 年国家对东北主产区实行了大豆目标价格直接补贴政策，2014 年新季大豆上市后，由于国际市场大豆价格低，国内失去了临时收储价格的支撑，大豆市场价格出现了近 6 个月的持续下跌走势。进入 3 月份，产区农民急需资金购买春耕所需生产资料以及承包土地资金，促使农民集中出售手中大豆，东北产区大豆价格加速下行。价格深度下跌的同时也刺激粮商以及企业入市抢收，进入 4 月中旬大豆价格开始低位反弹，之后进入区间震荡波动。7 月份山东港口对进口大豆分销进行检查，进口大豆停售近半个月，东北产区大豆销售量明显增加，受此提振，国产大豆价格迎来上涨契机，价格快速上行。但 8 月份后随着检查力度减弱，进口大豆重新逐步进入市场，且关内产区及东北产区新作大豆即将上市，国产大豆市场需求减弱导致价格承压下行。2015 年 9 月中旬东北主产区新季大豆上市收购平均价为 4 253 元/吨，至 2015 年 12 月 1 日降至 3 750 元/吨，收购价格下跌 503 元/吨，降幅达 11.8%。8 月下旬湖北、河南、安徽等地新季大豆相继上市，大豆价格出现了历史少有的大幅下跌行情。受新豆集中上市和进口大豆抢占市场的冲击，大豆收购价格由最初的 5 200 元/吨快速下跌至最低 3 700 元/吨，高点至低点下跌了 1 500 元/吨，跌幅高达 32.7%（见图 2-4-2）。

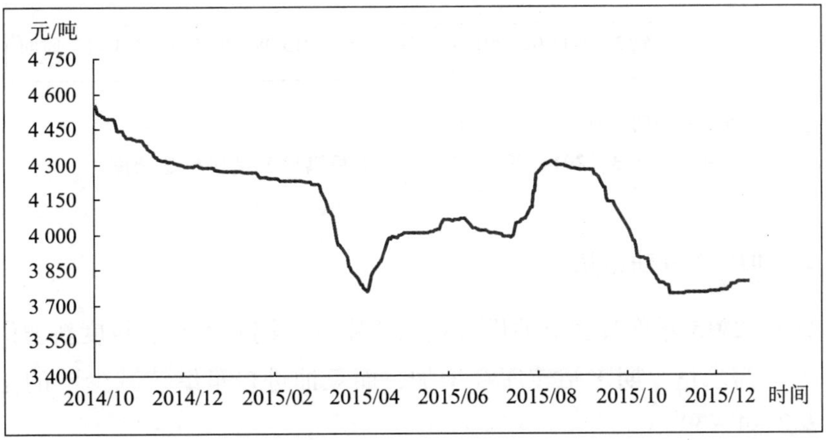


数据来源：博朗咨询 · 中国大豆网。

**图 2-4-2　2015 年东北大豆现货收购价格走势图**

受芝加哥期货交易所大豆期货价格反弹和我国大豆进口成本短期提高的影响，2014 年 10 月份国内港口进口大豆分销价格出现了近 150 元/吨的上涨，至 2014 年 11 月中旬最高达到 3 800 元/吨。随后在南美大豆产量大幅增加的预期下，芝加哥期货交易所大豆期货价格开始了近 8 个月的持续下跌，国内进口大豆港口分销价格 2015 年 6 月下旬跌至最低 2 945 元/吨，高点至低点下跌 855 元/吨，下跌幅度为 22.5%。价格在低位震荡近 2 个月后，由于美国农业部意外调低大豆库存，在芝加哥期货交易所大豆期货价格反弹的带动下，于 8 月中旬开始出现了近 200 元/吨的快速上涨。进入 9 月份，由于美国破纪录的单产和总产量已成定局，国内进口大豆港口分销价格跟随芝加哥期货交易所大豆期货价格再次进入跌势（见图 2－4－3）。

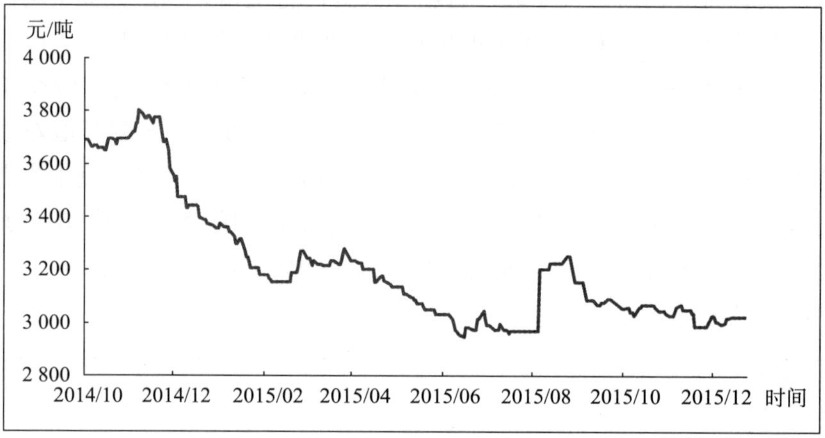


数据来源：博朗咨询 · 中国大豆网。

**图 2－4－3　2014/2015 年度进口大豆港口分销价格走势图**

### 2. 2015 年豆油市场

2014/2015 年度我国豆油供需状况总体呈“期初库存、年度新增供给量、年度需求量、期末结转库存增加，而豆油进口量继续减少”的态势（见表 2－4－3）。

**表 2－4－3　　2014/2015 年度中国豆油供需平衡表**　　单位：万吨

| 项　　目 | 2013/2014 年度 | 2014/2015 年度 | 增减幅（%） |
|---|---|---|---|
| **总供给量** | **1 592** | **1 702** | **6.9** |
| 期初库存 | 242 | 320 | 32.3 |
| 年度新增供给 | 1 350 | 1 382 | 2.4 |
| 生产量 | 1 215 | 1 304 | 7.4 |
| 进口量 | 135.3 | 77.3 | －42.9 |
| **年度需求量** | **1 272** | **1 349** | **6.1** |

续表

| 项　　目 | 2013/2014 年度 | 2014/2015 年度 | 增减幅（%） |
|---|---|---|---|
| 国内消耗 | 1 250 | 1 325 | 6.0 |
| 食用消耗 | 1 120 | 1 180 | 5.4 |
| 其他消耗 | 130 | 145 | 11.5 |
| 损耗量 | 12 | 13 | 7.3 |
| 出口量 | 9.5 | 10.7 | 12.6 |
| **期末库存** | **320** | **353** | **10.3** |

数据来源：博朗咨询·中国大豆网。

（1）豆油生产情况。博朗咨询·中国大豆网统计数据显示，2014/2015 年度国内大豆压榨总量比 2013/2014 年度增加，因此导致国内豆油生产量也随之增加。其中，国产大豆生产豆油量为 38 万吨，进口大豆生产豆油量为 1 321 万吨。2014/2015 年度通过油厂压榨对市场供应毛豆油数量为 1 359 万吨，折合一级豆油供应量为 1 304 万吨，比 2013/2014 年度增加 89 万吨，增幅为 7.4%。

（2）豆油进口情况。海关统计数据显示，2014/2015 年度豆油进口量为 77.3 万吨，比 2013/2014 年度骤减 58.0 万吨，降幅达 42.9%。按日历年度计算，2015 年中国豆油进口量为 81.8 万吨，比 2014 年减少 31.7 万吨，减幅为 27.9%（见图 2－4－4）。

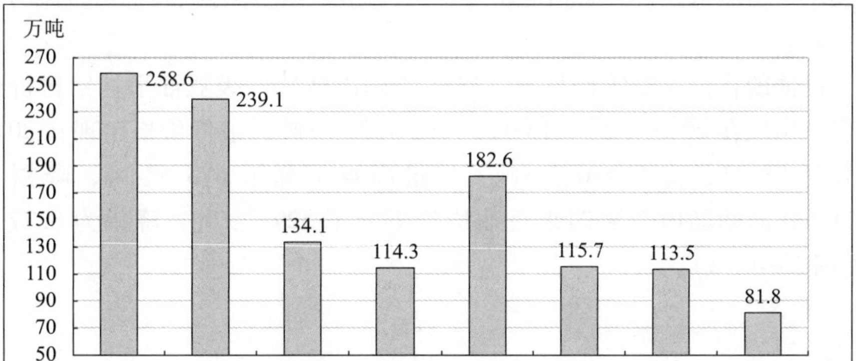


数据来源：中国海关总署。

**图 2－4－4　2008—2015 年中国豆油年进口量统计**

（3）豆油消费情况。2014/2015 年度，国内豆油消费包括出口在内的总量为 1 349 万吨，比 2013/2014 年度增加 77 万吨，增幅为 6.1%。其中，食用消费 1 180 万吨，比 2013/2014 年度增加 60 万吨，增幅为 5.36%，在总的消费需求中占比 87.5%；其他消费包括工业消费、损耗及出口在内的量为 168.7 万吨，比 2013/2014 年度增加 17.2 万吨，增幅为 11.2%，在总消费需求中占比 12.5%。海关数据显示，2014/2015 年度，我国共出口豆油预计为 10.67 万吨，比 2013/2014 年度增加 1.24 万吨，增幅为 13%。主要出口国家集中在朝鲜、韩国、新加坡等国家。

（4）市场行情走势。2014/2015 年度国内豆油市场整体表现为震荡筑底的过程，上方压制持续存在，下方支撑相对强劲，豆油期、现货价格年内走势呈区间波浪式轨迹，方向上始终未能形成实质性突破。与 2013/2014 年度相比，2014/2015 年度国内豆油市场面临的压制有增无减：美国、南美大豆产量在 2013/2014 年度高产基础上再创出新纪录、原油市场瀑布式下滑至近 12 年来最低位、美元升息从预期发酵到落实、全球特别是中国经济形势进一步放缓引发大宗商品市场普跌狂潮等，均在较大程度上压制国内豆油价格上行。其自身基本面状况对价格的主导作用相对弱化，尽管如此，第四季度油脂特别是豆油供需格局改善确实给豆油现货价格以较为坚实的底部支撑。在偏空的实体经济环境下，油脂终端消费持续低迷，贸易需求主体存货信心不足，低补高卖、低库存周转仍为主流的购销策略。

据博朗咨询跟踪统计显示，2015 年国内散装一级豆油平均销售价格最高点出现在 2015 年 5 月 13 日，为 6 153 元/吨，最低价格出现在 2015 年 8 月 28 日，为 5 580 元/吨，较最高点下降了 573 元/吨，降幅为 9.31%；同期国内散装四级豆油均价下降了 529 元/吨，降幅为 8.77%（见图 2－4－5）。

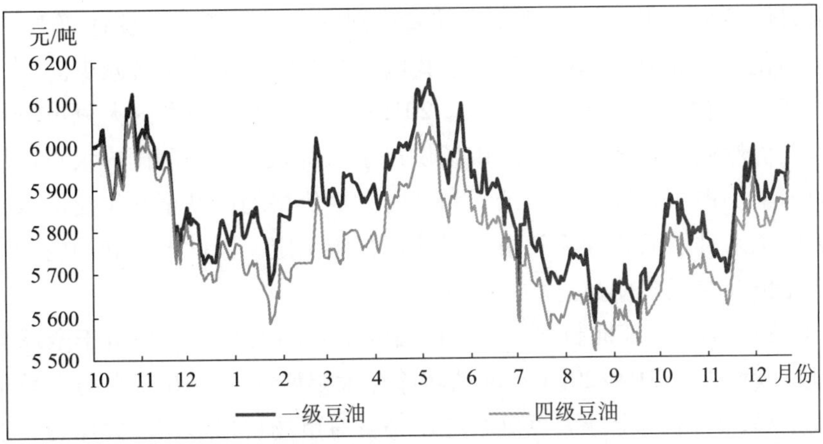


数据来源：博朗咨询·中国大豆网。

**图 2-4-5　2015 年国内豆油现货价格走势图**

## （二）2015/2016 年度我国大豆及豆油市场展望

### 1. 2015/2016 年度大豆市场展望

（1）国内大豆市场供需预计。2015/2016 年度，中国大豆新增供应量预计为 9 093 万吨，比 2014/2015 年度增加 13 万吨。其中，国产大豆产量预计 1 043.0 万吨，比 2014/2015 年度减少 202 万吨；进口大豆总量预计 8 050 万吨，比 2014/2015 年度增加 215 万吨。大豆消费总量预计为 9 238 万吨，比 2014/2015 年度的增加 338 万吨。其中，全年压榨总量为 7 650 万吨，比 2014/2015 年度增加 280 万吨。大豆食用与食品工业需求预计为 1 160 万吨，比 2014/2015 年度增加 20 万吨。2015/2016 年度末大豆结转库存预计为 1 875 万吨，比 2014/2015 年度减少 145 万吨。

2015/2016 年度我国大豆新增供应量增幅较小，主要是 2015 年国产大豆产量大幅降低，虽然进口大豆数量继续增加，但增速将有所放缓。由于国内 2016 年生猪饲养量及存栏量将出现恢复性增长，饲用豆粕需求量将继续增加，因此 2015/2016 年度国内大豆压榨量仍将继续提高。由于国家临时储备大豆很大部分已经超过或达到安全储存年限，预计 2016 年将拍卖消化，因此 2015/2016 年度末我国大豆结转库存将出现减少。

（2）国内大豆市场行情分析。2015/2016 年度影响国内大豆市场行情的因素仍然错综复杂，在国际市场供过于求背景下，抑制国内大豆市场行情的因素仍占主导地位。但国际和国内大豆价格均已跌至 6 年前低点，同时美国未来种植面积和天气情况目前还很难确定，因此国际和国内大豆价格变化仍存在很多变数。

2015/2016 年度抑制国内大豆价格的主要因素是：一是由于全球大豆产量连续增加，2014/2015 年度结转库存大幅增加，2016 年南美大豆丰产几成定局，本年度全球大豆供给过剩必将对市场价格形成巨大压力，进而影响到国内大豆价格。二是国家临时储备大豆库存近 600 万吨，而且 2010 年产的大豆还有一部分库存，2011 年和 2012 年产的大豆也已超过安全储存年限，临储大豆需竞价销售出库，这必然对国内大豆市场价格形成非常大的影响。三是进口转基因大豆进入食品加工市场对国产大豆价格影响巨大。由于进口大豆价格远低于国产大豆价格，在挤占国产大豆市场销售份额的同时，也必将严重冲击国产大豆价格。

2015/2016 年度支撑国内大豆价格的主要因素是：一是 2016 年美国大豆播种面积变化和作物期天气还有待于观察，如果 2016 年美国播种面积减少且天气出现较大问题，将对芝加哥期货市场大豆价格构成支撑，芝加哥期货市场大豆价格有由低位筑底转为上升的趋势，进而影响我国国内大豆价格。二是 2015 年国产大豆产量大幅减少，新产大豆满足不了 2015/2016 年度需求，虽然临储大豆将竞价销售补充市场，但新陈矛盾将对当年新大豆价格构成支撑，或出现阶段性上涨。

2015/2016 年度国内大豆市场利空因素居多，从市场实际购销情况看，产销两地的市场主体购销态度谨慎，因经营很难获利，缺少入市动力，这也是导致大豆价格软弱无力、市场交易难以活跃的重要原因。综合来看，2015/2016 年度国产大豆价格走势仍不太乐观。

**2. 2015/2016 年度中国豆油市场展望**

（1）国内豆油市场供需预测。2015/2016 年度全球植物油供需格局仍将以宽松态势呈现，身处其中，中国国内油脂特别是豆油市场料将难现供需偏紧格局，整体而言仍将在平衡与宽松之间徘徊。继美国大豆丰产之后，新年度南美大豆或再创纪录性的产量，国内大豆进口量也将继续保持高位，庞大的供应量也就预示着相应的压榨量会随之而生，加之国内菜油、棕油等其他油脂居高不下的库存量，不缺油的局面料将在新一年度继续呈现。油脂需求方面，预计2015/2016年度国内油脂消费还是处在上升趋势中，只不过近年受国内经济运行减速的影响，油脂消费量增速已经大大放缓。

初步预计，2015/2016年度国内豆油新增供应量为1 442万吨，比2014/2015年度增加60万吨，增幅为4.3%。其中，大豆压榨供应量1 362万吨，比2014/2015年度增加58万吨；进口豆油量83万吨，比2014/2015年度增加近6万吨。新年度需要关注的影响供应的几个主要因素有：第一，进口大豆逐月到港数量。虽然2016年国内经济形势更为严峻，且人民币经历大幅贬值，油粕市场行情均不理想，理论上看会影响到新年度的大豆进口量，但国内庞大的饲料及食品需求将难降，大豆进口量或有增无减。第二，国内大豆压榨能力已经在2014/2015年度完成进一步提升，部分新建油厂陆续建成并投产压榨，因此在2015/2016年度，国内大豆产业仍将展现其庞大的压榨能力。第三，全球油菜籽生长、产量及进出口情况，最主要是国内油菜籽的进口情况、国产油菜籽的种植及产量情况等，对菜籽油的供应状况会有影响。第四，厄尔尼诺背景下的棕榈油实际产量状况。

初步预计，2015/2016年度国内豆油需求量为1 410万吨，比2014/2015年度增加61万吨，增幅为4.5%。工业等其他需求量为145万吨，与2014/2015年度持平。损耗量为14万吨，此方面变化不大。新年度的国内油脂市场，小品种食用油将继续拓展高端路线，豆油、菜籽油、棕榈油在国内食用消费中的比重或将发生些微变化，豆棕、菜棕价差缩窄，有望使部分棕榈油需求转向豆油或是菜籽油。

（2）国内豆油市场行情预计。2016年国内豆油市场仍将处在多空交错、相互牵制的局面中，决定了豆油市场主基调以2015年为基础，难现极端性改变。但国内豆油价格在底部震荡徘徊了一年以后，目前看进一步下探较为困难，鉴于内外围市场出现一系列“新多”因素，新年度预计国内豆油价格在目前价位水平上有上移的空间和机会。我们预计，2016

年国内散装四级豆油销售均价向上有涨回 6 000 元/吨之上甚至攀至 6 500 元/吨的可能，期价向下有跌到 5 200 点位的风险。预计多数时间仍将在 5 300 ~ 6 000 元/吨区间展开波动，具体的走势还需视多方影响因素间此消彼长的配合程度而定。

（博朗咨询 · 中国大豆网　　刘兆福）

# 五、油菜籽及菜油市场分析

【内容提要】

2015年，国内油菜籽种植面积和总产量均比上年下降。自2008年连续7年实施菜籽（油）临时收储政策之后，2015年国家菜籽收储政策发生重大改变，国家不再进行临储收购，而是对主产省给予一定补贴，由主产省自行制定本省的收购政策。受此影响，2015年国内油菜籽价格大幅下跌，与进口油菜籽成本接轨。2015年，国内菜籽粕和豆粕之间的价差继续处于历史低位水平，由于豆粕对菜粕的替代和水产养殖不景气，菜粕消费降到了近5年最低，菜粕年底价格较年初下跌近30%。由于绝大多数时间压榨处于亏损状态，2015年进口油菜籽数量比上年减少近12%。国产油菜籽和进口油菜籽数量双双下降，由此带来的菜籽油减量需进口菜籽油来弥补，因此虽然国内菜油需求依然不太景气，菜籽油价格也持续处于10年来低位水平，但2015年菜籽油进口数量相对稳定，基本与2014年持平。由于2015年国内菜籽油价格大幅低于国家临储菜籽油成本，2015年临储菜籽油流出数量较少。在经历了2011年2月以来持续5年的下跌后，市场普遍认为2015年国内菜籽油价格已见底，2016年国内菜籽油价格区域将高于2015年。

## （一）2015年国内油菜籽、菜籽油供求情况分析

### 1. 官方油菜籽产量6年来首次下降

国家粮油信息中心数据显示，2015年中国油菜籽播种面积730万公顷，比上年758.8万公顷减少3.8%；单位产量为1.959吨/公顷，略高于上年的1.947吨/公顷，增长0.62%；预计2015年中国油菜籽产量1 430万吨，比上年的1 477.2万吨减少3.2%。

2015年我国油菜籽产量下降的主要原因是油菜种植比较收益较低所致。占我国油菜籽产量90%的夏收油菜和冬小麦基本处于同一生长期，由于油菜种植收益和同期生长作物小麦相比较低，且小麦机械化程度高，油菜处于竞地劣势，农民更倾向于种小麦而不是油菜。2015年国家不再实施菜籽（油）临储收购，除四川外，其他主产省油菜籽的收购价普遍在3 400～3 600元/吨之间，大幅低于2014年的5 100元/吨，考虑到人工成本，农民种植油菜已处于负收益。由于油菜种植收益继续大幅下降，市场预计更多的原种植油菜的土地将转种小麦或别的经济作物，预计2016年油菜籽产量将因种植面积减少而大幅下降（见图2－5－1）。

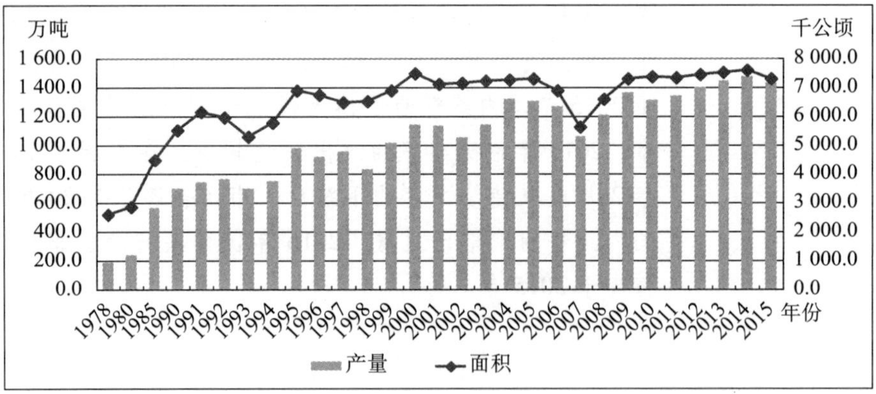


数据来源：2015年的数据来源于国家粮油信息中心；其他年份数据来源于部分国家统计局：《中国统计年鉴》，中国统计出版社出版。

**图2－5－1　我国历年油菜籽种植面积和产量**

### 2. 2015 年油菜籽和菜籽油进口量双双下降

海关数据显示，2015 年我国油菜籽进口量为 447 万吨，比 2014 年的 508 万吨大幅减少，减幅为 12%。2015 年我国油菜籽进口量下降的主要原因是：一是 2015 年除 3—5 月进口油菜籽压榨利润为正外，年内绝大多数时间压榨亏损幅度在 50 ~ 300 元/吨之间，且国内外植物油市场一直处于熊市，企业进口积极性下降。二是 2015 年国产油菜籽价格大幅下跌，与进口油菜籽到港成本基本接轨，进口油菜籽的优势下降。不过，国内油菜籽压榨产能严重过剩，东南沿海地区完全依靠进口油菜籽，企业的无序竞争和开机需求使得油菜籽进口保持在历史高位水平（见图 2 -5 -2）。

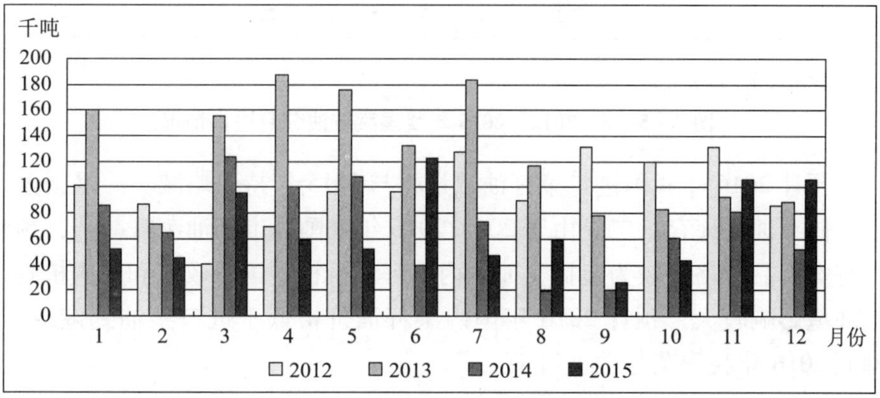


数据来源：海关总署。

**图 2 -5 -2 2012—2015 年我国油菜籽分月进口情况**

预计 2016 年我国油菜籽进口数量将继续保持在历史高位水平，将与 2015 年进口数量较为接近。一是由于我国油菜籽压榨产能严重过剩，国产油菜籽远不能满足压榨需求。二是市场预计 2016 年国内油菜籽产量将在 2015 年基础上进一步下降，让出来的这部分产能和市场需要进口油菜籽来填补。

海关数据显示，2015 年我国累计进口菜籽油 81.5 万吨，与 2014 年的 81 万吨基本持平，继续处于 5 年来的低位水平。2015 年我国菜籽油进口量继续处于 5 年低位的主要原因是：一是 2015 年油菜籽进口量虽然比 2014 年下降，但仍保持在历史高位水平；二是 2015 年国内菜籽油比豆油一直处于竞价劣势，其价格和需求受到压制，而国内外菜籽油价格多数时间处于倒挂状态，贸易商进口利润为负（见图 2－5－3）。

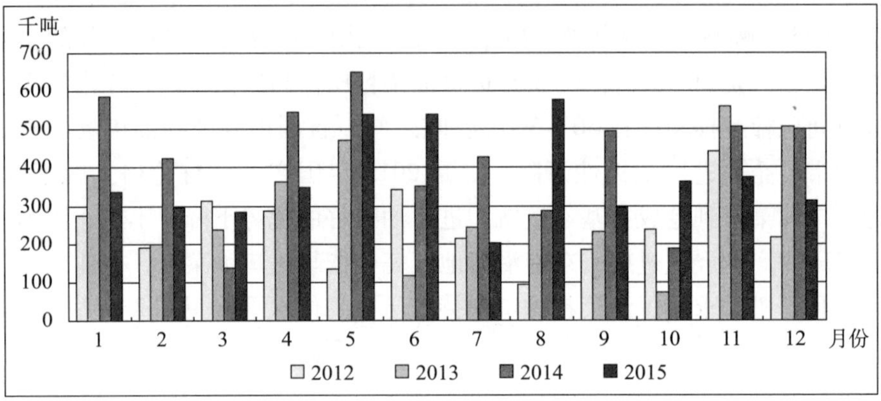


数据来源：海关总署。

**图 2－5－3　2012—2015 年我国菜籽油分月进口情况**

预计 2016 年我国进口菜籽油数量将与 2015 年持平略减。一是国家开始临储菜油去库存。二是由于 2015/2016 年度国际市场油菜籽减产，预计菜籽类商品价格将较为坚挺，而国内菜籽油价格受国家政策和国内植物油大环境影响较大，预计 2016 年国内菜籽油价格低于进口菜油到港成本，抑制 2016 年我国菜籽油进口量。

### 3. 国内油菜籽、菜籽油市场供需情况分析

国家粮油信息中心数据显示，2014/2015 年度，我国油菜籽新增供给量预计为 1 931 万吨，比上年度增加 50 万吨，其中，国内油菜籽产量预计为 1 477 万吨，油菜籽进口量预计为 454 万吨。预计该年度油菜籽榨油消费量为 1 870 万吨，比上年度增加 130 万吨，其中，包含 1 360 万吨国产油菜籽及 510 万吨进口油菜籽。该年度油菜籽供需缺口为 29 万吨。

2015/2016 年度，我国油菜籽新增供给量预计为 1 850 万吨，比上年度减少 81 万吨。其中，国内油菜籽产量预计为 1 430 万吨，油菜籽进口量预计为 420 万吨。预计该年度油菜籽榨油消费量为 1 800 万吨，比上年度减少 70 万吨，其中，包含 1 320 万吨国产油菜籽及 480 万吨进口油菜籽。该年度油菜籽供需缺口为 30 万吨。

2015年，我国油菜籽新增供给量和年消费量6年来首次双双减少，在国内油菜籽压榨产能持续提高的背景下，预计国内油菜籽压榨产能的开工率将比2014年的24%进一步降低，创下近几年新低。如此过剩的产能将继续使2015年国内油菜籽供需基本面呈紧平衡状态（见图2－5－4）。

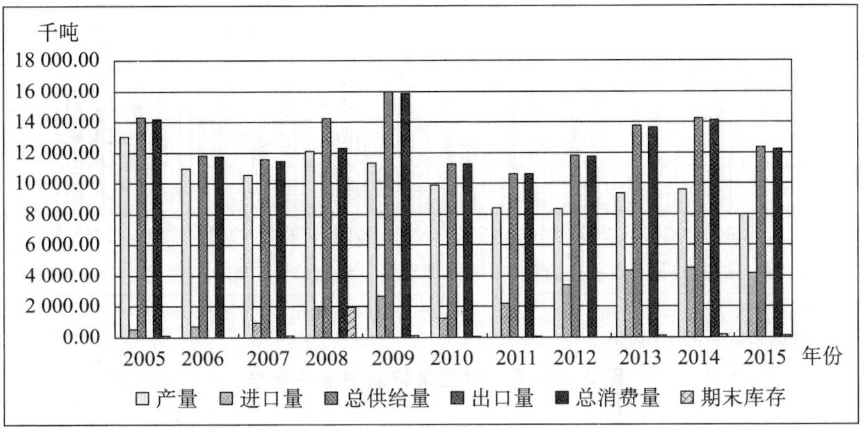


数据来源：WIND资讯。

**图2－5－4　中国油菜籽供需平衡表**

2014/2015年度，我国菜籽油新增供给量预计为752万吨，其中，菜籽油产量预计为689万吨，进口量预计为63万吨。该年度菜籽油国内消费量预计为630万吨，比上年度增加5万吨。年度菜籽油供需结余量预计为122万吨。

2015/2016年度，我国菜籽油新增供给量预计为713万吨，其中，菜籽油产量预计为663万吨，进口量预计为50万吨。该年度菜籽油国内消费量预计为680万吨，比上年度增加5万吨。年度菜籽油供需结余量预计为33万吨。

2015年，国内菜籽油仍然供大于求，基本面偏松，但供给比上年同比减少5.18%，而需求同比增长7.93%，国内菜籽油处于快速去库存状态。可以说，2015年国内几大植物油品种中，菜籽油的商业库存最低，基本面最好，这也是2015年菜籽油在熊市中比豆油和棕榈油抗跌，并成为投机资金阶段性多菜籽油空豆油或棕榈油的原因。不过，菜籽油也是国家储备最多的植物油，因此国内菜籽油走势是受政策影响最大的品种

（见图 2 –5 –5）。

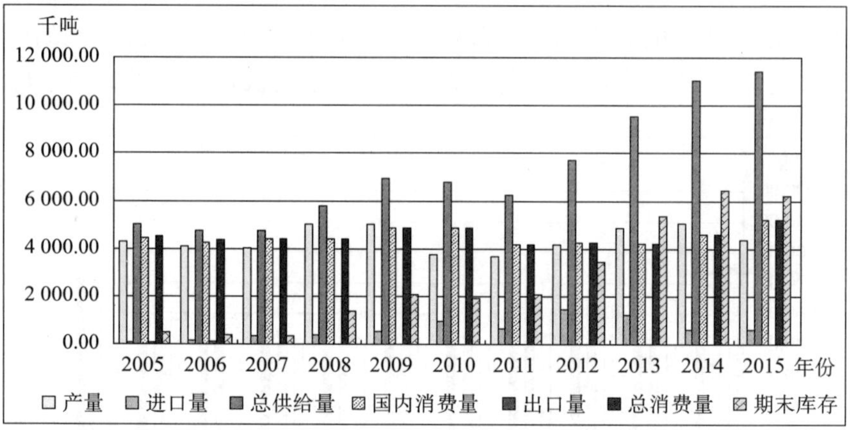


数据来源：WIND 资讯。

**图 2 –5 –5　中国菜籽油供需平衡表**

### 4. 2015 年国内油菜籽、菜籽油市场回顾

自 2015 年起国家不再实施菜籽（油）临时收储政策，由地方政府负责组织各类企业进行油菜籽收购。对湖北、四川、湖南、安徽、江苏、河南、贵州油菜籽主要产区，中央财政将适当予以补贴，支持地方鼓励加工企业收购、补贴种植大户，做好油菜籽生产工作。

在各主产省中，除四川省对国标三等油菜籽按 2. 3 元/斤（相邻等级按差价 0. 02 元/斤掌握）进行收购的企业给予 0. 25 元/斤的补贴外，湖北、江苏、安徽等主产省均在对油菜籽种植农民实行直补的基础上，实行市场化收购（见图 2 –5 –6）。

受政策重大调整影响，2015 年国内油菜籽收购市场呈现以下几个特点：

一是国产油菜籽收购价在 5 月下旬至 6 月下旬大幅下跌，从政策明朗前的 5 100 元/吨下跌到明朗后的 3 400 元/吨，跌幅达 33. 33%。主因是国内菜籽油和菜籽粕市场处于熊市，国产油菜籽压榨亏损，且企业不看好后市，失去政策支撑后，在市场作用下国产菜籽价格直线下跌。8 月下旬，国内植物油市场见底回升，油厂压榨利润略有好转及国产油菜籽供给减少后，国产油菜籽价格回升至 3 600 元/吨偏上。

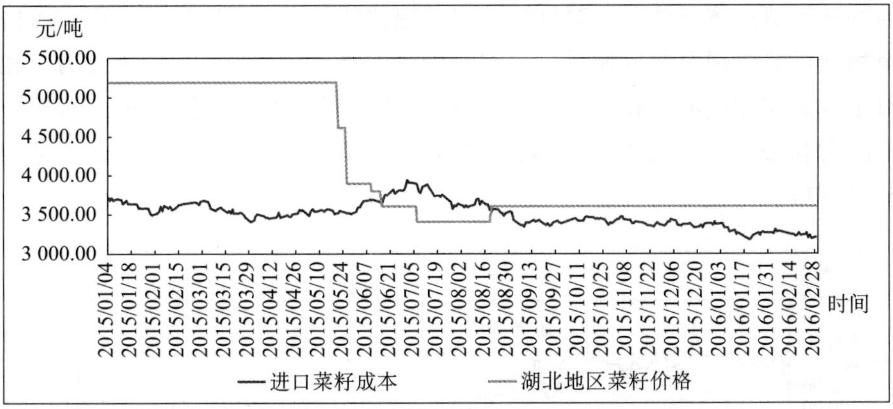


数据来源：WIND 资讯。

**图 2－5－6　2015 年湖北地区普通油菜籽价格和进口油菜籽成本走势对比图**

二是国产油菜籽与进口油菜籽价格接轨。相对于前两年国产油菜籽和进口油菜籽高达 1 500 元/吨的价差，随着国产油菜籽收购市场化，国产油菜籽与进口油菜籽价格快速接轨，6—7 月国产油菜籽集中上市期还出现国产油菜籽收购价低于进口油菜籽到港成本的局面，国产油菜籽长期处于竞价劣势的局面得到改变，有助于主产区以国产油菜籽为原料的压榨企业的生存。

三是主产区油菜籽贸易商普遍亏损。从调研来看，往年主产区油菜籽贸易商七挣三赔，而 2015 年却是三挣七赔。其主要原因是贸易商政策灵敏度不够，油菜籽压榨企业在政策不明朗观望时，贸易商却根椐往年经验认为在油菜籽已收获而企业没有开秤前是收购好时机，可以得到大幅低于托市价的收购价，短暂保存后卖给企业挣取价差，但 2015 年临储政策不再实施，国产油菜籽收购价急跌，部分油菜籽贸易商很受伤。

四是国产油菜籽商品量大幅下降。统计显示，截至 9 月 30 日，四川、湖北等 9 个主产区各类粮食企业收购新产油菜籽 160 万吨，比上年同期减少 188 万吨，减幅达到 54%。其主要原因是今年国产油菜籽价格太低，农民更愿意自留而不是销售。

2015 年，国内菜籽油价格全年呈区间震荡态势，并没出现趋势性行情。从年度行情来看，在经历了自 2011 年 2 月开始的持续近 5 年的震荡下跌后，2015 年菜籽油价格持续处于筑底阶段，上不去下不来。在国内植物油行情整体下跌时，菜籽油价格跌幅往往最小，表现抗跌；而在国内植物油行情出现大幅反弹时，菜籽油价格涨幅也往往最小，向上乏力。相对于豆油和棕榈油来说，2015 年菜籽油期、现货价格震幅较小，而在成本因素和金融因素影响下，菜籽油现货价格的震幅又小于期价（见图 2－5－7）。

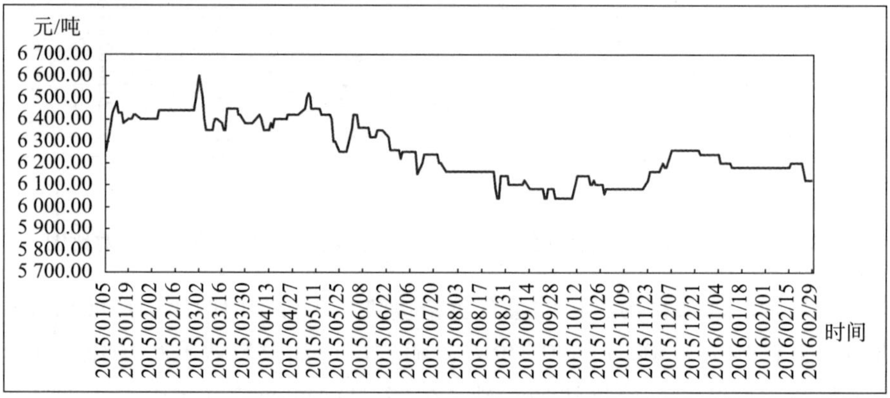


数据来源：WIND 资讯。

**图 2－5－7　2015 年湖北武汉四级菜油价格走势图**

影响 2015 年国内菜籽油价格的利空因素有：

一是全球宏观经济不景气，需求增速放缓，而以大豆为首的油脂油料供给增速却没有放缓，在基本面压力下，以大豆为首的油脂油料价格持续震荡下行，由于国内外植物油价格联动性较强，国内菜籽油价格难以一枝独秀。

二是由于近两年国内外菜籽类产品价格倒挂严重，业内预期 2015 年继续实施临储收购的可能性较小，随着靴子落地，国产油菜籽市场化定价，国产油菜籽价格大跌，原料成本对下游产品支撑作用减弱，国产菜籽油出厂成本下降。

三是自国家实施临储菜籽（油）收储政策以来，国内累积了近一年消费量的临储菜籽油，且部分临储菜油已过储存期，面临出库压力。国内菜籽油市场从年初到年底国家抛售临储菜油的传闻不断，抑制了国内市场对菜籽油的追涨热情，缩小了反弹行情时菜籽油的向上空间。

影响 2015 年国内菜籽油市场的利多因素有：

一是 2015 年绝大多数时间进口油菜籽和国产油菜籽，无论是从郑盘期价来看，还是从现货价格来看，压榨利润都处于负值，国内菜籽油成本对国内菜籽油期、现货价格支撑作用明显。

二是主要出口国加拿大和主要消费地区欧盟均出现油菜籽减产，国际市场油菜籽供需基本面偏紧，在全球大豆生产增速快于需求增速、以大豆为首的油脂油料价格下行压力较大的情况下，国际市场油菜籽价格虽然受到拖累，但明显较为坚挺，原料成本对下游产品价格起到支撑作用。

三是 2015 年国内菜籽粕需求降至近几年的谷底，价格也创 10 年新低，菜籽油和菜籽粕之间存在跷跷板效应，国内菜籽粕出厂价疲弱支撑了菜籽油出厂成本。

## （二）主产国减产，全球油菜籽基本面偏紧

《油世界》预计，2015/2016 年度全球油菜籽产量为 6 400 万吨，低于 2014/2015 年度的 6 903 万吨。其中，欧盟菜籽产量为 2 153 万吨，2014/2015 年度为 2 439 万吨；澳大利亚产量为 325 万吨，2014/2015 年度为 355 万吨；乌克兰产量为 190 万吨，2014/2015 年度为 233 万吨。预计 2015/2016 年度加拿大油菜籽产量为 1 380 万吨，为 5 年来最低水平，2014/2015 年度产量为 1 556 万吨，2013/2014 年度为 1 828 万吨。2015 年加拿大油菜籽出苗后经历严重干旱、倒春寒和霜冻灾害，尽管 7 月下旬迎来有利降雨，但单产受损及面积下降仍使产量下滑。国际谷物理事会（IGC）预计，2015/2016 年度油菜籽产量为 6 780 万吨，比 2014/2015 年度减少 360 万吨。其中，欧盟产量 2 190 万吨，同比减少 220 万吨；加拿大产量 1 490 万吨，同比减少 70 万吨。预计全球菜籽贸易量降至 5 年来低位为 1 290 万吨，比 2014/2015 年度减少 100 万吨，预计期末库存比上年下降 26%，至 410 万吨。

据加拿大农业暨农业食品部发布的最新报告显示，2015/2016 年度全球油菜籽产量预计减少约 540 万吨，为 6 250 万吨，因为欧盟、加拿大和澳大利亚产量下滑。印度的产量增长，但是增幅要小于上述国家的产量降幅。因而 2015/2016 年度全球油菜籽供应预计紧张，将会造成全球油菜籽

压榨量减少 380 万吨。

从以上数据来看，虽然绝对值不一样，但知名机构均对 2015/2016 年度全球油菜籽产量较上一年度做出较大幅度下调，下调幅度 5.05% ~ 7.95% 不等。加之减产幅度较大的国家还是传统的主要出口国，直接带来 2015/2016 年度全球可出口油菜籽数量和油菜籽期末库存数量同比下降，国际油菜籽基本面偏紧。因此，虽然 2015/2016 年度以大豆为首的国际油脂油料市场基本面偏空，由于油脂油料之间的替代效应，国际市场油菜籽价格也难免会受到拖累，但由于油菜籽自身基本面偏紧，预计国际市场油菜籽走势相对大豆将较为坚挺。

此外，2015 年 6 月 17 日中澳两国签订自由贸易协定，在货物领域，双方各有占出口贸易额 85.4% 的产品将在协定生效时立即实现零关税。减税过渡期后，澳大利亚最终实现零关税的税目占比和贸易额占比将达到 100%；中国实现零关税的税目占比和贸易额占比将分别达到 96.8% 和 97%。但是，根据协定规定，对进口自澳大利亚的油菜籽、菜籽油仍将保持基础税率 9% 不变，进口亚麻籽、棉籽、葵花籽、蓖麻、花生的关税都将分 5 年过渡期由当前的 15% 降至零，因此协定对国内外油菜籽和菜籽油市场基本无影响（见图 2 - 5 - 8 至图 2 - 5 - 10）。

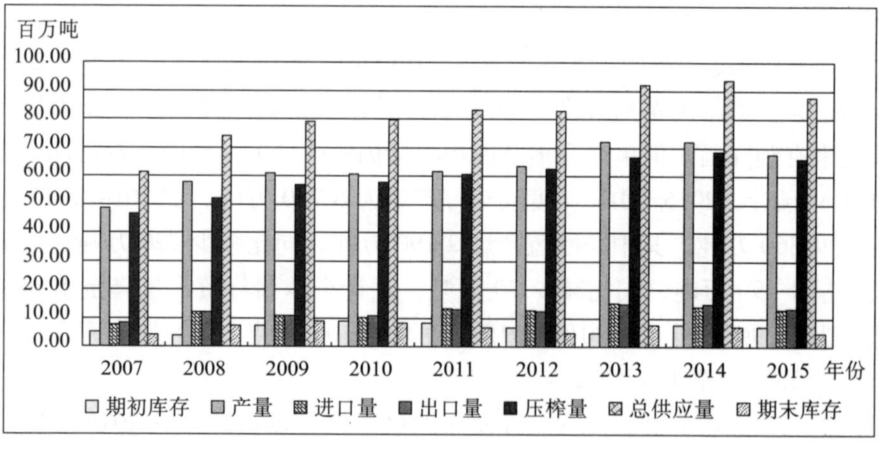


数据来源：WIND 资讯。

**图 2 - 5 - 8　全球油菜籽供需平衡表**

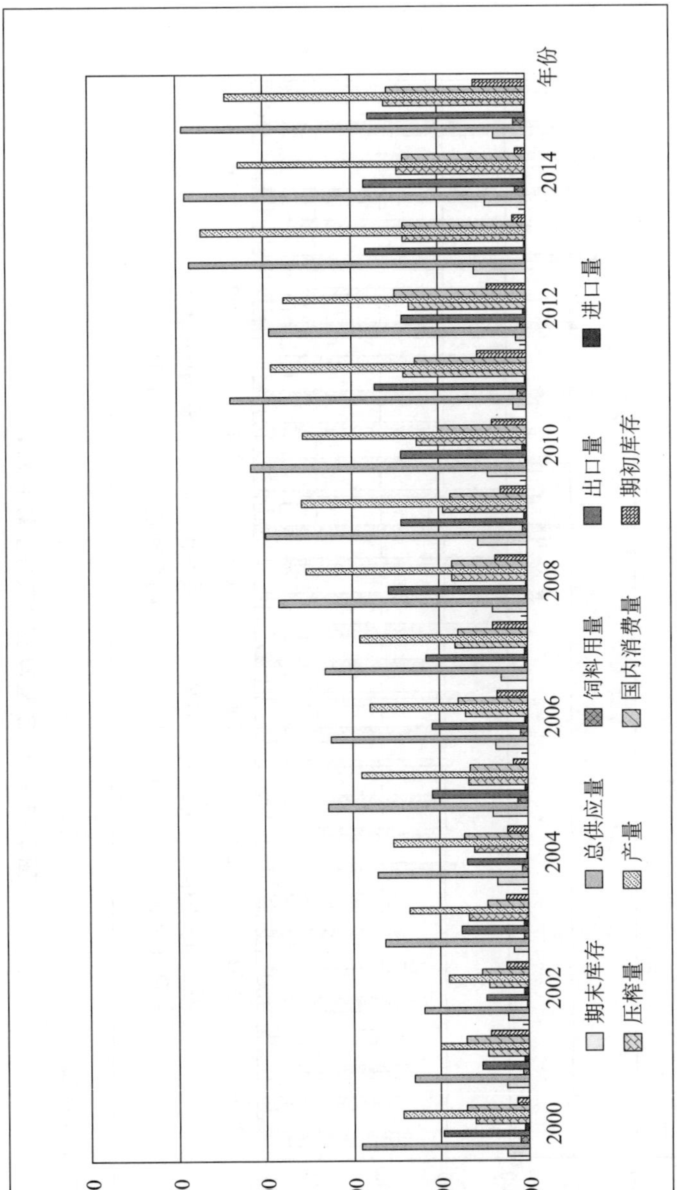


图 2-5-9　加拿大油菜籽供需平衡表

数据来源：WIND 资讯。

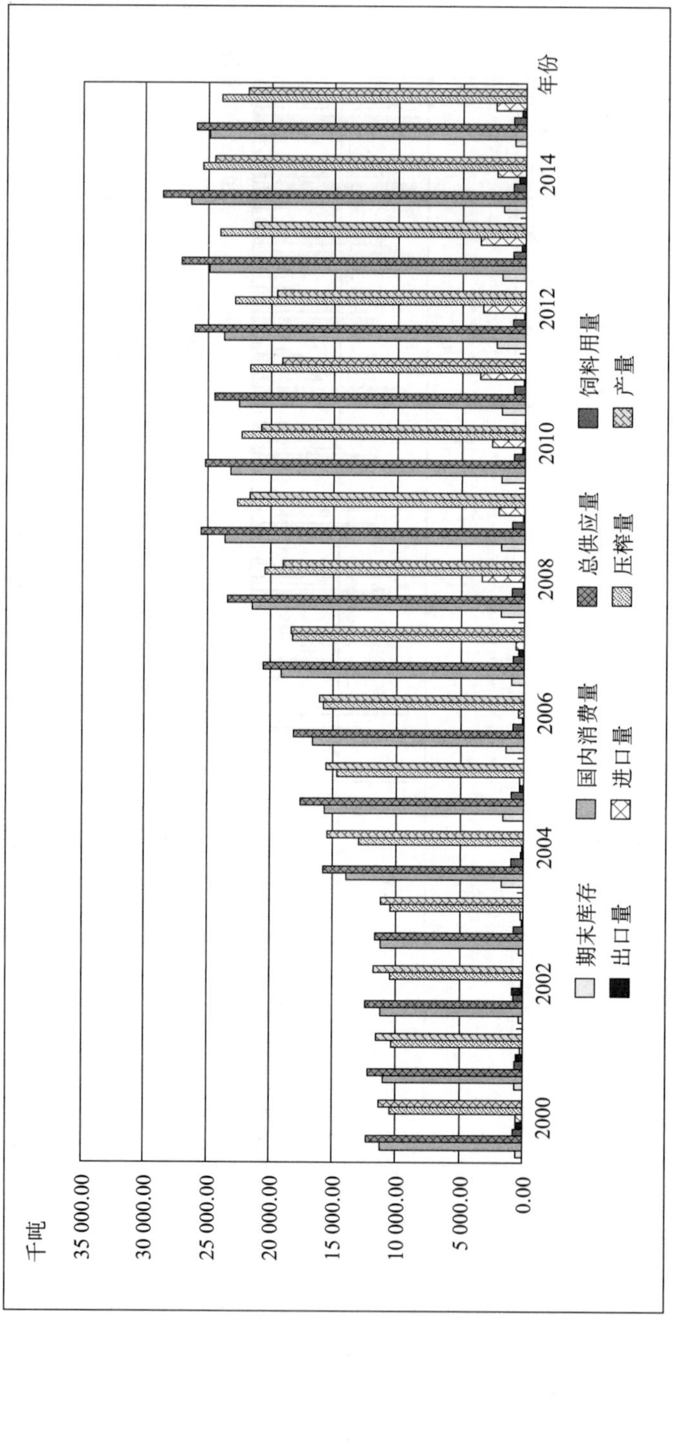


数据来源：WIND资讯。

**图2-5-10 欧盟27国油菜籽供需平衡表**

## （三）2016 年国内油菜籽、菜籽油市场展望

### 1. 预计 2016 年国内油菜籽价格运行区间将基本与 2015 年重叠

预计 2016 年国产油菜籽实际种植面积和总产量双双下降。其主要原因是：2015 年国产油菜籽收购市场化，价格比 2014 年大幅下跌，农民种植收益同比大幅下降，在比较效应下，农民更倾向于种小麦或其他经济作物，部分地区有撂荒出现。市场预期 2015 年秋冬播油菜籽面积将同比下降 10% 以上，个别机构甚至下调至 30% 以上。2015 年国产油菜籽因天气良好，单产和质量均处于 5 年来最好水平，2016 年即使天气理想，单产和质量继续上升的空间较小，因此 2016 年国产油菜籽总产量将随着种植面积大幅下降。

预计 2016 年国内油菜籽价格运行区间将基本与 2015 年重叠，在 3 200～4 600 元/吨之间运行，新菜籽上市后，低开高走的可能性较大。其主要考虑因素是：

一是 2015 年国产油菜籽价格市场化以后，国产油菜籽价格已与进口油菜籽价格接轨，而 2015/2016 年度国际市场油菜籽基本面偏紧，进口油菜籽价格稳定在 3 200 元/吨以上，未来也是易上难下，进口油菜籽对国产油菜籽的下拉作用有限。而 2015 年国产油菜籽种植利润已为负，这也表明了国产油菜籽价格的底部，低于这价位农民宁可自用而不是出售，因此 2016 年国产油菜籽收购价不太可能低于 2015 年。

二是 2015 年无论是国产油菜籽还是进口油菜籽，绝大部分时间压榨利润都处于负数。预计 2016 年油菜籽压榨利润将有所好转，这将提高油菜籽压榨企业采购油菜籽的积极性。一方面，由于 2015 年国内菜籽粕需求量已降到极值，2016 年国内菜籽粕需求将随水产养殖好转而有所提高，但国内菜籽粕供给量将随国产油菜籽的大幅减产而减少，在国产油菜籽上市期，国内菜籽粕价格走高的可能性非常大；另一方面，国内菜籽油价格在 2015 年下半年已出现拐点，2016 年随着国内植物油市场震荡向上的可能性较大。油粕价格回升有利于油厂压榨利润好转。不过 2016 年国际大

豆市场基本面压力较大，仍处于去库存状态，豆油和豆粕价格将抑制菜籽油和菜籽粕价格向上空间，间接影响国内油菜籽价格向上空间。

三是由于2015年国产油菜籽经纪人基本全线亏损，加之2011年以来的熊市，在惯性思维下，预计在国产油菜籽上市初期市场观望情绪较浓，不过农民惜售和菜籽压榨利润的好转将推动国产油菜籽价格稳步向上，因此收购初期很可能是年内油菜籽价格的低位水平区域，建议经纪人和企业趁机囤一部分货。

**2. 预计2016年国内菜籽油价格呈宽幅区间震荡，重心逐步上移的态势**

2015年下半年国内菜籽油期、现货价格已探寻到2011年2月下跌以来的长线大底，并出现拐点，2016年将呈宽幅区间震荡、重心逐步上移的态势，操作上逢回调择机买多。郑菜油主力合约价格在5 500～7 500元/吨运行的可能性较大，而国内菜籽油现货因混入进口菜籽油情况不同，报价相对混乱。

分析后市，主要利空因素有：

一是从2015年12月开始，国家开始定期拍卖临储菜籽油，拍卖底价远低于市场价，考虑到精炼费用后才和市场价基本持平。业内传言国家将把2014年产的约100万吨临储菜籽油转为常规储备，通过正常轮换实现以新旧交替，其他约400万吨2014年以前产的临储菜籽油将每周定期向市场投放。如传言成真，则低价临储菜籽油的抛售将增加阶段性的供给，延长国内菜籽油期、现货价格在底部区域的盘整时间。

二是2015/2016年度美豆销售量较上年同期减少15%，开春后农民需要资金购买种子、农药、化肥，后期面临较大销售压力；巴西大豆产量虽然生长期遭受北旱南涝，但从气象规律来看，厄尔尼诺天气多有利于大豆生长，2015/2016年度巴西大豆丰产的可能性仍较大；2015年最后两个月，中国进口大豆压榨利润为负，采购步伐放缓。由于供给充裕而需求疲软，2016年上半年国际以大豆为首的油料市场基本面仍然偏空，芝加哥期货交易所大豆期价中期仍有创新低的可能。由于国内外油脂油料市场高度联动，国内主要植物油品种之间因替代效应关联性也较强，因此国内菜籽油价格难以独秀。

分析后市，主要利多因素有：

一是原料成本支撑。由于国际市场油菜籽减产供应偏紧，进口油菜籽到港成本基本已无向下空间；国产油菜籽市场化后价格已与进口油菜籽接轨，2016 年新油菜籽在农民惜售、压榨企业利润好转的共同推动下，低开高走的可能性较大。由于原料价格坚挺，支撑下游产品价格。

二是市场不看好 2016 年上半年粕类商品价格，在油粕跷跷板效应下，粕弱则油强。如上所述，2016 年一季度末二季度初来自于国际市场大豆基本面的压力很可能爆发，国内进口大豆成本在可以预期的未来半年将继续在 10 年来的历史底部区域，而国内生猪在春节前集中出栏后往往进入 3 月才开始补栏，国内豆粕需求阶段性下降，预计来自于大豆的压力更多集中在豆粕而不是豆油。在库存压力下，油厂也更倾向于降粕保油。因此，菜籽粕受到来自于大豆的不利影响要大于菜籽油。

三是经过近 5 年的持续震荡下跌，国内包括菜籽油在内的植物油市场在 2015 年下半年见底并出现拐点，市场已处于 U 型底的右半侧底部区域，资金杀跌意愿不强，反而逢低买入进场积极性较高。

四是 2015 年 12 月美联储进入加息周期，人民币渐进式贬值，由于国内植物油 67% 都来自于国际市场，人民币贬值将推高植物油进口成本，国内菜籽油的运行区间也将因此上移。

（郑州粮食批发市场　陈艳军）

# 六、花生及花生油市场分析

【内容提要】

我国是世界花生生产、消费和出口大国，花生产量和出口量均是世界第一。与其他传统的油料作物相比，花生具有国际竞争力强、增产潜力大、出油率高、经济效益好、营养价值高和种植适应性强等方面的优势。推动花生产业稳定发展，对于调整我国农业结构、增加农民收入、提高食用油脂自给率、增强农产品出口创汇能力具有重要而深远的意义。

近两年来，国内花生行情相对疲软，对农户种植积极性有一定的影响。在油厂收购缩减、中间商谨小慎微的态度影响下，市场购销热情不高，整体行情稳定，市场缺乏活力。花生油市场一直波澜不惊，出现旺季不旺的特点。在整体去库存的形势下，主力油厂开工不足，对花生市场没有形成推动力。

2015年南方产区早花生上市后，花生收购价格高开，但后期价格快速下滑，尤其是在河南产区春花生大批上市后，价格逐步下滑至谷底。后期花生价格虽有小幅波动，但整体购销氛围清淡，交易未出现高峰。虽然部分产区因干旱而减产，但减产并未出现“物以稀为贵”的预期，自上市以来，农户出售积极性一直偏弱，市场走货缓慢，然而进口花生米仍大量到港，对农户的心理带来沉重打击。

近几年形成花生行情清淡的原因是什么？如何保障花生产业健康发展？面对日益沉重的进口产品压力，中国花生产业的突破点在哪里？地广人稀的新疆地区能否发展成为中国花生种植业的支撑点？农户、经销商、出口加工企业和油厂如何紧密配合迎接2016年新的挑战？本文作者将在文中做具体论述，为广大农民、经销商和相关企业提供决策参考。

## （一）2015年国内花生及花生油市场分析

### 1. 2015年国内花生市场回顾

（1）2015年我国花生种植面积和产量延续下滑趋势。2012年是我国花生种植面积最大的年份，种植总面积为463.853万公顷，但2013年以后，花生种植面积持续小幅缩减。2014年种植总面积为460.385万公顷，总产量1 648.17万吨，单产3 579.98千克/公顷，与2013年相比同步下滑。2015年种植面积当前尚无权威数据，据中国花生交易网对合作经纪人及种植合作社所作不完全统计，2015年国内花生种植面积与2014年相比减少了10%～15%，就2014年数据估算在420万公顷左右。受天气干旱影响，山东半岛及东北吉林、辽宁等产区花生均出现减产情况。据当地经纪人反映，干旱地区花生单产减产20%～30%，花生品质下降，空果增多。结合河南及其他产区，2015年花生总产量不足1 550万～1 580万吨，单产在3 200千克/公顷左右。

近几年花生行情低迷是导致种植面积下降的主要原因。花生行业进入前所未有的低迷阶段，花生价格跌破种植成本，严重打击了农民的种植积极性。油厂收购不积极，进口花生及花生米大量到港，低价冲击国内花生市场，价格大幅波动的频率也越来越高。在持续两年的低迷行情影响下，国内花生种植面积持续小幅缩减。由于花生具有抗旱性及耐贫瘠性的特点，多数山丘地、河滩沙化土地仍选择种植花生。同时，形成规模效应的山东省莒南县、河南省正阳县等产区，种植面积调整不大。其他分散种植的区域呈现缩减态势。由于新疆产区地广人稀，以沙质土壤为主，成为花生种植的新兴产地，但当前种植面积仍然较少，尚未形成影响力（见表2－6－1）。

**表2-6-1 2009—2014年我国花生种植面积、产量及单产**

单位：万公顷，万吨，千克/公顷

| 年 份 | 总面积 | 总产量 | 单 产 |
|---|---|---|---|
| 2014 | 460.385 | 1 648.17 | 3 579.98 |
| 2013 | 463.299 | 1 697.22 | 3 663.33 |
| 2012 | 463.853 | 1 669.16 | 3 598.46 |
| 2011 | 458.144 | 1 604.64 | 3 502.47 |
| 2010 | 452.730 | 1 564.39 | 3 455.55 |
| 2009 | 437.652 | 1 470.79 | 3 360.64 |

数据来源：国家统计局。

（2）2015年农民种植成本及收益分析。为了更好地分析2015年农民种植成本及收益情况，通过对农户花生种植机会成本的分析，更好地预测2016年的种植情况。从山东省临沭县和沂源县种植调查情况来细化分析：

2015年12月31日至2016年1月7日，据临沭县物价局对9户花生种植户的成本收益调查，与2014年相比，2015年花生亩均产量下降，产值减少，收益减少。受干旱影响，2015年沂源县花生产量与收购价格明显双降，农户连续两年呈现负收益。其主要原因是：

一是产量下降，产值减少。2015年花生亩均产量290.63千克，较2014年下降35.86千克，减幅为10.98%。主要是受天气干旱影响，产量减少，花生质量下降，空壳增加。尤其是岭地种植户，亩均产量仅200千克左右。亩均产值1 616.88元，比2014年减少459.37元，减幅为22.12%。

二是利润较低，调查户出售意愿不强。亩均利润342.34元，比2014年减少469.11元，减幅为57.81%。花生平均出售价格（皮果）5.35元/千克，比2014年下降13.63%。花生收购价格下降的主要原因是受国内外大环境影响，花生出口减少，花生收购价格低位运行。

三是产量及收购价格下降。产量方面，2015年所调查的9户农户亩均花生产量为179.1千克，与2014年同期相比下降21.1%。通过农户了解到，2015年天气过于干旱，而沂源县花生种植多为沙山地种植，土地自身储水量差，且供水设施不到位，水量无法满足花生生长的需求，导致2015年花生空壳、瘪壳、烂果率比往年有所增加，饱满花生产率下降。

四是收购价格下降。2015 年沂源县皮花生收购价格为 5.00 元/千克左右，与 2014 年同期相比下降 7.4%。收购价格下降的主要原因是受国内大环境影响，各类农副产品价格走低，在一定程度上影响了花生收购价格，而如此低的价格使农户宁愿自己留用也不愿出售，2015 年所调查的 9 户中均无花生出售。

五是成本投入上升，收益下降。每亩种植成本大约是 1 791 元，与 2014 年同期相比上涨 6.15%；其中上涨较为明显的为：化肥费用 246.4 元、农药 12.5 元、农膜费 42.36 元、人工费 1 066 元，与 2014 年同期相比分别上涨 27.85%、54.62%、15.14%、13%。2015 年亩均收益为 891.33 元，扣除成本后，亩均净利润为 -828.29 元。在产量和收购价格同时下跌的情况下，直接导致了净利润的减少。此外，种植总成本上升也加速了净利润的下降。

从两地物价局调查来看，花生种植各种成本均有不同程度的上涨，各地区生产资料成本相差不大，主要在于地膜、肥料、良种之间的差异，人工成本成为花生种植成本的主要组成部分。随着我国经济的发展，农户外出务工人数增多，劳动力成本成为农户选择种植品种的主要条件之一。与玉米相比，花生种植机械化程度相对较低，对人工占用较多，机械化的推进成为降低花生种植成本的重要途径。

（3）2015 年花生价格情况统计与分析。根据图 2-6-1 可知，2015 年 7—9 月份，花生价格以下行为主，其中白沙统货米价格下滑较为明显。

2015 年 7 月份持续高温使花生储存难度加大，变质率提高，致使花生经销商出货意愿增强，但市场成交依然不太理想。各地停收停机现象陆续增加，引发市场各方普遍谨慎观望。国内花生市场品种分化走势延续，油料花生仍维持偏弱调整。由于国内花生收购基本接近尾声，各地采购积极性普遍下降，花生出口行情也不容乐观。同时，麦收后市场供应量有所增加，导致短期内市场强势格局难以显现。由于 7 月份国内花生市场正处于需求淡季，经销商补库心理较为谨慎，补库量有限，花生价格大幅上涨缺乏有力支撑。

自 8 月份以来，各地新花生逐步上市，除南方江西、湖南等上市较早的产区开秤价格较高外，至河南产区大量上市后，价格持续快速下滑。产区间上市时间差缩小，新花生集中上市，形成下滑趋势。江西 2015 年播

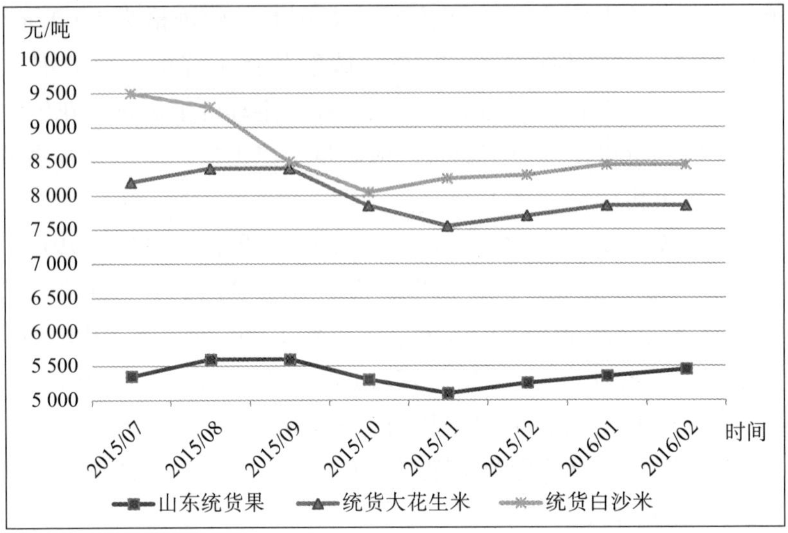


数据来源：中国花生交易网。

**图 2－6－1　2015 年 7 月至 2016 年 2 月花生价格走势图**

种时间受持续降雨影响而推后，上市时间略推迟一周，8 月中旬开始陆续上市，与河南产区上市时间差缩小。河南产区新花生由于水分较大，经销商普遍存在停收观望心理，收购商收购较为谨慎，市场需求不旺，各地成交量相对平淡。

9 月中下旬，全国范围内新花生大量上市进程加快，新花生供应量继续增大，供应压力仍然是近期行情的主要利空因素。油厂停收局面依然存在，9 月份价格逐步走低。

10 月国庆节过后，国内花生市场整体平稳，部分地区互有涨跌。由于正处于农忙时节，市场上货量不大，经销商采购积极性普遍不高，需求清淡。由于收购价与经销商和农户的心理价位存在一定差距，市场又缺乏明显的利好引导，经销商普遍采取随进随出的采购策略，各地交易呈现购销两难局面，因此市场价格上涨动力明显不足，农户惜售或成为花生价格平稳的主要原因。

11 月受国内阴雨及降雪天气影响，同时由于价低农户惜售，各地上货量偏小，导致部分产区花生价格稳中偏强。然而，油料米与商品米之间的价差进一步扩大，制约了整体行情的波动，各地花生价格稳中有涨。

12 月份以来，农户惜售心理浓厚，同时受产区降雨降雪影响，干货少，运输受阻，价格偏强上涨。由于花生下游产品需求疲软，油厂收购谨慎，限制了花生上涨空间。商品米价格小幅上涨，油料米价格低迷，销售困难。

2016 年 1 月份随着春节的临近，国内花生市场陆续进入年底备货期，各购销主体入市信心复苏，农户挺价心理进一步增强，但受市场整体需求依然较为清淡以及进口米陆续抵港等因素的影响，花生价格以平稳略强走势为主。主力油厂收购意愿提高，对整体花生行情起到提振作用，油料米走货有所加速，经销商入市信心恢复，加上产区上市量小、优质货源较少，成为价格走势偏高的有利支撑。市场消化缓慢和进口米到港压力，将花生价格限制在小区间震荡。

2016 年 2 月初期，国内花生市场总体维持平稳态势，但局部地区市场价格小幅震荡，而各地花生市场购销基本结束，仅有少量交易。其中，山东、河南、河北、吉林、辽宁等地交易基本停止。国内花生市场总体库存不高。农户和中间商整体花生库存水平低，挺价心理强，春节后至今，价格呈现小幅上涨走势。

（4）2015 年花生出口分析。2015 年中国花生、花生仁、花生油出口量比 2014 年小幅缩减，金额基本持平，单价略有上涨。其中，花生出口约 12.77 万吨，同比下降 7.63%；出口金额约 2.15 亿美元，同比上涨 7.09%；单价约 1 684.27 美元/吨，同比上涨 15.94%。花生仁出口约 9.82 万吨，同比下降 2.41%；出口金额为 1.74 亿美元，同比上涨 12.36%；单价约 1 771.10 美元/吨，同比上涨 15.14%。花生油出口约 0.951 万吨，同比下滑 2.11%；金额 0.217 亿美元，同比增长 2.62%；单价约 2 282.94 美元/吨，同比下滑约 2.26%。我国花生产品出口数量比 2014 年出口数量逐步减少，单价略有提高，但花生油制品单价及数量同步小幅减少（见表 2－6－2）。

全球花生种植国家主要是印度、中国、美国、阿根廷等四国，此外西非塞内加尔花生也逐步出口至中国。由于经营模式不同，相对成本也不同。作为发展中国家的印度、中国、阿根廷三国，印度、中国种植面积最大，由于人口众多，生产方式以小农生产为主，机械化水平较低；印度劳动力价格低廉，相对于中国日益增加的劳动力成本，其价格有竞争优势，

表 2－6－2　　2015 年中国花生、花生仁、花生油月出口数据与同比分析

单位：千克，美元，%

| 品 种 | 月 份 | 当 月 | | 同 比 | |
|---|---|---|---|---|---|
| | | 数 量 | 金 额 | 数 量 | 金 额 |
| 花 生 | 1 | 12 944 500 | 22 406 677 | －28.75 | －16.71 |
| | 2 | 9 194 224 | 16 174 527 | 11.95 | 43.92 |
| | 3 | 8 973 377 | 15 871 440 | －45.22 | －34.21 |
| | 4 | 16 214 053 | 28 209 747 | －3.40 | 18.56 |
| | 5 | 18 265 948 | 31 519 619 | 15.84 | 36.51 |
| | 6 | 14 278 256 | 24 064 946 | 10.38 | 33.45 |
| | 7 | 6 078 591 | 10 057 124 | －38.81 | －25.11 |
| | 8 | 4 544 415 | 7 504 034 | －43.57 | －31.31 |
| | 9 | 4 341 747 | 7 085 728 | －25.78 | －11.98 |
| | 10 | 6 604 999 | 10 340 016 | 10.41 | 21.41 |
| | 11 | 10 458 730 | 16 296 437 | 15.31 | 19.61 |
| | 12 | 15 765 045 | 25 490 547 | 42.33 | 33.71 |
| | 总 计 | 127 663 885 | 215 020 842 | －7.63 | 7.09 |
| 花生仁 | 1 | 10 620 316 | 19 221 021 | －29.32 | －16.71 |
| | 2 | 7 271 467 | 13 642 189 | 27.71 | 67.52 |
| | 3 | 7 269 875 | 13 572 246 | －35.49 | －23.23 |
| | 4 | 12 799 669 | 23 348 621 | 7.53 | 30.66 |
| | 5 | 13 632 221 | 24 939 342 | 19.13 | 39.58 |
| | 6 | 10 162 891 | 18 137 046 | 20.84 | 43.82 |
| | 7 | 4 342 338 | 7 634 579 | －32.37 | －18.20 |
| | 8 | 3 219 180 | 5 621 368 | －37.37 | －25.60 |
| | 9 | 3 540 924 | 5 922 219 | －16.70 | －4.06 |
| | 10 | 5 173 706 | 8 360 855 | 6.97 | 16.22 |
| | 11 | 7 947 181 | 12 971 745 | 12.10 | 17.48 |
| | 12 | 12 253 128 | 20 620 322 | 33.52 | 26.50 |
| | 总 计 | 98 232 896 | 173 991 553 | －2.41 | 12.36 |

续表

| 品　种 | 月　份 | 当　月 | | 同　比 | |
|---|---|---|---|---|---|
| | | 数　量 | 金　额 | 数　量 | 金　额 |
| 花生油 | 1 | 892 208 | 2 175 813 | -25.23 | -20.18 |
| | 2 | 750 453 | 1 942 752 | 17.51 | 14.89 |
| | 3 | 523 027 | 1 340 151 | -50.63 | -40.96 |
| | 4 | 547 549 | 1 410 185 | 6.32 | 8.42 |
| | 5 | 601 408 | 1 562 029 | -37.75 | -25.09 |
| | 6 | 245 777 | 688 327 | -66.49 | -55.44 |
| | 7 | 729 847 | 1 943 193 | 13.73 | 32.93 |
| | 8 | 567 034 | 1 418 984 | -38.88 | -29.22 |
| | 9 | 617 037 | 1 585 190 | 1.17 | 7.72 |
| | 10 | 683 409 | 1 761 907 | -4.20 | 6.58 |
| | 11 | 1 902 183 | 2 304 243 | 171.04 | 41.05 |
| | 12 | 1 451 776 | 3 581 855 | 42.78 | 45.82 |
| | 总　计 | 9 511 708 | 21 714 629 | -2.11 | -2.62 |

数据来源：海关总署。

价格低廉；阿根廷地广人稀，以大农场的模式种植，机械化程度相对较高，成本较低。美国科技发达，机械化程度更高，价格优势明显。由于美国开展新品种研究及基因育种等技术，使其平均单产达到5吨/公顷以上，而且还有再增长的空间。这种高科技带来的农业成本下降，在国际市场极具竞争力。阿根廷和美国都积极开展高油酸花生的商业化种植，作为增强国际市场竞争力的砝码。尤其是阿根廷，通过高油酸花生的大面积种植（超过整体面积的70%），一举夺得欧盟主要零食厂商的订单，抢夺了中国出口花生的市场。中国花生进口出现增长趋势，美国花生协会（APC）认为，中国已成为花生产品的净进口国，而美国可以部分满足中国花生市场需求。

2015年11月20日塞内加尔农业部长塞克宣布，2015年塞内加尔将向中国出口花生25.5万吨，2014年为15.5万吨。塞内加尔2015年花生产量为112万吨，比2014年增产40%。

在国际供应相对充足的情况下，中国花生出口价格走低，但与其他国家相比，其价格仍相对较高。据国际市场商品价格网的信息，同期阿根廷花生仁 FOB 价格为 963.00 美元/吨，低于我国出口花生仁约 700 美元/吨。随着花生出口的缩减和进口量的增加，将对国内花生产业带来不利影响。

**2. 2015 年国内花生油市场回顾**

据相关资料可知，我国花生油年生产量基本在 230 万吨左右，仅占国产食用植物油生产量的 20% 左右。而国内植物油年消费总量为 2 900 万吨，花生油占比不足 1/10。在大豆超量进口、大豆油的低价冲击下，花生油价格行情稳定，仅有小幅波动，销售不畅。

2015 年 9 月初，随着秋季的深入，天气转凉，大专院校开学，市场消费需求逐渐回升，花生油市场行情有所回暖。9 月下旬，随着中秋节的到来和国庆节的临近，厂商提前备货，对油脂价格提供了支撑，加之成本因素，使油厂挺价心理强烈。

2015 年 10 月上旬，由于国庆期间油厂开机率下降，油脂库存回落，供应出现阶段性紧张，油厂挺价心理强烈，推动油脂行情向好。后期随着大部分油厂陆续开机，油脂供应逐步恢复，供应阶段性紧张的局面逐渐缓解，加之花生油价格在油脂品种中价格较高，市场份额处于相对弱势，10 月中下旬花生油市场行情以平稳运行为主。国内花生油供应充足，油脂价格上方承压，国内市场处于传统的需求淡季，价格涨跌不大。

2015 年 11 月中上旬，国内花生油市场供应充足，需求有限，行情基本稳定。11 月下旬，受油脂期货提振，国内油脂现货市场行情总体向好，花生油价格稳中有涨。

2015 年 12 月以后，临近春节，采购商备货收购积极性较高，有利于花生油上涨，但供应充裕，花生油价格以平稳运行为主。

2016 年以来，春节并未带来花生油价格的走高，2 月份以后，国内油脂市场进入传统消费淡季，供需两端均现不旺，行情以持稳为主（见表 2－6－3）。

表 2-6-3　　2015 年 7 月至 2016 年 2 月山东、河南、广东花生油价格　　单位：元/吨

| 日　期 | 山东花生油 | 河南花生油 | 广东花生油 |
|---|---|---|---|
| 2015 年 07 月 | 14 500 | 13 000 | 21 000 |
| 2015 年 08 月 | 14 500 | 13 000 | 21 000 |
| 2015 年 09 月 | 14 500 | 13 000 | 21 000 |
| 2015 年 10 月 | 14 500 | 13 000 | 21 000 |
| 2015 年 11 月 | 14 000 | 13 300 | 21 000 |
| 2015 年 12 月 | 14 000 | 13 300 | 21 000 |
| 2016 年 01 月 | 14 000 | 13 500 | 21 000 |
| 2016 年 02 月 | 14 000 | 13 500 | 21 000 |

数据来源：中国花生交易网。

### 3. 2015 年国内花生、花生油市场行情总结

虽然 2015 年花生受种植面积缩减、单产减产等影响，花生价格却未出现预想的上涨行情，价格持稳在低位，小幅震荡前行；花生油市场低迷，销售不畅，价格基本持稳。综合来讲，这种是由于以下四点原因：

（1）农户惜售心理。由于花生种植面积缩减，部分产区受灾害性天气影响，出现减产情况，整体货源不足，农户成本上涨，对价格预期较高，惜售心理较为浓厚。农户的惜售心理使花生供应在一定程度上处于偏紧的状态，有力支撑了价格的稳定。但农户毕竟处于产业链的弱势地位，惜售仍不能改变花生行情偏弱的状况。

（2）花生消费类型有所变化。一直以来国内花生产量的 60% 左右用于榨油，由于食用花生部分利润增厚，这两年油用花生占比有所下降。国内植物油价格大幅下跌，花生油市场份额下降、价格下跌，花生油厂开工率处于 3 年来低位水平，花生的油用需求同比下降。更多的花生进入利润更高的食品行业，花生需求增长点更多的来自于食用需求，商品花生米价格上涨较为明显，而油料米由于销售困难，呈价格走弱的局面。

（3）许多花生转而从越南通过广西边贸形式进口，在海关数据上得不到体现。业内估计，前两年每年通过越南进口的印度和美国等国的花生可高达 50 万 ~70 万吨。美国花生协会（APC）认为，中国将逐步成为花

生产品的净进口国，国外花生对国内市场形成冲击，补充了花生总体供给量。虽然国内出现总量减少的情况，但在国际低价货源涌入的条件下，花生价格上涨困难。

（4）大豆、油菜籽、棕榈等油用作物全球性丰产丰收，国内大豆进口超过8 000万吨，大量低价大豆油、菜籽油充斥市场，降低了花生油的市场份额，花生油行情低迷，压制国内纯花生油需求和价格，花生油厂为规避风险严控开工率和花生收购成本，更倾向于在成本价以下收购花生。

## （二）2016年花生及花生油市场预测

2016年行情可以分以下两个阶段预测：

### 1. 2016年产新花生上市前价格预测

2016年春节后，国内花生市场喜忧参半，归纳利好、利空因素如下：

利好因素：一是国内花生市场整体库存不多，据调查显示，目前市场经销商库存量比往年同期偏少三四成，库存压力有所缓解，后续货源不太充足。二是花生市场仍有一定刚性需求，油厂、批发市场有一定的市场需求。

利空因素：一是油厂库存充裕，节前花生油销售不佳，节后入市采购积极性将不会太高。二是节前印度、塞内加尔等国进口花生米陆续到港，节后集中补充国内市场，将对国内花生米价格带来一定冲击。三是节后各地气温将会逐渐升高，农户存储条件简陋，部分产地出货节奏将会加快。

据笔者常年研究估计，2016年产新花生上市前，国内花生供应整体处于偏紧的状态，农户、中间商手中存货远低于往年同期水平，虽然有外部货源到港，但其销售主要为油厂原料收购，对消费市场影响相对较小。在9月份之前，仍有半年以上的销售期，货源供应缺口较为明显，市场花生米价格上涨潜力较大。

### 2. 2016年产新花生上市后价格预测

从当前行情看，由于2015年花生减产，部分产区农户收益偏低，甚至低于成本，在劳动力成本提高的条件下，平原部分地区改种的可能性较大，河北、河南、山东及东北部分地区，2016 年花生种植面积缩减的可能性较大。由于花生主要种植偏向于河滩地、沙质土壤以及丘陵山地，我国山地、丘陵面积较广，花生仍有相当大的种植空间。

随着政府对花生的政策性扶持，花生良种补贴活动的进行，部分花生集中种植区域种植面积相对稳定，面积变化有限。我国花生生产机械化程度低，人工成本较高，与其他经济作物相比，种植收益波动大；与粮食作物相比，国家补贴少，影响花生发展的不稳定因素较多。因此，在产业发展对策上，一是需要国家政策层面的支持，建议建立花生最低收购价制度，保障农民种植收益，进一步落实花生良种补贴政策并扩大花生种植补贴范围，稳定花生种植面积。二是在生产层面，从种植模式、良种推广、社会服务等各个环节入手降低花生种植成本，提高科技含量，培育新型经营主体，提升花生产业核心竞争力。

值得注意的是，新疆地区花生种植面积扩大，由于其气候、土质条件适合花生生长，同时大规模种植有利于花生机械化水平的提高，对内地花生缩减面积有一定的补充。

如果 2016 年 4 月份之前花生价格上涨明显的话，花生种植面积或能维持在 450 万 ~460 万公顷。上市价格或有明显提高。预计统货米价格区间在 9 000 ~11 000 元/吨。

（中国花生交易网　　张修志）

# 第三部分

## 中国粮食市场专论

# 一、我国粮价政策改革：逻辑与路径

【内容提要】

日益严重的粮食高库存、进口激增等问题凸显了临储等粮价政策改革的紧迫性。目前我国粮价政策调整的倒逼机制已经形成，正处于改革的重要关口。2015 年调低临储价格属于过渡性调整，虽然有利于保护种粮农民利益，但可能无助于缓解当前玉米高库存问题，政策调整远未到位。与此相反，若不及时采取配套措施，2015 年玉米库存可能会继续增加，而且还可能引发更加严峻的新问题。建议按照“定向施策、价补分离，创新调控、综合配套”的思路，采取“退出粮价支持”+“种粮收益补贴”的组合改革方式，创新粮食调控体系，用两三年时间使粮价调整到位，形成以市场定价为基础的粮食价格形成机制、以直接补贴为主体的农民利益保护机制。要当机立断，按“分类处置、分期消化”的思路，降价销售处理粮食临储库存。

2012 年以来，我国粮食临储库存迅速累积，目前已处于历史最高水平。截至 2015 年 4 月底，玉米临储库存达 1.54 亿吨，稻谷最低收购价库存超过 6 000 万吨。日益严重的粮食高库存、进口激增等问题，凸显了改革临储等粮价政策的紧迫性。目前我国粮价政策调整的倒逼机制已经形成，正处于改革的重要关口。对此我们进行了专题调研，初步提出粮价支持政策改革的思路和建议，现报告如下：

## （一）2015 年临储价格调整尚未到位

根据玉米库存问题突出的实际，2015 年国家对玉米临时收购价格做出重大调整，从 2014 年的 1.12/斤降到 1 元/斤。经初步评估，我们认为，2015 年调低临储价格属于过渡性调整，虽然有利于保护种粮农民利益，但可能无助于缓解当前玉米高库存问题，政策调整远未到位。与此相反，若不及时采取配套措施，2015 年玉米库存可能会继续增加，而且还可能引发更加严峻的新问题。

第一，2015 年的临储价格仍属较高水平，临储收购量仍将比较大。根据调研情况看，2015 年东北玉米有所减产，但华北、西北等地增产，供应充裕，预计全国产量与 2014 年基本持平，而玉米需求基本面并未发生较大变化，供求格局仍处于较宽松阶段。

2015 年华北玉米收购价格一路走低，年底已经降至 0.9 元/斤以下，远期广东进口高粱价格也低于 1 900 元/吨，按此倒推到东北产区，玉米价格只有调低到 1 500 元/吨（即 0.75 元/斤）才可与之竞争，因此国家公布的 1 元/斤东北玉米临储价格仍属较高水平。在国家严控收储质量标准（霉变严格控制在 2% 以内）的前提下，预计 2015 年东北玉米临储收购量将达到 5 000 万 ~ 6 000 万吨。若后期放宽对霉变的控制，收购量将进一步放大。

第二，有可能导致粮食产能向稻谷等品种转移集中。近年来水稻在最低收购价政策的刺激下（2008 年以来稻谷最低收购价提高了约 1 倍），2015 年底库存高达 6 200 万吨，压力仅次于玉米。2015 年国家调低玉米临储价格，给农民发出玉米降价减产信号，如果水稻最低收购价不随之调低，水稻比价优势将更为明显，部分农民可能由种玉米转向种水稻，这将使稻谷库存压力进一步增大。特别需要注意的是，稻谷容易陈化，品质风险高，新陈价差大，相对玉米而言，消化库存的难度会更大。

第三，有可能引发部分地区的土地流转违约和纠纷。在临储政策的支撑下，由于玉米种植有利可图，极大推动东北地区的土地流转，黑龙江土地流转面积甚至达到 70% 以上。2015 年调低临储价格，反应最为强烈的是那些流转土地的规模经营主体，认为这大大压缩了他们的利润空间。因此，调低临储价格，有可能会改变高临储价下形成的土地流转与规模经营格局，部分地区也有可能出现土地流转违约与纠纷，对此需早作应对准备和化解预案。

## （二）粮价政策改革的时机与逻辑

从国内外宏观环境看，目前已具备推进粮价政策调整的有利条件，是启动改革的最佳时机。

一是国内库存充足、全球粮食供求关系宽松为改革临储等政策奠定了坚实的物质基础，提供了足够的回旋空间。如目前玉米临储库存可以满足国内一年的需求，即使出现粮食显著减产的极端情况，国家也有足够的库存来调控市场，确保国内市场供应。

二是具有稳定的粮食产能基础，这是推进粮价政策改革的根本保障。产能在，粮食就在。若主要品种出现供需结构失衡，即使库存已经消化，只要采取一定的刺激措施，粮食产能就能够转化为实际生产，也能确保满足国内市场需求。

三是已经形成改革共识和预期。近几年临储政策对粮食产业影响深远，各方早已期待国家改革这项政策。2015 年临储价格调低以来，各类市场主体已对粮价政策改革达成共识，且普遍认为玉米临储价格调整还未到位，对今后国家政策进一步调整形成预期。

四是 2014 年以来对大豆、棉花实行的目标价格补贴改革试点，探索改革农产品价格的形成机制，为新一轮粮价政策改革积累了难得的操作经验和实践基础。

那么，究竟应该怎样推进粮价政策改革？改革的基本逻辑是什么？

第一，必须系统谋划，顶层设计。既然目前的粮食高库存问题是临储等粮价政策对国内市场过度干预和扭曲影响的结果，那么解决粮食高库存问题就不能仅仅限于采取某些消化某个单一粮食品种库存的专项措施，而是要系统谋划、顶层设计政策改革方案，从根本上消除库存形成机制。从改革的逻辑看，关键在于必须纠正价格支持政策对各粮食品种价格的过度干预，消除市场扭曲机制，建立以市场定价为基础的粮食价格形成机制。

第二，必须定向施策，价补分离。改革的逻辑虽然清晰，但为什么改革难以推进？究其实质，是因为最低收购价、临储等粮价政策目标多重、功能错位，既要保障粮食有效供给（即“保供给”），也要保护农民种粮利益（即“保收益”）；形成的利益关系复杂，既关乎粮食安全等国家利益，也涉及地方政府、粮食产业和农业生产者的多重利益，但财政成本全部由中央负担。因此，若调整甚至是退出临储等价格支持政策必然会导致一系列利益关系的变化和冲突，引发对政策改革的疑虑。尤其是相对直接补贴等政策工具而言，粮价支持政策具有操作简单、受益直接、效果明显等特征，因此调低政策性收储价格、退出临储等改革一般容易引发对保供给、保收益以及农民种粮积极性谁来保护等担忧。

从本质上看，保供给、保收益是我国包括粮价支持措施在内的全部农业政策的两个基本目标。在国内粮食供给不足、国内价格低于国际市场时，若施策得当，两个目标可同时得到兼顾，反之，两者将相互冲突。如2005—2010 年期间，我国通过稳步提高粮食收储价格，有效刺激农民种粮积极性，在保护种粮农民利益的同时，也实现了粮食稳定增产、保障供给的目标。但 2011 年以来，国际国内粮食进入供大于求、国内价格高于国际市场阶段，持续提高国家收储价格虽然在表面上有利于保证种粮农民收益，也刺激粮食大幅增产，但由此形成的高库存、进口激增等外部性问题已使政策实施难以为继，最终并不能真正有效保护农民利益，更不利于农业的可持续发展。

因此，推进粮价政策改革，必须调整长期以来对保供给、保收益两个目标二位一体、不加区分的做法，要优化政策功能配置，按照桥归桥、路归路的原则，对两个目标分而治之。在此基础上，退出粮价政策的保收益功能，将其回归到“解决农民卖粮难”的设计初衷。如此，就可通过调低乃至取消价格支持来消除其对市场的干预和扭曲影响，把粮食价格形成还给市场机制，另外通过直接补贴措施来“保收益”，实现定向施策、价补分离。

第三，必须统筹兼顾，利益补偿。降低临储价格乃至退出临储政策等改革必然会在一定程度上损害农民现有利益，因此必须在改革中统筹兼顾，配套建立粮价改革利益补偿机制，使种粮农民在改革中利益不受损、收益不减少，种粮积极性得到有效保护，亦即需要配套实施既不扭曲市场、又能实现“保收益”目标的粮食收益补贴措施。

与此同时，国外支持和保护农业的政策经验表明，粮价等农业政策调整改革并没有固定的目标模式，也没有一项政策能够一劳永逸、“以不变应万变”，均需因时制宜，动态调整。如美国自 20 世纪 30 年代大萧条实施农业保护政策以来，基本上每 5 年更新一次农业法案，对农业政策目标与措施进行动态调整、渐进式改革，逐步形成了目前系统完整的农业支持政策体系。相比之下，我国实施的粮食最低收购价政策、临时收储政策已经分别连续实施 10 年和 7 年，部分补贴政策已经实施 13 年，目前也到了需要总结评估、调整完善的阶段。同时也要求，今后政策制定和实施必须因地、因时制宜，与时俱进，动态调整。

## （三）粮价政策改革要点及实施方案

有观点认为，解决目前粮食库存过高、市场扭曲严重等问题，必须立即全面退出临时收储政策，使粮价改革一步调到位。我们认为，根据我国的国情粮情，为确保市场稳定和政策平稳过渡，宜按照“定向施策、价补分离，创新调控、综合配套”的思路，采取“退出粮价支持” + “种粮收益补贴”的组合改革方式，创新粮食调控体系，用两三年时间使粮价调整到位，形成以市场定价为基础的粮食价格形成机制、以直接补贴为主体的农民利益保护机制。初步考虑，改革设计的要点和方案为：

### 1. 逐步退出粮价支持政策的市场扭曲机制

要用两三年的时间逐年同步将水稻、小麦的最低收购价和玉米的临时收储价格降至不扭曲市场的合理水平。调整到位后，对水稻、小麦等重点粮食品种采取不扭曲市场、随行就市的最低保障临时收储措施，为农民卖粮提供基本保障。具体政策设计要求如下：

第一，用两三年时间同步退出水稻、小麦以及玉米的价格支持措施，逐年减少市场扭曲效应。政策调整到位后，最终不再保留具有生产刺激作用的价格支持政策。其中，玉米在价格调整到位后不再纳入最低保障收储，2014 年已经退出价格支持的大豆等品种也不再纳入。今后农民根据各粮食品种的市场价格信号来决定扩大或减少种植面积。

第二，最低保障临时收储作为市场调控措施，其基本功能是解决农民卖粮难问题，不以保障农民收益为目标。

第三，价格调整到位后，最低保障临储价格要能够与进口替代产品的价格竞争，挡得住进口替代。以玉米为例，按照目前的进口到岸价测算，东北产区玉米最低保障临时收购价格若在 0.75 元/斤，基本可以挡住进口玉米、高粱等进入国内市场。另一方面，国家发改委公布的全国平均种粮成本，将土地和劳动力的机会成本均纳入计算，而对于拥有承包地的农民来说，土地成本不应纳入收益测算，因此估计种粮成本时需扣除土地租金成本。根据 2014 年数据，全国平均玉米成本为 2 129 元/吨，扣除土地成本后为 1 680 元/吨（即 0.84 元/斤）。按照逐步调整到位的原则，2016 年可将临储价格过渡性调至 0.9 元/斤，2017 年可进一步调低至 0.8 元/斤左右（具体需根据当时的进口价格确定）。如此，既可弥补农民种粮的大部分成本，也基本挡得住进口产品竞争，还可理顺国内外以及上下游价格关系，也避免刺激产量继续增加。特别是可以避免地租和生产资料价格的非理性上涨，有利于提高我国玉米的国际竞争力。在此基础上，进一步考虑将玉米全面退出临储政策。

当然，由于美国等主产国自 2012 年以来已经连续 4 年减少玉米种植面积，国际玉米价格有可能在今后几年回升，因此也可考虑将玉米临储价格在 2016 年一步到位调低到 0.85 元/斤，亦即用 2 年的时间退出玉米临储收购。

价格调整到位后，今后设定水稻、小麦等最低保障临储价格时，既要考虑进口产品竞争、种粮成本因素，也要考虑不同粮食品种之间的比较收益关系，避免出现新的资源集中、结构失衡问题。

### 2. 配套实施种粮收益补贴

种粮收益补贴是粮价政策改革的配套措施，主要用于补偿粮价改革对农民收益的影响，有效保护农民种粮积极性。种粮收益补贴实质上是目标价格补贴的升级版，其不与具体粮食品种挂钩，任何粮食品种均有获得补贴的权利，属非特定产品补贴（即对所有粮食品种的种植补贴）。其具体原则建议为：

第一，按面积进行补贴，单位面积补贴标准根据改革过程中价格调低后种粮收益减少的情况确定，并随价格调低逐年提高补贴标准。例如，假定 2016 年玉米临储价格下调到 0.9 元/斤，比 2015 年降低 0.1 元/斤，按照平均亩产 1 000 斤计算，需补贴 100 元/亩；若 2017 年调低到 0.8 元/斤，则补贴 200 元/亩，这样相当于农民每斤玉米仍得到 1 元，与 2015 年国家实施 1 元/斤临储政策的效果相当，但不会扭曲市场，也不增加库存，还能挡住进口。从财政成本看，假定政策调整到位后，补贴标准定为 200 元/亩，按照玉米平均单产 500 千克/亩测算，相当于 400 元/吨，明显低于国家玉米库存 2 年 504 元/吨的成本（其中，收购费 50 元/吨，做囤费 70 元/吨，保管费 92 元/吨·年 ×2 年 =184 元/吨，资金利息 2 000 元/吨 ×5%/年 ×2 年 =200 元/吨）。

今后价格调整到位后，种粮收益补贴标准应保持相对稳定，可根据粮食供求状况以及调控总体要求进行增减调整。

第二，不与具体品种挂钩。即不论生产者种植何种粮食品种（包括杂粮杂豆），单位面积均获得相同的补贴。这样有利于发挥市场机制作用，避免资源向单个品种转移，逐步优化粮食品种结构，同时也有利于规避世界贸易组织特定产品“黄箱补贴”的“微量允许”约束，有效利用我国非特定产品补贴较大的政策空间。

第三，补贴只针对法定承包地的种植面积，可与土地承包权脱钩，谁种补谁。同时，要简化政策操作，避免出现类似目标价格补贴试点执行困难等问题。建议按省市包干补贴总量，据实补贴到实际生产者。

### 3. 创新粮食市场调控体系

要建立与粮价政策改革配套的新型粮食调控体系，推动政策从目前的以价格支持直接干预为主导的增产取向向以价补分离、市场机制为基础的供求基本平衡转型，逐步形成以政策补贴为基础，预期引导、风险管理、储备调控、贸易补充等工具相结合的新型调控体系。在粮食供给紧张时，采取综合支持措施，既保供给也保收益，统筹发挥进口贸易的积极作用，提高国内有效供给水平；在粮食供给相对宽裕时，要弱化价格政策作用，以补贴政策“保收益”为基础，重点管理好生产，严控进口，实现国内供需基本平衡。具体政策工具和调控机制建议如下：

第一，实施粮食产能补贴。粮食产能补贴是新型粮食调控体系的结构调整工具。其目的在于，通过提供收益补偿，引导农民对耕地轮作休耕，退出超载粮食产能，促进粮食结构调整，推进农业生态修复、环境保护，增强农业可持续发展能力。该政策应按世界贸易组织“绿箱”政策条款设计，不与任何农产品生产挂钩。

在当前库存压力较大的背景下，建议粮食产能补贴标准与同期实施的种粮收益补贴相当。这样可以为农民在种（获得非特定生产补贴）与不种（获得产能补贴）之间提供自由选择的机会。今后若出现粮食供给紧张，再相应调低或者停止“粮食产能补贴”。

从政策的可操作性看，建议以行政区划为单位，集中连片在部分地区先行试点实施土地轮作休耕计划，对计划内土地面积纳入产能补贴；对其他地区主动进行粮食结构调整的农户，也可考虑给予“粮食产能补贴”。

第二，建立预期管理机制。这是促进政策改革措施发挥有效作用的关键。建议尽快确定粮价改革以及相关配套政策措施，并在年底前抓紧通过多种途径（如官方半官方研究机构、权威人士等）对外发文发声，强化政策前期舆论解读，有效引导社会预期。在此基础上，在春节前正式公布详细政策方案和措施，并通过多种方式广泛宣传。其中，要重点组织县乡村组培训宣传，做到户户知晓、人人明白，让每个基层干部和种粮农民熟悉新政策、了解新办法，确保政策能够不折不扣落地、扎扎实实到位。

第三，加强粮食市场风险管理。要根据粮价政策改革后的新形势新要求，抓紧开发研究市场风险管理工具，加快推出适合新型农业经营主体的期货、保险等产品，有效分散和管理农业生产者市场风险。

第四，增设粮食调控储备。今后粮价政策改革到位后，对主要粮食品种实施保障性临时收储措施，在解决农民卖粮难的同时，可将收储的部分粮食转为调控储备。建立粮食调控储备，目的在于高抛低吸、调峰填谷，维护粮食市场的稳定。如此，将有利于进一步增强国家粮食宏观调控的物质基础，使粮食专项储备定位于保障粮食安全、应对突发事件，粮食调控储备主要负责维护市场稳定，形成分工明确、职责清晰的国家粮食储备体系。建议参照粮食专项储备管理办法，对粮食调控储备进行制度化、法制化管理。

第五，严厉打击走私，有效调控粮食进口。据估计，按照目前国内外粮价测算，若采取措施严控粮食进口，可为国产玉米增加近3 000万吨的饲用需求和1 500万吨的深加工需求，比不采取措施分别增加50%、80%。因此，要严厉打击走私，多措并举防控走私产品对粮价政策改革的冲击。要管好用好粮食进口关税配额制度，加强进口检验检疫，有效调控主粮、杂粮及肉类产品进口，为推进粮价改革、消化临储库存，确保国内市场稳定提供有效支撑。

## （四）消化粮食临储库存建议

妥善解决好粮食临储库存问题，既是当前推进粮价政策改革的重要保障，更是当务之急。特别是2015年粮食市场预期不稳、价格波动剧烈，收储矛盾尤为突出，对加快消化临储库存的要求更加紧迫。我们建议：

第一，降价销售是基本选项。在全球粮价低迷、国家调低临储价格的背景下，目前临储库存粮食已经不存在顺价销售的可能。因此，要想有效消化临储库存，就必须考虑降价销售。但究竟需降价多少？以临储库存玉米为例，在国际原油价格为50美元/桶时，若临储库存玉米价格降至1 800元/吨，燃料乙醇等深加工企业就可实现盈亏平衡，与2 240元/吨的临储收购价格相比，相差440元/吨。若按目前国内市场价格以及低档玉米进口替代品的价格要求，目前需降至1 700元/吨才能顺利销售出库，价差达540元/吨。这意味着，降价销售1.54亿吨的库存，将产生677.6亿~831.6亿元的价差亏损。

但是，若不降价销售，按2 240元/吨临储价格计算，每年每吨玉米的库存成本至少204元（其中，保管费92元/吨，资金利息2 240元/吨×5% =112元/吨，收购费用和做囤费用为沉没成本，不再列入计算），每年玉米临储库存总成本将达314.2亿元。更为重要的是，2013年产的玉米存储已超过2年，品质风险日益增大，若不尽快处理，损失将更大。按降价价差440元/吨计算，相当于2年2个月的库存成本。可见，降价销售实质上是玉米临储库存成本的贴现，是最为有效的库存减损方式。因此，我们建议应当机立断，采取降价方式消化库存。

第二，分类处置，分期消化。当前消化玉米库存要注意把握好销售节奏，避免对当期市场形成冲击。调研表明，目前临储库存中，2012 年及以前产的超期储存玉米达 1 000 万吨，品质已基本劣变；同时，还有 1 700 多万吨品质较低的德美亚品种，也不具备使用价值。另外，其他库存玉米霉变超标非常严重，有专家估计，霉变严重超标玉米占比可能达到 50%。因此，要采取分类处置、定向销售措施，分期、分批消化品质较差的玉米库存。

综合考虑，处理品质较差的库存玉米，以燃料乙醇加工较为适宜，既有利于环境整治，也可避免对粮食加工产业和市场造成冲击，而且目前国内也已具备相应的产能。建议加大国内燃料乙醇消费，在全国范围推广燃料乙醇。在现有基础上新增 770 万吨燃料乙醇需求，使燃料乙醇需求量达到 1 000 万吨/年，由此可新增 2 400 万吨玉米消费，年消化量可达 3 000 万吨，这样用 4 年左右的时间基本可消化差品质的玉米库存。同时建议按照市场机制方式操作，不鼓励、不支持增加新的燃料乙醇产能，以现有国家定点燃料乙醇生产企业为主，由企业自主对现有过剩酒精产能进行并购、租赁或委托加工（据估计，现有酒精过剩产能可处理玉米约 1 100 万吨），短期内可迅速形成燃料乙醇产能。今后若库存玉米消化殆尽或玉米供求关系发生逆转，可考虑采取如下方式保持 1 000 万吨燃料乙醇供给：一是直接进口燃料乙醇；二是发展纤维素乙醇，逐步替代粮食乙醇。

对于其他库存玉米，建议采取分期公开降价拍卖方式，由企业自主决定加工使用用途。

第三，划转部分临储库存为调控储备。建议将 2013 年收储的部分玉米（建议 2 000 万吨）划转为调控储备，实行轮换管理。这样既可避免玉米降价销售大规模入市冲击市场，也可以为未来收购腾出库容、缓解收储压力，还可减少降价销售的损失。

（国务院发展研究中心　　程国强）

# 二、“十三五”时期粮食价格支持政策改革总体思路

【内容提要】

深入推进粮食价格支持政策改革，增强价格支持政策的灵活性和有效性，充分发挥价格信号的作用，对转变农业发展方式、优化生产结构、提高资源配置效率至关重要。应从国家粮食安全战略出发确定粮食价格支持政策的扶持重点，从国内外农产品价差走势出发确定粮食价格支持水平的调整步伐，从“黄箱”补贴空间出发确定粮食价格的支持力度。综合考虑过去10年我国农产品价格支持政策执行的实际效果、先行国家类似发展阶段农业支持政策的实践经验、“十三五”时期我国农业发展的基本方向和农业支持政策空间等多种因素，应按“价补统筹、水平适度，一品一策、精准发力，分步实施、央地分担”的总体思路，重构“十三五”时期的粮食价格支持政策框架。

以粮食最低收购价和重要农产品临时收储为主要内容的农产品价格支持政策是2004年以来农业支持保护政策的重要组成部分。这一政策如何改革，对农业发展方式转变、生产结构优化、资源配置效率提高至关重要。应从国家战略、发展阶段、资源禀赋、世贸组织规则等出发，统筹推进“十三五”时期粮食价格支持政策改革。

## （一）对近两年农产品价格支持政策改革的评价

针对农产品价格支持政策带来的问题，近两年国家采取了一系列改革举措：改革食糖临时收储办法，不再实行国家收储，改由制糖企业自主储存、自负盈亏，国家仅对企业储存补贴半年利息；国家不再实行统一的油菜籽临时收储政策，改为地方自主决策，中央财政仅给予地方一定补助。这些改革，增强了农产品价格支持政策的弹性，但也降低了约束力和支持水平。最引人注目的是棉花和大豆目标价格补贴改革试点。2014年中央1号文件提出“启动东北和内蒙古大豆、新疆棉花目标价格补贴试点”；2015年中央1号文件进一步强调“总结新疆棉花、东北和内蒙古大豆目标价格改革试点经验，完善补贴方式，降低操作成本”。实行目标价格补贴改革试点的基本背景是：按高于长期市场均衡价的价格水平托市收购容易给农民发出增产信号，造成国家库存成本居高不下，国家收储的产品难以顺价销售，既造成库存增加、潜亏加重，又抬高了下游企业的原料成本，甚至导致低价进口的农产品进入国家库存。因此，衡量农产品目标价格补贴改革试点成功与否的标准，应是以下三个方面：国内外价格是否并轨、农民是否按市场信号调整生产结构、“黄箱”补贴力度是否在允许的上限之内。从2014年新疆棉花目标价格补贴改革试点情况看，第一个标准得到了实现，国内棉花价格与进口到岸税后价的价差基本消失；第二个标准未能得到实现，补贴仍与农民种植面积或（和）交售量挂钩，影响农民按市场价格决定其资源配置行为；第三个标准也未能实现，按目标价格与市场平均价格的价差、试点地区棉花产量计算的“黄箱”补贴有可能超过8.5%的上限。

农产品目标价格制度包括目标价格收购、目标价格补贴、目标价格抵押贷款和目标价格保险等多种具体形式。2014年和2015年中央1号文件均提出鼓励探索农产品目标价格保险，但国家层面未出台任何具体政策。近年来这方面的实践主要由地方政府自行开展。如北京市顺义区开展的生猪价格指数保险，上海、浙江、江苏等地开展的蔬菜价格保险。受地方财力、农民种植面积和市场价格数据采集困难等因素影响，农产品目标价格保险的实施范围和实际发挥的作用有限。

## （二）农产品价格支持政策改革必须在约束条件下进行

### 1. 从国家粮食安全战略出发确定农产品价格支持政策的扶持重点

实施农产品价格支持政策要以公共资源为支撑，因而要服从和服务于国家公共政策目标，在农业领域就是要服从和服务于国家粮食安全战略。在 2013 年底召开的中央经济工作会议和中央农村工作会议上，习近平总书记提出了“以我为主、立足国内、确保产能、适度进口、科技支撑”的国家粮食安全新战略和“进一步明确粮食安全的工作重点，合理配置资源，集中力量首先把最基本最重要的保住，确保谷物基本自给、口粮绝对安全”的国家粮食安全新要求。2014 年中央 1 号文件强调，要更加积极地利用国际农产品市场和农业资源，有效调剂和补充国内粮食供给；抓紧制定重要农产品国际贸易战略，加强进口农产品规划指导，优化进口来源地布局，建立稳定可靠的贸易关系。2015 年中央 1 号文件进一步强调，科学确定主要农产品自给水平，合理安排农业产业发展优先序。这些重要政策表述表明，在需求增长和资源环境约束趋紧的双重压力下，我国主要农产品必须有保有放，以更加积极的姿态利用国内国外两个市场两种资源。面向未来，我国不能再追求所有品种粮食都自给自足，关起门来解决吃饭问题，而是要适度进口；不能再追求所有农产品都靠自己解决，关起门来支撑工业化城镇化，而是要科学确定各种农产品的自给水平。实际上，各种农产品自给率水平的敏感性、相对重要性有较大差异。农产品价格支持政策要把稻谷和小麦作为扶持重点，集中使用公共资源和“黄箱”政策空间。

### 2. 从国内外农产品价差走势出发确定农产品价格支持水平的调整步伐

过去十多年来，我国之所以能够通过不断提高粮食最低收购价和重要农产品临时收储价来促进农业增产、农民增收，是因为我国农产品国内价格普遍低于进口到岸税后价，有提价的空间。但随着近年来国内外价格的反向变化，主要农产品国内价格逐步超过进口到岸税后价，顶破了国际价格的“天花板”。我国加入世贸组织时做出承诺，对大豆、植物油等多数产品只征收单一关税；同时也争取到对部分农产品实行关税配额管理的政策，配额内实行低关税，配额外实行高关税，因而根据关税的不同有两层国际价格“天花板”。第一层“天花板”是根据配额内低关税计算的进口到岸税后价，第二层“天花板”是根据配额外高关税或单一关税计算的进口到岸税后价。从目前已经达到的倒挂程度和未来价差走势看，可以分为以下三种类型：

一是已经持续性顶破第一层“天花板”，与第二层“天花板”尚有一定距离。主要包括大米和小麦。据农业部市场与经济信息司监测，大米和小麦分别于 2013 年 7 月和 6 月开始出现持续性价格倒挂，配额内 1% 关税到岸税后价持续低于国内市场价。从未来走势看，我国大米和小麦单产提高潜力有限，劳动生产率提高缓慢，在人工成本和土地成本的推动下，生产成本将长期持续上升，国内价格有长期持续上涨的内在推力；而大米和小麦主要进口来源国的价格上涨空间有限。综合判断，“十三五”期末，大米和小麦国内价格有可能持续性顶破按配额外 65% 关税计算的到岸税后价，即第二层“天花板”。

二是已经持续性顶破第一层“天花板”，部分时点也已顶破第二层“天花板”。主要是食糖和玉米。食糖于 2011 年 2 月开始出现持续性价格倒挂，配额内 15% 关税到岸税后价持续低于国内市场价。玉米于 2013 年 7 月开始出现持续性价格倒挂，配额内 1% 关税到岸税后价持续低于国内市场价。值得注意的是，据农业部市场与经济信息司监测，配额外 50% 关税的巴西糖到岸税后价已于 2015 年 2 月以来连续低于国内市场价，且价差从 2015 年 2 月的 99 元/吨扩大到 2015 年 7 月的 1 061 元/吨。据农业部农业贸易促进中心监测，玉米已于 2014 年 7 月和 9 月短期出现过配额外 65% 关税进口到岸税后价低于国内市场价的情形，2015 年 4 月 15 日以来美国 2 号黄玉米配额外 65% 关税进口到岸税后价再次低于国产玉米价格，且持续 2 个多月。从未来走势看，我国食糖原料生产成本极高，提高甘蔗生产效率、降低成本的潜力不大；巴西货币贬值，能源化利用需求疲软，蔗糖出口潜力和竞争力很高。国内玉米提高单产、扩大经营规模、提高劳动生产率等方面有较大潜力，但人工成本和土地成本仍将继续上涨；受国际市场石油价格疲软影响，玉米的能源化利用需求不振，国际海运费难以提高，玉米国际市场价格将长期走低。展望未来，食糖国内价格持续性顶破第二层"天花板"的趋势已经确立，玉米国内价格顶破第二层"天花板"极有可能在"十三五"期间常态化。

三是已持续性顶破第二层"天花板"。主要包括大豆和棉花。加入世贸组织以来，由于大豆仅实行3%的单一关税，国内大豆片面追求含油率、未能发挥蛋白质含量高和非转基因的差异化竞争优势，国内价格与进口到岸税后价几乎完全重合，国内市场几乎完全受国际市场左右；但从2012年10月开始，大豆的国内外价格出现持续性倒挂，按3%单一关税计算的到岸税后价持续低于国产大豆市场价。棉花于2011年10月开始出现持续性价格倒挂，按滑准税计算的进口到岸税后价格持续低于国产棉花市场价，直到2015年1月国内外价格倒挂现象基本消失。如果考虑质量等因素，目前国内外棉花价格已完全并轨。

### 3. 从"黄箱"补贴空间出发确定农产品价格支持力度

按世贸组织规则，我国现行粮食最低收购价和重要农产品临时收储价属于典型的对生产和贸易有扭曲作用的"黄箱"补贴，各种财政支付性补贴中，与当期生产和贸易挂钩的补贴也是典型的"黄箱"补贴。我国加入世贸组织时承诺，我国"黄箱"补贴必须遵从两个8.5%的上限约束，即特定产品"黄箱"补贴不得超过该产品产值的8.5%，非特定产品"黄箱"补贴不得超过农业总产值的8.5%。

从特定产品"黄箱"补贴来看，多数产品的"黄箱"补贴还有一定空间，但如果支持价格继续逐年提高并有较大的托市收购量，则很快就会遭遇8.5%上限的实质性约束。2004年以来，国家实行的财政支付性补贴政策呈现出比较规则的变化趋势，这也是各产品"黄箱"补贴额中比较固定的组成部分。尽管支持价格在逐年提高，但年度间和品种间实际托市收购量差异较大，因而年度间和品种间"黄箱"性质的价格支持水平波动较大。这表明，控制特定产品"黄箱"补贴水平，关键在于控制托市收购行为。需要注意的是，部分产品在个别年份的"黄箱"补贴已接近上限约束，如2009年的玉米（5.3%）、2012年的大豆（7.2%）。

从非特定产品“黄箱”补贴来看，我国还有很大空间。最低收购价和临时收储都是针对具体农产品的，因而在非特定产品“黄箱”补贴中不存在价格支持部分。大致而言，目前我国非特定产品“黄箱”补贴力度不大。以2014年为例，全国农业总产值（不含渔业）为91 892亿元，按8.5%计算的非特定产品“黄箱”补贴上限值为7 811亿元，而实际的非特定产品“黄箱”补贴仅1 300亿元左右，仅占农业总产值的1.4%，补贴空间还很大。尤为重要的是，未来我国农业总产值还会继续增长，按8.5%计算的非特定产品“黄箱”补贴上限值也会因此“水涨船高”。

## （三）粮食价格支持政策改革的思路与建议

综合考虑过去10年我国农产品价格支持政策实施的实际效果、先行国家类似发展阶段农业支持政策实践经验、未来我国农业发展基本方向和农业支持政策空间等多种因素，重构粮食价格支持政策体系的总体思路是：“价补统筹、水平适度，一品一策、精准发力，分步实施、央地分担”。

### 1. 价补统筹、水平适度

价补统筹、水平适度就是要统筹运用价格支持和财政支付性支持，统筹运用“黄箱”补贴和“绿箱”补贴，统筹运用特定产品“黄箱”补贴和非特定产品“黄箱”补贴，使“绿箱”补贴水平符合国家财政承受能力，使“黄箱”补贴水平符合世贸组织规则要求。

（1）调整最低收购价、临时收储价、目标价格的定价原则。按现行“成本加合理利润”和“成本加基本收益”的定价原则制定的托市价、目标价，本质上是一种促进增产增收的价格，也势必是一种高于市场长期均衡价的价格。国内外的实践已经充分表明，这么做的结果就是高产量、高收购、高库存、高亏损。我国农产品生产成本已经很高，部分农产品生产成本甚至超过国际市场价格，今后农业生产成本还将继续抬升，而国际市场价格将长期疲软。按现行定价原则，不断抬升的成本

“地板”将不断推高托市价或目标价，国内外农产品价格倒挂现象将越发严重。因此，必须尽快调整定价原则，使支持价格低于市场长期均衡价，使政策目标从增产增收转向止损或保本，使托市收购从几乎年年都要启动的常态化行为转向仅在市场供求关系发生重大变化时才启动的非常态化行为。

（2）打好财政支付性支持和价格支持、“绿箱”和“黄箱”、特定产品“黄箱”和非特定产品“黄箱”的组合拳。能用财政支付性支持解决的不用价格支持，能用“绿箱”政策解决的不用“黄箱”政策，能用非特定产品“黄箱”政策解决的不用特定产品“黄箱”政策，把支持空间尽可能留给未来、留给稻谷和小麦。

（3）加强部门协调。价格支持政策、财政支付性政策、“绿箱”和“黄箱”政策分别由不同部门负责实施，做好这些政策工具之间的协调，必须做好相关部门之间的沟通协调。

**2. 一品一策、精准发力**

一品一策、精准发力就是要对目前价格支持政策覆盖的稻谷、小麦、玉米、食糖、棉花、大豆和油菜籽 7 个重要农产品进行分类，按政治敏感性和自给率要求、未来支持政策空间、价格倒挂程度和走势等多种因素，确定国家支持保护的政策目标和政策工具组合。

（1）稻谷和小麦是最重要的口粮品种，自给率要求高，必须把“保产能”作为政策目标。可长期维持目前已经实行的最低收购价政策工具，但要掌握好最低收购价的调整节奏和幅度，扩大经营规模，降低生产成本，尽可能延缓顶破第二层“天花板”时点的到来。财政支付性补贴要向粮食主产区和粮食适度规模经营者倾斜。

（2）玉米是重要的饲料作物，需求增长快，进口压力大，必须把“增强竞争力”作为政策目标。近期内可继续实行临时收储政策，但要调整操作办法：调整定价原则，按国内市场价不高于第二层“天花板”的原则倒推主产区临时收储价；调整实施区域，将东北地区低积温带退出价格支持范围，促进边际产能退出；调整实施规模，每年只收购固定数量的临储玉米，不再敞开收购，让农民分担一定的市场风险。从中长期看，应将玉米“黄箱”支持量中的价格支持部分调剂给财政支付性支持，并按照不超过8.5%上限约束的原则，在种子、机械作业等方面定向加大对玉米生产的财政支付性支持，同时配套实施“绿箱”支持和非特定产品“黄箱”支持，协同解决制约玉米单产提高的“瓶颈”因素，切实提高我国玉米的生产效率和竞争力。

（3）棉花、大豆、糖料和油菜籽是重要的区域性作物，对新疆、黑龙江、广西和长江中游等特定区域的农民生计影响大，但进口依存度已经很高、进口来源稳定可靠，应把“调结构”作为政策目标。现行棉花和大豆目标价格补贴办法不利于边际产能退出，可考虑以2014年或2015年差价补贴为基数，在过渡期内固定几年不变或逐年递减，过渡期结束后只给予财政支付性支持而不再实行价格支持。其理由是：节省操作成本，不必年年核实面积或产量；与当期面积或产量挂钩属于“黄箱”，而只与基期挂钩不属于“黄箱”，有利于为财政支付性“黄箱”政策腾出空间；有利于促进农民调整种植结构，促进非适宜地区和低效率生产者退出棉花和大豆生产。食糖的第二层“天花板”对国内市场价形成压制，进而对国内甘蔗收购价格形成压制，甘蔗收购价格下降倒逼甘蔗生产方式转变和当地种植结构调整，这一方向应该坚持。2015年开始实行的将油菜籽价格支持事权移交地方政府的方向应当继续坚持，同时应加大对油菜生产机械化的支持力度，降低劳动强度。

### 3. 分步实施，央地分担

分步实施、央地分担就是要在整体框架的指导下，根据价格倒挂、库存积压等情况，区分轻重缓急，逐步推进改革，并在中央和地方之间合理分配农产品价格支持事权。当务之急是完善棉花和大豆的目标价格补贴办法，慎重稳妥地制定玉米临时收储新政策，总结推广农业补贴改革试点经验。考虑到目前的社会生态、政策执行成本，要妥善应对中央与地方、地方与农户的利益博弈。在2014年大豆目标价格补贴改革试点中，目标价格的制定、市场价格的采集和大豆产量的统计掌握在中央手中，有利于锁定中央财政补贴总额；由地方按补贴总额和总种植面积确定单位面积补贴、按农户种植面积确定每户所得补贴，操作成本较低。尽管这种做法不利于维护单产水平高的种植地区和种植户的利益，从而不利于促进单产水平低的地区和农户退出，但有利于增强中央对地方、地方对农户在利益博弈中的主导权，值得在棉花目标价格补贴中参考借鉴。对生猪、蔬菜等产品的目标价格保险，宜继续由地方自主探索。

（国务院发展研究中心农村经济研究部　　叶兴庆）

# 三、2015年中国粮食支持政策回顾与2016年展望

【内容提要】

2015年中国在基本稳定小麦和稻谷最低收购价以及继续推进大豆目标价格试点等基础上，下调了玉米的政策性临时收储价格水平，并对粮食和农业补贴政策进行了调整和改革试点。这些政策与改革举措虽然短期内曾引起粮食市场各类主体预期的改变和不确定性的上升，但总体上没有带来粮食市场运行的明显波动，同时价格反映市场供求关系的机制效应有所呈现，从下半年开始粮食市场价格不断下跌，第四季度下跌幅度高于第三季度。按照2016年中央1号文件部署，国家将继续执行并完善小麦和稻谷最低收购价政策，更多更好地发挥市场机制调节玉米供求关系的作用，估计国家政策性收储将对减少过高的国内粮食库存水平和粮食生产结构调整等供给侧结构性改革产生积极作用。同时，国家在全国范围内将粮食直补、良种补贴和农业生产资料综合补贴合并，这无疑有助于保护和提高粮食生产能力以实施藏粮于田战略，将有利于粮食生产经营的新型主体培育及其适度规模经营的发展，从而推动粮食发展方式转变为以确保口粮绝对安全和谷物基本自给。

小麦和稻谷最低收购价与玉米临时收储政策以及农业补贴等已经成为中国重要的惠农政策措施，对于粮食产业发展、粮食市场运行和农民增收等具有广泛的影响。2015年国家在继续执行多年形成的粮食支持政策的同时，也对其中的一些措施进行调整，对市场产生了一定的效应。针对粮食政策性收储矛盾增多和处理难度

加大的实际情况，估计2016年中国粮食支持政策的稳定与调整都会对粮食市场产生影响，必将受到社会高度关注。

## （一）2015年中国粮食支持政策的主要实施措施

为了防止谷贱伤农，保护种粮农民利益，2015年国家继续对稻谷和小麦执行最低收购价政策，小麦（三等，下同）最低收购价为1.18元/斤，稻谷最低收购价为1.43元/斤，与2014年持平。其中，早籼稻、中晚籼稻和粳稻最低收购价格分别为1.35元/斤、1.38元/斤和1.55元/斤，保持2014年水平不变。

2015年在东北四省区（内蒙古自治区、吉林省、辽宁省和黑龙江省，下同）对玉米实施临时收储政策，到库收储价格水平统一为1元/斤，这是自2008年实施玉米临时收储政策以来连续多年不断提高玉米收储价格后的首次较大幅度下调。

2015年继续对东北四省区大豆实行目标价格改革政策，大豆目标价格水平为4 800元/吨，与2014年持平。2014年，国家在东北四省区启动大豆目标价格试点，目的在于发挥市场机制作用，以控制国内库存过快增长，避免财政负担不断加重，同时通过实际市场价格与目标价格之间的差价补贴以调动豆农的生产积极性。

2015年，中国将安徽、山东、湖南、四川和浙江五省份的粮食直补、良种补贴和农业生产资料综合补贴合并为农业支持保护补贴。

2015年，在全国范围内调整20%的农业生产资料综合补贴资金用于支持粮食适度规模经营，即从农业生产资料综合补贴中调整20%的资金，加上种粮大户补贴试点资金和“三项补贴（粮食直补、良种补贴和农业生产资料综合补贴）”增量资金，统筹用于支持粮食适度规模经营。支持对象为主要粮食作物的适度规模生产经营者，重点向种粮大户、家庭农场、农民专业合作社、农业社会化服务组织等新兴经营主体倾斜，体现“谁多种粮食，就优先支持谁”。其中，国家安排支持粮食适度规模经营资金达到234亿元，用于支持粮食适度规模经营，重点向专业大户、家庭农场和农民合作社倾斜。

2015 年，在全国范围内将 80% 的农业生产资料综合补贴资金，加上粮食直补和农作物良种补贴资金，用于耕地地力保护，补贴对象为所有拥有耕地承包权的种地农民，享受补贴的农民要做到耕地不撂荒、地力不降低。

2015 年，中央财政继续实行种粮农民直接补贴，安排补贴资金 140.5 亿元，原则上要求发放给从事粮食生产的农民；继续实行种粮农民农资综合补贴，拨付补贴资金 1 071 亿元；继续实行粮食等良种补贴政策，安排补贴资金 203.5 亿元。

2015 年，国家对水稻、小麦、玉米以及东北和内蒙古的大豆实行良种补贴。其中，水稻补贴 15 元/亩；新疆地区小麦良种补贴 15 元/亩，其他地区的小麦补贴 10 元/亩，玉米和大豆在全国范围内都是补贴 10 元/亩，对马铃薯一、二级种薯补贴 100 元/亩。

为了推进农机购置补贴普惠制改革，2015 年，国家重点要求粮食主产省（区）选择粮食生产关键环节急需的部分或全部机具品目敞开补贴，主要包括深松机、免耕播种机、水稻插秧机、喷雾喷粉机、谷物联合收割机、玉米收获机、薯类收获机、秸秆粉碎还田机、粮食烘干机等。吉林等省份农机购置补贴政策调整后，重点是补贴粮食生产全程机械化所需机具。

值得说明的是，广义的粮食支持政策还应包括农田水利基本建设、粮食生产大县奖励政策和技术补助政策等，本文没有列举。

## （二）2015 年中国粮食支持政策实施的主要影响

虽然自 2004 年起中国就放开了粮食收购市场，但目前中国三大主粮收购市场基本上由国家收储政策及其执行力度和范围来主导。从 2015 年中国粮食市场的变化情况来看，售粮农民和粮食加工收储主体等对粮食收购价格、收购进度、质量把控等明显地受国内粮食收储政策影响，粮食收购市场相关主体普遍地高度关注并依赖国家收储，认为中国粮食市场是一个“政策市”。当收储政策不确定时，粮农往往会惜售，加工收储企业购进时也比较谨慎，粮食市场购销相应地也比较清淡。

2015 年中国夏粮早稻收购市场基本平稳。由于秋粮在全年粮食总产量中所占比重大，加上粮食市场主体受到中国粮食连续多年增产、库存较多和新粮收储库容不足、国际国内粮价差较大等影响，不同主体对国内粮食收储政策调整预期出现了分化，直接带来了中国粮食收购市场在 10 月份的波动，进入 11 月份后随着国家启动玉米临时收储政策和公布 2016 年小麦最低收购价政策，粮食收购市场才逐渐恢复平稳。

2015 年上半年，中国粮食市场价格基本上继续沿袭 2003 年以来的总体趋于不断上涨的态势，但是自第三季度开始粮食收购价格普遍地呈现出下跌扩大态势。

2003 年以来，中国粮食生产价格除了 2005 年和 2015 年外其他多数年份同比都是上涨的，但消费价格一直保持上涨态势。2015 年中国粮食生产价格虽然同比下跌了 1.3%，但是粮食消费价格仍然同比上涨 2.0%（见图 3－3－1）。2015 年中国粮食生产价格下跌虽然主要是由粮食供求关系决定的，但也受到收储政策影响，特别是政策性收储的玉米价格下调直接带来市场价格的下行，以及国家收储粮对品质的更加严格要求，致使质量不高的粮食市场价格下跌明显。

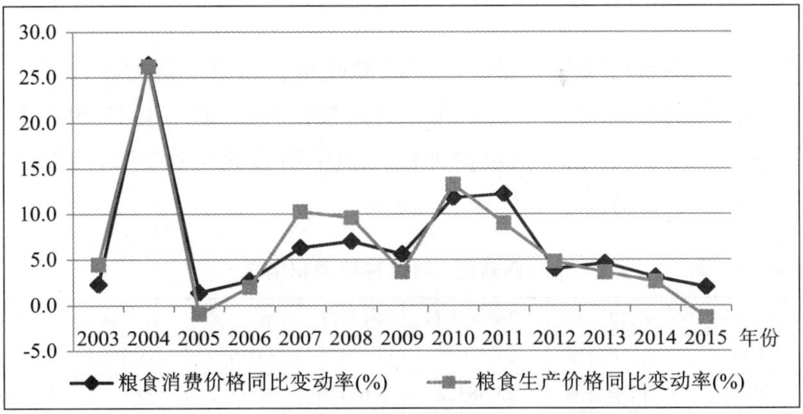


**图 3－3－1　2003 年以来中国粮食价格变动情况**

2015 年，优质小麦收储压力总体比较小，但湖北、安徽和江苏等偏南地区小麦品质不高，部分地区小麦收获季节遭遇连绵阴雨，出现霉变，销售困难；而北方优质小麦市场供求关系相对较好，价格相对较高。国家规定的三级麦价格 1.18 元/斤，对于南方小麦市场价格偏高，政策性收储压力较大，而北方优质麦市场价格偏低，政策性收储压力相对较小。稻谷最低收购价南方多数省份按合同订购来执行政策性收储，北方粳稻与国际市场错位竞争，供求平衡矛盾并不十分突出。但是，南方籼稻受到进口和走私大米等冲击，收储政策执行的矛盾相对较多。

国家调整粮食收储政策对市场的影响在2015年下半年呈现得更加明显。第三季度粮食生产价格同比下跌1.9%（见表3-3-1），而第四季度粮食生产价格同比下跌了5.7%，跌幅扩大了近3个百分点。第三季度稻谷生产价格同比仍然是上涨的，到第四季度则同比下跌了0.6个百分点。在三大主粮中，玉米生产价格下跌幅度最大，第三季度和第四季度同比分别下跌3.9%和12.9%。

**表3-3-1　　2015年分季粮食生产价格同比变动情况**　　单位：%

| | 粮 食 | 谷 物 | 小 麦 | 稻 谷 | 玉 米 |
|---|---|---|---|---|---|
| 一季度 | 1.7 | 1.8 | 3.7 | 2.4 | 1.3 |
| 二季度 | 1.4 | 1.6 | 1.4 | 2.6 | 1.3 |
| 三季度 | -1.9 | -2.1 | -3.2 | 1.5 | -3.9 |
| 四季度 | -5.7 | -5.7 | -5.8 | -0.6 | -12.9 |

资料来源：国家统计局网站。

由于东北四省区实施玉米等临时收储政策，国家支持力度较强，玉米种植面积扩大明显。2015年，东北四省区粮食种植面积达到2 586.7万公顷（见表3-3-2），在全国粮食种植面积中所占比重达到22.8%，比上年上升了0.1个百分点。

**表3-3-2　　东北四省区*粮食种植面积情况**

| 年 份 | 单 位 | 四省区小计 | 内蒙古 | 辽 宁 | 吉 林 | 黑龙江 |
|---|---|---|---|---|---|---|
| 2008 | 千公顷 | 23 670.5 | 5 254.5 | 3 035.9 | 4 391.2 | 10 988.9 |
| 2014 | 千公顷 | 25 583.2 | 5 651.0 | 3 235.1 | 5 000.7 | 11 696.4 |
| 2015 | 千公顷 | 25 867.3 | 5 726.7 | 3 297.4 | 5 078.0 | 11 765.2 |
| 2008年至2014年期间年均增长 | % | 1.3 | 1.2 | 1.1 | 2.2 | 1.0 |
| 2015年比2014年增长 | % | 1.1 | 1.3 | 1.9 | 1.5 | 0.6 |

资料来源：国家统计局：《2009中国统计年鉴》、《2015中国统计年鉴》，中国统计出版社出版；国家统计局：《国家统计局关于2015年粮食产量的公告》。

说明：*东北四省区是指内蒙古自治区和辽宁、吉林与黑龙江省。

2015年，内地很多原来的棉花产区棉农因废除棉花临时收储政策而退出棉花种植，改种玉米。国家统计局资料显示，江淮部分地区棉花播种面积减幅近三成。同时，东北四省区粮食种植积极性仍然相对较高，2015年东北四省区粮食种植面积比上年增长1.1%，仍然是全国粮食种植面积增长速度的2倍多。

不可否认，中国现有的农业支持政策产生了广泛的积极影响，粮食生产“十二连增”，避免了历史上反复出现的粮食波动周期，促进了国内粮食等大宗农产品市场的平稳运行，特别是中国近年来国内大宗农产品生产价格波动明显地低于国际市场；有效地遏制了农业比较效益恶化的态势，为农民持续较快增收做出了突出贡献；也对农民收入分配产生了均等化效应，对农村脱贫和缩小农村内部收入差距产生了良好的效果。但是，中国现有的农业支持政策所带来的不良后果呈现出累积性效应，负面影响越来越大，已经到了绝不可忽视的程度，否则不仅影响当前中国经济社会发展大局，也会损害中国长远发展和农业可持续发展。

2015年，尽管国家对粮食收储政策进行了一些调整，粮食市场购销矛盾暂时得到缓和，但是粮食收储的深层次矛盾和累积性矛盾仍然没有有效解决。因此，调整完善粮食收储政策，发挥好粮食收储政策影响力，显得更加重要和迫切。

## （三）2016年中国粮食支持政策展望与分析

中国粮食“十二连增”之后出现了粮食产量、库存和进口都创历史新高，国家政策性收储的粮食总体上进多出少，出清难度不断加大，财政负担不断加重，粮食等农产品供给数量过于充裕而价格下行压力加大可能会出现的影响农民增收的新情况，而全面建成小康社会必须确保农民收入继续保持较快增长。同时，我们也必须考虑长期以来困扰着我国农业发展的资源环境和农产品质量等问题。面对农业、农村和农民方面的“三农”新难题，中共中央、国务院发布了《关于落实发展新理念　加快农业现代化　实现全面小康目标的若干意见》（2016年中央1号文件），要求用党的十八届五中全会提出的发展新理念来解决农业供给等方面库存、成本、产能以及短板和投入等难题，显著提高农业供给体系质量和效率。

推进农业包括粮食在内的供给侧结构性改革，意味着不能完全延续过去的农业支持政策，当然也不意味着彻底抛弃粮食“十二连增”的所有支持政策，另起炉灶再搞一套支持政策，而必须对现有的农业支持政策措施有留有舍并进一步改进。

为了保护农民利益，我国曾连续多年实施粮食收储政策，经过2014年的政策性收储制度改革，目前只有小麦、稻谷和玉米保留托市收购。根据2016年中央1号文件意见，出于去库存和降成本需要，2016年小麦最低价收储政策基本稳定，而稻谷和玉米收储政策可能会做出调整，其中，稻谷政策性收储价格已经调整，收储范围也可能调整，而玉米收储政策改革的力度可能比较大。但是，稻谷和小麦一样，与新形势下国家粮食安全战略有关，确保口粮绝对安全决定了稻谷收储政策不会发生急剧改变，而玉米不属于口粮且种植效益偏高，农民将玉米作为“铁杆”庄稼而不愿调减，国家必然会显著地调整玉米收储政策。

推进农业供给侧结构性改革，必然会探索农业结构调整新途径和发展方式转变新突破，相应地农业补贴政策也会显著地调整并进一步完善，其中，在全国范围内归集粮食直补、农业生产资料综合补贴和良种补贴并归并为农业支持保护补贴的可能性比较大，同时让适度规模经营新型农业主体能够成为农业支持保护补贴收益主体的一部分。国家在支持农业新型经营主体的同时，也会十分注重农民能够共享发展红利。

无论是三大主粮的收储政策稳定调整和改革，还是大豆的目标价格改革，应该在严格执行中央财政预算的前提下，增加粮食支持政策措施执行的弹性，扩大地方自主权，调动地方政府探索创新的积极性。2016年一些地区的粮食收储政策调整可能会与三项农业补贴政策改革协调配套起来，一些地方可能会合并粮食直补、农资综合补贴和良种补贴，相应地将收储费用补贴转变为这三项补贴的增量，根据农民粮食销售情况发放价外补贴。

2016年的中央1号文件从创新发展和绿色发展等新理念出发，明确提出要优化农业生产结构和区域布局，特别针对我国玉米种植面积过大和国家库存水平过高等问题，要求“适当调减非优势区玉米种植”。适当调减非优势区玉米种植，既有利于绿色发展，又可以提高玉米品质，更可以改善玉米供求关系，为玉米库存调减和市场出清创造有利条件。

（中国社会科学院农村发展研究所　　李国祥）

# 四、探索和创建农村新型合作制

【内容提要】

本文从培育新型农业经营主体、加快农业现代化进程必须创建新型农村合作制切入，全面阐述了新型农村合作制的性质、原则和宗旨。它是社会主义公有制经济的重要组成部分，是农村先进的社会经济制度和先进文化的体现。文章概述了我国农民专业合作社组织的发展特点及发挥的重要作用，以及现存的问题。从“问题倒逼改革”的方法论出发，文章着力提出创建我国新型农村合作制的“五加强”措施：加强农村合作制普及教育；加强农村合作制规范化建设；加强农村合作制服务能力建设；加强农村合作制人才培养；加强对农村合作制的支持。

在20世纪80年代初农村改革大潮中诞生的农户联产承包责任制奠定了我国农村经济制度的基石。这一制度曾经迸发出巨大的生产力。其精髓在于确立和保持农业生产者的主体和主人地位，在于激发和加强农业生产者的积极性和主动性，而归根结底在于激活生产力和创新力。然而，任何一种先进制度都需要随着客观环境的变化而进行调整和完善。

## （一）新型农村合作制是农业现代化的必须与必然

随着农村改革的深化和农业结构的变化，一家一户的小农生产方式越来越不适应农业现代化、市场化、国际化的需要：一是生产规模狭小，难以使用现代农业技术装备，难以采用现代技术方法；二是组织化程度低，市场地位低下，相比国内外大市场竞争力弱小；三是农户身单力薄，面对自然灾害无能为力，损失严重；四是生产成本高，效益低，尤其是只能供应初级农产品，加工附加值完全失去，农户增收困难；五是大批农村青壮年劳力外出打工，务农种粮者后继乏人。透过这些问题使人看到，小农生产方式已在多方面不适应生产力发展的需要，产生资源浪费、效率降低、甚至无人种地、阻碍农业现代化进程的消极后果。尤其是在农业市场化程度不断提高和农产品供求关系快速变化的条件下，大批集约化经营程度较高的农业生产者，包括粮食业、林果业、养殖业、畜牧业、特色农业等，遭遇到信息、技术、资金、销售以及劳力短缺等多种忧愁和困难。为农民排忧解难的根本途径在于自我组织、自我发展、自主自助、自我强大起来。这就是探索和发展真正的农民专业合作制。探索和发展农民专业合作制，是深化我国农村改革、加快农业现代化步伐的必须和必然。

农民专业合作制是一种新型的农村合作制。它既是先进的农村经济制度，也是一种先进的文化。以农民专业合作制形式体现的合作经济，在马列主义经典著作及宪法和共同纲领的条文规定中都被称为“合作社经济”。具有重大历史意义的党的十一届三中全会后，农村实行家庭承包经营责任制，促进了农业生产的发展，农民要求发展新的联合，出现了诸如新联合体、协作体以及协会等合作形式。虽然他们不是农民专业合作社组织，但也属于合作经济范畴，是合作经济发展的不同形式，因此都称“合作经济”。合作经济与个体企业、合伙企业、私营经济等有着本质的区别。

农村合作经济是我国基本经济制度的一种形式，也是推进农业现代化的最佳形式。其客观理论依据和实践依据包括：一是在我国，合作经济属于社会主义性质。合作制的本质和社会主义的本质是一致的，合作制是劳动群众联合起来，通过互助合作，发展生产力，反对剥削，谋求共同富裕。二是在我国，合作经济是公有制经济的重要组成部分。合作经济中虽然保留入股劳动者的个人所有权，但不是私有制，而是社会主义公有制的一种形式。合作经济与其他公有制经济一起在国民经济中处于主体地位。

三是合作经济组织的宗旨是为农服务。农村合作经济组织的唯一宗旨是为农业、农村和农民服务，满足农民日益提高的生产与生活需求，积极推进农业专业化、市场化、产业化、现代化，促进实现农村全面小康社会。四是合作经济是规模经济。各种类型的合作社组织可以对生产要素优化配置，提高适度规模经营水平，从而有力提高中国农业的竞争力。五是合作经济具有独特的优越性。它是在尊重个人利益的基础上，将个人利益与共同体利益乃至国家利益相结合。合作经济是民主经济，参加合作经济组织的劳动者是企业的主人，享有广泛的民主权利，每个成员的积极性、主动性、创造性都有充分发挥的机会。

## （二）我国农民专业合作社组织发展的特点

适应培育新型经营主体、扩大土地适度规模经营、加快农业现代化的需要，我国农民专业合作社组织像雨后春笋一般在广大农村涌现，并呈现出以下三大特点：

第一，规模大，领域广。截至2015年10月底，全国农民专业合作社数量达到147.9万个，比2014年底增长15.5%；入社农户9 997万户，覆盖全国41.7%的农户。在合作社总数中，各级示范社约有13.5万多个。而在2011年上半年，全国注册登记的农民专业合作社数量为44.6万个，实有入社农户3 000万左右，约占全国农户总数的12%。大体4年间，农民专业合作社增加了103.3万个，年均增加25.8万多个。与农村改革深化和农业分工细化相适应，农民专业合作组织的合作领域、合作方式呈现多元化，涉及多个领域，包括种植业、畜牧业、加工业、林果业、水产业及劳务合作社等。

第二，形式活，样式多。农村新型合作组织因地制宜，形式灵活多样，主要包括四种模式：一是实体型专业社模式。即以承包土地经营权入股的土地股份合作社和集体资产折股量化的社区股份合作社方兴未艾，农民以入股形式成为社员，与组织的关系较为紧密，实行盈余返还，社员与合作社成为利益共同体。二是公司带动合作模式。其特点是：以公司或集团企业为主导，以农产品加工、运销企业为龙头，以市场为导向，实行市场牵“龙头”、“龙头”带基地、基地连农户，进行一体化经营。三是股份合作模式。这是按照章程或协议，自愿以资金、实物、技术、承包土地使用权等作为股份，依法从事各种农业生产经营服务活动，实行按劳分配与“按股份分红”相结合的分配办法。四是集中资源联合经营。即以村组为单位、将集体资产折股量化，或将农民分散资源集中起来联合经营，进行规模化种养。公共收益用于本村民组公益事业建设，改善生产、生活条件。

第三，业态新，机制活。在上述各种形式的专业合作社中，实体型专业社和股份合作社组织实现了土地、资产、技术、劳动等资源要素的合作，也是资源的优化配置。在经营业态上，许多专业合作社积极探索和开展种养循环，产加销一体化，发展农村一、二、三产业融合，推进农业产业链整合和价值链提升，培育农民增收新途径。此外，许多地方的专业社还采取电子商务、会员制、认购式销售等新形式。值得注意的一种倾向是，农村专业合作社向多种领域延伸。此外，集新型经营主体与传统农户于一身、融生产与服务为一体的开放式、复合式合作组织成为参与主体多元化、利益分配多样化、管理决策灵活化的运行机制。

## （三）我国农民专业合作社组织发挥的作用与问题

方兴未艾的农民专业合作社对我国农业发展适度规模经营、提高农业生产、增加农民收入，以及促进农村流通都发挥了有利的作用，具体表现为五个有利于。

第一，有利于提高农民组织化程度。2013 年中央 1 号文件提出培育新型经营主体，鼓励和支持农民承包土地经营权向专业大户、家庭农场、农民合作社流转。以此为契机，全国各地纷纷出台相关政策，推动了新型农业经营主体的快速发展，农业现代化步伐不断加快，原有乡村治理结构也随之发生明显变化。其中，各地涌现数以百万计的农民专业合作社，将分散经营的农民组织起来，一定程度上克服了家庭经营规模小、生产成本高、市场竞争力弱的局限性，提高了农民进入市场的组织化程度。这带来了扩大适度规模经营、培育新型经营主体、增强抗御市场风险能力的效应。与专业大户、家庭农场及农业企业等经营主体相比，农民专业合作社组织具有更多优越性，是扩大农业适度规模经营、加快农业现代化的最佳形式。

第二，有利于推广现代技术装备。与提高农民组织化程度、扩大适度规模经营、培育新型经营主体相关，农民专业合作社组织创造性地使用和推广农业机械和现代植保技术方法的条件，特别是大大提高了农业机械化水平。新世纪以来，在培育新型经营主体的同时，国家加大了农机具购置补贴力度，激发了农民购买农机的热情，重点在耕整地、种植、收获、植保、烘干、秸秆处理等六大领域，促进了主要农作物生产全程机械化。目前，我国农机化水平达到61%以上，提前一年实现了“十二五”规划目标。这意味着我国农业生产方式已实现由人力、畜力为主向机械作业为主的历史性跨越。

第三，有利于增加农民收入。各类农村专业合作社组织采用科学种田技术，提高了产量和质量，相应促进了农民增收。同时，农村合作社组织不断完善利益分配机制。不同类型的专业合作社组织采取了不同的保护农民利益形式：一是农民以土地入股形式组成的专业合作社组织，农民社员既可获得土地红利，又可获得劳动的工资报酬，收入显著增长。二是采取合同农业形式的合作社组织，收购社员农产品的价格由市场价格向上浮，保护农民利益免受市场价格波动带来的损失。三是采取二次分配的合作社组织，将提取一定比例的经营利润按社员的交易额进行分红，促进农民既增产又增收。

第四，有利于提高农产品的质量。专业合作社组织在生产过程中通过采用和推广科技、优良品种，以及推广测土配方的科学施肥，既缩减了面源污染，又提高了产品质量。特别是专业合作社组织注重推进专业化、标准化、规范化生产，更有效提高了农产品的品质质量和市场竞争力。更有意义的是，专业合作社注重发展无公害农产品、绿色食品、有机农产品和农产品地理标志，即所谓农产品“三品一标”质量认证。相当一部分农民专业合作社通过了这种认证，拥有了注册商标。

第五，有利于促进产销对接。一家一户的小农几乎没有市场谈判能力，更是市场竞争的弱者。农民专业合作社的发展有利于提高农民在市场上的地位，帮助分散的农民根据市场信息做出更理性的生产经营决策，生产出适销对路的农产品。此外，各类农村专业合作社以不同形式架起了小生产与大市场之间的桥梁。像发展直销，或与超市、企业、学校等主体对接，直接进入销售终端，可以大大减少流通环节，降低成本。

然而，在为农民专业合作社取得明显进展而鼓舞的时候，还必须清醒意识到，我国农村的新型合作制在总体上还处于起步阶段：认识还不到位，发育还不成熟，组织还不规范，实力还不大，带动力还不强。如果以真正规范的农村合作社制度衡量，目前我国农民专业合作社组织还存在相当大差距，或必须切实解决以下问题：

第一，思想观念落后。由于在我国曾经发生的把农村合作经济异化为“归大堆”的历史教训，所以多年来社会上一直存在“谈合变色”的恐惧感，缺乏对发展合作经济价值的认同感。又由于长期受小农生产方式传统的影响，农民合作意识淡薄。这导致我国普遍存在误解或歧视合作经济组织的思想观念。另外，只片面认为专业合作社是经济组织，而对农村专业合作社组织的先进理念、价值观和人文精神却几乎没有认识。

第二，制度尚不健全。迄今，我国农民专业合作社组织的法人地位还不明确，初始条件不理想，组织内部运行机制不健全。为数不少的农民专业合作社内部组织不健全，合作社的理事会、监事会、社员代表大会等“三会”结构不全。这导致了民主管理机制不落实、财务制度不规范等问题。

第三，“离农”和“离粮”倾向。相当多的城市工商企业下乡办合作社或农业企业，采取租赁农户承包土地的形式，租赁大面积耕地，期内支付较高租赁费，对农民具有较大吸引力。但这种做法大大抬高了土地成本，单纯从事农业粮食生产无法收回成本，于是不少下乡的工商企业表现出“离农”和“离粮”倾向，从事其他收益更高的经营活动。这是违背农村合作社经济原则的失当做法。

第四，发展规模偏小。迄今，具有一定规模和较强竞争力的农民专业合作社组织数量不多，应对市场风险能力不强，产品规模和档次不高，服务层次较低。目前大多数专业合作社组织对成员的服务停留在信息服务、技术咨询及贩销大户销售服务方面，而更高层次的、规范化的产供销一体化的专业合作社还凤毛麟角。当然，发展专业合作社也必须坚持适度规模。

第五，合作社融资难。农民专业合作社普遍面临的一个“瓶颈”是自有资金不足和融资困难。其主要原因有二：专业合作社组织贷款时缺少抵押物品或必要的担保；贷款手续繁杂，授信额度低。由于专业合作社组织的融资需求得不到有效满足，束缚了其正常发展。

## （四）对发展我国农村新型合作制的对策建议

认识和正视问题是解决问题的开端。党的十八大以来，形成了“问题倒逼改革”的方法论。运用这一思维方法，针对现存的问题，当前和今后一个时期对我国农民合作社组织的改革应着重采取以下“五加强”措施：

第一，加强农村合作制普及教育。针对我国社会上对农村合作制知识贫乏甚至误解，需要加强农村合作制科学知识的普及教育。这是对我国健康发展农民专业合作社组织，或者说健康发展农村合作经济的思想建设。首先，要普及农民专业合作社和农村专业合作经济的农村合作制的理念、价值观和人文精神。它是我国公有制经济的重要组成部分，既是农村先进的经济制度，又是一种先进的文化，与社会主义核心价值观是一致的。其次，要普及专业合作社经济的性质。即农民专业合作社是农民群众兴办的，属民主、民办、民用、民有等“四民”性合作经济组织。再次，要普及专业社合作经济的宗旨。即真正按照合作制原则建立的自愿、自主、自助、自治等“四自”服务型合作经济组织。只有普及和加强全民农村合作制的理念、价值观和人文精神，以及农村专业合作制的性质、宗旨、先进性和优越性，才能促进其持续健康发展。

第二，加强农村合作制规范化建设。农村合作制的普遍原则是坚持自愿、民主和监督。加强农村合作制规范化建设，最基本的就是加强和完善专业合作社组织的自主自愿和民主制度，即加强民主管理、民主决策和民主监督。为此，需要加大理事会、监事会权力的行使，建立健全入社审批制度、财务管理制度、风险保障制度等；规范“龙头企业+专业合作社+农户”的组织形式；引导龙头企业通过委托生产、订单农业、入股分红、盈余返还等方式，与合作社建立自愿平等、利益共享、风险共担的利益机制。为保障专业合作社组织的规范化，还需要采取以下必要措施：修改和完善农民专业合作社法；健全合作社运行机制；培育和提高合作社带头人的素质；创建示范社，引导合作社依法建社、依章办社、依制管社。

第三，加强农村合作制服务能力建设。农村合作制的宗旨就是为农服务。其前提是必须以多种方式加强服务能力：一是建立联合社。鼓励专业合作社组织通过协商，采取共同出资、共建品牌、兼并、整合等方式建立联合社。二是组成产业联合体。农村专业合作社组织与其他农业经营主体以及普通农户建立合作关系，组成产业联合体。三是拓展农业产业链建设。发挥专业合作社组织的优势功能，带动农民调整产业结构，开发特色产业，发展支柱产业，开拓农产品加工业、休闲观光业，积极运用“互联网+”的新商业模式发展流通业。四是注重培育农产品品牌，增强农产品市场竞争力，提高农民融入产业链、价值链的话语权和收益权，让广大农民通过专业合作社的综合化服务共享产业发展成果。

第四，加强农村合作制人才培养。人才资源是农村专业合作事业持续发展的首要条件，有必要实施“人才兴社”，即通过人才振兴农村专业合作事业。为此，要通过多种形式培育和造就农村合作制人才队伍：（1）以多形式加强合作社带头人的教育与培养。诸如专家授课、示范指导、技术交流，提高合作社领导人及广大社员的科技文化素质；（2）鼓励农技人员到专业合作社任职，提高专业合作社领导班子的能力。（3）充分发挥实训基地作用，组织开展合作社各类人才培训，增强培训的针对性和实用性。（4）专业机构培育专业人才。要在相关专业院校和研究机构培育农村合作制的专业人才。

第五，加强对农村合作制的支持。发展具有本国特色的农村合作制是建设新农村及实现农村全面小康社会的好形式，目前正在初创阶段，需要国家以不同形式提供必要的支持和帮助：对农村专业合作社为农业生产提供的服务应享受税收优惠、融资优惠；对农业技术咨询、农资服务、农产品销售、品牌宣传等减免营业税；对从事农产品深加工的合作社减免增值税；要落实农民专业合作社从事农业种植、养殖及农产品初加工、仓储、冷藏等生产经营活动的用水、用电的价格优惠。

我国是缺乏合作制传统和合作意识的国家，亚细亚小农生产方式是通往农业现代化道路上的障碍。在加快农业现代化和建设全面小康社会的当下，打通这一障碍，探索和创建具有中国特色的新型农村合作制已成为时代课题，必须提上日程。

（中国粮食经济学会　　丁声俊）

# 五、基于粮食供给侧结构性改革视角的休耕制度分析[①]

【内容提要】

目前，我国粮食产业发展面临诸多供给侧矛盾的制约，包括粮食出现阶段性与结构性过剩、面临前所未有的库存压力、降成本的任务非常艰巨、补短板压力非常巨大。按照“创新、协调、绿色、开放、共享”的发展理念，通过休耕推进粮食供给侧结构性改革是必然选择。休耕有利于土地休养生息，对调整粮食供求关系、提高耕种效益、实现农业可持续发展具有重要意义。中国实行休耕制度，将会在粮食去产能、去库存、降成本、补短板等方面发挥重要作用。在科学设定休耕政策目标、原则的基础上，正确制订休耕试点总体方案，合理确定休耕补贴标准与补贴方式，与新一轮退耕还林规划协同联动，进一步完善国家粮食对外开放战略，是休耕制度试点的基本路径选择。

供给侧改革、农业供给侧改革、粮食供给侧改革无疑成为经济领域、农业领域、粮食领域改革的热点、难点。在这种大背景下，如何推进休耕制度改革是摆在我们面前的重大课题。

① 本文为教育部人文社会科学研究规划基金项目（11YJA790178）和上海市教委创新项目（12ZS180）的阶段性研究成果。

## （一）粮食发展面临诸多供给侧矛盾的制约

### 1. 农业供给侧结构性改革的基本内涵

2015年中央经济工作会议在分析国际国内经济形势的基础上，明确提出着力推进供给侧结构性改革。这是面对困难和挑战，尤其是经济发展的结构性矛盾，按照“创新、协调、绿色、开放、共享”的发展理念，深化我国经济改革的必然选择。所谓供给侧结构性改革，就是从提高供给质量出发，用改革的办法推进结构调整，矫正要素配置扭曲，扩大有效供给，提高供给结构应对需求变化的适应性和灵活性，提高全要素生产率，促进经济社会持续健康发展。

供给侧结构性改革的关键就是要抓好去产能、去库存、去杠杆、降成本、补短板五大任务。农业作为国民经济的基础，同样面临各种结构性矛盾。农业供给侧改革是我国供给侧改革的重要内容，其改革是否成功也直接影响供给侧改革的成效。因此，在2016年中央农村工作会议上中央首次提出了“农业供给侧结构性改革”。农业供给侧结构性改革就是通过提高农业供给体系质量和效率，使农产品供给数量充足、品种和质量契合消费者需要，真正形成结构合理、保障有力的农产品有效供给。保障国家粮食安全是农业结构性改革的基本底线。很明显，粮食供给侧结构性改革是农业供给侧结构性改革的核心内容。立足粮食行业的实际，粮食供给侧结构性改革同样面临去产能、去库存、降成本、补短板的艰巨任务。

推进粮食供给侧结构性改革既是落实中央经济工作会议精神的需要，也说明我国粮食供给侧结构性矛盾非常尖锐，因而成为改革的重点。

### 2. 我国粮食供给侧结构性矛盾的主要体现

（1）粮食出现阶段性与结构性过剩。长期以来，我国党和政府高度重视“三农”问题，尤其是2004年以来，我国连续13年出台有关“三农”的中央1号文件，出台了种粮直补、托市收购、取消农业税等一系列惠农政策，极大地调动了农民种粮的积极性。2004年实际是我国农业发展的重要拐点，从此开始，实现了粮食播种面积“十二连增”、粮食产量“十二连增”、粮食人均产量“十一连增”（其中2008年、2009年持平），这是新中国成立后我国农业发展史上从未取得的成就。2007年以来，我国的粮食产量已经连续9年稳定在50 000万吨以上，2013年开始连续3年跨上60 000万吨台阶，2015年粮食产量达62 143.5万吨的历史最高水平（见表3-5-1）。

**表3-5-1　　我国粮食播种面积、总产量及人均产量情况**

| 年　份 | 播种面积（千公顷） | 总产量（万吨） | 人均产量（千克） |
| --- | --- | --- | --- |
| 2004 | 101 606 | 46 946.9 | 362 |
| 2013 | 111 956 | 60 193.8 | 443 |
| 2014 | 112 723 | 60 702.6 | 445 |
| 2015 | 113 340.5 | 62 143.5 | — |

资料来源：数据主要来源于国家统计局：历年《中国统计年鉴》，中国统计出版社出版；2015年数据来源于《国家统计局关于2015年粮食产量的公告》。

粮食连年增产丰收以及人均产量的不断提高，极大地确保了我国的粮食安全。但是应该看到，随之而来的是我国的粮食也出现了阶段性过剩与结构性过剩。即粮食供给总量出现阶段性过剩，总供给大于总需求；某些粮食品种出现结构性过剩，我国玉米和稻谷结构性过剩情况明显，尤以玉米最为突出。综合来看，我国粮食既出现了总量过剩，也出现了结构过剩。同时，粮食行业还存在高能耗、低水平、粗放式的落后加工产能，存在长期亏损、资产负债率高、停产半停产的“僵尸”企业。也就是说，粮食生产、粮食加工都存在去产能的问题。如何在保证粮食安全的前提下解决粮食供给总量与供给结构的矛盾，去产能或者储产能是摆在粮食供给侧改革面前的重大课题。

（2）粮食面临巨大的库存压力。在粮食连年增产丰收、政府托市收购的大背景下，我国粮食库存面临巨大的压力。在我国，粮食库存数据保密，但从各方面的数据综合看，粮食库存应在2亿吨以上，其严峻形势在2016年全国粮食流通工作会议上可以清晰体现出来。在本次会议上，国家发改委和国家粮食局的领导明确提出，“当前，全国粮食库存处于历史高位，安全储粮形势异常严峻、压力巨大”，“粮食高产量、高价格、高库存‘三高’特征更加明显”，“粮食产量、库存量均创历史最高，给粮食收购、安全储粮和消化库存带来前所未有的压力”，“面对粮食库存之高前所未有、简易仓囤储粮之多前所未有”，等等。据联合国粮农组织预测，2016 年全球谷物产量、库存量将继续保持较高水平，分别达到 25.3 亿吨、6.4 亿吨。而我国的粮食库存至少应该占到全球谷物库存量的 1/3 以上，难怪有行业专家说“全世界最庞大的库存已经建立起来了”。去库存也是我国粮食供给侧改革面临的重大问题。

（3）粮食面临降成本的艰巨任务。在连年托市收购支撑下，当前国内粮食价格处于全球“高地”，呈现产区与销区、原粮与成品粮、国内市场与国际市场粮食价格三个“倒挂”的局面。“十二五”期间（2011—2015 年），累计粮食产量 59 823.7 亿斤，其中谷物产量为 54 821.86 亿斤；累计托市收购粮食 8 460 亿斤，占谷物产量的 15.4%。托市收购在有效保护种粮农民利益的同时，也带来了粮食补贴、粮食收购、粮食仓储成本高企。去成本是我国粮食供给侧改革面临的又一重大问题。

（4）粮食面临补短板的巨大压力。随着我国农业快速发展，制约农业与粮食的一些“短板”问题也越来越突出，主要包括：农田水利、仓储等基础设施薄弱；农业生产方式粗放，农业资源利用效率低下；水土资源污染严重，农业可持续发展面临挑战；农业科技相对落后，制约农业现代化的进程；农民整体素质较低，缺少新型的职业化农民队伍，等等。农业在金融服务、保险服务、智能装备、信息技术等现代生产要素方面同样存在短板问题。补短板是我国粮食供给侧改革面临的另一重大问题。

## （二）休耕是粮食供给侧结构性改革的重要选择

长期以来我国对土地休耕有些讳莫如深，很少有人讨论，一个基本的看法是我国人多地少，粮食安全压力非常大，基本不具备休耕的条件。实际上，在我国人们非常崇尚人与自然的和谐，休耕制度在我国古而有之。班固在《汉书·食货志》中就记载了西周以来的“民受田，上田夫百晦，中田夫二百晦，下田夫三百晦，岁耕种者为不易上田，休一岁者，为一易中田；休两岁者，为再易下田，三岁更耕之，自爰其处”休耕制度。1999 年以来，我国启动的两轮退耕还林还草也可在某种程度上视为休耕。

而美国、欧盟则有比较成熟的休耕制度。正是在粮食供给出现阶段性过剩、库存压力空前、生态环境恶化、全球供应过剩的情况下，中国政府开始建议在部分地区实施耕地轮作休耕制度。因此，在粮食供给侧矛盾的倒逼下，不得不让我们重新审视休耕制度。

土地休耕制度是指在政府宏观调控下，土地所有者或使用者有计划、有组织、有步骤地将一部分耕地在一定时期内闲置起来或进行科学轮作，从而实现储粮于地、保护耕地、保护生态的制度安排。休耕有利于土地休养生息，对提高耕种效益、实现土地可持续有效利用具有重要意义。在粮食过剩的情况下，也是调整粮食供求关系的重要政策选择。中国实行休耕制度将会在粮食去产能、去库存、降成本、补短板等方面发挥重要作用。

### 1. 休耕是粮食储产能的蓄水池

我国粮食出现阶段性过剩与结构性过剩，这意味着不仅要调整粮食供给总量，还要调整粮食供给结构。所以，我们应该正视这个矛盾，粮食阶段性去产能不容回避。但是粮食领域去产能与工业领域去产能应有很大的区别。工业领域去产能意味着要彻底淘汰部分落后与过剩产能，粮食领域去产能并不是要把耕地非农化，而是应使部分耕地暂时退出耕种，实现藏量于地，与其说是去产能，不如说是储产能。这取决于对我国粮食安全的形势与粮食生产的特点两个基本判断：一是人多地少的国情决定了我国粮食供需将长期处于紧平衡状态；二是人口增加、气候变暖、水资源短缺、环境恶化等因素决定了全球粮食供给在较长时间内将处于偏紧状态。同时，粮食的生产周期比较长，很容易出现“多了多了，少了少了”的情况。这决定了我国粮食领域去产能不可能把大量耕地非农化。因此，通过休耕实现粮食产能的暂时退出与储存将是一种合理的选择。

### 2. 休耕是粮食去库存的安全垫

伴随粮食产量的“十二连增”，我国粮食库存量已创历史最高，给粮食收购和储存带来了前所未有的压力。中国的粮食库存消费比远高于联合国粮农组织规定的17%的粮食安全标准。因此，去库存是粮食供给侧改革的必然选择。在没有休耕制度下，粮食安全实际只有一道安全垫，即库存（含进口粮食）。而在休耕制度下，粮食安全将会增加一道安全垫。去库存的同时进行休耕制度改革，则可以提高去库存的操作空间。休耕实际是把存粮于库改为存粮于地，必要之时可以快速释放粮食产能，保障国家粮食安全。

**3. 休耕是粮食降成本的调节阀**

粮食从生产到收购、从储存到流通要经过一系列环节，从国家的角度来看，每个环节都要支付成本。从生产看，政府要支付生产资料补贴、良种补贴、种粮直补等；从收储看，政府要为托市收购付出巨大的财力；从储存看，政府要进行大量的仓储建设，要提供大量的仓储补贴；从流通环节看，政府要投入流通设施，建设流通市场，支付流通费用，等等。保障必要的粮食安全与必要的库存，相关的成本是政府必须要付出的。但超过粮食安全标准的生产与库存，必然给政府带来额外的负担，高成本必然带来市场的高价格，高价格又会形成粮食加工企业的高负担，进而降低我国粮食的竞争力。休耕则可对粮食高成本、高价格、高库存起到有效的缓解作用。

**4. 休耕是粮食补短板的助推器**

通过休耕补粮食短板主要可体现在以下几个方面：使部分土地得到休养生息，可更好地保护耕地资源；缓解地力透支、水土流失、污染加重等带来的环境问题，利于农业可持续发展；通过减量提质，可有效提升我国粮食安全的质量；通过结构调整，可把更多的资源投向粮食科技创新，有效提升粮食产业的竞争力；有利于推进农民转型，培育新型农业经营主体，逐步建设职业化农民队伍，等等。

由以上可见，粮食供给侧存在的诸多矛盾既是对我们提出的挑战，也为休耕等制度创新提供了难得的机遇。

## （三）休耕制度试点基本政策建议

**1. 科学设定休耕政策目标**

（1）平衡粮食供求。从各国实施休耕制度的实践来看，一个基本的原因就是由于粮食供过于求，出现粮食过剩，通过休耕以达到储粮于地，调节粮食供求关系。这是休耕政策的基本目标，基于此种目的的休耕可称为“产能过剩休耕”。

（2）保护生态环境。粮食的“十二连增”实际上也带来我国耕地开发利用强度过大的问题，一些地方地力严重透支，水土流失、地下水严重超采、土壤退化、面源污染加重已成为制约农业可持续发展的突出问题。从各国实施休耕制度的实践来看，保护生态是休耕政策的另一基本目标，基于此种目的的休耕可称为“生态休耕”。

（3）稳定农民收入。在休耕情况下，对参与政府休耕计划的农民的直接影响就是收入减少。因此，为了保障休耕计划的顺利实施，必须对农民进行休耕补贴，以稳定农民收入。休耕补贴是休耕制度的核心内容之一，对政府来说是休耕成本，对农民来说是收入。补贴的方式可以采用粮食或现金补贴。

（4）优化财政支持。我国目前是按“成本加合理利润”和“成本加基本收益”的定价原则来制定托市价格和目标价格，这样做必然使粮食价格长期高于市场均衡价格，出现“高产量、高收购、高库存、高进口、高亏损”，财政支出“高成本”。因此，通过休耕调整供求关系，完善粮食价格形成机制，优化财政支持也是休耕应有之义。

**2. 休耕制度试点应坚持的原则**

（1）粮食安全原则。我国进行粮食休耕制度试点必须深入贯彻国家粮食安全战略，确保“谷物基本自给、口粮绝对安全”。保障国家粮食安全既是粮食供给侧改革的基本底线，也是休耕制度试点的基本底线，休耕一定要避免非农化倾向。粮食安全原则界定了休耕制度的操作空间。

（2）循序渐进原则。对耕地进行轮作休耕情况比较复杂，尤其在中国这样一个人多地少的大国实施，情况则更为复杂，改革不可能一步到位。渐进式改革是我国经济体制改革的成功经验。因此，要坚持先行试点，探索可复制可推广的成功经验。这决定了我国的休耕制度应该有计划、有步骤的实施。

（3）综合改革原则。休耕制度试点会涉及粮食生产、粮食收储、粮食流通、粮食监控等一系列体制机制、政策的调整，这决定了休耕制度试点不能单兵突进，应遵循综合改革的原则。

（4）自愿参加原则。目前我国耕地绝大部分为农户承包，土地承包人对其依法承包的土地享有占有、使用、收益和一定处分的权利。在试点期间，应坚持农民自愿、政府引导的原则。

**3. 休耕制度试点的路径选择**

（1）科学制订休耕试点总体方案。可结合农业发展的“十三五”规划，在对国际、国内粮食供求形势分析判断的基础上，制订土地休耕试点的总体方案，提出土地休耕的指导思想、目标、任务、试点周期，这样有利于粮食宏观调控，落实国家粮食安全战略。在总体规划的基础上，通过制订年度计划，利于试点的顺利推进。通过一个周期的试点，应该可以形成比较成熟的可推广、可复制的休耕经验。

（2）合理选择休耕试点区域。我国疆域辽阔，各地的耕地情况、耕种制度有很大差别，这意味着可供选择的休耕区域很多。但休耕试点区域的选择要能够体现过剩休耕与生态休耕的不同要求。因此，根据我国不同粮食品种过剩的情况和生态面临的问题，建议重点选择两类区域进行试点：一是对粮食绝对过剩的品种选择一定区域进行试点；二是在生态问题非常突出的地区选择一定区域进行试点。因为过剩休耕与生态休耕的要求会有所不同，休耕的时间、补贴的办法也会有所区别。这样通过试点就可以为我们积累过剩休耕与生态休耕的经验。具体而言，面对玉米严重过剩的情况，可在玉米种植区选择一定的区域进行过剩休耕试点；针对生态问题严重的区域，可选择在地下水漏斗区、重金属污染区和生态严重退化区等区域开展生态休耕试点。在保障国家粮食安全的基础上，合理确定年度休耕减产的计划指标，通过减产指标来控制休耕面积。

（3）合理确定休耕补贴标准与补贴方式。休耕试点要坚持自愿原则，同时休耕后不能降低农民收入。因此，这就需要合理制定补贴标准，补贴标准应体现以下要求：一是对农民自愿休耕有吸引力；二是政府可承受；三是与种粮收入保持合理比例。

从理论上讲，休耕补贴方式可采用实物补贴，也可采用货币补贴。实物补贴就是按休耕面积与单位面积补贴粮食数量，对休耕农户补贴粮食；货币补贴就是按休耕面积与单位面积补贴现金，对休耕农户补贴现金。根据我国粮食供求与库存的现状，建议采用补贴粮食的方式，这有利于减轻国内粮食供求与库存压力。补贴现金可能会出现农民把现金用于粮食的替代消费，会影响粮食供给侧改革的效果。

（4）与新一轮退耕还林规划协同联动。休耕与退耕还林无论在目的、实施的方式方法上都有所不同，但是也有相同的地方，如都会减少粮食产量、都需要补贴，等等。退耕还林在某种程度上是对不适合种粮的一些陡坡地和沙化地等进行永久休耕。1999 年我国启动了第一轮退耕还林还草，截至 2006 年底，累计完成退耕地造林 1. 39 亿亩，配套实施荒山荒地造林和封山育林 2. 25 亿亩，取得了较好的生态、经济和社会效益。从 2014 年开始，我国启动了新一轮退耕还林还草，规划的基本目标是到 2020 年将全国具备条件的约 4 240 万亩耕地退耕还林还草。因此，我国的休耕制度应该与退耕还林还草规划衔接起来，这样才能更好地实施粮食安全战略，使休耕制度更好地发挥作用。

（5）进一步完善国家粮食对外开放战略。随着经济全球化和贸易自由化向纵深推进，国内外粮食市场的关联度越来越强，国际粮食形势对我国粮食市场的影响更加直接。进一步完善国家粮食对外开放战略，运用国际国内两种资源、国内国外两个市场，进一步提高我国粮食安全的保障水平是必然选择。因此，在休耕背景下，应主动对接“一带一路”等国家对外开放战略，通过“引进来”、“走出去”，加快形成互利共赢的国际合作关系，更好地保障国家粮食安全。

另外，休耕是一项政策性很强的改革，涉及国家、农民、企业利益关系的调整，客观上需要尽快出台相关法规制度，以保证休耕改革的顺利推进。

（上海立信会计学院　　杨光焰）

# 六、我国农业补贴政策评估及改革思路

【内容提要】

当前，我国已建立了以直接补贴和价格支持为核心的农业补贴政策体系，对农业增产增收、农产品价格稳定和农业发展方式转变发挥了重要作用，但是我国农业补贴水平低、结构不合理、精准度不高、代价大等问题突出。在我国经济进入新常态的背景下，我国农业补贴政策改革应借鉴发达国家经验，按照“扩总量、优结构、转方式、提效率”的思路，扩大农业补贴总量，优化调整“四项补贴”政策，新设农户基础设施投资补贴制度，分步实施目标价格制度，探索土地休耕补贴试点，大幅增加农业保险补贴。

农业补贴是指政府为引导农业生产活动，对农业生产经营者提供的财政转移支付。对农业进行补贴是各国进入工业化中后期的普遍做法。加入世贸组织以后，我国逐步建立了符合世贸组织规则的农业补贴政策框架，对推动农业发展和农民增收、促进经济健康发展发挥了重要作用，但运行中也暴露了一系列问题和缺陷，亟须调整和完善。

## （一）建立了以直接补贴和价格支持为核心的农业补贴政策体系

21世纪以来，中央把“三农”作为全党工作的重中之重，不断加大支农强农惠农力度，建立了以“四项补贴”（粮食直补、良种补贴、农资综合补贴、农机具购置补贴）和“三项价格支持”（最低收购价、临时收储、目标价格）为核心的农业补贴政策体系。一是补贴规模持续较快增长。2004—2014 年中央财政用于“四项补贴”的资金从 146 亿元增加到 1 681 亿元，增长了 10.5 倍，年均增长 27.7%；用于“三项价格支持”的资金从 2005 年的 183 亿元增加到 3 890 亿元，累计增长了 20.2 倍，年均增长 35.7%。二是补贴范围不断扩大。累计出台农业补贴 50 多项，补贴范围从农业生产、农产品流通到农民教育培训、农产品质量安全、农村生态建设等领域，补贴品种既包括粮棉油糖大宗农产品，也包括猪、牛、羊等大型畜产品。三是补贴对象惠及所有农户。农户无论规模大小、家在何处，只要拥有承包土地，都可获得粮食直补和农资综合补贴。

## （二）农业补贴政策对农业增产增收、农产品价格稳定和农业发展方式转变发挥了重要作用

一是促进粮食“十二连增”和主要农产品产量稳定增长。粮食产量由 2003 年的 43 070 万吨增加至 2014 年的 60 710 万吨，累计增长 41%；棉、油、糖和猪肉的产量分别增长了 27%、25%、39% 和 34%，有效保障了国家粮食安全和城乡居民不断增长的消费需求。二是促进农民收入持续较快增长。农民人均纯收入从 2003 年的 2 622 元增加到 2014 年的 9 892 元，年均增长 12.8%，比 1978—2002 年平均增速高 5.3 个百分点，其中 2014 年“四项补贴”直接增加农民人均收入近 300 元，占当年农民家庭经营收入的 7% 以上。三是促进农业发展方式加快转变。良种补贴助推全国粮食良种覆盖率提高到 96% 以上，农机购置补贴提升了农业机械化水平，2004—2014 年全国共补贴购置各类农机超过 3 500 万台，农机总动力增长了 78%。测土配方施肥补贴面积接近 14 亿亩，占新公布耕地面积 20.3 亿亩的 69%。四是保持主要农产品价格水平总体稳定。2007—2014 年，我国大米、小麦、玉米、菜籽油、食糖、猪肉等产品的价格波动系数分别为 0.1660、0.1426、0.1428、0.1439、0.225、0.1366，明显低于同期国际市场同类产品的价格波动幅度（分别为 0.2158、0.2464、0.2653、

0.2213、0.3387、0.2236）。

## （三）我国农业补贴水平低、结构不合理、精准度不高、代价大

随着农业生产成本快速上升，国内主要农产品价格已高于国际市场价格，特别是我国经济进入新常态后，农业可持续发展面临严峻挑战，农业补贴政策已不能适应新形势、新要求。

第一，补贴总量严重不足，人均水平低。相对于发达国家巨额的农业补贴和国内庞大的农业人口基数，我国农业补贴水平仍然很低。首先，从国际比较看，2014 年我国财政用于“三农”的支出为 1.4 万亿元左右，扣除农业固定资产投资、各项农业事业费、农村社会事业发展等不属于世贸组织界定的农业补贴项目后，实际农业补贴资金只有 3 150 亿元，仅占全国财政总支出的 2.1% 左右，农民人均获得农业补贴只有 500 元左右，仅占当年农民人均纯收入的 5%，明显低于美国、欧盟、日本等发达国家和地区（农业补贴占农民收入一般在 20% 以上，高的达到 40% ~50%）。其次，从农业微量补贴水平看，根据农业部农业贸易中心测算，2013 年我国非特定产品的“黄箱”补贴规模为 1 300 多亿元，仅为许可上限（占当年农业总产值比重 8.5%）的 18.4%，尚有 5 700 多亿元的补贴空间可以利用。最后，从国内农业生产成本收益比较看，农业补贴增长速度赶不上农业生产成本上涨幅度。以谷物为例，2009—2013 年，我国稻谷、小麦、玉米每亩总成本分别增长 68.5%、61.3% 和 83.6%，明显高于“四项补贴”44.6% 的增幅，导致三大粮食生产成本利润率分别从 2009 年的 36.8%、26.5%、31.8% 下降到 2013 年的 13.5%、－1.4%、7.7%。

第二，补贴结构不合理，可持续性差。主要表现为“三重三轻”。其一，重“黄箱”轻“绿箱”，除小麦、稻谷外，2013 年玉米、棉花、油菜籽、食糖的“黄箱”补贴水平分别达到 18%、27.7%、18.3% 和 11.1%，超过了 8.5% 的上限标准，而“绿箱”政策尚有 6 项没有使用。其二，重小农轻大户，小农户只要拥有承包土地就会得到补贴，而转包土地搞规模经营的专业大户、家庭农场、农民合作社等新型经营主体却得不

到补贴，不利于农业适度规模经营和现代农业发展。其三，重产量轻质量，补贴政策主要围绕增产设计，长期透支粮食生产能力，导致耕地过度开发，地下水过度抽取，化肥、农药过量使用，农业可持续发展面临严峻挑战。

第三，玉米临时收储政策代价高，难以为继。玉米临时收储政策在一定程度上保护了农民利益，但却损害了养殖户、加工企业和国家三方利益（保一损三），弊大于利。其一，国家不断提高玉米临时收储价格，导致国内价格明显高于国际价格，进口压力大，同时造成加工企业和养殖户原料成本高企、经营困难，不利于玉米加工业和养殖业健康发展。其二，不限量保价收储，一方面导致国家收储玉米数量急剧攀升、仓满为患，收储资金和仓储设施投入大量增加，另一方面为消化库存玉米补贴加工和运销企业，财政负担不断增加。2012—2014 年，国家玉米临时收储量从 3 083 万吨增加到 8 330 万吨（占当年玉米产量的比例从 14.8% 提升到 38.6%），收购资金从 610 亿元增加到 1 866 亿元，两年内分别增长了 1.7 倍和 2.1 倍，分别占三大谷物总收购量和金额的 58.0% 和 52.3%。其三，临时收储政策人为抬高了玉米和大豆比价，扭曲市场价格信号，过度刺激玉米生产，导致资源错配，大豆主产区农民减大豆、扩玉米，大豆面积和产量逐年萎缩。

第四，棉花、大豆目标价格试点效果有待观察，机制有待完善。从新疆、东北试点情况看，目标价格政策实现了“价补分离”，发挥了市场在资源配置中的决定性作用，促进了棉花、大豆收购价格合理回归，棉花价格从 2012/2013 年度最高的 32 000 元/吨下降到 2014/2015 年度的 13 500 元/吨左右，大豆从 4 800 元/吨下降到 4 000 元/吨左右，既减轻了国家财政负担（国家财政用于棉花和大豆目标价格的补贴资金分别为 300 亿元和 34 亿元左右，不到 2013 年棉花、大豆临时收储支出 1 350 亿元和 153 亿元的 1/4），也有利于下游纺织服装业健康发展。但在农业生产成本上升和 2015 年目标价格不变和下调（大豆不变，棉花下调到 19 100 元/吨）的背景下，棉花、大豆种植收益持续走低，影响农民种棉、种豆的积极性和两个产业的发展。目前，各方面对目标价格试点效果评价褒贬不一。我们认为，目标价格试点刚进入第二年，其综合效果评价要放在更长的时间尺度去考察，目前下结论还为时过早。

## （四）按照“扩总量、优结构、转方式、提效率”的思路，完善农业补贴政策

在我国经济进入新常态的背景下，农业补贴政策改革必须综合考虑国家财政收入增长放缓、农业生产成本上升和更好发挥市场决定性作用等因素，加强顶层设计和整体谋划，遵循有利于保障国家粮食安全和重要农产品供给、有利于增加农业生产者收入、有利于现代农业发展和不违背市场机制、不违背世贸组织规则“三有利、两不违背”的原则，按照“扩总量、优结构、转方式、提效率”的总体要求，围绕重点地区、重点品种、重点人群“三个重点”，改革完善直接补贴、价格支持、保险补贴三大政策工具，提高农业补贴的精准度和有效性。

第一，扩大农业补贴总量。在农业生产比较效益逐年下降的背景下，要调动农民生产积极性，确保农业特别是粮食生产不滑坡、农产品竞争力不下降、农民收入不徘徊，必须加大农业补贴力度，这既是农业与非农产业均衡配置生产要素的客观需要，也是应对国外农业高补贴挑战的迫切要求。要按照农业补贴增幅明显高于财政支出增幅和农业生产成本增幅“两个明显高于”的原则，继续扩大农业补贴总量规模，逐步将农业补贴占财政支出的比重提高至5%以上，农业补贴占农民收入的比重提高到10%以上。新增农业补贴主要用于增加对农户的收入补贴、基础设施投入补贴和转变农业生产方式补贴（如测土配方施肥等），不与农产品产量挂钩，避免过度刺激某种农产品生产，避免扭曲市场价格，造成资源要素“错配”。

第二，优化调整“四项补贴”政策。由于粮食直补、农资综合补贴、良种补贴只与承包土地面积挂钩，不与品种、产量挂钩，在农民心中已被当作普惠性收入补贴，是国家给农民的一项福利。可按照“三并一、两不变、两倾斜、一提高”的思路进行调整，将功能相近、操作相同的这三项补贴合并为一项补贴，统称为“农业生产者收入补贴”，明确与产量脱钩，保持补贴对象不变、补贴面积不变，根据生产成本变化逐步提高补贴标准，同时将农机具购置补贴资金向粮棉油糖等主产区倾斜、向适度规

模经营农户和合作社倾斜。

第三，新设农户基础设施投资补贴制度。针对我国“绿箱”补贴严重不足的现实，从有利于推进农业现代化的考量出发，利用中央新增财政农业补贴设立农户基础设施投资补贴制度，鼓励农户加大对农业基础设施的投资。补贴方式采取普惠制，按照“谁投资补贴谁”的原则，对所有农户一视同仁。但在时序上，可优先安排粮食等重要农产品、重点生产区域和新型农业经营主体。同时鼓励有条件的地方政府增加配套补贴，加大对农业基础设施投资支持力度。

第四，分步实施目标价格制度。近期，继续完善棉花、大豆目标价格试点，建立目标价格动态调整机制，确保目标价格富有弹性，增强政策导向性和精准性。完善玉米临时收储政策，根据市场变化调整收储价格，有升有降，避免财政过度“兜底”和过度刺激玉米、糖料等生产，同时实施限量收储，收储数量控制在前 3 年平均总产量的 30% 以内，并把收储指标分配到农户，允许指标公开交易。中远期，逐步将目标价格制度由棉花、大豆向玉米、油菜籽、糖料、稻谷、小麦等品种延伸，并同步取消玉米、糖料、油菜籽临时收储政策和稻谷、小麦最低收购价政策。

第五，探索土地休耕补贴试点。利用我国粮食库存较多和国际粮价低迷的时机，开展土地休耕补贴试点，一方面可让土地休养生息、保护耕地生产能力，另一方面又可调减粮食产量、稳定农产品价格。休耕土地的重点是过度开发导致地力下降、地下水超采、重金属污染严重等三类耕地。每年休耕土地规模控制在 5 000 万亩以内，补贴标准为前 3 年亩均收益的 80%。按粮食亩均纯收益 500 元计算，休耕补贴水平为每亩 400 元，5 000 万亩休耕土地合计补贴金额 200 亿元，中央财政完全能够承受。可将休耕补贴试点和消化大量的库存玉米结合起来，将补贴金额折合成等量玉米，以票券形式发放给签订休耕计划的农民，票券可在市场上公开交易。

第六，大幅度增加农业保险补贴。大力发展重要农作物保险、重要“菜篮子”品种保险，提高中央、省级财政对农作物保险的保费补贴比例，加大保险保费补贴力度。完善畜牧业保险补贴政策，增加畜禽保险种类，调整养殖业保险补贴比例和标准，取消或减少养殖业保险县级保费补贴比例。支持发展养殖业互助合作保险，引导养殖场（户）以互助合作形式开展养殖保险。创新农业保险提供方式，开展综合性农业收入保险补贴，实现一张保单涵盖多种农产品。

（国家发展和改革委员会产业经济与技术经济研究所
黄汉权　蓝海涛　王为农　涂圣伟　张义博　卞靖）

# 七、促进亚太地区低收入群体粮食安全与营养可持续发展

**【内容提要】**

为实现亚太经合组织（APEC）各经济体持久的粮食安全，促进经济体实现千年发展目标、2015 年饥饿目标和联合国 2015 年后可持续发展议程目标，解决亚太地区低收入群体的粮食安全与营养可持续问题显得十分迫切。APEC 及其经济体已经认识到解决这个问题的紧迫性，正在采取积极行动，加强低收入群体粮食安全与营养可持续发展的研究和实践，推动落实和巩固 APEC 关于粮食安全宣言、路线图、行动计划成果，增强粮食供应链互通，提高效率，减少产后损失和浪费，畅通贸易渠道，改善粮食体系结构，重点促进低收入群体买得起安全、营养的粮食。

## （一）低收入群体粮食安全与营养可持续亟待解决

2015 年是联合国千年发展目标 2015 年饥饿目标的最后一年，也是联合国可持续发展议程目标的第一年。全球贫困人口显著下降，从 1990 年的 19.58 亿人、占比 37.1% 到 2012 年的 9.02 亿人、占比 12.8%，再到 2015 年的 7.02 亿人、占比 9.6%（见表 3－7－1）。但是，低收入群体粮食安全与营养状况不容乐观。为促进各成员经济体持久的粮食安全，促进经济体实现千年发展目标 2015 年饥饿目标和联合国可持续发展议程目标，解决低收入群体粮食安全与营养可持续问题显得十分

迫切。

表 3 –7 –1　　　　全球贫困人口估计

| 区域 | 1990 年 | 1999 年 | 2011 年 | 2012 年 | 2015 年 |
|---|---|---|---|---|---|
| 人均低于 1.90 美元/日的人口占比（%，2011 年平价购买力） | | | | | |
| 东亚和太平洋 | 60.8 | 37.5 | 8.5 | 7.2 | 4.1 |
| 欧洲和中亚 | 1.9 | 7.8 | 2.7 | 2.5 | 1.7 |
| 拉丁美洲和加勒比海 | 17.7 | 14.1 | 6.5 | 6.2 | 5.6 |
| 中东和北美洲 | — | — | — | — | — |
| 南　亚 | 50.6 | 41.2 | 22.3 | 18.8 | 13.5 |
| 撒哈拉以南的非洲 | 56.0 | 58.1 | 44.3 | 42.6 | 35.2 |
| 发展中世界 | 44.3 | 34.2 | 16.6 | 15.0 | 11.9 |
| 全世界 | 37.1 | 29.0 | 14.2 | 12.8 | 9.6 |
| 人均低于 1.90 美元/日的人口（百万，2011 年平价购买力） | | | | | |
| 东亚和太平洋 | 999.3 | 689.7 | 173.1 | 147.2 | 82.6 |
| 欧洲和中亚 | 9.0 | 36.6 | 12.7 | 12.0 | 4.4 |
| 拉丁美洲和加勒比海 | 78.0 | 72.2 | 37.7 | 37.1 | 29.7 |
| 中东和北美洲 | — | — | — | — | — |
| 南　亚 | 574.5 | 560.1 | 362.3 | 309.2 | 231.3 |
| 撒哈拉以南的非洲 | 284.0 | 375.4 | 393.5 | 388.5 | 347.1 |
| 全世界 | 1 958.5 | 1 746.6 | 987.4 | 902.0 | 702.1 |

数据来源：世界银行：《2015/2016 人口变化时代的发展目标》。

### 1. 联合国各成员经济体粮食安全战略的需要

近年来，由于粮食价格波动和供应周期的问题，粮食安全已经受到 APEC 各经济体的日益关注。由于每个经济体的不同特性，其在粮食生产、流通、消费方面临着不同的粮食安全问题，在自然资源、技术、资金、管理经验等方面具有不同的比较优势，具有不同的粮食消费需求、模式和习惯，因此，在粮食资源、贸易投资、技术合作、基础设施建设等方面有较大的需求和潜在的合作机遇，迫切需要经济体之间的政策沟通、交流与合作（见表3－7－2）。

表3－7－2　　亚太地区粮食获取基础设施研究

| 铺平公路占所有公路的比例（%） | | | | |
|---|---|---|---|---|
| | 东亚地区 | 东南亚地区 | 南亚地区 | 大洋洲 |
| 1990 年 | 43.7 | 38.3 | 46.2 | 9.9 |
| 2011 年 | 63.1 | 40.0 | 52.8 | 11.5 |
| 公路密度（平方米/平方千米） | | | | |
| | 东亚地区 | 东南亚地区 | 南亚地区 | 大洋洲 |
| 1990 年 | 16.3 | 17.2 | 37.9 | 5.8 |
| 2011 年 | 37.7 | 29.4 | 81.2 | 6.3 |
| 铁路线密度（平方米/100 平方千米） | | | | |
| | 东亚地区 | 东南亚地区 | 南亚地区 | 大洋洲 |
| 1990 年 | 0.5 | 0.4 | 1.5 | — |
| 2011 年 | 0.6 | 0.4 | 1.4 | — |

数据来源：联合国粮农组织。

**2. 促进经济体实现联合国千年发展目标2015年饥饿与营养不良目标和可持续发展议程目标的需要**

联合国粮农组织公布的数据显示，2014—2016年间，全球约有7.95亿人面临饥饿和营养不良，其中亚太地区是全球饥饿和营养不良人口最多的地区，达4.90亿人，约占全球饥饿和营养不良人口的62%。APEC各经济体内贫困地区、弱势群体的粮食安全与营养仍面临不可低估的威胁（见表3－7－3）。

表3－7－3　　亚太地区营养不良人口粮食获取情况

| 营养不良人口比例（%） | | | | |
|---|---|---|---|---|
| | 东亚地区 | 东南亚地区 | 南亚地区 | 大洋洲 |
| 1990—1992 年 | 23.2 | 30.6 | 23.9 | 15.7 |
| 2014—2016 年 | 9.6 | 9.6 | 15.7 | 14.2 |

续表

| 粮食缺乏的深度（千卡/人/日） | | | | |
|---|---|---|---|---|
| | 东亚地区 | 东南亚地区 | 南亚地区 | 大洋洲 |
| 1990—1992年 | 182.0 | 232.0 | 169.0 | 101.0 |
| 2014—2016年 | 76.0 | 73.0 | 114.0 | 94.0 |
| 粮食不足的比例（%） | | | | |
| | 东亚地区 | 东南亚地区 | 南亚地区 | 大洋洲 |
| 1990—1992年 | 32.6 | 40.1 | 32.8 | 23.3 |
| 2014—2016年 | 16.2 | 16.6 | 24.5 | 22.0 |

数据来源：联合国粮农组织。

**3. 落实和巩固联合国可持续发展议程目标，APEC关于粮食安全宣言、行动计划成果的需要**

APEC粮食安全部长级会议先后通过了《APEC粮食安全新泻宣言》(2010年)、《APEC粮食安全喀山宣言》(2012年)、《APEC粮食安全北京宣言》(2014年)。APEC第22次领导人非正式会议宣言第46条指出：我们欢迎《APEC减少粮食损失和浪费行动计划》《APEC粮食安全商业计划（2014—2020)》《APEC面向2020年粮食安全路线图（2014年版)》和《加强APEC粮食标准和安全确认互通行动计划》；我们呼吁APEC成员努力增进共识，建立开放、包容、互利、多赢、长期的粮食安全伙伴关系。为更好地推动落实和巩固联合国可持续发展议程目标和APEC关于粮食安全宣言、路线图、行动计划成果，增强粮食供应链互通，提高效率，减少产后损失和浪费，畅通贸易渠道，改善粮食体系结构，重点促进低收入群体买得起、安全、营养的粮食，有必要促进APEC增强低收入群体的粮食安全与营养可持续。

## （二）APEC及其粮食安全有关机构正在采取的行动

基于上述情况，APEC及其粮食安全有关机构积极采取行动，呼吁各经济体采取措施和行动，对改善低收入群体粮食安全与营养可持续达成共识。

APEC 粮食安全政策伙伴关系机制（PPFS）于 2015 年 5 月 13—15 日在菲律宾召开了第一次会议，会议成果包括：

第一，确定了 PPFS 2015 年主题是“建设农业与渔业包容性增长，确保粮食安全”，确保所有粮食行业特别是小农户和渔民的收入增长和福利改善。

第二，PPFS 的首要任务是建设、维持和继续 PPFS 相关文件的战略和行动，诸如《APEC 面向 2020 年粮食安全路线图（2014 年版）》《APEC 粮食安全商业计划（2014—2020）》《APEC 粮食减少损失和浪费行动计划》《增强 APEC 粮食标准和安全保证的互通行动计划》。

第三，PPFS 2015 年粮食安全关注的重点领域主要有技术合作、知识分享和能力建设，粮食储藏、供应链和冷链技术方面的合作，减少粮食损失和浪费，贸易合作和便利化，投资和基础设施合作，标准和质量安全保证，政策和规则交流与协调。

PPFS 于 2015 年 10 月 2—3 日在菲律宾召开第二次会议，PPFS 2015 年副主席（中国）回顾了 PPFS 推动各经济体粮食减少损失和浪费开展的活动和取得的成效，呼吁推动落实和巩固 APEC 关于粮食安全宣言、路线图、行动计划成果，呼吁各经济体采取技术和政策创新等措施提高贫困群体和小农户的收入水平，重点促进低收入群体买得起安全、营养的粮食。会议成果包括：

第一，呼吁 PPFS 和 APEC 有关论坛继续实施和督促 APEC 粮食安全路线图，优先关注亚太地区粮食安全高效进展的议题和活动。重申私营部门在粮食安全活动中的重要作用，鼓励包括小农户、微小中型企业和妇女在内的私营部门和其他有关业主主动、有益地参与粮食安全活动（由 PPFS/盘点和面向 2020 年粮食安全路线图工作组提议）。

第二，为了取得可持续发展，鼓励 PPFS 重点推动研究、开发和技术推广，增强小业主和妇女组织合作和活力，保护小业主和妇女的合法权益，减少气候等因素对当前和未来粮食的负面影响，促使他们参与粮食供应和价值链，加强服务和培训，推动自然资源可持续管理和使用，促进可持续生产粮食的消费（由 PPFS/农业和渔业部门的可持续发展工作组提议）。

第三，认识到可持续的粮食安全和营养在低收入群体中的迫切需要，呼吁APEC各经济体推动有关项目，同时高度重视投资和基础设施开发对实现可持续的粮食安全和营养的重要作用和贡献（由PPFS/投资和基础设施开发便利化工作组提议）。

第四，建议PPFS重点鉴别非关税壁垒，探索建立有用的关税清单，推动建立强劲的未来贸易协定框架。注意到全球标准使用与开发的可能性，以及粮食欺诈和防护挑战，促进有关能力建设，减少贸易摩擦，推动粮食贸易透明、流动、可追溯，促进冷链和有效的跨境实践价值链等可持续商业实践的发展，减少粮食损失和浪费，促进亚太地区粮食安全（由PPFS/促进贸易和市场工作组提议）。

APEC 2015年部长级会议2015年11月16—17日在在菲律宾召开，会议通过了《APEC 2015年部长会议联合声明》。该声明强调，加强区域粮食供应的安全，呼吁成员经济体重视投资和基础设施开发对粮食获取的关键作用，支持经济体努力实现可持续的粮食安全和改善低收入群体的营养。

APEC第23次领导人非正式会议于2015年11月18—19日在菲律宾召开，会议发表了APEC第23次领导人非正式会议宣言——《打造包容性经济，建设更美好世界：亚太大家庭愿景》。“领导人宣言”强调，我们认识到包括人口老龄化和城镇化在内的区域流动人口将对区域粮食体系产生深远影响，我们将加强努力改进区域粮食供应的数量和质量安全，通过城市、农村和偏远地区较好的互通、投资和基础设施的便利化，使粮食价值链上减少粮食损失和浪费，增加居民粮食的可获取程度。

## （三）下一步推进行动的提议

要加快研究APEC增强低收入群体粮食安全与营养可持续政策、措施和行动，主要包括：促进粮食安全政策沟通；努力减少粮食损失和浪费；改善粮食质量安全和营养；促进粮食贸易便利化；增强粮食安全伙伴关系的互联互通；改善农民和小企业主的收入和福利。APEC/PPFS中国政府代表兼PPFS 2015年副主席在2015年APEC/PPFS会议、粮食安全与蓝色经济高级别政策对话会议上提出了“增强亚太地区低收入人群的粮食安全和营养可持续性政策研究”的建议。其主要内容包括：

**1. 推动实施 APEC 减少粮食损失和浪费行动计划的进度与重点**

2016 年项目重点包括：一是收集整理相关组织粮食减损活动信息。包括：联合国粮农组织（FAO）、世界粮食计划署（WFP）、国际农业发展基金会（IFAD）、APEC 粮食安全政策伙伴关系机制（PPFS）、APEC 农业技术合作工作组、APEC 食品安全合作论坛合作培训网、APEC 妇女与经济论坛等开展的粮食减损活动。二是开展减少粮食损失创新技术和最佳实践的调查。三是加强在供应链和减少粮食损失方面的公共部门和私营部门的合作伙伴关系。

2017 年项目重点包括：一是研究适合炎热潮湿地区的粮食储存技术、方法与设施。二是研究小农户粮食储存技术、方法与设施。三是研究爱粮节粮政策、技术与设施。

2018 年项目重点包括：一是鼓励各 APEC 经济体私营部门加强能力建设，减少粮食损失。二是研究减少粮食损失和浪费的技术交流和推广。三是完成推动实施 APEC 减少粮食损失和浪费行动计划项目报告。

**2. 促进实施加强亚太经合组织粮食标准和安全确认互通行动计划的进度与重点**

2016 年项目重点：一是交流和研究亚太地区各经济体现行的粮食标准；二是研究促进亚太地区各经济体粮食标准沟通与合作的可行性。

2017 年项目重点：一是交流和研究亚太地区各经济体粮食质量检验检测技术；二是交流和研究亚太地区各经济体粮食质量安全风险管理控制技术和措施。

2018 年项目重点：完成促进加强亚太经合组织粮食标准和安全确认互通行动计划项目报告。

**3. 推动实施亚太经合组织粮食安全商业计划关于促进投资和基础设施建设的进度与重点**

2016 年项目重点：一是收集整理相关组织促进投资粮食活动的信息。

包括：联合国粮农组织（FAO）、世界粮食计划署（WFP）、国际农业发展基金会（IFAD）、APEC 粮食安全政策伙伴关系机制（PPFS）、APEC 农业技术合作工作组、APEC 食品安全合作论坛合作培训网、APEC 农业生物技术高层政策对话、全球农业和营养公开数据库等开展的促进投资粮食活动。二是促进投资粮食最佳实践的调查。三是研究促进投资粮食便利化。

2017 年项目重点：一是收集整理相关组织促进粮食基础设施建设的活动信息。包括：联合国粮农组织（FAO）、世界粮食计划署（WFP）、国际农业发展基金会（IFAD）、APEC 粮食安全政策伙伴关系机制（PPFS）、APEC 农业技术合作工作组、APEC 食品安全合作论坛合作培训网、APEC 农业生物技术高层政策对话、全球农业和营养公开数据库等开展的促进粮食投资活动。二是促进粮食基础设施建设最佳实践的调查。三是研究促进粮食基础设施建设便利化。

2018 年项目重点：一是研究促进投资粮食便利化试点。二是研究促进粮食基础设施建设便利化试点。三是完成推动亚太经合组织粮食安全商业计划关于促进投资和基础设施建设项目报告。

该提议可以通过 APEC 粮食安全政策伙伴关系机制（PPFS）年度工作计划等形式推进实施，特别是通过 PPFS 下设的促进贸易和市场发展工作组、促进投资和基础设施建设工作组来具体推动，各经济体 PPFS 代表及其团队直接参与研究。

（国家粮食局政策法规司　　韩继志）

# 八、我国粮油产品电商营销模式创新

【内容提要】

本文论述了粮食电商发展的五个阶段，介绍了粮食流通领域11个电商模式、粮食加工领域6种电商模式，论述了网上支付手段、移动商务发展趋势、粮食网络金融、“三网融合”+物联网。本文将我国粮油产品电商营销国家政策归纳为：粮食电商促进政策、监管政策、长期发展政策，并对2015年涉粮政策进行了总结。本文还对我国粮油产品电商营销和总体框架进行了论述，包括我国粮食电商产业链和我国粮油产品电商营销总体框架。最后，本文论述了我国粮油产品电商营销模式创新趋势，如规模化、多样化、融合化等13个趋势。

## （一）我国粮油产品电子商务发展过程

第一阶段，1995—2002年：1995年，郑州商品交易所集诚现货网成立，1998年12月开始第一笔粮食网上交易。自1998年以来，通过中华粮网电子商务平台参与网上交易的粮油企业已有3 000多家。

第二阶段，2003—2005年：2003年开始，国家发改委利用国债资金支持重点粮食批发市场信息化建设，2003年中国（衢州）网上粮食市场建立。

第三阶段，2006年：《国家临时存储粮食销售办法》出台，国家有关部门第一次明文许可粮食可以在网上进行流通，安徽等地推出网上粮食交易。

第四阶段，2007—2013年：2007年，国家通过中储粮总公司现货电子交易平台，实现了全年国内小麦市场价格的总体稳定。中储粮总公司网上物资采购平台建立，首次 200 万条塑料编织袋网上采购顺利完成，粮食电子交易平台逐渐成为国家宏观调控的重要载体。

第五阶段，2014 年至今：全国各地粮食批发市场在积极利用电子交易手段开展地方粮油的购销交易活动的同时，一些粮食批发市场电子交易模式不断创新，差异化经营。粮食企业通过建立电子商务平台在网上销售自己的产品；某些贸易商转型的企业通过建立农产品专业电子商务网站提供高端、精品农产品销售等。

## （二）我国粮食电商模式创新

近年来，我国出现的粮食电商有中华粮网、中国网上粮食市场、中国安徽粮食批发市场交易网、中国谷物网、宁波网上粮食市场、台州网上粮食市场、黑龙江中米网、哈尔滨网上粮食交易市场、北京买粮网、京粮点到网、易谷网、易粮网等。

### 1. 粮食流通领域电商模式创新

（1）中华粮网、中国郑州粮食批发市场、河南粮食交易物流市场、易谷网。2015 年，以中华粮网为代表的电子商务服务平台共举办国家临时存储小麦竞价销售交易会 48 场，交易总量 1 368 万吨，共成交 670 万吨，总成交率 49%。郑州粮食批发市场积极开发商品粮场际交易新模式，2014 年成交粮油 100 余万吨，成交金额近 30 亿元。河南省粮食交易物流市场联合相关企业专门经营豆粕现货业务，逐步促进上游企业在电子商务盘中挂单、下游企业通过电子商务买单，从而推进豆粕电子商务的发展。

在 B2B、B2C、OPO 模式日益成熟的基础上，衍生出 O2O 模式、O2O +本地化经营模式，促进了企业线上线下资源的有机融合。

2014 年 8 月 27 日，中粮招商局（深圳）粮食电子交易中心有限公司——易谷网成立。该网站以服务粮食产业链为己任，利用 B2B、O2O 等多种交易模式，搭建起衔接南北产销区、连通国际市场的粮食空中交易平台，利用云计算、物联网等现代信息科技手段，积极打造国内粮食行业信息中心、结算中心、物流中心、定价中心、服务中心、大数据分析中心。

（2）中国网上粮食市场模式。2014 年 8 月 7—8 日，中国网上粮食市场早稻交易会在江西省上饶市举行。当日举行两场网上交易，网上共竞价交易成交 4. 27 万吨粮食，成交额 1. 23 亿元；网下洽谈成交 10. 45 万吨粮食，成交额 3 亿元。

2015 年 8 月 7 日，由江西省、浙江省、福建省和安徽省八市（区）粮食局共同主办的“2015 年中国网上粮食市场早稻交易会”在上饶市举行。当天举行了两场网上竞价投标，共成交早稻 4. 38 万吨，成交金额 1. 31 亿元。此次早稻网上交易会是上饶与衢州等市第 6 次联合举办的交易会。

（3）我买网双品牌运营模式。2014 年我买网完成 B 轮 1 亿美元融资，该笔资金由 IDG 资本领投，赛富基金继 A 轮投资后再次追投。2015 年获得百度、泰康人寿领投的 2. 2 美元融资。2014 年我买网预计销售额在 20 亿元，目前尚未实现盈利。我买网采取“中粮集团”、“我买网”双品牌运营模式，主要经营粮油、食品、水果、蔬菜等，还经营其他产品。

（4）天津粮油商品交易所。2014 年 5 月 9 日，天津粮油商品交易所推出了一种崭新的“OPO”电商模式——“找粮网”。这种模式基于绿色产品库，延伸出“委托买”、“微顾问”、“微行情”、“微金融”等新服务。“委托买”是为中小粮油店及超市量身打造的特色服务，基于“永远免费帮买家找到最具性价比的粮油产品”的原则，通过“找粮网”庞大的产品库及粮油企业大数据平台，将小订单汇集成大订单，提高买家的议价能力，为买家提供精准的交易信息及价值帮助。

（5）在淘宝网上开“吉林大米馆”。2014 年，吉林东福米业、梅河大米公司和柳河国信米业等 8 家企业入驻淘宝“吉林大米馆”。2014 年网上销售小包装大米超过 10 万件，共销售大米 510 吨，销量居全网大米之首。吉林省政府与阿里巴巴签订战略合作协议，合作销售吉林大米。通过参与淘宝“挑食吉林鲜米”等活动，吉林大米一跃升至淘宝大米网页首页，吉林大米“营养、好吃、更安全”的整体形象得到充分展示，品牌影响得到快速提升。在 2014 年 9 月淘宝网组织的 5 省 6 款大米“秋收新米香”促销活动中，吉林大米（东福有机稻花香）劲销 1. 2 万单，名列第一（黑龙江五常大米 5 700 单，排名第二）。

（6）苏州粮食批发交易市场良粮网上线。2015 年 1 月苏州市粮食批发交易市场的良粮网上线，涵盖门户网站、交易管理、电子结算管理、会员体系等相关子系统。该电商系统除了为粮食经营单位提供了储备粮轮换、大宗粮食及农产品采购与销售的交易平台外，还在城乡居民与批发市场之间架起了一座桥梁——当地百姓只要上网点点鼠标，就能浏览良粮网的最新消息，看到经济实惠的产品、优质的品牌产品，选购到自己需要的放心粮油产品。

（7）杂粮电商平台——“饭中有豆”上线。2015 年 8 月 23 日，山西首家杂粮电商平台——“饭中有豆”在忻州市上线，2014 年来，忻州被授予“中国杂粮之都”称号。平台以家庭厨房服务为核心，开通了 PC 端、手机端、微信商城等多种网上入口。其主要服务内容有：“产地直供”、“精品馆”、“团购”、“今日特惠”、“健康饮食”、“供求信息”、“健康论坛”等八个模块，发布特色小米、特色杂粮豆、石磨杂粮纯粉、杂粮面条、土特产、大米、小麦面粉、食用油等八大系列 100 多个品种。“饭中有豆”目前体验店已开通忻府区、保德、代县等三个区域，下一步将开通忻州市其他区域，最终实现全国 1 000 个体验店的目标。

（8）中米网及其中国大米产业联盟。2015 年 7 月 17 日，“2015 年东北稻米产业营销高峰论坛”在黑龙江哈尔滨召开，同期举办了中国电子商务协会东北稻米产业电子商务联盟揭牌仪式。与会专家和近 200 家企业代表围绕如何通过“互联网 + 大米”实现东北大米营销模式升级和“瓶颈”破解进行了深入的探讨，并宣布组建电子商务联盟。

（9）长春市打造“大米白金城”。长春市农产品电子商务交易平台 2014 年正式上线运营，打造与“汽车城”、“电影城”并列的“白金城”（长春松花江大米）。

（10）“左权模式”——“田农宝”网上易货贸易。所谓“左权模式”，就是拿玉米换手机，用高粱换衣服，不出村就能用地头上的庄稼把吃穿用度全部换回家。该模式是由田农宝公司首创的一种“以粮换物”电子商务模式，2015 年左权县被列入国家电子商务进农村示范县后，政府主动抛来了合作的“绣球”，并在山西进行推广。

目前，田农宝公司在左权县已建起一个运营中心及一个上行下行综合仓储中心，建立 10 个乡镇综合服务站以及 150 多个行政村级服务店，初步实现以农产品搬到网上叫卖为轴心，让农民通过田农宝这个交易平台支现金、换农资、换商品、换服务和缴费用。长期以来，在粮食缺少的时候，粮食哗哗都能卖了；在粮食供大于求的时候，市场价格不高，农民就把粮食压在家里。现在有了田农宝，农民卖粮食不愁了。“田农宝”切实解决了卖粮难和支付难的问题，让老百姓足不出户分享网络经济的红利。除了田农宝模式外，田农宝公司还衍生推出了田农购（第三方电子商务交易）、田农通（第三方物流配送）等生态交易系统。

（11）东方粮仓的众筹模式——品牌农产品优质优价。东方粮仓的众筹模式较好地解决了农产品劣币驱逐良币问题。2015 年 7 月，东方粮仓联手民生易贷大胆尝试首次推出“可以吃的理财产品”，即“大米理财”。该次大米理财总额度 500 万元，项目期为 3 个月，项目在民生易贷平台发布融资标的，以东方粮仓在五常市自有园区种植的 2015 年第一批五常有机稻花香二号为交易标的。五常有机稻花香二号是东方粮仓自主研发培育的有机食品，是优质保真的五常大米。项目到期后，由东方粮仓从原产地直接邮递给消费者。该众筹项目在上线短短 5 小时内就完成了 500 万元的销售目标，共有 8 865 个消费家庭参与了该活动。这种全新形式的大米理财在国内尚属首例，首次将“互联网 + 农业 + 金融”有机结合，是对“互联网 + 农业”战略的一次新尝试。

**2. 粮食加工领域电商模式创新**

目前，大多数粮油加工企业主要通过第三方电子商务平台进行产品交易。因为自建电子交易平台需要大批资金，对于绝大多数中小粮油加工企业来说不易成功。

（1）京粮点到网。北京粮食集团于 2011 年投资上线的食品类 B2B 电子商务网站点到网，2014 年“双 11”当天，点到网销售额达 500 多万元。2015 年点到网正式上线运营，主要产品为米面、粮油、食品、酒饮等，打破以往传统商超模式。同时，也促进新产品快速上市，保证新产品的成功率。依托京粮集团的研发能力，点到网推出了众多特色产品，如冷冻面团、特色进口食品等，用微波炉稍微加热即可进食，方便快捷。因为地处北京，网站内部还做了一个专属频道叫作“北京味道”，全面服务北京市民，维护北京市场。除点到网以外，其他线上商城有淘宝商城京粮食品专营店和京粮商务网。

（2）金龙鱼在知名平台上开旗舰店。金龙鱼进军电商起步晚，不是自建平台，而是采用与1号店、易迅、京东商城等合作的方式，目前在几大电商的粮油份额与实体店份额相近。此外，由于豆油等中低端产品进行线上售卖利润薄，金龙鱼主要瞄准中高端产品如橄榄油等。2013年开通了淘宝旗舰店，发挥传统渠道优势，进展比较顺利。但由于供销体系和传统供销体系需要磨合，为了平衡电商和传统渠道的差异，金龙鱼下一步将朝着“定制化”方向发展，对其定制化产品、规模、组合，最终把优惠回馈给消费者。

（3）西安爱菊粮油“电商+店商”O2O模式。2014年9月22日，西安爱菊粮油集团全面启动社区电子商务项目——“电商+店商”O2O模式，依托西安市700多个连锁网点，按照“预约订货、就近取货、验货付款、买退自由”的原则，消费者可以通过网站、手机、预约机和电话订货的方式任意选择爱菊放心产品。订单下达后，客服中心将根据预定时间分两个时间段安排配送。爱菊集团进入电商以爱菊系列米、面、油、主食、豆制品作为核心产品，并以全国各地的名牌副食产品作为补充。

（4）恒大粮油自营平台与第三方平台“双运行”。一是自营平台。2015年4月15日，恒大粮油产品分别在自营平台恒优米App、恒优米官方商城以及京东商城、天猫、我买网等五大电商平台实现全面上线，构建起了传统渠道、商超渠道与电子渠道的立体化的恒大粮油销售体系。二是依托第三方平台。恒大粮油在天猫、京东商城、我买网等第三方电商平台建立旗舰店，起到互为补充、最大化整合资源的重要作用。更重要的是，第三方电商平台的成熟运作模式、丰富的实践经验，对恒大粮油着力打造的自营电子销售服务平台——“恒优米”能够起到积极的借鉴作用。

（5）易粮网——第一家成品粮B2B交易平台。易粮网是在大连粮食批发市场基础上建设的第一家成品粮B2B+O2O交易平台，它将采购方用户与加工厂、仓库三方通过平台连接起来，然后引入农业发展银行，形成第三方结算关系。2015年交易额达到8 665.27万元（见图3-8-1）。

（6）B2B食材配送平台。2015年我国餐饮业年营收超过3万亿元，食材采购规模超过8 000亿元。中小餐厅有诸多痛点，如采购量小无法获得议价权、采购人力支出以及可能发生的灰色收入支出、采购菜品质量无

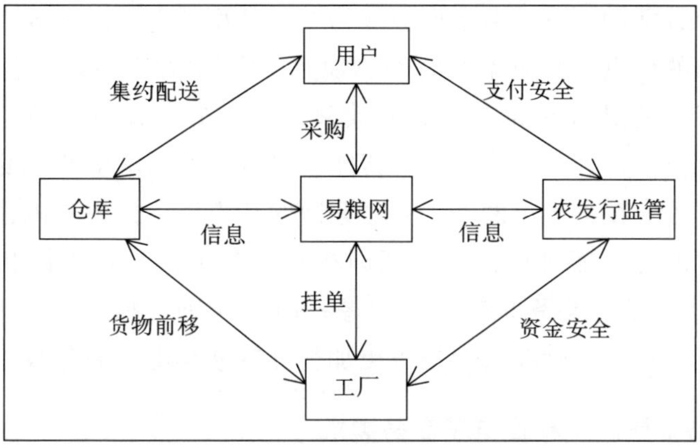


**图 3－8－1　易粮网电子交易流程**

法保证等。针对存在的问题，B2B 食材配送平台能够较好地解决相应的问题。

### 3. 网上支付手段不断升级

粮食作为大宗商品，交易额往往比较大，对资金的安全性、到账速度等的要求比普通商品贸易更高，因此解决大额支付问题是中国粮食电子商务发展不可回避的问题。粮食电子交易市场发展至今，所采取的支付手段经历了从传统的汇票支付到最新的银商通道支付的发展历程。作为电子商务的核心环节，网上支付随着粮食电子商务平台的发展不断优化升级，传统网银这种落后的支付渠道已跟不上现阶段电子商务奔跑速度，银行和第三方支付机构“快捷支付”的方式应运而生，弥补了网银的不足。未来第三方支付将是促进中国网上支付完善和发展的主要途径和必然趋势，成为粮食电子商务发展的助推器。例如，西安爱菊进入电商后，与电信天翼、拉卡拉进行合作，推行“预约订货、就近取货、验货付款、买退自由”的销售模式，消费者可通过网站、手机、预约机和人工预订等方式任意选购爱菊的产品。

### 4. 移动商务成为粮食电子商务发展趋势

随着移动通信技术、互联网技术和信息处理技术的快速发展，人们已经不再满足于传统的电子商务活动，而是更加迫切地希望能够随时随地地进行各种商务活动。移动电子商务作为一种新型的电子商务方式，利用移动无线网络的优点，具有不受时间、地点、空间限制，以及灵活、简单、方便等特点，能显著提高电子商务效率，大大节省客户交易时间。2014 年我国手机用户达到 12. 86 亿户，智能手机成为助力电子商务发展的一个重要因素。各类粮食电子商务平台也紧随时代发展，推出手机客户端、微信公众号等服务，实现粮油资讯实时推送、各类信息自由订制、随时查询。通过利用移动设备的扫描、图像、语音识别、感应、地理化、GPS 等，将逐步实现移动端在线交易等更加智能的移动电子商务服务。

### 5. 网络金融满足粮食电子商务需求

网络融资模式是利用互联网技术、电子商务与银行业务管理系统结合的产物，目前已经成为我国电子商务行业发展的标志性业务，对我国电子商务业务尤其是 B2B 大宗商品网上交易的支撑作用明显，有效解决了长期以来粮食市场电子交易融资“瓶颈”问题，助力粮食电子商务快速发展。

2015 年 1 月 9 日，中华粮网完成了粮食行业的第一笔网络融资贷款服务，授信总额度为 3 000 万元，首次投放金额 500 万元，实现了全国粮食行业网络银行业务的新突破。

2015 年，地大物博公司全面推出农产品交易 + 互联网金融扶持计划，向农产品的供应商、分销商提供全方位的交易担保、保险、授信、支付结算、理财、投融资等金融增值服务，9 月份正式上线技术领先、功能强大便捷的农产品 B2B 大型在线交易服务平台，为交易双方提供全方位的线上线下综合保障服务，创新我国农产品大流通的新模式。

### 6. “三网融合” + 物联网成为粮食电商行业发展新趋势

随着“三网融合” + 物联网，手机下单、手机销售、手机采购、手机管理、手机发布、手机交流、手机寻找物流都将会实现，并成为一种趋势。智能粮食预订单、智能粮食交易、智能粮食市场、智能粮食支付、智能粮食通关、智能粮食物流、智能粮食仓配一体化、智能快递都将会成为发展趋势。随着三网融合 + 物联网，移动商务将在新一代电商中发挥越来越大的作用，微博、微信、微店“三微”营销，也会促进粮食电商进入一个精准营销新阶段。

目前，一些粮油加工企业广泛开展了微信营销，开设微信公众号，将其作为一个展示公司形象与品牌的平台，除了向消费者推送一些了解大米品质的文章外，还适时推广公司的新品。

未来农产品电商发展趋势将由平台型主导，因其商品品类多、交易规模大、服务能力较强，如结算、物流、标准化、信用等，平台越强，其获得的交易能力越强。未来粮食行业 B2B 的平台将率先“跑起来”。

另外，还可以从不同的角度创新交易模式，如从平台、驱动、市场体系、B2B、粮食电商、淘宝村镇县、生鲜等角度创新粮食网上交易模式。

## （三）我国粮油产品电商营销国家政策

### 1. 促进、监管、长期发展政策

（1）促进政策。2014 年、2015 年、2016 年中央连续发布的 1 号文件都把农产品电子商务作为重要内容。相关文件包括《关于促进内贸流通健康发展的若干意见》《物流业发展中长期规划（2014—2020 年）》《关于开展电子商务进农村综合示范的通知》《关于进一步加强农产品市场体系建设的指导意见》《关于促进商贸物流发展的实施意见》《关于大力发展电子商务加快培育经济新动力的意见》《关于建立百家百亿市场联系制度的通知》《“互联网” +流通指导意见》《“互联网 +” 行动指导意见》等，明确了 11 项重点行动等。

（2）监管政策。相关文件包括《关于清理整顿各类交易场所　切实防范金融风险的决定》《关于清理整顿各类交易场所的实施意见》《商品现货市场交易特别规定（试行）》《关于网络交易管理办法》《关于整治用网络平台擅自售彩行为通知》，国家发改委《关于〈禁止价格欺诈行为的规定〉有关条款解释的通知》，国务院办公厅发布的《关于运用大数据加强对市场主体服务和监管的意见》等。

（3）长期发展政策。相关文件包括《关于加快生态文明建设的指导意见》《社会信用体系建设规划纲要（2014—2020 年）》等，对促进我国粮食电子商务生态链建设、诚信体系建设具有重要的指导意义。

### 2. 2015年以来的涉粮电商政策

（1）《关于开展电子商务进农村综合示范的通知》。2014年7月24日，财政部、商务部发布《关于开展电子商务进农村综合示范的通知》，在河北、黑龙江、江苏、安徽、江西、河南、湖北、四川进行综合示范，即在8省56个县开展电子商务进农村综合示范，建立适应农村电子商务发展需要的支撑服务体系，发展与电子交易、网上购物、在线支付协同发展的物流配送服务。2015年发展到26个省市的200个综合试点县，投入财政资金总额37亿元。2014—2015年商务部、财政部联合在256个县开展农村电商综合示范活动，并将这一活动延续到2016年。

（2）连续三个中央1号文件都强调农产品电子商务。

2014年中共中央、国务院颁布了《关于全面深化农村改革 加快推进农业现代化的若干意见》，其中指出：启动农村流通设施和农产品批发市场信息化提升工程，加强农产品电子商务平台建设。

2015年2月1日，中共中央、国务院颁布了《关于加大改革创新力度 加快农业现代化建设的若干意见》，其中指出：创新农产品流通方式，“发展农产品期货交易，开发农产品期货交易新品种。支持电商、物流、商贸、金融等企业参与涉农电子商务平台建设。开展电子商务进农村综合示范”。

2016年中共中央、国务院颁布《关于落实发展新理念 加快农业现代化 实现全面小康目标的若干意见》，其中指出：促进农村电子商务加快发展，形成线上线下融合、农产品进城与农资和消费品下乡双向流通格局。加快实现行政村宽带全覆盖，创新电信普遍服务补偿机制，推进农村互联网提速降费。加强商贸流通、供销、邮政等系统物流服务网络和设施建设与衔接，加快完善县乡村物流体系。实施“快递下乡”工程。鼓励大型电商平台企业开展农村电商服务，支持地方和行业健全农村电商服务体系。建立健全适应农村电商发展的农产品质量分级、采后处理、包装配送等标准体系。深入开展电子商务进农村综合示范。加大信息进村入户试点力度。

（3）网上卖食品先领证，无证经营最高罚3万元。2015年8月，国家食药监总局发布《网络食品经营监督管理办法（征求意见稿）》。根据这份意见稿，网络食品经营者须取得食品经营许可或者备案凭证，这意味着粮食生产者和经营者在网上、微信圈卖食品也要办证备案。

（4）国家重视“粮油网络经济”。2016 年 1 月，全国粮食流通工作会议在京召开。会议研究粮食行业“十三五”发展思路，部署 2016 年粮食流通重点工作。会议提出，2016 年突出抓好粮食产业经济发展，加快“互联网＋粮食”电商平台建设，打造“粮油网络经济”。

## （四）我国粮油产品电商营销产业链和总体框架

### 1. 我国粮食电商产业链

粮食电商产业链主要分为产前、产中和产后。产前包括农资产销。农资生产主要是指 B2C、采购 O2O、代购云农场等；农资流通主要有种苗、农药、化肥、饲料、兽药、农机的流通等。产中分为粮食生产和粮食加工。粮食生产是指种植及服务业等；粮食加工包括粮食加工品和深加工品。产后包括最终产品流通、零售终端销售、消费者。最终产品流通是指物流服务；零售终端销售是指贸易商，主要包括 B2B、批发、B2C、零售、直供淘宝、顺丰优选等等（见图 3－8－2）。

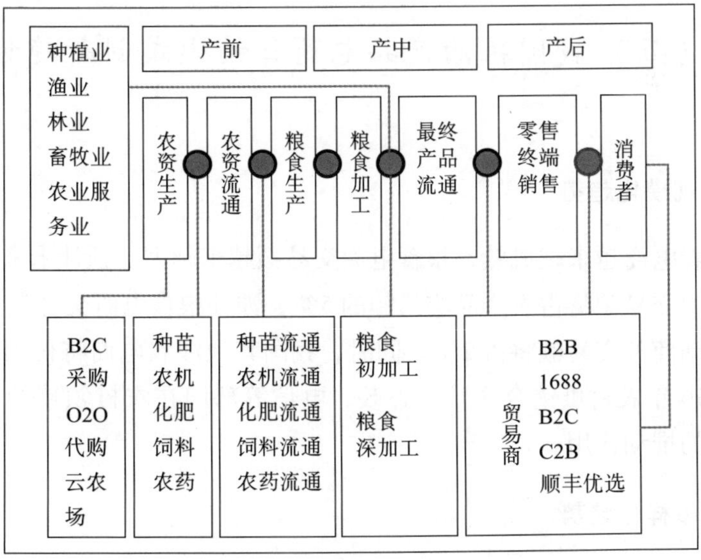


**图 3－8－2　我国粮食电商产业链**

**2. 我国粮油产品电商营销总体框架**

我国粮油产品电商营销总体框架主要包括借用、引进、培育，三者之间相互关联。借用是指借用阿里巴巴、京东等一些有特色的大平台；引进是指跨境电商和移动电商等都可以引进一些特色平台；培育主要是指培育社区商务和电商园区等一些本地电商（见图3－8－3）。

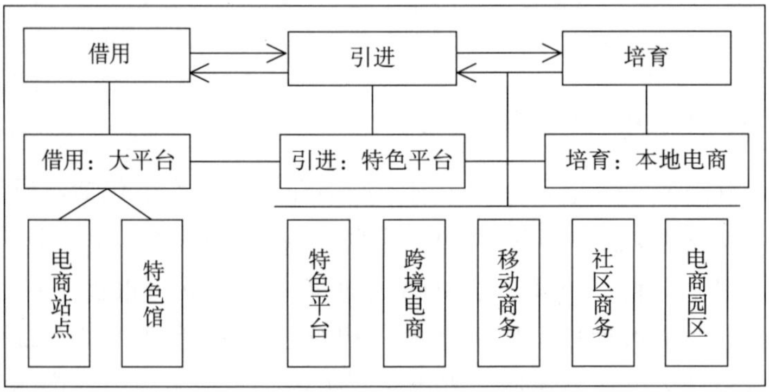


**图3－8－3　我国粮油产品电商营销总体框架**

## （五）我国粮油产品电商营销模式创新趋势

**1. 规模化趋势**

随着电商越来越成熟，粮食电商交易额越来越大。预计未来5年我国粮食电商交易额将占农产品交易额的5%，涉外粮食电商交易额将占1%，粮食移动商务交易额将占2%。同时，我国其他涉农电商将得到较大的发展，2016年农村供销合作社、邮政、电信等部门在农村领域的发力将起到重要的推动作用。

**2. 多样化趋势**

从平台角度来看，粮食电商模式主要有五种：政府粮食网站、粮食期货市场网络交易平台、大宗粮食商品电子交易平台、粮食零售网站等。

从驱动的角度看粮食电商模式，主要有供应链驱动型、营销驱动型、产品驱动型、渠道驱动型、服务驱动型五大类型。

从生鲜角度看网上供应链模式，生鲜电商从最基本的 B2C 模式，后来发展衍生出来 F2C（农场直供）模式、C2B（消费者定制）模式、C2F（订单农业）模式、O2O 模式和 CSA（社区支持农业）模式等。从采用的网络工具而言，生鲜电商常用模式有五种：自建电商平台、借助公共平台、委托电商平台代办、合作共建平台（O2O 模式）、“三微营销”（如微博、微信、微店营销）。

从 B2B 角度而言，出现了许多新型的农产品电商模式，如中华粮网、沁坤农产品、B2B 食材网、美菜、链农、大厨网、小农女、优配良品、菜筐子、饭店联盟、一亩田、中国惠农网等。2015 年 B2B 农产品大宗商品交易平台达 470 个，交易额突破 20 万亿元。

如果从专业电商的角度来看，粮食电商发展模式也是多样的，如中华粮网、中国网上粮食市场、中国安徽粮食批发市场交易网、中国谷物网、宁波网上粮食市场、台州网上粮食市场、黑龙江中米网、哈尔滨网上粮食交易市场、北京买粮网、京粮点到网，应引起关注。

从淘宝的角度看农产品电商模式，2014 年主要有淘宝村模式、特色馆模式、O2O 模式三种形式。2015 年底全国出现 780 个淘宝村、71 个淘宝镇，到 2016 年又出现了 300 个亿元淘宝县。以上案例可分为 14 种模式等等。

成功的模式主要表现为六个方面的特征，即有效性、整体性、差异性、适应性、可持续性、生命周期性。

### 3. 融合化趋势

O2O 融合是发展趋势，即网上与网下相互融合，形成一个有机的整体，真正解决现在存在的网上渠道资源与网下渠道资源相互冲突、相互矛盾的问题。推进粮食电商模式创新，如平台模式、自营模式、平台 + 自营模式多样化发展，引导“平台 + 自营模式”主导地位，引导粮食电商发展的趋势。

#### 4. 标准化趋势

随着电商越来越成熟，粮食全产业链过程工厂化，粮食电子商务越来越规范，越来越标准，粮食“三品一标”产品占整个电商的比例将超过80%。

#### 5. 多功能趋势

随着电商越来越成熟，粮食交易平台的功能越来越多样化，交易功能、展示功能、信息功能、外向型功能、上下延伸的供应链功能、融资功能等将更多地表现出来，经过5~10年的努力，冷链物流效应将得到充分发挥：一是成本降低，二是效率提高，三是品质提高，四是给“新农人”带来新的利润增长点。

#### 6. 全渠道趋势

随着电商越来越成熟，网上与网下由相互对立到相互融合，网上渠道更加多样，这里指的是平台、自营、平台+自营相融合的多种模式创新。网下渠道是指社区店、便利店网络及其电子菜箱、智能菜柜等新型业态涌现。

#### 7. 体系化趋势

网上期货交易、大宗商品交易、各类批发交易、各类零售交易、各类易货贸易等多种方式、多种市场逐渐体系化，期货市场与现货市场形成相互联系、相互融合的关系，而不是“板块化”关系，这样就形成了我国粮食大市场。

#### 8. 国际化趋势

随着我国经济的一体化，两个市场和两种资源的充分利用，2015年我国粮食进口超过1.2亿吨（其中大豆8 169万吨）。随着电子商务发展，粮食跨境电子交易将发挥越来越重要的作用，商务部在互联网+流通行动计划中提出在国外建设100个海外仓。

### 9. 智能化趋势

随着“三网融合” + 物联网 + 大数据 + 云计算等新技术的应用，移动商务在新一代电商中发挥越来越大的作用，微博、微信、微店“三微”营销促进农产品电商进入一个精准营销新阶段，智能交易、智能支付、智能物流、智能配送、智能仓储等新的信息技术革命将给我们带来新的机遇和挑战。

### 10. 区域化趋势

粮食电商是电子商务的皇冠，生鲜、油脂、油料电商是皇冠的皇冠。随着经济和社会的发展，生鲜农产品电商的区域化特征将越来越明显。随着区域化电商的发展，也使其越来越有效率。粮油电商交易中，有的通过平台建设进行专业化分工，基地只负责产品生产环节，电商只管发展用户和服务用户，物流外包给专业生鲜物流企业，可以同时解决标准化、产品安全性、冷链物流等三大难题，其业务也越来越区域化。

### 11. 社区化趋势

随着城镇化和粮食农业现代化加速推进，社区电商将扮演重要的角色，粮食的性价比会很高，比以往通过传统渠道购买的还要高，以社区为主力的移动端涉农电子商务占主体，产地影响力降低，粮油电商物流冷链等问题可以得到很好的解决。

### 12. 品牌化趋势

我国粮食生产、流通、消费的品牌化趋势十分明显，五常大米现象应引起人们的高度重视，一方面需要保护“三品一标”粮食产品的品牌效应，另一方面要保护我国优质的粮食产品卖出好的价钱来，粮食既要“种得好”，更要“卖得好”。

### 13. 法制化趋势

2016 年 6 月《中华人民共和国电子商务法》将出台，与之相适应，我国电子商务法律、法规、标准体系将不断完善。同时，国家工商总局、质监总局、商务部、农业部、海关、税收、银行等金融部门加强电商管理，相继出台了《流通领域商品质量监督管理办法》《网络销售商品质量抽检有关规范》《电商企业落实新〈消费者权益保护法〉7 日无理由退货指引》等，将会提高消费者维权规范化、程序化、法治化。

（北京工商大学经济学院　　洪涛）

# 九、现行粮食政策存在的突出问题及政策建议①

【内容提要】

过去的2015年，中国粮食产量达到了12年来的最高水平，世界粮食价格波动比较稳定，全球食物不足的人口数量已经由20世纪初的10亿人下降了1.6亿人，世界范围内的粮食问题正在不断好转。中国方面，农业主体仍然是生计型农业，即“绝大多数农民还是要依靠种地来吃饭”。按照最新的统计结果，农业经营收入仍然占到农民家庭收入的39.4%，这一比例在粮食主产区会更高一些。2008年以后，中国城镇化进程加快，给粮食生产带来了一系列问题，对粮食生产效率提出了更高的要求。与此同时，中国已经由一个粮食净出口国转变为全球最大的粮食净进口国。

在国内外环境的深刻变化中，党中央于2013年中央农村工作会议上明确做出了实施“以我为主、立足国内、确保产能、适度进口、科技支撑”的国家粮食安全新战略的重要决定。作为2014年国家社科基金重大项目“基于改革视角下国家粮食安全问题研究”的阶段性成果，本文提出为构筑更加稳固牢靠的国家粮食安全保障体系，实现新常态下的国家粮食安全，迫切需要加快我国现行粮食政策的调整步伐。

① 2014年国家社会科学基金重大项目《基于改革视角下国家粮食安全问题研究》，编号：14ZDAZ041；中国农业科学院科技创新工程资助项目，编号：ASTIP－IAED02。

## （一）中国粮食“十二连增”背后呈现四大隐患

### 1. 中国粮食的供给将长期处于结构性紧平衡

根据国家统计局最新发布的粮食产量公告，2015 年我国粮食总产量达到 6.21 亿吨，比 2014 年增加 1 440.8 万吨，增长率为 2.4%。其中，谷物总产量 5.72 亿吨，比 2014 年增加 1 484.6 万吨，增长 2.7%。至此，我国的粮食产量已经连续 12 年实现增长。但是，2015 年城乡居民口粮消费总量估计大约为 2 亿吨，饲料用粮 3 亿吨，再加上种子用粮、工业用粮和生产加工流通等环节不可避免的损耗，中国粮食消费和消耗总量可能接近 6 亿吨。与此同时，考虑到城镇化导致中国每年城市新增人口超过 1 000 万人，“总体基本平衡、结构性紧缺”将成为中国粮食供给的常态。

### 2. 中国粮食价格保持高位运行

2004 年以后，我国启动主要粮食作物托市收购政策，释放价格托底信号，成为粮价上涨的重要支撑，并导致“政策市场”不断扩大，市场调节空间相对萎缩。2008 年世界金融危机之后，随着国际粮价回落，国内外粮价倒挂明显。2015 年三大主要谷物（玉米、小麦、水稻）进口完税价格比国内价格低 300 ~ 500 元/吨，以小麦为首的谷物进口量大幅增加。考虑到我国作为全球最大的粮食消费国，谷物消费量是国际谷物贸易量的 2 倍，如果进口增长加速常态化，可能使我国丧失粮食市场话语权，陷入进口时国际粮价暴涨、丰收时国际粮价暴跌的被动局面，进一步带来政治、外交、贸易风险。

### 3. 中国粮食持续增产的动力不足

过去的十多年中，我国粮食增产主要得益于单产水平的提高，而维系其间的却是极其粗放的发展手段，即过度的地力开发与化肥、农药施用。目前，我国土壤有机物质含量水平较建国初期明显下降，近四成耕地出现不同程度的退化；平均每公顷土地的化肥使用量约为 480 千克，是世界平均水平的4.1倍，农药利用率只达到30%，未被充分吸收的化肥、农药至少使10%的耕地受到污染，我国粮食生产可持续发展的生态与环境基础受到了严重破坏。

#### 4. 转基因主粮商业化仍然遥遥无期

面对人多地少的资源性约束，2008年，转基因作为我国农业领域的唯一项目，和大型飞机一起，进入了16个中长期重大科技专项。这个重大专项计划在15年内投入240亿元，是有史以来投入资金最多的农业科技项目。目前，我国转基因水稻和玉米种子的研发技术已经处于国际领先水平，然而有关转基因食品的争论却使中国政府面临着两难困境。2015年的中央1号文件并未提到推进培育转基因新品种及促进产业化，只是强调了加强农业转基因生物技术研究和安全管理。可见，在转基因作物已经大量进入我国食用油和饲料消费链的事实前提下，这一可能成为保障我国粮食生产与生态安全的现代技术将被继续搁置。

### （二）中国粮食政策体系产生“两大”困局

目前，“四取消”、“四补贴”、“一支持”、“一保险”以及“一奖励”构成了中国粮食政策体系的主要内容，但在支持方式、补贴标准、执行成本等方面均存在着一些问题，导致出现“最低收购价格刚性化发展”与“粮食生产区域分工制度危机”两大突出矛盾。

#### 1. 最低收购价格刚性化发展

2004年，为了应对国内粮食市场的价格波动，保障粮食生产积极性，中国开始对水稻和小麦等粮食作物实行最低收购价；2008年，又开始对玉米和大豆开展临时收储。2013年中央财政粮油事务支出已超过900亿元，主要用于提高粮食最低收购价补贴利息和储备粮油包干费标准等，每生产一斤粮食，财政就要补贴0.08元。为弥补成本上升，国内粮食支持价格至少维持每年6%～8%的增幅。同时，联合国粮农组织、世界银行预计未来10年国际粮价呈“稳中偏弱”走势，预计未来10年国际粮价涨幅将低于国内 4 ~ 5 个百分点，届时将会有更多财政支出用于粮食价格支持。目前，最低收购价政策呈现刚性化趋向，推动国内粮食市场价格逐年上升，并将成本向产业链下游传导，不仅无法形成市场价格机制，还造成了财政负担和仓储压力，更不利于农业生产经营方式转型和技术进步。

**2. 粮食生产区域分工的制度危机**

2001 年我国粮食流通体制改革以后，全国被正式划分为 13 个粮食主产区、7 个主销区和 11 个基本平衡区，由粮食主产区承担保障国家粮食生产和安全的责任。然而，随着土地、劳动力和农资价格的不断上涨，各粮食主产区逐步陷入“粮食大省、经济弱省、财政穷省”的窘况。近 10 年以来，粮食主产区人均财政收入 6 136 元，仅相当于全国平均水平的 80%。随着种粮收益持续下降，从事种粮的农民中青壮年越来越少，且年龄多在 50 岁以上。有相当多的耕地，由于种粮不如打工赚钱而被抛荒。13 个主产区中，只剩 5 个有稳定的商品粮可输出（黑龙江、吉林、内蒙古、河南、安徽），主产区商品粮输出省份的减少将使粮食生产进入徘徊期的可能性越来越大。

此外，粮食主产区的地理集聚效应在带来规模效益的同时，区域分布和品种结构矛盾导致的粮食安全隐患也日益突出，已经成为国家粮食安全的主要威胁。从区域分布上看，13 个主产省粮食产量占比为 76%，北方 7 个省产量占主产区的比重达到 61%；从品种结构上看，单品种粮食集中趋势更加明显，其中，小麦集中在黄淮海地区，籼稻集中在长江流域，粳稻集中在东北和江苏，玉米集中在东北和冀鲁豫；从仓储与流通上看，目前主产区和主销区粮食库存分别占全国的 75% 和 9%，而消费量分别占 62% 和 17%，由于库存集中，粮食长距离跨区域流通量较大，每年省际间粮食净调入量达 1 600 多亿千克，一旦粮食主产区发生自然灾害或粮食运输受阻，这种隐患将发展成阶段性粮食短缺，对我国社会稳定和经济发展的危害难以预料。

## （三）中国粮食政策体系调整的政策建议

### 1. “按需生产、强化储备、高效流通、节约消费”应成为制定粮食新政的重要理念

粮食消费受到人口年龄结构、职业结构以及城乡划分的显著影响。随着中国人口平均热量需求的下降，可以通过调节粮食供给丰裕度、价格、消费习惯等，改变粮食消费弹性，使粮食消费量增速低于人口增速，以减轻粮食供需压力。考虑到粮食生产丰歉交替的波动性，应进一步强化粮食储备的重要性，平衡波谷的阶段性减产与波峰的连续丰收；并挖掘流通环节的粮食安全保障潜力，实施粮食收储供应安全保障工程，以此改变目前粮食的“掠夺式”生产与“漫灌式”流通，减少从田间到餐桌等各环节的浪费，更好地适应居民食物消费结构升级和满足人们生活水平提高的需要。

### 2. 进一步完善粮食的价格形成机制，逐步建立目标价格制度，发挥价格机制的市场调节作用

从欧美国家的农业支持政策演变逻辑来看，目标价格并不直接影响农产品市场，因而更加符合市场经济的基本要求，有利于农产品市场价格机制的形成，符合我国粮食政策调整的基本方向。应尽快完善粮食生产经营单位的基础数据调查，建立粮食市场价格监测体系和公共信息服务平台；逐步形成粮食的市场价格、目标价格和最低保护价格“三元”价格体系，开展粮食生产主体营销贷款试点，并做好时段性过剩（不足）的应急措施；同时，利用粮食期货市场进行风险管理，应对实行目标价格后市场波动的风险。

### 3. 探索可持续的粮食生产方式，走自主研发的技术产业化之路

开展农业资源休养生息试点，抓紧编制粮食主产区生态环境突出问题治理的总体规划，加快中低产田的改造步伐，并通过土壤改良、培肥地

力、耕地修复，努力提高土地产出率和资源利用率；加快高产、抗逆、优质的粮食突破性新品种的选育应用与新技术的集成创新推广，走依靠科技进步提高单产的内涵式发展道路；根据不同区域的季节性降水特点，合理调整粮食种植结构，按照“压劣扩优、压夏扩秋”的思路，再结合相应的旱作技术，把旱作农业的潜力充分挖掘出来，打造我国粮食生产新的增长极。除此以外，要将建立本土转基因农业产业化体系纳入现代农业发展规划，积极引导社会客观认识转基因技术及其发展趋势，加快转基因品种审定标准的出台，帮助现代种业公司恢复转基因技术自主研发的活力，争取缩小与跨国公司的差距。

#### 4. 保障国家粮食安全既要注重总量平衡，更要注重区域和品种平衡

实现总量平衡的主要途径是粮食生产，调节总量平衡的主要手段是储备和进出口，实现区域性、结构性、阶段性供求平衡的主要方式是顺畅流通。在粮食收储技术上，要继续推进“小型铁皮粮仓”科学储粮专项工作，加大科技投入，通过采纳烘干、机械通风等先进方式，改善粮食存储条件，减少仓储与运输损耗，逐步实现粮食储备由粮食主产区向主销区转移，加强粮食主产区与主销区的对口协作。

#### 5. 重新构建综合性粮食安全责任体系

保障我国的粮食安全，不能仅仅强调中央政府和主产区的责任，而应重构粮食安全的责任分担体系，尤其是主销区的生产责任。研究引入粮食作物碳汇功能的农业生态补偿机制，加大对粮食主产区的补贴与支持力度，加快主产区储备与流通基础设施建设，完善主销区的粮食应急保障机制，通过体制机制创新来挖掘生产潜力。同时，加快构建新型农业经营体系，促进粮食的适度规模经营，大力发展农业社会化服务组织，降低种粮成本，扩大农业保险的品种和覆盖面，要积极发展深加工，提高粮食产业的增值效益。

（中国农业科学院　　蒋和平　詹琳）

# 十、走中国特色规模化道路 提高中国农产品竞争力

【内容提要】

中国粮食产量“十二连增”与谷物大量进口形成巨大反差，其原因主要是国内外存在的较大的价差。价差形成受国内粮食价格政策和汇率影响较大，但更为麻烦的是，中国农产品生产成本在快速上升，中国农产品生产成本已全面显著高于主要农产品出口国。近些年中国人工成本和土地成本的快速上涨是导致农产品生产成本快速上涨的主要原因。交通等基础设施的快速发展使农民外出务工更加方便，而通信和互联网等的发展则有效改变了劳动力市场信息不对称，加剧了农业生产机会成本的快速上升。在劳动力机会成本快速上升的背景下，机械化程度没有跟上，造成农产品人工成本的快速增加。作为土地成本上升的主要外部因素，国家的各种补贴和支持政策使种地利润较好，推动了土地租金上涨。

坚定推进粮食市场化改革，正确引导土地规模化，严格执行土地用途管制，可有效控制土地成本上涨。提高农业生产的机械化水平是有效降低农产品生产成本，提高竞争力的有效举措。土地流转集中不是农业生产规模化的必要条件。大力推动农机社会化服务是中国全面实现农业机械化较为现实和有效的手段，是符合小农经济特征的、具有中国特色的规模化道路。

2003 年以来，中国粮食生产实现“十二连增”，粮食总产量从 4.3 亿吨增长到 2015 年的 6.2 亿吨，稻谷、小麦、玉米三大谷物的增长贡献率分别达到 25%、23% 和 57%。与此同时，2009—2011 年，小麦、玉米、

大米相继变为净进口；2003—2015年，谷物进口量从209万吨增至3 271万吨。谷物的大量进口与国内以三大主粮为主的粮食增产形成巨大反差。以玉米为例，目前国内的饲用玉米需求大量被进口玉米以及玉米酒糟、大麦、高粱等玉米替代品所替代，国产玉米大量进入仓库，库存持续高位。由此，在造成粮食资源闲置的同时，政府收购保管这部分粮食也付出了巨大的成本，导致了不必要的资源浪费。

谷物进口有结构性短缺的因素，比如强筋小麦和弱筋小麦，但更主要还是价差因素。目前，配额内大米的国内外价差接近800元/吨，配额内小麦的国内外价差接近200元/吨，配额内玉米的国内外价差超过600元/吨。

国内外农产品的巨大价差受国内粮食价格政策和汇率影响较大，但更为麻烦的是，中国农产品的生产成本也在快速上升，如果不能有效遏制生产成本上涨或降低生产成本高企问题，未来较大规模的非供求因素进口将不可避免。本文通过比较国内外农产品生产成本，分析影响农产品成本的各要素，发现成本增加主要是劳动力成本和土地成本增加所致，进而提出走中国特色规模化道路、提升中国农产品竞争力的建议。

## （一）主要农产品国内外生产成本比较

基于国内外各农产品数据的可获取性，对小麦、玉米、大豆、棉花等四种主要农产品国内外生产成本进行比较，可以发现，中国农产品在生产成本上明显处于劣势。2014年，小麦、玉米、大豆和棉花的单吨生产成本比主要出口国分别高出300元、900元、2 400元和9 000元以上（见表3－10－1）。

**表3－10－1　中国、美国、巴西主要农产品生产成本比较**　单位：元/吨

| | 中国 | 美国 | 巴西 |
|---|---|---|---|
| 小麦 | 2 255 | 1 926 | — |
| 玉米 | 2 189 | 980 | 1 261 |
| 大豆 | 4 647 | 2 245 | 1 693 |
| 棉花 | 23 232 | 14 061 | — |

资料来源：国家发改委：《全国农产品成本收益资料汇编》，中国统计出版社出版；巴西国家商品供应公司（CONAB）。

单产水平对农产品的生产成本有一定影响，美国大豆、玉米单产水平高于中国，每公顷分别高出 1 吨和 3.2 吨，而小麦、棉花低于中国，每公顷分别低出 3.9 吨和 0.7 吨（见图 3－10－1）。因此，如果剔除掉单产水平的影响，中国大豆和玉米的生产成本依然高于美国，而小麦和棉花的生产成本与美国的差距更大，下文仍以元/吨进行分析。

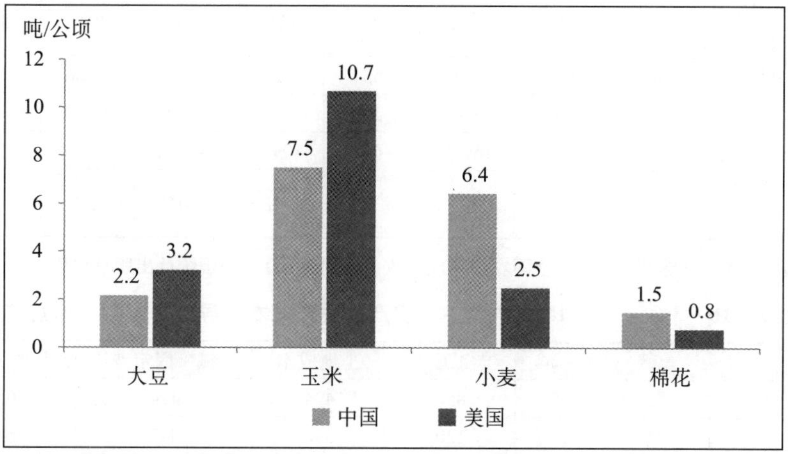


资料来源：国家发改委：《全国农产品成本收益资料汇编》，中国统计出版社出版。

说明：此数据为成本收益资料中计算时采用的单产，数据与根据总产量和面积计算出来的单产有差异。

**图 3－10－1　2014 年中美主要农作物单产比较**

对土地和人工等生产成本进一步分析可以发现，2014 年同 2003 年相比，中国小麦、玉米、大豆、棉花等四种农产品的土地成本上涨了 1～2 倍，同期的美国土地成本也有所上涨，但上涨幅度相对较小，仅为 30% 左右。中国人工成本同样上涨了 1～2 倍，而同期美国人工成本则呈下降趋势，下降幅度约为 20%～40%（见表 3－10－2）。在土地成本对中、美两国小麦、玉米、大豆和棉花四种农产品总成本差异的贡献分别达到了 8%、17%、41%、11%，人工成本对差异贡献更是分别达到了 222%、79%、59%、147%（见表 3－10－3）。因此，可以得出结论，近些年中国人工成本和土地成本的快速上涨是导致农产品生产总成本高企，同主要出口国相比成本明显处于劣势的主要原因。

**表3-10-2　　中美主要农产品土地和人工成本变化**　　单位：元/吨

| | | 小麦 | | 玉米 | | 大豆 | | 棉花 | |
|---|---|---|---|---|---|---|---|---|---|
| | | 中国 | 美国 | 中国 | 美国 | 中国 | 美国 | 中国 | 美国 |
| 土地成本 | 2003年 | 202 | 299 | 136 | 195 | 474 | 703 | 1 222 | 1 295 |
| | 2014年 | 424 | 398 | 449 | 250 | 1 725 | 748 | 2 803 | 1 767 |
| | 涨　幅 | 110% | 33% | 230% | 28% | 264% | 6% | 129% | 36% |
| | 年均复合增长率 | 7% | 3% | 11% | 2% | 12% | 1% | 8% | 3% |
| 人工成本 | 2003年 | 403 | 149 | 353 | 65 | 722 | 155 | 4 536 | 1 237 |
| | 2014年 | 852 | 120 | 950 | 39 | 1 509 | 100 | 14 630 | 882 |
| | 涨　幅 | 111% | -19% | 169% | -40% | 109% | -35% | 217% | -29% |
| | 年均复合增长率 | 7% | -2% | 9% | -5% | 7% | -4% | 11% | -3% |

资料来源：国家发改委：《全国农产品成本收益资料汇编》，中国统计出版社出版。

**表3-10-3　　2014年中美主要农产品生产成本差异**　　单位：元/吨

| | | 总成本 | 人工成本 | 土地成本 | 机械+固定费用 | 其他成本 |
|---|---|---|---|---|---|---|
| 小麦 | 中　国 | 2 255 | 852 | 424 | 414 | 565 |
| | 美　国 | 1 926 | 120 | 398 | 947 | 461 |
| | 中美差异(1) | 329 | 732 | 26 | -533 | 104 |
| | 对差异贡献(2) | — | 222% | 8% | -162% | 32% |
| 玉米 | 中　国 | 2 129 | 950 | 449 | 295 | 435 |
| | 美　国 | 980 | 39 | 250 | 292 | 399 |
| | 中美差异 | 1 149 | 911 | 199 | 3 | 36 |
| | 对差异贡献 | — | 79% | 17% | 0.2% | 3% |
| 大豆 | 中　国 | 4 647 | 1 509 | 1 725 | 694 | 719 |
| | 美　国 | 2 245 | 100 | 748 | 807 | 590 |
| | 中美差异 | 2 402 | 1 409 | 977 | -113 | 129 |
| | 对差异贡献 | — | 59% | 41% | -5% | 5% |
| 棉花 | 中　国 | 23 232 | 14 360 | 2 803 | 2 197 | 3 872 |
| | 美　国 | 14 061 | 882 | 1 767 | 6 072 | 5 340 |
| | 中美差异 | 9 171 | 13 478 | 1 036 | -3 875 | -1 468 |
| | 对差异贡献 | — | 147% | 11% | -42% | -16% |

资料来源：国家发改委：《全国农产品成本收益资料汇编》，中国统计出版社出版。

说明：

（1）中美差异即用中国的生产成本-美国的生产成本。

（2）对差异的贡献即用相应项的成本差异/总成本差异。

## （二）中国人工成本和土地成本快速上涨的原因

### 1. 人工成本上涨原因分析

高速公路、高铁等交通基础设施的快速发展极大改变了农村出行不便的状况，使农民外出务工日趋便利，许多农村适龄劳动人口选择外出打工就业；通信和互联网的蓬勃发展则有效改变了劳动力市场雇佣双方信息不对称的状况，农民在家务农的机会成本大幅提高。近年来，农民工月平均收入显著提高，意味着务农的机会成本也显著提高（见图3－10－2）。

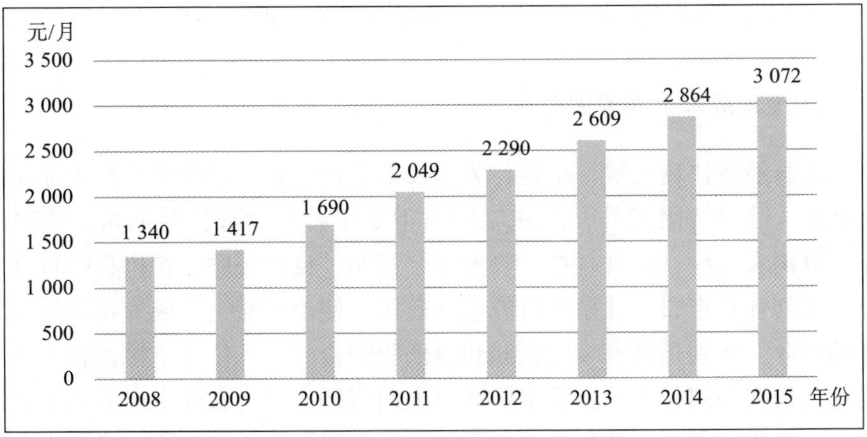


资料来源：国家统计局、WIND资讯。

**图3－10－2　农民工月平均收入**

在劳动力机会成本快速提高的情况下，中国农业生产机械化程度却比较低，用工需求偏高，这必然导致农产品生产成本中人工成本占比偏高。从小麦、玉米、大豆、棉花四种主要农产品来看，中国人工成本均显著高于美国。机械化必然带来折旧等固定资产费用高，美国的机械＋固定成本普遍高于中国。但是，将这三种成本加在一起，可以看到，中国的这三种成本显著高于美国，剔除掉单产差异，中国的这三种成本比美国更高（见表3－10－4）。可见，中国的机械化程度比较低是导致总成本较高的重要因素。从每亩用工量来看，以稻谷为例，尽管2003—2014年稻谷生产的每亩用工量从13.10个工日下降到6.43个工日，下降了一半以上，但即便是与同样以小规模农业生产为主的日本稻谷亩均用工约2个工日相比，中国的粮食用工量依然偏高。

**表3-10-4　　2014年中美人工、机械和固定成本比较**　　单位：元/公顷

| | 人工成本 | | 机械+固定成本 | | 人工+机械+固定成本 | |
|---|---|---|---|---|---|---|
| | 中　国 | 美　国 | 中　国 | 美　国 | 中　国 | 美　国 |
| 小　麦 | 5 472 | 300 | 2 661 | 2 355 | 8 133 | 2 655 |
| 玉　米 | 7 120 | 424 | 2 212 | 3 123 | 9 332 | 3 546 |
| 大　豆 | 3 251 | 321 | 1 497 | 2 596 | 4 748 | 2 917 |
| 棉　花 | 21 126 | 678 | 3 273 | 4 666 | 24 399 | 5 344 |

资料来源：国家发改委：《全国农产品成本收益资料汇编》，中国统计出版社出版。

### 2. 土地成本上涨原因分析

随着经济快速发展，土地作为重要的生产资料，其价格不断上涨是必然趋势。除经济因素外，近些年国家不断出台粮食最低收购价、临时收储、取消农业税、粮食直补、农资综合补贴、良种补贴、农机具购置补贴等一系列强农惠农、补贴支持农业的政策，使得农业生产成为投资回报较高的产业，特别是国家临时收储和最低收购价政策，使得主粮作物生产可以获得较高利润。各种经营主体通过土地流转，参与农业生产的积极性高涨。土地流转需求增长导致土地租金不断上涨，在东北地区，近年来土地流转租金可以达到500元/亩以上。

适度规模经营是国家鼓励的方向，有些地方政府为了政绩，强行推动土地流转或者对流入土地生产者给予各种补贴。前一种形式的土地流转违背了农民意愿，必然要付给农民更高的租金；后一种形式的土地流转，流入土地者有政府补贴做支持，愿意付出更高的租金给农民。这两种形式的土地流转均可导致土地租金上涨，从而导致农产品生产成本增加。

此外，粮食生产的收益相比其他产业总体还是较低，在土地用途管制执行不够严格的地区，就会存在其他经营主体从农民手中将土地流转过来后打“擦边球”，擅自改变土地用途，获取高收益，反过来也助推了土地

租金的提高。

## （三）推进中国特色的农业规模化，降低农业生产成本

**1. 坚定推进粮食市场化改革，正确引导土地规模化，严格执行土地用途管制，有效控制土地成本上涨**

随着 2014 年国家启动新疆棉花和东北地区大豆目标价格改革试点，2015 年国家不再实行油菜籽国家临储收购政策，2016 年中央 1 号文件明确提出要“积极稳妥推进玉米收储制度改革”等一系列政策的实施和调整，农产品价格将主要由市场机制来形成，土地赢利能力受其影响将有所下降，土地租金快速上涨势头必然得到有效遏制，且将显著下降至正常水平。正确引导土地规模化，避免过多行政干预。随着农民外出务工，短期内有将其耕地流转给其他人耕种的动力。随着城镇化的推进，农民在城里定居就业，在子女上学、医疗、社会保障等方面获得与城镇户口的居民同等待遇后，其退出在农村的耕地是顺理成章的事情。通过适度引导，让有意愿、有能力的农业经营主体通过流转获得土地，形成适度规模经营，可以有效提升土地资源的使用效率，提高农业生产力。但是，要注意避免在推进土地流转形成规模化经营过程中出现过多的行政干预。以高租金吸引农民流转土地虽然不违背自愿原则，但客观上导致生产成本上升，降低了竞争力。

某些土地经营者之所以愿意付出高租金来流转土地，是因为其土地可能用于非农用途，因此，严格的土地用途管控有助于将许多以“非农化”经营为目的的社会资产挤出土地流转市场，降低土地流转租金。

**2. 提高机械化生产水平，降低人工成本，走有中国特色的农业规模化之路**

针对中国目前农村劳动力不足、农业生产中人工占比过高的现状，用机械化生产替代人工劳动，提高农业生产的机械化水平，是有效降低农产品生产成本、提高竞争力的有效举措。

在发展农业机械化过程中，要避免日本的教训，即每家每户均购买农业机械（政府大量补贴），农业机械利用率低，浪费严重，生产成本也相对较高。

农业机械化是不是必须要先实现土地流转集中？我们认为，土地流转集中不是农业生产规模化的必要条件，农业生产规模化既可以是以土地流转集中为基础的规模化，也可是以农业服务集中为基础的规模化。目前新兴农业经营主体不断涌现，但传统农户仍占中国农业经营主体的多数。中国小农经济的基本国情，决定了以土地流转集中为基础的规模化难以成为主要形式，土地流转规模必须与城镇化进程相适应，大力推动农机社会化服务是中国全面实现农业机械化较为现实和有效的途径。通过这种方式，可以在不改变农户耕地承包权的情况下实现统一的机械化耕种收，从而实现农业规模化生产，其实质是将经营权外包，是符合小农经济特征的、具有中国特色的规模化道路。

通过社会化服务为主要形式实现农业机械化，是包括农机研发、育种等农业生产全环节的系统工程，建议着重加强以下三个方面的工作：

第一，加快农业机械技术的研发创新，使农业机械可以适应不同作物生产和地形条件。中国农产品众多，许多农作物，如棉花、薯类、蔬菜等生产机械化程度还比较低。此外，中国地形条件复杂，东北地区多为平原，西南地区多为丘陵，西北地区则多为高原，目前中国的农业机械，特别是大型机械多适于在平原地区作业，在丘陵地带等则难以用于农业生产。因此，要加快农业机械技术创新，研发和制造适合不同农作物品种和地理条件的农业机械。

第二，加快适应机械化作业的育种创新。农业机械化进程的推进对作物品种提出了更高要求。中国现已拥有一些较为适合机械化作业的农作物品种，如目前在新疆种植的加工番茄，因果实含水量低、表皮较厚，实现了机械采收，减少了人工劳动的使用，与普通番茄相比生产成本大幅降低。但目前多数农作物品种仍不适合现代化机械作业。以玉米为例，中国的玉米品种有不少为高秆大穗，穗位高低不齐，成熟时间不完全一致，脱水慢，不利于机械化作业。再比如，中国的油菜籽品种在成熟后通常易出现倒伏现象，豆荚也易裂开，机械收割难度较大，且会造成大量损耗。因此，要推动农业机械化发展，培育新品种，使农作物适合密植，在抗倒性、脱水性、早熟性等重要农艺性状上取得新突破十分必要。

第三，大力扶持农机大户和专业合作组织发展，继续推广跨区作业等农机社会化服务模式。提供机械化服务的主体可以多元化，专业大户和合作社、专业提供农机服务的企业或农产品贸易和加工企业都可以提供服务，发挥多主体积极性，共同推进中国农业机械化进程。

（中粮集团战略部　　顾善松　车进）

# 十一、我国粮食仓容现状、存在的问题及对策研究

【内容提要】

粮食仓储是粮食流通工作的重要组成部分，确保粮食“存得好”对保障国家粮食安全、提高粮食流通效率、促进社会经济发展具有重大意义。受到国际宏观经济疲软和国内经济结构调整的影响，粮食供应出现了阶段性过剩，加之受仓储设施布局不合理等因素影响，现有粮食仓容总体紧张，部分地区严重不足，储粮安全形势趋于紧张，破解粮食仓容不足问题已迫在眉睫。为此，本文在系统分析我国粮食仓储设施现状的基础上，指出了当前我国仓储设施存在仓容总量不足、地区布局不合理、配套设施和技术水平落后等问题；进一步深入分析了造成当前粮食仓容紧张的主观和客观原因；最后，为解决粮食仓容缺口提出了近期增加仓容建设力度、把过剩的产量暂时“储存”起来的对策。同时，加大对粮食主产区产地加工的支持，促进粮食产地加工转化；打通“北粮南运”物流通道。长远来看，要深化粮食流通体制改革，畅通粮食产销衔接渠道，依靠市场自主调节的力量，扭转价格倒挂困局。

受耕地、淡水等资源环境约束，我国粮食连续增产的难度越来越大，而随着人口增加、消费结构升级、城镇化进程加快，粮食需求将继续刚性增长，“紧平衡”将成为我国粮食供求的长期态势。一方面，近年来由于“人努力、天帮忙”，我国粮食生产连年丰收。通过整理国家统计局发布的数据，2015 年，全国粮食总产量 62 043. 2 万吨，比 2014 年增加 1 438. 6 万吨，增长

2.4%，创历史新高，实现了半个多世纪以来粮食产量“十二连增”。另一方面，我国粮食进口量2015年达到11 282.6万吨，其中，谷物及谷物粉3 270.7万吨，大豆8 174.1万吨，粮食进口量创历史新高。国内供应增加和进口增加的叠加效应，为增加国内粮食有效供应和增强国家粮食安全保障能力奠定了重要物质基础。然而，受到国际宏观经济疲软和国内经济结构调整的影响，粮食供给出现了阶段性过剩，加之受仓储设施布局不合理等因素影响，现有粮食仓容总体紧张，部分地区严重不足，储粮安全形势趋于紧张，破解粮食仓容不足问题已迫在眉睫。

2014年6月25日，国务院总理李克强主持召开国务院常务会议，部署做好粮食收储和仓储设施建设工作，加强收储和仓储设施建设。7月初，李克强总理又考察了湖南中储粮直属库，指出要解决好收储问题，避免出现农民“卖粮难”，确保粮食颗粒归仓。2015年中央1号文件明确提出加快千亿斤粮食新建仓容建设进度，尽快形成中央和地方职责分工明确的粮食收储机制，提高粮食收储保障能力。如何提高粮食仓储设施能力，缓解粮食供应阶段性过剩与长期紧平衡的关系，对于一头连着亿万农民、一头连着亿万消费者的粮食环节，确保粮食“存得好”，对保障国家粮食安全、提高粮食流通能力、加快农业现代化建设意义十分重大。

## （一）我国粮食仓储设施现状和存在的主要问题

### 1. 我国粮食仓储设施现状

经过1998—2003年的三批国债投资中央储备粮库项目建设，以及近年来各省（区、市）“退城进郊”粮食仓库置换建设、民营企业收储库点自行投资建设和中央粮食企业仓储物流项目支持的粮食仓房建设，我国粮食仓储设施总体得到较大改善。据国家粮食局统计，2012年底全国共有粮油仓储企业近2万家，总仓容44 145万吨，有效仓容38 590万吨，比1992年前分别增加了265%和275%。有效仓容量达到粮食总产量的66%。

从粮食仓容量规模来看，10万吨以上规模企业粮食仓容占有效仓容的比例为33.8%，5万～10万吨规模企业仓容占有效仓容的比例为22.5%；

2.5 万~5 万吨规模企业仓容占有效仓容的比例为 19.2%，小于 2.5 万吨规模企业仓容占有效仓容的比例为 24.5%。仓容规模主要以大型和小型为主，大型仓容主要用于满足粮食大规模中转流通需求和国家长期静态储备需求；小型仓容主要用于满足企业粮食周转储存的需求。

从粮食仓储设施的仓型来看，在现有粮食仓储设施中，粮食仓房主要以平房仓为主，占有效仓容的比例为 84.3%，立筒仓、浅圆仓占有效仓容的比例为 13.5%，楼房仓和地下仓占有效仓容的比例为 2.3%。平房仓主要适合粮食静态储存，立筒仓和浅圆仓则较适合快速周转的粮食储藏，楼房仓主要用于成品粮的储存，地下仓主要是用于一些山区或者丘陵地带的粮食储存。从现有粮食仓房的建设年度来看，1998 年前建设的仓房占有效仓容的比例为 33.2%，1998 年及以后建设的仓房占有效仓容的比例为 66.8%。可见，我国目前有 1/3 的粮食仓房是在 20 年前建设，还有一部分仓房是在上个世纪 50 年代建设而成的，存在仓房老旧、条件差、不能安全储粮的问题。

从现有仓房的权属和地区分布来看，粮食仓房产权属于中央政府的仓房占有效仓容的比例约为 16.7%，属于各省（区、市）以及以下地方政府和企业的仓房占有效仓容的比例约为 83.3%，也即仓房权属的中央与地方的比例为 1∶5。其中，粮食仓房国有与社会企业的比例约为 3∶1。这些仓房主要分布在粮食主产区，主销区和产销平衡区粮食仓房所占比例较少。据国家粮食局统计，现有仓房粮食主产区、主销区、产销平衡区的分布比例为 7∶1∶1。

**2. 当前我国粮食仓储设施存在的主要问题**

（1）仓容总量不足，储粮安全隐患突显。粮食供求的阶段性过剩致使粮食总库存高。考虑到不同粮食品种占用仓容和粮食倒仓时的粮食空仓等综合因素，理论上目前全国的仓房几乎全部装满了。同时，有效仓容占当年全国粮食总产量的比重偏高，已经不能满足粮食收获后及时收储和各级政府长期储存的需要。加之，粮食仓房的地区布局不平衡和政策性粮食执行主体的垄断性，粮食主产区和中储粮直属企业则不得不出现露天储粮。从粮食市场来看，当前，全国粮食市场存在高产量、高收购量、高库存量“三高”叠加，特别是玉米连续增产和消费需求持续下降同步出现，阶段性过剩特征明显；稻米市场也呈现供大于求，销售不畅。库存粮食积压较多，主产区夏粮和秋粮收购将面临无仓可用的局面。粮多仓少，很多粮食只能露天存放在用草围成的临时粮囤中，过火粮食约 5 万吨。此外，露天储粮也很容易引发粮食发霉腐烂变质，严重影响粮食质量。

根据资料显示，美国、加拿大、澳大利亚等粮食出口大国的仓容量高于粮食产量，美国的农场粮库与中转粮库仓容量约为粮食产量的 2 倍。日本、韩国等粮食进口国的仓容量也都超过粮食总消费量。随着我国城镇化、工业化进程的不断推进，粮食生产的集约化、规模化、商品化不断提高，仓容总量不足问题将更为突出。

（2）有效仓容地区布局不合理，加剧了区域粮食仓储困难的矛盾。从仓容布局来看，粮食生产和粮食仓储布局不协调，部分粮食主产区仓容严重不足。目前，东北地区和长江中下游主产区仓容不足问题突出，特别是黑龙江、吉林、湖南、湖北、江苏等省仓容不足问题突出。黑龙江、吉林的库存更高，仓房不能满足粮食的储藏需要，只得采用露天或者罩棚等暂时存放。

（3）配套设施和技术水平落后，安全储粮风险增大。中央和地方储备粮库普遍配备了粮情检测、机械通风、环流熏蒸、谷物冷却等四项新技术，中央储备粮库还进行了仓储管理智能化建设，智能通风、智能烘干和气调储粮技术示范推广。但是，广大的基层收纳粮库设施简陋、功能不齐全，没有采用科学保粮技术，仓储设施普遍存在老化现象，难以满足安全储粮的基本要求，更不能保证储粮品质良好。一些民营企业建设的粮库投资标准低、配套设施不全、技术水平落后，有的甚至存在安全隐患。

## （二）我国当前粮食仓容紧张的主要原因

### 1. 粮食连年增产，粮食仓容客观需要增加

（1）我国粮食供给不断增长，客观上需要粮食仓容随之增加。我国粮食产量和进口量双双连续增加，2015 年粮食产量实现“十二连增”，全国粮食总产量 62 043.2 万吨，比 2003 年增加 18 848.8 万吨，增幅达到了

43.6%；粮食商品率由2003年的39%增加到2014年的65.57%；粮食收购数量不断增加，2014年全国各类粮食企业收购量首次超过35 000万吨。2015年粮食进口量达到11 282.6万吨，比2003年增加8 992.6万吨，增幅达392.7%。粮食供给数量和商品量的绝对增加客观上要求增加粮食仓容。

（2）农户存粮习惯变化，集中化的粮食仓储需求增加。随着粮食商品率的增加，农户存粮下降，原先由农户家庭"蓄水池"存粮向集中化的国家和企业存粮转变，放大了粮食仓储设施需求效应。特别是随着城镇化的推进和农村老龄化的发展，家庭人口数量减少，农民存粮意愿下降，种粮商品意识增强，粮食收获后即出售。特别是在小麦、稻谷托市收购政策下，粮价波动性降低，供求稳定性增强，中小规模经营粮户选择降低储粮水平，出现粮食出售数量增加、农户储粮数量减少等储粮结构变化。随着城镇化、工业化和农业现代化的协同推进，以及种粮大户和新型家庭农场的发展，农户层面的存粮水平还将呈现进一步下降态势。因此，对集中化的粮食仓储需求增加将成为未来粮食和农业农村发展的一个重要趋势。

（3）粮食产销格局变化，造成了地区间粮食仓储设施需求不均衡。随着经济发展和地区经济发展的不平衡性，我国粮食生产重心由南向北、由东向中西部转移。当前，我国粮食生产主要集中在东北地区、黄淮海地区、长江中下游地区和新疆粮食生产后备基地四个主要区域。其中，东北地区已经成为我国最大的粮食生产区和净调出区域，粮食外运量占全国粮食跨省运输量的35%以上。粮食生产布局的调整形成了"北粮南运"跨省粮食大流通的格局，同时也要求调整原有粮食仓储设施地区布局，不仅要求新增粮食仓储设施总量，而且需要进一步优化粮食仓储设施地区布局，以适应粮食生产形势的发展和变化。

### 2. 粮食收储政策效应致使政府仓容紧张

从2005年开始实行的托市收购政策多次提高粮食最低收购价格水平。以政策性收储为支撑，当国外粮食价格高于国内价格时，其他市场主体在国内市场收购较为积极；而当国际粮食价格低于国内粮食价格时，其他市场主体为了规避市场风险，在国内收购市场不入市。为了保护种粮农民利益，政策性收储主体则增加其收购量，出现了农民卖粮靠政策启动，加工企业等多元主体不敢入市，中央政府承担了全部的收储责任、经济成本和仓容压力，造成了产量高、收购量高、库存高的“三高”现象。

（1）粮源向政府集中，国有粮食企业仓容爆满。受粮食最低收购价连续“单边持续上涨”影响，过去10年来，我国粮食市场价格也呈现出“单边持续上涨”的非自然变动状态。受价格导向作用，粮源不断向政府手中集中。2012年最低收购价粮食和临储粮共3 063万吨，占国有粮食企业收购量的25%，2013年两项政策性收购占国有粮食企业收购总量的近60%。粮源的集中和国内外市场价差导致粮食销售不畅，国有粮食企业仓容不能满足需要。

（2）临时性政策被常态化，粮食经营变成了以政府为主体的政策性经营。临时性收储政策制定的初衷是为了维护粮价稳定，应对粮食市场短期异常波动，保护农民利益。但在实际执行过程中，短期政策被长期化，临时性政策被常态化。一方面，受国内外粮食市场价格影响，多元市场主体入市不积极，导致国家粮食收购量刚性增加。另一方面，由于部分国有粮食企业从事政策性经营，政府给补贴，导致政策性粮食收购是一个非竞争的市场，中储粮总公司及其委托的国有粮食收储企业能够享受到国家的优惠贷款和保管费用、出库、调运补贴，甚至比承储中央储备粮补贴还多，以至不少国有收储企业又重新捧起了吃财政补贴政策的“铁饭碗”。

（3）国内粮食高价格政策刺激农民扩大粮食种植，甚至一些质量不合格粮食被生产出来而由国家收购。近几年来，受农业结构调整、气候变化、水源和土壤污染等影响，我国部分地区粮食水分、杂质、霉变、重金属、农药残留超标等问题日益突出。受到粮食价格较高并且相对稳定的激励，在一些不适合粮食生产的区域，农民生产出镉超标大米、高水分玉米和赤霉病超标小麦等受劣质粮食。造成“问题粮”的原因在于政府连年提高粮食价格水平，农民为追求产量选择高产品种，降低质量要求。如在黑龙江、吉林等地越区种植并不适合本地无霜期短的高产玉米品种，造成收获时水分含量高，收获后在田间地头和农户储粮环节霉变现象严重。而为保护农民利益，国家托市收购又不得不放宽收购质量标准，国家承担巨大的财政支出，造成仓容紧张矛盾突出。

（4）粮食市场价格倒挂，销售不畅。由于国际市场粮食价格从2011年连续走低，而国内粮食最低收购价和政策性收购价格连年提高，国内粮食市场价格全面高于国际粮食市场价格。目前，广东港每吨国产玉米、大米、小麦分别比同品种进口完税价高出750元、900元和500元左右，玉米价差甚至一度超过1 000元，三大谷物品种配额外进口（缴纳65%关税）的价格逼近“天花板”。国际粮食市场价格低，导致国内粮食输入性压力增大。加之国内在粮食主产区实行政策性收储，使得国内粮食市场价格信号被扭曲，造成国内与国际粮食价格倒挂、产区与销区倒挂，粮食原料与成品价格倒挂，粮食销售不畅。大量粮食积压在仓房，加剧了仓容紧张现象。南方加工企业不愿到东北采购和储存粮食，宁愿进口或等待政府低价拍卖，导致东北等粮食主产区仓容紧张矛盾愈加显著。

### 3. 仓储设施布局不合理，造成阶段性和区域性仓容紧张

2003—2015年间我国粮食生产结构发生了较大改变，粮食生产重心从南向北转移、粮食消费重心则向东南沿海地区和京津沪等大城市集聚，主销区粮食产量占全国比例持续下降，主产区粮食产量和占比都持续增加（见表3－11－1）。当前能够净调出粮食的只有黑龙江、吉林、内蒙古、河南、安徽和新疆6个省区。预计到2020年，江西、河北、江苏、湖北等主产省和甘肃、宁夏等平衡省将转变成粮食净流入省份，山西、陕西、浙江等省的粮食净流入比例将有较大幅度增加，原有粮食仓储设施布局不能适应新的粮食供求关系调整需要，粮食仓容布局和新建仓容布局将面临新的更大挑战。

**表3－11－1　　我国粮食产量区域变化状况**

| 年份 | 全国总计（万吨） | 13个粮食主产区 小计（万吨） | 13个粮食主产区 占全国百分比（%） | 7个主销区 小计（万吨） | 7个主销区 占全国百分比（%） | 11个产销平衡区 小计（万吨） | 11个产销平衡区 占全国百分比（%） |
|---|---|---|---|---|---|---|---|
| 1984 | 40 706.8 | 28 220.9 | 69.33 | 5 228.6 | 12.84 | 7 257.3 | 17.83 |
| 1996 | 50 927.9 | 36 261.6 | 71.20 | 5 246.6 | 10.30 | 9 419.7 | 18.50 |
| 2003 | 43 291.0 | 30 707.7 | 70.93 | 3 464.2 | 8.00 | 9 119.2 | 21.06 |
| 2004 | 46 957.0 | 34 124.3 | 72.67 | 3 451.0 | 7.35 | 9 381.8 | 19.98 |
| 2012 | 58 958.0 | 44 609.8 | 75.66 | 3 422.9 | 5.81 | 10 925.3 | 18.53 |
| 2015 | 62 143.5 | 47 341.2 | 76.18 | 3 311.8 | 5.33 | 11 490.5 | 18.49 |

资料来源：根据国家粮食局：《中国粮食年鉴》（经济管理出版社出版）、国家统计局网站数据整理得到。

以东北地区为代表的主产区近年来粮食产量大幅增加，增大了该区域的仓容建设需求。同时由于粮食品种结构调整，与仓容建设配套的相关设施需求进一步增加。如受粮食种植比较效益影响，东北地区玉米替代大豆种植比例增加，甚至一些农民采取跨区种植，增加种植收益，但是引发玉米收获后水分高，若不及时烘干会导致玉米霉变等质量安全问题，又对东北地区相关的烘干设施提出了更高的要求。

## （三）解决我国粮食仓容缺口的对策

党的十八届三中全会指出：经济体制改革是全面深化改革的重点，核心问题是处理好政府和市场的关系，使市场在资源配置中起决定性作用和更好发挥政府作用。解决我国当前的粮食仓容问题，同样需要发挥市场的决定性作用，并与政府调控有机结合。中央政府负责与省长负责制要有效结合，各有侧重，中央政府既不能大包大揽，也不能推卸责任，撒手不管。解决好仓容缺口问题，长远来看要深化粮食流通体制改革，畅通粮食产销衔接渠道，依靠市场自主调节的力量，扭转价格倒挂困局，调动加工企业积极性，发挥社会仓储力量的作用。短期来看，要加大主产区，特别是适宜种粮存粮的东北地区仓储设施建设力度，把过剩的产量暂时“储存”起来。同时，加大对粮食主产区产地加工的支持，促进粮食产地加工转化；打通“北粮南运”物流通道，确保需要时调运周期短、效率高、费用低。此外，必须强调仓储技术配套，全面采用绿色生态保质储粮技术，避免 15 年前的陈化粮问题再度发生。

### 1. 全面改革政策性粮食收储政策

单纯依靠敞开收购、提高托市收购价格来保护农民种粮积极性的空间越来越小，效应越来越弱，现行粮食收储政策体系面临前所未有的挑战和考验。迫切需要研究调整最低收购价和临时收储政策，使之更加有效地支持粮食市场体系的建立，发挥保护农民利益和维护粮食市场稳定的作用。国家粮食收储政策要重在鼓励产销衔接机制的建立，要通过完善储备保管费用结算机制等政策引入竞争机制，鼓励符合条件的多元市场主体参与收储。我国粮油加工企业应通过承担国家任务充分发挥作用。要区分不同的粮食品质，采取不同的支持政策，鼓励优质优价、高质高价，在考虑保护农民利益的同时，要严格执行粮食质量标准，使农民承受质量问题造成的市场风险，提高重视粮食质量的意识。

**2. 推进粮食收储模式变革**

根据我国粮食生产以小农户为主要单元，同时正在向种粮大户、家庭农场、合作社等大农户规模化经营方式发展的实际，今后应采取不同的收储模式。在继续改善传统一家一户小农家庭储粮设施的基础上，应通过“两代”服务（代农储存、代农烘干）和“粮食银行”等多种形式，建立先服务后结算制度，鼓励农户在田间地头将收获后的粮食直接卖给粮食产后收储中心或者粮库，进行统一集中烘干储存。这样既可避免农户储粮数量和质量损失，保证农民收入，又可充分发挥国家粮食仓库和社会仓容的作用，实现规模化收储处理，提高粮食仓储设施的综合利用效率，提高粮食流通效率。对于种粮大户、家庭农场和专业合作社等大农户，要通过财政补助支持他们自建烘干塔和清理设施，自建钢板仓、立筒仓等便于散粮储运、装卸的设施。

根据我国粮食产销区空间分布和不同储粮生态区的自然条件特点，国家应在完善物流运输设施的同时，把收储重点布局在东北地区、西部产粮大县等自然条件较好的地方，建设国家“大粮仓”。应充分利用东北地区常年气温低、冬季漫长的储粮有利自然条件，集中力量改善东北主产区收储条件，增加长期收储仓容，把国家储备粮的主要库存和南方销区地方储备粮的部分库存放在东北地区，以节省保管费用，延缓粮食品质劣变，同时也能有效调节粮食购销不畅年份的收储矛盾。

**3. 继续增加重点地区仓储设施能力**

根据国务院总理李克强在2014年6月25日国务院常务会议上的部署，要创新投融资方式，引导社会资本积极参与仓储设施建设。以东北地区和南方稻谷产区为重点，“今明两年新建仓容1 000亿斤”①。支持主产

---

① 国家粮食局：《贯彻落实国务院第52次常务会议精神　六部门多措并举做好粮食收储和仓储设施建设工作》。

区农民合作社、专业大户等建设有烘干设备的储粮设施。强化地方政府特别是销区责任，严格落实地方储备任务，2014 年增加地方储备。督促销区按照不低于 6 个月市场供应量要求，确保粮食储备到位。

预计到 2020 年全国需要再新建仓容 1 亿吨，维修改造提升功能仓容 3 亿吨。要建立分级负责的粮食仓储设施建设和维护长效机制。中央财政重点支持主产区和产销平衡区的仓储设施建设和危仓老库维修改造，重点支持连接产销区的重大粮食物流通道和节点的设施建设，支持提高粮食库存监管水平和物流信息化水平的智慧粮库建设。主销区的设施建设和维修改造主要由地方财政负责。

#### 4. 增强粮食产地加工转化能力

化解当前粮食库存高、仓容缺口大的有效途径之一就是要加大粮食的产地加工转化能力。支持粮食主产区发展畜牧业，特别是东北地区每年“北粮南运”的粮食数量巨大，粮食运到南方大部分用于饲料加工。而主产区发展畜牧业则可引导种粮农民实现种植、养殖一体化经营，集约化经营，提高粮食的综合利用效率和增值，促进可持续生态农业发展，增加农业经营收入。当前，在国内粮食市场出现阶段性、结构性过剩的情况下，应适度发展粮食精深加工，促进粮食产地加工增值，消化粮食主产区库存粮食，解决仓容爆满、储粮安全隐患问题。同时，粮食的精深加工还能带动地方经济发展，缓减地方政府财政压力。

#### 5. 畅通粮食物流通道

解决困扰我国多年的粮食物流通道不畅，包粮运输为主，效率低、成本高问题的关键在于切实发挥好政府的宏观管理和组织引导作用。建立由国家上层机构统一协调各部委及粮食管理机构，建立和完善粮食行业协会对粮食仓储与运输企业的管理，形成以政府调控和市场调节为基础的粮食储运机制。以建设“北粮南运”大动脉为主目标，通过制定散粮火车入关返空运费政策为主要抓手，组织产销区粮食企业和中国铁路总公司、中储粮、中粮等大型粮食企业建立合理的组织形式和利益分配机制，鼓励产区战略装车点和销区战略卸车点、粮食集散地的建设，切实推进散粮火车入关运营。要充分发挥大型粮油加工企业，特别是饲料企业在衔接产销、畅通物流方面的作用，依托南方销区的大型加工企业建设“北粮南运”物流集散地和战略卸车点，较快形成开通散粮班列的条件。

（国家粮食局科学研究院　　亢霞　钟昱　张庆）

# 十二、大豆、棉花目标价格实施情况及政策建议

【内容提要】

目标价格实施以来，农产品价格的形成与政府补贴脱钩，减少了对市场的扭曲，成为农产品支持补贴政策调整的基本方向。但在实施过程中还存在不少问题，如补贴方式陷入两难、补贴资金到位晚于预期、农民收益存在不确定性、中央和地方在认定种植面积与实际种植面积上存在分歧、政策责任部门权责不清等，有待于在今后落实中不断完善。

在目前市场行情和收益决定农民种植决策的情况下，虽然有目标价格补贴，种植大豆的收益也不到玉米的一半。即使取消玉米临储政策，调减玉米种植面积，但如何确保农民种植大豆的收益还是一个考验。

在地权预期不稳定的情况下，农民土地追加投资动力不足，土地经营短期化行为普遍，造成土地资源的粗放式经营和级差地租Ⅱ的流失，农民增产增收困难。而且，土地流转价格的大幅攀升让经营主体望而却步，农民种植收益抵不过高企地租的侵蚀。地租价格出现回落，对土地流转和集约化经营是个利好。

从长远看，要增强国际竞争力必须强化顶层设计，采取全方位扶持和保护政策，完善现有补贴办法，试点差异化补贴标准；组织搞好收购，防止出现销售难现象发生；以市场为导向，实施种粮目标收益保险；稳步推进改革，完善农产品市场调控政策体系，以确保棉花和大豆目标价格政策顺利实施。

最低收购价和临时收储政策实施以来，国内粮食价

格稳步上升，棉花、油料、食糖价格总体高位运行，保持了主要农产品生产基本稳定，农民收入平稳较快增长，为稳定物价总水平、保持国民经济持续较快发展起到了重要支撑作用。但是，最低收购价和临时收储政策能够有效实施的前提条件是国内市场价格低于国际市场价格。当这个前提不复存在，必然扭曲市场价格的形成机制。开展目标价格改革试点，探索推进农产品价格形成机制与政府补贴脱钩的改革，就是充分发挥市场在资源配置中的决定性作用，价格形成由市场决定，以促进产业协调发展。

2014 年中央 1 号文件首次提出目标价格改革试点，当年 6 月 25 日召开的国务院常务会议确定，推动最低收购价、临时收储和农业补贴政策逐步向农产品目标价格制度转变，从棉花和大豆入手，分品种推进补贴试点。2015 年中央 1 号文件继续提出要“坚持市场定价原则，探索推进农产品价格形成机制与政府补贴脱钩的改革，逐步建立农产品目标价格制度”。

## （一）目标价格实施中的主要问题

目标价格实施以来，农产品价格的形成与政府补贴脱钩，有效调动了农民生产积极性，减少了对市场的扭曲，较好地发挥了市场配置资源的决定性作用，成为农产品支持补贴政策调整的基本方向。调研发现，在实施过程中还存在着不少问题，很多地方不尽人意，有待于在今后落实中不断完善。

一是补贴方式选择陷入两难。2014 年新疆开展棉花目标价格改革试点工作，分别试点了按照播种面积、交售量以及两种方式综合操作的多种补贴方式。2015 年根据各地情况，对补贴方式做出了进一步调整。按播种面积补贴，问题主要包括土地面积核实确认过程工作量大，成本较高，寻租现象时有发生，非法开荒地的确认、补报和漏报现象频发，承包土地的种植者并未享受补贴等。按交售量补贴，优势在于操作成本相对较低，有利于提高籽棉品质。但操作过程中存在非法虚开收购票据等现象，同时非法开荒土地种植的棉花也可享受补贴，不利于保护新疆脆弱的生态环境，维持农业可持续发展。东北大豆补贴标准的选择也面临同样的问题。

二是补贴实施初期漏洞叠出。目标价格采价点的确定不够科学，偏差较大；补贴对象为农业生产者，但农业生产者如何界定？对于拥有土地承包经营权的农民来说，拿不到补贴是否会心理不平衡？农民提高租金将会增加种植成本；目标价格的公布时间晚，实施细则出台也晚，种植面积和单产的确定不够准确；地方政府对目标价格的宣传力度不够，对目标价格实施的核查与监管的力度也不够等。

三是补贴资金到位晚于预期。2014 年自治区方面补贴金额分别与实际种植面积和籽棉交售量挂钩，按每亩 191 元和 33 元的标准分两批兑付给棉农，其中第二批补贴资金计划应于次年 2 月底前兑付至基本农户和农业生产经营单位。在实践中发现，由于前期土地面积核实上报过程中存在偏差，导致截至 2015 年 6 月，尽管补贴资金已逐级拨付至各级财政，但部分地区补贴资金尚未兑付给农户，严重挫伤了棉农种植积极性。

四是农民收益存在不确定性。生产成本，特别是人工成本上升造成棉花和大豆种植利润持续走低，严重影响农民的生产积极性，已成为新疆棉花和东北大豆产业发展面临的突出“瓶颈”之一。由于国家财政资金有限，造成补贴标准相对较低，部分地区并未实现保证农民种植收益的政策目标。此外，新疆、黑龙江地域辽阔，地区间人均耕地面积、水土、气候等生产条件差异较大，实施单一的补贴标准不利于条件落后地区产业发展。

五是政策责任部门权责不清。中央层面，目标价格补贴政策主要由国家发改委牵头制定，会同农业部、财政部等有关部门发布执行。但在地市州及以下层面，政策执行中参与的部门数量多、工作量大，部分地区政策实施牵头单位不够明确，参与部门职能交叉、权责不清、多头管理的现象时有发生。

## （二）政策困境：中央与地方的博弈

目标价格实施两年来，中央财政对各省区拨付目标价格补贴时与棉花、大豆总产、目标价格同市场价格的差价挂钩，而各省区对种植者兑付目标价格补贴时与种植者大豆合法实际种植面积挂钩，中央认定面积与实际种植面积成了中央和地方在目标价格实施中的主要分歧。

棉花、大豆目标价格补贴对象为本省行政区划范围内棉花、大豆合法实际种植面积的实际种植者。未经过申报、公示、审核的种植面积，在国家和省有明确退耕要求的土地上种植的面积，在未经批准开垦的土地或者禁止开垦的土地上种植的面积不享受目标价格补贴。对于在合法耕地上实施作物间种、套种棉花、大豆的，按实际比例认定种植面积。但是，很多农民恰恰是在未经批准的开垦土地或者禁止开垦土地上种植棉花或大豆，自然希望一样获得政府补贴，而中央政府却明文规定不给补贴，这在很大程度上挫伤了农民种植的积极性。

实际上，在目标价格实施上，地方政府认为补贴面积低于实际面积，中央政府则觉得地方虚报面积。中央和地方政府的博弈导致目标价格补贴的实施效果打了折扣，补贴小于地方和农户预期。从目标价格本身来看，2014 年的棉花目标价格为 19 800 元/吨，2015 年为 19 100 元/吨，而 2016 年则为 18 600 元/吨，三年来目标价格水平不断下降，与新疆棉农的期望有很大的差距。

## （三）机会成本的考量：种植大豆还是玉米

开展大豆目标价格补贴政策有利于破除我国大豆市场国内外价格倒挂、南北价格倒挂的死结，为国产大豆发展提供了重要历史机遇。2014 年、2015 年确定大豆目标价格均为 4 800 元/吨，比前几年大豆临储收购价和市场平均价格稍高。由于玉米和大豆种植存在争地关系，农民习惯用玉米种植收益做比较，而大豆种植收益则远不如玉米。以黑龙江省为例，2014 年该省在册大豆实际种植面积 4 700 万亩，产量 648. 6 万吨，亩种植成本 648. 6 元。2014 年黑龙江大豆亩单产为 138 千克，每亩产值 681. 17 元，亩纯收益（按市场收购价）33 元，加上目标价格补贴，亩纯收益 90 元左右。虽然 2014 年黑龙江大豆产量增加，有目标价格补贴，但农民种植大豆的收益不到种植玉米收益的一半。

根据国家统计局数据，2015 年全国玉米产量 4 491. 6 亿斤，同比增加 178. 7 亿斤；而相关机构估算 2015 年玉米消费量仅 3 500 亿斤左右。此外，受国外低价玉米和大麦、高粱、木薯干和酒糟蛋白质饲料等玉米替代品进口数量激增的影响，国内玉米市场受到较大冲击，玉米库存不断增加，市场消费低迷、加工转化开工不足等都使得新粮收储和安全储粮压力突出。据市场机构估计，截至 2016 年 2 月底，临储玉米库存已达 2.5 亿吨之巨，每年仅利息和仓储费就高达 500 亿元，其中存储时间超过或即将超过 3 年的临储玉米数量达 7 000 万吨，面临陈化质变和存储安全等极大风险。从机会成本的角度来看，为了减轻玉米的库存和供应压力，提升大豆种植收益迫在眉睫。

在农业调结构、降产能、去库存的过程中，需要政府大力给予政策、资金和技术支持，依靠科技手段降低大豆的种植成本，提高大豆的产量和质量；通过实施目标价格，提高大豆种植补贴，使之能趋近甚至超过种植玉米效益，才能化解玉米天量库存的压力和陈化变质的风险，实现农业结构调整的目标。

值得高兴的是，2016 年 3 月底，国家取消了东北三省和内蒙古的玉米临时收储政策，调整为市场化收购加补贴的机制。玉米价格由市场形成，各类市场主体自主入市收购；建立玉米生产者补贴制度，中央财政补贴资金拨付到省区，由地方政府统筹补贴资金兑付给生产者，以保持优势产区玉米种植收益基本稳定。为应对出现大范围卖粮难等风险，政策将安排符合条件的企业入市托底收购。玉米临储政策的终结，有利于平衡玉米和大豆的种植收益差距，优化农产品种植结构。

## （四）地租对目标价格补贴的侵蚀

2015 年中央 1 号文件指出，要充分发挥县乡农村土地承包经营权、林权流转服务平台作用，引导农村产权流转交易市场健康发展。2016 年 1 号文件又提出，支持多种类型的新型农业服务主体开展代耕代种、联耕联种、土地托管等专业化、规模化服务。健全县乡农村经营管理体系，加强对土地流转和规模经营的管理服务。农业经营体制的不断创新，土地流转和专业化规模化经营的实现，都离不开地租这个绕不过去的话题。

地租是土地所有者凭借对土地所有权获取的一部分剩余价值，任何地租都是以土地所有权存在为前提。土地价格是地租的资本化，是地租收益的实现形式。马克思把地租分为级差地租和绝对地租。绝对地租是由土地所有权垄断产生，一切租用土地都必须支付的地租。级差地租分两种形式：因土地肥沃程度和位置差别而形成的级差地租 I，因对同一块土地连续追加投资而带来不同生产率所形成的级差地租 II，后者意味着集约化经营。

农业地租不仅能够真实反映农业生产经营对土地资源配置的市场需求信号，同时也代表农民切身利益发展的制度化诉求。在我国的地租分配格局中，绝对地租和级差地租 I 归集体所有毋庸置疑，国家为农村提供农田水利等基础设施建设，理应获得地租收益；级差地租 II 应归追加投资的广大农民所有。农户对土地追加投资力度的大小取决于对地权稳定性预期。在地权预期不稳定情况下，农民追加土地投资动力不足，土地经营短期化行为普遍，对土地的开发利用往往竭泽而渔，忽视农地土壤改良及农田水利建设。长此以往，必将大大降低土地流转意愿和土地投入积极性，造成土地资源的粗放式经营和级差地租 II 的流失，农民增产增收困难，严重违背国家“十三五”规划提出的“藏粮于地”和“藏粮于技”战略。

仍以黑龙江省为例，2014 年全省农村土地流转面积达 6 507 万亩，比上年增长 16.2%；农村土地规模经营面积达 5 971 万亩，比上年增长 17.1%。土地规模经营的开展对土地投入的各项要素进行优化配置，降低了诸如资金、人才、机械等方面的成本，而土地向经营能力更强的生产者流动，也提高了土地产出效率，成本降低和产出增加大大提高了劳动生产率。在过去几年里，土地流转价格的大幅攀升增加了农民的财产性收入，但成本过高也让经营主体望而却步。如果地租价格持续上涨，即使有目标价格政策扶持，农民种植收益也抵不住高企地租的侵蚀，成为土地流转和规模化专业化经营的不利因素。

目前转机已经出现，由于目标价格补贴等政策的实施，2015 年地租开始止涨回跌。2015 年，东北临储玉米收购价格调低至 1 元/斤，加之局部旱情影响，令不少玉米种植农户收益缩水，租地农户更是赔钱。大豆、玉米种植收益下降，在一定程度倒逼东北土地租金在 2016 年开春就走“下坡路”。随着玉米临储政策的取消，这一趋势在未来一段时期内还将持续下去。由于种棉收益的持续下降，新疆个别地区甚至出现了零地租的现象。

在去库存、调结构背景下，土地租价回落不但降低种粮成本，也有利于推进玉米种植结构调整，降低农户在改种其他作物过程中可能产生的经营风险，有利于农村土地的流转和农业生产的集约化经营。

## （五）完善目标价格制度的建议

从目标价格政策的初衷来看，政府是为了在稳定农户收益的前提下，将农产品的价格交由市场来决定，但实际效果是农户种植大豆和棉花的收益均出现较为明显的下滑。从长远发展看，要增强国际竞争力，国家必须强化顶层设计，重视农业结构调整，采取全方位扶持和保护政策，尤其对主产区更要给予政策倾斜。建议采取有效措施，确保棉花和大豆目标价格政策顺利实施。

### 1. 注重顶层设计，完善现有补贴办法

从中央到相关省区必须高度重视目标价格政策的落实，深入调研，科学分析，不断完善，促进棉花、大豆以及玉米等品种生产转方式、调结构，不断提高国内农产品的竞争力。应研究综合参考历史单产水平和当年播种面积为标准的办法，与当期交售量脱钩，在保障农民收益的同时，也确保中央财政支出总量的基本稳定。补贴标准可表示为：补贴金额 = 当地历史 5 年单产平均值 × 当年播种面积 ×（目标价格 - 市场价格）。逐步建立主产区目标价格补贴信息库，包括补贴对象、种植面积、金额、地区、产量、单产等。采用高科技手段辅助测定棉花和大豆种植面积，解决按照面积补贴信息不对称的难题。建立公开透明、执行高效的奖惩机制。公开领取价格补贴的程序和关键细节接受村民监督。要创新管理机制，完善配套设施，加强风险管理，防控财政补贴道德风险，不断提高财政补贴的政策效能。

**2. 完善政策方案，试点差异化补贴标准**

要打破身份界限，遵循“种植者得补贴”原则，明确补贴对象；目标价格采价点应尽量设在产区，而不是收购点，种植面积越大，采价点的设置应越多；及早公布目标价格和当期补贴标准，使农户对新季粮食种植结构做出科学预判；加大对目标价格的宣传、核查与监管力度；实现供需接轨，让市场主导资源配置，减少政策壁垒；大幅提高大豆补贴标准，有效遏制国内大豆种植面积逐年下滑的势头，提高国产大豆的自给率和竞争力。新疆地域辽阔，南北疆、各地州之间自然条件差异较大，农业发展的基础也不同。特别是南疆地区，水利、气候、地力等自然条件较北疆有一定差距。这些都造成了地域间产业发展的巨大差异。因此，目标价格补贴标准应充分考虑不同地区发展条件，采取区别化的补贴标准，对生产基础薄弱的地区给予适度倾斜，从而促进棉花产业区域间均衡发展。

**3. 组织搞好收购，防止出现销售难现象发生**

引导具备一定加工、仓储和资金实力的市场主体积极参与大豆收购，并研究制订相关预案，防止出现大面积“卖难”现象，加强收购市场监管，维护市场秩序。长期看，人工成本持续上涨将是制约新疆棉花产业发展的主要“瓶颈”之一。新疆人均耕地面积较大，土地平整，适合推广机采棉技术。未来通过积极开展适合我国种植模式的机采棉技术攻关，加快推广机采棉技术，降低生产成本。目标价格政策制定时可适度对机采棉农户予以倾斜，提高补贴标准，加快提升集约化和规模化水平。

**4. 以市场为导向，实施种粮目标收益保险**

把农业保险作为支持农业的重要手段，扩大农业保险覆盖面，增加保险品种，提高风险保障水平。积极开发适应新型农业经营主体需求的保险品种。探索开展重要农产品目标价格保险以及收入保险、天气指数保险试点。探索建立农业补贴、涉农信贷、农产品期货和农业保险联动机制，进一步完善农业保险大灾风险分散机制。

**5. 稳步推进改革，完善农产品市场调控政策体系**

要采取积极稳妥策略，借鉴新疆棉花和东北大豆目标价格补贴试点工作的经验做法，分区域、分品种逐步推广目标价格政策。选择农业基础好、条件相对成熟的地区先行试点，待时机成熟时考虑全国范围内推广。从品种上看，下一步要稳步向关系国计民生的水稻、小麦、玉米等主要口粮作物推广，并以此为契机，抓紧调整现有补贴和贸易管理政策，加快完善我国农产品市场调控政策体系。

## （六）结　　语

国家“十三五”规划和2016年中央1号文件都指出，要牢固树立和深入贯彻落实创新、协调、绿色、开放、共享的发展理念，用发展新理念破解“三农”新难题，厚植农业农村发展优势，加大创新驱动力度，推进农业供给侧结构性改革，加快转变农业发展方式，保持农业稳定发展和农民持续增收，着力构建现代农业产业体系、生产体系、经营体系，提高农业质量效益和竞争力，走产出高效、产品安全、资源节约、环境友好的农业现代化道路。

实施目标价格补贴政策为我国农业产业探索发挥市场配置资源作用，应对国际竞争提供了有效借鉴，对提升我国农业国际竞争力具有现实而深远的意义。我国应结合试点改革的内容，不断完善目标价格制度，坚定不移持续推进。

（郑州粮食批发市场　史振厚　杨京）

# 第四部分

## 2015 年中国
## 粮食相关政策法规

# 一、推进种植业结构调整 打赢供给侧改革攻坚战

【内容提要】

2016 年是全面建成小康社会决胜阶段的开局之年，也是推进农业供给侧结构性改革的攻坚之年。种植业发展面临着不少困难和问题，也迎来了难得的发展机遇。必须把握机遇、应对挑战，贯彻发展新理念，加快种植业结构调整，促进种植业转型升级。“镰刀弯”地区是典型的旱作农业区，也是生态脆弱区，农业基础设施薄弱，玉米产量低而不稳，是这一轮农业结构调整的重点区域。按照适宜性调、种养结合型调、生态保护型调、种地养地结合型调、有保有压地调、围绕市场调的技术路径，力争到 2020 年玉米面积调减 5 000 万亩，2016 年调减 1 000 万亩以上。

“十二五”以来，种植业发展取得了显著成绩，粮食实现“十二连增”，产量、质量、效益稳步提升，农业转方式取得新进展，成为经济社会发展的突出亮点。2016 年是全面建成小康社会决胜阶段的开局之年，也是推进农业供给侧结构性改革的攻坚之年。种植业发展面临着不少困难和问题，也迎来了难得的发展机遇。必须把握机遇、应对挑战，贯彻发展新理念，加快种植业结构调整，促进种植业转型升级。

## （一）推进农业结构调整是适应经济发展新形势的必然选择

### 1. “十三五”种植业发展面临的挑战

当前，我国农业发展环境正发生深刻变化，老问题不断积累，新矛盾不断涌现，种植业发展面临不少困难和挑战。一是品种结构不平衡。小麦、稻谷口粮品种供求平衡，玉米出现阶段性供大于求，大豆供求缺口逐年扩大。棉花、油料、糖料等受资源约束和国际市场冲击，进口大幅增加，生产出现下滑。优质饲草短缺，进口逐年增加。二是资源环境约束的压力越来越大。工业化、城镇化快速推进还要占用一部分耕地，并挤压一部分农业用水空间。耕地质量退化、华北地下水超采、南方地表水富营养化等问题突出，对农业生产的“硬约束”加剧，靠拼资源消耗、拼物质要素投入的粗放发展方式难以为继。三是消费结构升级的要求越来越高。经济的发展使城乡居民的支付能力和生活水平不断提高，消费者对农产品的需求由吃得饱转向吃得好、吃得安全、吃得健康，进入消费主导农业发展转型的新阶段。四是产业融合的程度越来越深。现代农业产业链条不断延伸，产业附加值不断提升，需要开发农业的多种功能和多重价值，推进农牧结合，实现第一、二、三产业融合发展。五是国内外市场联动越来越紧。经济全球化和贸易自由化深入发展，国内与国际市场深度融合，资源要素和产品加速流动，竞争优势不足，进口压力加大。

### 2. “十三五”种植业发展仍有难得的机遇

种植业发展面临挑战的同时，也迎来难得的机遇。一是有发展新理念的引领。“创新、协调、绿色、开放、共享”五大发展新理念为调整优化种植结构提供了基本的遵循。二是有巨大市场消费的拉动。还有 5 年的时间我国就实现第一个百年奋斗目标，加之工业化、城镇化快速推进，进入消费需求持续增长、消费结构加快升级、消费拉动经济作用明显增强的重要阶段，蕴藏着巨大的市场空间，外在动力持续增强。三是有科技创新加速的支撑。以生物、信息、新材料、新能源技术为中心的新一轮科技革命和产业变革正蓄势待发，物联网、智能装备、DNA 生物记忆卡等一批新技术不断涌现，国家科技创新驱动战略和“大众创业、万众创新”的深入实施，智慧农业、生态农业等新业态应运而生，内在动力持续增强。四是有农村改革的深入推进。农村集体产权制度改革，改革完善粮食等农产品价格形成机制和收储制度，健全农业、农村投入持续增长机制，推动金融资源更多向农村倾斜，将进一步释放改革红利。五是有国际国内的深度融合。我国已深度融入全球化格局中，“一带一路”战略加快实施，统筹国际国内两个市场、两种资源，为调整优化种植结构拓展了空间。

**3. 在发展现代农业中推进种植业结构调整势在必行**

面对新形势、应对新挑战，必须主动作为、顺势而为，加快转变农业发展方式，推进种植业结构调整，提升农业效益和市场竞争力。第一，这是适应消费结构升级的需要。适应市场需求和消费升级的新变化，因地制宜调整种植业结构，在注重数量增加的同时，更要注重品种结构优化和产品质量提升，满足消费者多样化的需求。第二，这是适应产业结构转型升级的需要。农业现代化的重要标志是产业不断升级，生产链条不断延伸，产业附加值不断提升。适应这种新的变化，必须加快推进种植业结构调整。第三，这是缓解资源环境压力的需要。农业连年丰收，资源利用的弦绷得越来越紧，生态环境的承载能力接近极限。适应这种新的形势，必须推进种植业结构调整，走出一条资源节约、生态友好的农业可持续发展之路。第四，这是应对国际市场冲击的需要。随着经济全球化和贸易自由化的发展，国内与国际市场进一步融合，农业开放程度还会进一步提高。与小麦、玉米、大豆等世界主产国相比，我国不具备竞争优势，必须加快种植业结构调整，以应对日益激烈的国际竞争。

## （二）推进种植业结构调整的思路原则和目标任务

### 1. 总体思路

按照新形势下国家粮食安全战略和藏粮于地、藏粮于技战略的要求，牢固树立创新、协调、绿色、开放、共享的发展理念，坚持市场导向、科技引领、生态保护，优化品种结构和区域布局，巩固提升粮食产能，形成粮经饲统筹，农牧结合，种养加一体，一、二、三产业融合的农业发展格局，实现生产与市场需求相适应、产业升级相匹配、资源环境相协调。

### 2. 基本原则

基本原则就是做到“六个坚持”。一是坚持底线思维，确保粮食安全。立足我国国情和粮情，集中力量守住“谷物基本自给、口粮绝对安全”的战略底线。加强粮食主产区建设，建立粮食生产功能区和重要农产品保护区，提升粮食产能。二是坚持市场导向，推进产业融合。发挥市场配置资源决定性作用，引导农民安排好生产和种植结构。以关联产业升级转型为契机，推进农牧结合，发展农产品加工业，扩展农业多功能，实现一、二、三产业融合发展，提升农业效益。三是坚持突出重点，做到有保有压。根据资源禀赋及区域差异，做到保压有序、取舍有度。优化品种结构，重点是保口粮、保谷物，兼顾棉、油、糖、菜等生产，发展适销对路的优质品种。优化区域布局，发挥比较优势，巩固提升优势区，适当调减非优势区。优化作物结构，建立粮经饲三元结构，推进农牧结合。四是坚持创新驱动，注重提质增效。推进科技创新，强化农业科技基础条件和装备保障能力建设，提升农业科技水平。推进机制创新，培育新型农业经营主体和新型农业服务主体，发展适度规模经营，提升集约化水平和组织化程度。五是坚持生态保护，促进持续发展。树立尊重自然、顺应自然、保护自然的理念，节约和高效利用农业资源，推进化肥、农药减量增效，建立耕地轮作制度，实现用地养地结合，促进资源永续利用、生产生态协调发展。六是坚持着眼全球，统筹两个市场。在保障国家粮食安全底线的前提下，充分利用国际农业资源和产品市场，保持部分短缺品种的适度进口，满足国内市场需求。

**3. 发展目标**

发展目标的重点是提升粮食等主要农产品供给能力，主要是保口粮、保谷物，稳定棉花自给率、稳定食用植物油自给率、稳定糖料自给率，促进蔬菜生产与需求协调发展、饲草生产与畜牧养殖协调发展。提升农业质量效益和竞争力，通过增产增效、节本增效、提质增效等措施，种植业产品的质量效益和竞争力明显提升。提升持续发展能力，建立合理轮作制度，开展耕地休耕试点，构建资源节约、环境友好的绿色发展格局，实现种植业的永续发展。

**4. 重点任务**

重点任务就是“四个构建”。一是适应现代农业发展的要求，建立粮食作物、经济作物、饲料作物三元结构，构建粮经饲均衡发展的作物结构。二是发展优质农产品、专用农产品、特色农产品，构建适应市场需求的品种结构。三是根据农业资源的承载能力、环境容量、生态类型和发展基础等因素，分类施策，梯次推进，构建生产生态协调的区域结构。四是根据不同区域的资源条件和生态特点，建立耕地轮作制度，构建用地养地结合的耕作制度。

## （三）“镰刀弯”地区玉米结构调整是这一轮种植业结构调整的重中之重

“镰刀弯”地区主要包括黑龙江和内蒙古第四、五积温带的冷凉地区、北方农牧交错区、西北风沙干旱区、太行山沿线区及西南石漠化区。上述区域在我国地形版图中呈现由东北向华北—西南—西北镰刀弯状分布，故称“镰刀弯”地区。该区域玉米种植面积 1.5 亿亩以上，占全国玉米种植面积的 1/4 以上，是近 10 年我国玉米面积增长最快、产量增加最多的区域。按照《农业部关于“镰刀弯”地区玉米结构调整的指导意见》，力争到 2020 年玉米面积调减 5 000 万亩，2016 年调减 1 000 万亩以上。

**1. 推进“镰刀弯”地区玉米结构调整的必要性**

“镰刀弯”地区玉米结构调整是一项复杂的系统工程，面临不少困难和问题。一是玉米库存量高。目前，我国玉米库存量高，出现阶段性供大于求。特别是东北地区玉米库存量占全国玉米库存量的 3/4，区域性供大于求矛盾突出。二是市场竞争力偏弱。“镰刀弯”地区不同程度存在干旱缺水、低温寒害、土地沙化、石漠化等因素制约，玉米生产成本高，加之地处边远区域，外运成本也高，处于竞争劣势。三是作物结构单一。“镰刀弯”地区玉米“一粮独大”，挤压了轮作倒茬、牧草种植、节肥降耗等耕作模式的发展空间，种植结构由多元化向单一化演变。四是基础设施薄弱。“镰刀弯”地区多处在农牧交错、高寒高纬、坡地岗地、沙重盐重、跑水跑肥等立地条件较差的地区，中低产田占比较高，抗御自然灾害能力较弱。五是生态环境脆弱。“镰刀弯”地区是北方水资源匮乏的集中区域，也是退耕还林还草和生态涵养建设的重点区域。近些年，该区域玉米种植面积快速扩张，资源环境约束与生产发展的矛盾日益突出。

**2. 推进“镰刀弯”地区玉米结构调整的可行性**

“镰刀弯”地区优化调整玉米结构时机成熟，条件具备。一是调整有空间。粮食生产实现“十二连增”，粮食生产能力迈上新的台阶，特别是玉米市场供应充足、价格平稳，保数量的压力有所缓解，为调整优化种植结构腾出了空间。二是发展有需要。农产品消费结构加快转型升级，膳食结构多元化，营养健康、生态安全的农产品市场广阔，特别是畜牧业的快速发展，“镰刀弯”地区优质专用饲料需求旺盛，可实现粮食等农作物的就地转化和过腹转化。三是种植有基础。“镰刀弯”地区属于多元种植区，适宜多种作物生长，而且有多种作物轮作的传统和习惯。特别是“粮改饲”和粮豆轮作试点取得初步成效，为大面积推广积累了经验。四是调减有意愿。由于玉米收储政策调整，“镰刀弯”地区农民有意调减玉米种植面积，发展高效种养。

### 3. 推进“镰刀弯”地区玉米结构调整的技术路径

围绕“镰刀弯”地区结构调整的目标任务，重点是推进“六个调整”。一是适宜性调整。重点是调减高纬度、干旱区的玉米种植，改种耐旱的杂粮杂豆和生育期短的青贮玉米。二是种养结合型调整。重点是粮饲兼顾，调减籽粒玉米、发展青贮玉米和苜蓿，以养定种，把“粮仓”变为“粮仓” + “肉库” + “奶罐”。三是生态保护型调整。重点是调减石漠化地区的玉米种植，改种有生态涵养功能的果桑茶等经济林、牧草饲草、饲油兼用的油莎豆等，既保护生态环境，又促进农民增收。四是种地养地结合型调整。重点是东北地区恢复大豆、玉米轮作，因地制宜发展苜蓿、玉米轮作，华北地区实行冬小麦、夏花生（豆类）种植，发挥豆科作物固氮养地的作用。五是有保有压调整。重点是稳定玉米核心产区，调减北方农牧交错带和西南石漠化区等非优势区的玉米种植，特别是调减黑龙江第五积温带及部分第四积温带的玉米种植。六是围绕市场调整。重点是发挥龙头企业和新型经营主体的带动作用，实行订单种养、产加销融合。

（农业部种植业管理司　　潘文博）

# 二、加大改革创新力度 加快推进农业现代化

【内容提要】

2015 年是“十二五”规划的收官之年。面对适应、引领经济发展新常态提出的新要求和农业农村发展的新挑战，中央 1 号文件继续以党中央、国务院坚持“三农”重中之重地位不动摇，发出了以“加大改革创新力度　加快推进农业现代化”为主题的指导 2015 年农业农村工作文件。文件以深化农村改革、加快农业现代化、促进农业可持续发展、强化农村法治保障为重点，对农业农村工作进行了全面部署，提出了一系列重大政策和举措。在中央 1 号文件的有力推动和全国上下的共同努力下，全国粮食继续增产，农民收入继续较快增长，农业农村发展继续保持稳中有进的良好态势，继续成为经济社会发展的突出亮点，为“十二五”农业农村工作画上圆满句号，也为“十三五”乃至更长一个时期的农业农村发展奠定了坚实基础。

2015 年 1 月，中共中央、国务院发出了《关于加大改革创新力度　加快推进农业现代化的决定》（中发［2015］1 号），对 2015 年农业农村工作进行了全面部署。

## （一）政策出台背景

2015 年的中央 1 号文件是党的十八大以来中央发出的第 3 个 1 号文件。中央决定 1 号文件不仅继续姓

“农”，而且继续以深化农村改革为主线、以推进农业现代化为目标。这既是基于国内外发展形势深刻变化、经济社会深刻转型的时代特征，又是针对农业、农村发展面临的困难和挑战，是利当前、惠长远的重大决策部署。

首先，引领“新常态”，必须依靠深化农村改革、加快推进农业现代化。在新常态下，整个经济社会发展都在转型升级。作为国民经济的基础、“四化同步”发展的短板，农业转型升级的要求更加迫切。随着农村经济社会结构的深刻变革，特别是农业劳动力向外转移、农业生产要素减少的趋势持续发展，农业发展的原有格局不断被打破，“谁来种地、怎么种地”等问题日益突出。随着城乡居民收入增长，农产品消费加快升级，人们不仅要求农产品供给充足，而且要求更加多元化、个性化，更加关注“舌尖上的安全”和“舌尖上的美味”，保障粮食等重要农产品有效供给的任务更加艰巨。随着经济增长速度不断放缓，农产品产量增加、价格提高和工资性收入的增长也都相应放缓，继续保持农民收入较快增长面临严峻考验。只有加快转变农业发展方式，不断推进产业升级，才能适应经济社会发展的需要，在引领新常态中不断开创农业发展、农民增收新局面。

其次，应对“天花板”，出路在于深化农村改革、加快推进农业现代化。我国农产品关税只有世界平均水平的1/4，是世界上农业开放程度最高的国家之一。随着对外开放的继续深化，国内市场与国际市场的进一步融合，农业对外开放程度持续提高，农业发展面临的“天花板”制约越来越突出。从价格天花板来看，到 2014 年底，我国主要大宗农产品的国内市场价格普遍接近或超过了进口税后价格，部分粮食品种已超过了配额外完税价格，价格的“封顶效应”已经显现出来，保持农产品市场价格基本稳定困难重重。从支持天花板来看，我国加入世贸组织时承诺对特定农产品的“黄箱”支持不超过该产品产值的 8.5%，对非特定农产品的支持不超过农业总产值的 8.5%。而我国对主要粮食品种等特定农产品的价格支持已经接近承诺上限，继续增加支持的余地很有限。从库存天花板来看，由于我国农业连年丰收和部分农产品进口持续增加，农产品库存屡创新高。2014 年，虽然稻米、小麦、玉米三大主粮的净进口量比上年减少了近 300 万吨，但高粱、大麦等替代品进口量却成倍增长。据专家推算，仅玉米替代品进口的大量增加，就至少导致国产玉米新增 1 000 多万吨库存。只有加快转变农业发展方式，创新支持保护政策，才能有效化解农业发展面临的各种制约，在日益激烈的国际竞争中把握主动。

最后，破解“紧箍咒”，唯有通过深化农村改革、加快推进农业现代化。我国农业资源禀赋先天不足，特别是人均耕地和淡水资源分别只有世界平均水平的1/2和1/4。这些年，我们主要依靠国内生产解决了13多亿人的吃饭问题，成绩十分突出，但也付出了巨大的资源环境代价，成为农业持续稳定发展的“紧箍咒”。一方面，经过持续的高强度开发利用，尤其是过度开采地下水和过量施用化肥、农药、农膜等化学投入品，使农业资源环境不堪重负、农产品质量安全受到威胁，已经到了难以为继的地步，一些地方甚至频频亮起了“红灯”。另一方面，我国仍处在工业化、城镇化快速推进的发展阶段，耕地面积减少、农业用水紧张加剧的趋势仍将持续。如果继续沿着拼资源消耗、拼农资投入、拼生态环境的粗放式增长老路走下去，农业发展就会根基不保。只有加快转变农业发展方式，提高资源利用效率，才能节约资源、保护环境，实现农业的永续发展。

## （二）主要政策内容

2015年的中央1号文件以深化农村改革、加快农业现代化、促进农业可持续发展、强化农村法治保障为重点，对农业农村工作进行了全面部署，提出了一系列重大政策和举措。其中与农业特别是粮食生产直接相关的内容可以归纳为以下四个方面：

### 1. 加快转变农业发展方式

一是不断增强粮食生产能力。全面开展永久基本农田划定工作，统筹实施全国高标准农田建设总体规划，实施耕地质量保护与提升行动；探索建立粮食生产功能区；实施粮食丰产科技工程和盐碱地改造科技示范，深入推进粮食高产创建和绿色增产模式攻关。二是深入推进农业结构调整。开展粮改饲和种养结合模式试点，促进粮食、经济作物、饲草料三元种植结构协调发展；推进农业综合开发布局调整；支持粮食主产区发展畜牧业和粮食加工业，发展农产品深精加工。三是提升农产品质量和食品安全水平。落实重要农产品生产基地、批发市场质量安全检验检测费用补助政策，建立全程可追溯、互联共享的农产品质量和食品安全信息平台，大力发展名特优新农产品，培育知名品牌。四是强化农业科技创新驱动作用，健全农业科技创新激励机制，加快农业科技创新。五是创新农产品流通方式。加快全国农产品市场体系转型升级，加快千亿斤粮食新建仓容建设进度，开展电子商务进农村综合示范。六是加强农业生态治理。实施农业环境突出问题治理总体规划和农业可持续发展规划，开展西北旱区农牧业可持续发展、农牧交错带已垦草原治理、东北黑土地保护试点，启动新一轮退耕还林还草工程。七是提高统筹利用国际国内两个市场、两种资源的能力。加强农产品进出口调控，完善粮食、棉花、食糖等重要农产品进出口和关税配额管理。

**2. 加大惠农政策力度**

一是优先保证农业农村投入。坚持把农业农村作为各级财政支出的优先保障领域，持续增加财政农业农村支出，中央基建投资继续向农业农村倾斜；优化财政支农支出结构，重点支持农民增收、农村重大改革、农业基础设施建设、农业结构调整、农业可持续发展、农村民生改善。二是提高农业补贴政策效能。逐步扩大“绿箱”支持政策实施规模和范围，调整改进“黄箱”支持政策；实施农业生产重大技术措施推广补助政策；健全粮食主产区利益补偿、耕地保护补偿、生态补偿制度。三是完善农产品价格形成机制。继续执行稻谷、小麦最低收购价政策，完善重要农产品临时收储政策；积极开展农产品价格保险试点；落实新增地方粮食储备规模计划，建立重要商品商贸企业代储制度。四是强化农业社会化服务。抓好农业生产全程社会化服务机制创新试点；加大中央、省级财政对主要粮食作物保险的保费补贴力度；将主要粮食作物制种保险纳入中央财政保费补贴目录。

**3. 全面深化农村改革**

一是加快构建新型农业经营体系。创新土地流转和规模经营方式，积极发展多种形式适度规模经营；鼓励发展规模适度的农户家庭农场，完善对粮食生产规模经营主体的支持服务体系；引导农民以土地经营权入股合作社和龙头企业；鼓励工商资本发展适合企业化经营的现代种养业、农产品加工流通和农业社会化服务企业。二是推进农村集体产权制度改革。探索农村集体所有制有效实现形式，创新农村集体经济运行机制。三是稳步推进农村土地制度改革试点。四是推进农村金融体制改革。推动金融资源继续向“三农”倾斜，确保农业信贷总量持续增加、涉农贷款比例不降低；开展大型农机具融资租赁试点。五是深化水利和林业改革。建立健全水权制度，开展水权确权登记试点，推进农业水价综合改革，深化集体林权制度改革，稳步推进国有林场改革和国有林区改革。六是加快供销合作社和农垦改革发展。

#### 4. 加强农村法治建设

一是健全农村产权保护法律制度。抓紧修改农村土地承包方面的法律，明确现有土地承包关系保持稳定并长久不变的具体实现形式。加强农业知识产权法律保护。二是健全农业市场规范运行法律制度。健全农产品市场流通法律制度，营造农产品流通法治化环境。完善农产品市场调控制度，适时启动相关立法工作。三是健全“三农”支持保护法律制度，研究制定规范各级政府“三农”事权的法律法规，明确规定中央和地方政府促进农业农村发展的支出责任。四是依法保障农村改革发展。加强农村改革决策与立法的衔接。

### （三）政策实施效果

2015 年，在中央 1 号文件的有力推动和全国上下的共同努力下，全国粮食继续增产，农民收入继续较快增长，农业农村发展继续保持稳中有进的良好态势，继续成为经济社会发展的突出亮点，为“十二五”农业农村工作画上圆满句号，也为“十三五”和更长一个时期的农业农村发展奠定了坚实基础。其成效主要表现在以下四个方面：

一是农业生产实现新发展。全国粮食总产量达到 62 143 万吨，比 2014 年增长 2.4%，连续第 3 年超过 60 000 万吨；棉油糖、肉蛋奶、果蔬茶、水产品等都获得丰收，主要农产品市场供应充足。这标志着我国农业综合生产能力尤其是粮食综合生产能力已稳定迈上一个新台阶，农业现代化发展已提升到一个新水平。

二是农民收入取得新突破。全国农村居民人均可支配收入达到 11 422 元，比 2014 年增长 8.9%，扣除价格因素实际增长 7.5%，增长速度连续第 6 年高于城镇居民收入和国内生产总值的增长速度。这反映出我国城乡居民收入差距持续扩大的态势已经得到明显扭转，城乡协调发展的格局正在加快形成。

三是农业转方式、调结构打开新局面。2015 年，三大主要粮食作物的化肥和农药利用率分别比 2013 年提高 2.2、1.6 个百分点，畜禽养殖规模化率提高到 39.6%，粮改饲、粮豆轮作试点全面启动。这体现了我国农业发展正由主要依靠增加资源要素投入向主要依靠科技进步转变，科技进步对农业增产、农民增收的贡献率在进一步提高。

四是农村改革取得新进展。全国土地承包经营权确权登记面积超过 3 亿亩，家庭农场、种养大户、农业合作社、龙头企业等新型农业经营主体达到近 250 万家，多种形式适度规模经营加快发展，农村集体产权制度改革迈出重要步伐，深化农村改革综合性实施方案正式印发。这证明了深化农村改革蕴藏的巨大潜力，为培育农业农村发展接续新动能指明了努力方向。

（国务院研究室农村司　　张顺喜）

# 三、加强农业生态治理 促进可持续发展

**【内容提要】**

随着我国农业综合生产能力的不断提升，农业生态环境问题日益凸显。党的十八大以来，以习近平总书记为首的新一届领导集体高度重视生态文明建设，多次强调绿水青山就是金山银山，在粮食连续增产的形势下，从战略高度提出了“在重视粮食数量的同时，更加注重品质和质量安全；在保障当期供给的同时，更加注重农业可持续发展”的新要求。当前，国家财力日益雄厚，利用国际市场调剂余缺的能力增强，主要农产品供给充足，有条件通过财政奖补、结构调整等综合措施，开展农业资源休养生息试点，治理农业环境突出问题的时机已经成熟。2015 年国务院正式批准了《农业环境突出问题治理总体规划》和《农业可持续发展规划》。

## （一）政策背景

民以食为天。我国是一个人口大国，增加农产品供给、保障国家粮食安全是头等重要的大事，建国 60 年来，历届政府为此进行了不懈的努力。特别是 2004 年以来，国家加大了对农业的支持力度，农业综合生产能力不断跨上新台阶。2015 年，我国粮食生产实现了“十二连增”，连续 3 年产量超过了 12 000 亿斤。

但是，由于我国自然资源禀赋不足，人均耕地、人均水资源占有量均低于世界人均水平，人口分布、经济发展与资源环境配置不均衡，加上长期粗放的发展方

式，水土资源约束亮起了红灯，农业生态环境问题凸显。长期以来，一些地区和企业片面追求经济效益，废气废水废渣等排放不达标造成土壤污染，农田过度利用，化肥、农药使用量大，利用效率偏低。我国粮食产量占世界 16%，但化肥年使用量占世界 31.7%；农药施用利用率仅为 35%，比发达国家低 20～30 个百分点；农膜残留率高达 40%；畜禽粪污中一半未经处理就直接排放；农业面源总氮、总磷年排放量已占全国排放总量的一半以上，长期积累的水土污染问题导致农产品质量安全事件多发。同时，地表水过度开发和地下水超采、水土流失、草原退化、湿地萎缩等问题日益严重。迫切需要统筹规划、分类指导，有序推进农业环境突出问题治理工作，开展大规模整治。

对生态环境的关注源于上世纪 90 年代末长江水灾，朱镕基总理提出了“封山植树、退耕还林，平垸行洪、退田还湖，以工代赈、移民建镇，加固干堤、疏浚河道”32 字方针，生态环境问题纳入了我国经济社会发展的重要议事日程。国家加大了投入，加强了治理力度，但由于经济发展模式和理念相对落后，治理技术研发滞后，对治理难度及长期性、复杂性认识不足，以及法律法规和治理机制不健全，农业环境突出问题治理工作仍未全面系统展开。党的十八大以来，以习近平总书记为首的新一届领导集体高度重视生态文明建设，多次强调绿水青山就是金山银山，在粮食连续增产的形势下，从战略高度提出了“在重视粮食数量的同时，更加注重品质和质量安全；在保障当期供给的同时，更加注重农业可持续发展”的新要求。当前，国家财力日益雄厚，利用国际市场调剂余缺的能力增强，主要农产品供给充足，有条件通过财政奖补、结构调整等综合措施，开展农业资源休养生息试点，治理农业环境突出问题的时机已经成熟。

2013 年下半年，国务院分管领导同志主持召开促进农业可持续发展专题会议，明确要求国家发改委会同有关部门组织编制农业环境突出问题治理总体规划。2014 年中央 1 号文件明确提出，要抓紧编制农业环境突出问题治理总体规划。同年，中央将“调整严重污染和地下水超采区耕地用途，有序实现耕地、河湖休养生息”确定为改革任务。2015 年中央 1 号文件提出启动实施农业环境突出问题治理总体规划和农业可持续发展规划。同年，国务院正式批准了《农业环境突出问题治理总体规划》和《农业可持续发展规划》。

## （二）治理工作的总体思路、目标、任务

总体思路：坚持节约资源和保护环境的基本国策，坚持节约优先、保护优先、自然恢复为主的方针，充分认识各类农业环境问题的复杂性和治理的长期性，以确保国家粮食安全和农民增收为前提，统筹国际国内两个市场、两种资源，妥善处理好农业增产与可持续发展、稳定国内生产与利用国际市场、保障供给与保护环境的关系，通过政策引导、结构调整、机制创新、科技支撑、试点示范、依法监管，着力推进发展方式转变，加强水土资源节约利用和污染防治，充分调动各方积极性，加快发展环境友好、资源节约、优质高效的现代农业，推动美丽中国和和谐社会建设。

基本原则：统筹规划，重点突破；多措并举，试点示范；政策引导，多方参与；建管并重，巩固成果。

目标与任务：鉴于农业环境治理难度及长期性、复杂性，按照分步目标实施。一是按照“有限时间、有限范围、有限目标”的要求，在摸清底数、试点示范的基础上，探索各类农业环境突出问题的治理模式和运行机制，并在试点范围内初步解决或缓解现存的问题。二是力争到2018年，通过试点探索，总结出一批成功治理范例和适用模式，为在全国范围内实施农业环境问题治理奠定基础，并有计划、分步骤推广。

## （三）重点工程及保障措施

针对水土污染严重影响农产品质量安全、资源利用过度影响农业可持续发展、土地垦殖无序影响生态环境等三个方面的问题，整合为七大工程。并根据现有治理技术、模式提出了相关工程的重点，如耕地重金属污染治理和农业面源污染综合治理尚无成熟的治理模式，主要以试点示范为主；其他技术路线成熟、问题边界明确的治理任务，可适当扩大治理范围等。经过5年努力力争达到以下治理成效：治理区污染物削减能力、土壤有机质和耕地基础地力有所提高，有利于保证农产品质量安全；治理区地

表水过度开发和地下水超采状况将得到缓解，水资源利用效率提高；治理区林草植被盖度将大幅增加，有利于涵养水源、调节气候和维护生物多样性。同时，可总结形成一批治理模式和经验，为全面治理农业环境问题奠定基础。

七大工程如下：

一是耕地重金属污染治理。以治理镉、砷和复合重金属污染耕地为重点，建设耕地重金属污染治理示范区，通过治理，使轻、中度污染治理区耕层土壤有效态重金属含量降低 30% 以上，食用农产品基本达标生产，重度污染治理区改种非食用农作物或花卉林木。治理区实现耕地及农产品分类、分级管理和长期监控。

二是农业面源污染综合防治。在典型流域和水源地等重点区域，建设农业面源污染综合治理示范区，实施化肥、农药控施替代，建设农药包装废弃物回收试点，控制氮、磷流失，合理处理和资源化利用畜禽粪污，水产养殖废水废物净化循环利用，降低示范区内化学需氧量、总氮、总磷排放量。建设农田残膜回收与再生利用示范区，大幅提高地膜当季回收率。建设农作物秸秆综合利用示范区，基本实现项目区内秸秆全部利用。

三是地表水过度开发和地下水超采综合治理。对试点地区实施治理，有效缓解试点地区地表水过度开发和地下水超采问题，初步形成与区域水土资源条件相匹配的农业发展格局，有效实现农业资源休养生息，改善农业环境和水生态环境。

四是新一轮退耕还林还草。在尊重农民意愿的基础上，根据不同地理、气候和立地条件，对符合条件的 25 度以上坡耕地、严重沙化耕地和重要水源地 15 ~ 25 度坡耕地实施退耕还林还草，增加植被盖度，减缓和控制水土流失。

五是退耕还湿。对试点地区具备条件的已围垦湿地实施退耕还湿，恢复试点地区已退化湿地，提高湿地质量，恢复湿地生态系统功能。

六是农牧交错带已垦草原治理。通过大力推广多年生优良牧草品种及其旱作栽培技术，在农牧交错带已垦撂荒草原区建设多年生旱作人工牧草地，有效提高植被覆盖度。

七是东北黑土地保护。实施黑土综合治理，使项目区耕层厚度恢复到 25 厘米以上，土壤有机质含量提高 3% ~ 5%，土壤保水保肥能力显著提高，耕地地力提高 0.5 个等级。

八项保障措施为：一是坚持改革创新，探索建立治理和保护长效机制；二是健全法规标准，依法推进治理工作；三是完善扶持政策，调动各方治理积极性；四是做好调查监测，为治理提供科学依据；五是加强技术研发，为治理提供科技支撑；六是强化监督管理，巩固治理成果；七是把握治理节奏，统筹兼顾粮食安全和生态保护；八是明确部门分工，落实地方责任。

## （四）实施情况

2015 年国家加大了新增 1 000 亿斤粮食生产能力建设预算内资金规模，其中专门安排了 4 000 多万元在黑龙江双城实施黑土地治理试点，在江苏金坛县开展了面源污染治理试点。安排预算内资金 30 多亿元用于退耕还林和湿地建设。中央财政也安排资金用于地下水超采区、土壤重金属污染区种植结构调整补助。

（国家发改委农村经济司　　方言）

# 四、2015年粮食信贷政策与管理

【内容提要】

2015年，为应对错综复杂的国内外经济形势，党中央、国务院采取了一系列政策措施，避免了经济大起大落。但经济运行中结构性矛盾仍然突出，经济回稳基础不牢。同时，国内粮食市场供大于求，出现了产销区、产成品价格倒挂，加工企业经营困难等一系列问题。为此，国家启动了粮食去库存和粮食收储制度改革等一系列政策，这必将对粮食市场以及粮食信贷政策带来重大影响。为应对形势变化，农发行及时调整粮食信贷政策，进一步明确粮油信贷工作的指导思想和发展战略，全力支持粮食收购，及时提供粮食收购资金，确保粮食市场稳定和国家粮食安全；在风险可控的前提下积极支持粮食加工企业经营发展，帮扶企业渡过难关；加强信贷管理，防控信贷风险，提高信贷服务水平。

## （一）政策背景

2015年，世界经济仍处于深度调整之中，呈现出低增长、不平衡、宽震荡、多风险的特征。我国经济进入结构调整和动力转换的关键阶段，潜在增长率趋势性回落与长期结构性、短期周期性问题叠加，经济下行压力加大。面对错综复杂的国内外经济形势，党中央、国务院采取了一系列稳增长、促改革、调结构、惠民生、防风险的政策措施，坚持稳中求进的总基调，避免了经济的大起大落。但经济运行中的结构性矛盾仍然突出，部分领域的困难和风险还在增加，经济回稳基础不牢。同时，国内粮食市场供大于求，粮食产量高、库存高、价格高，出现了产销区、产成品价格倒挂，加工企业经营困难；粮食流通不畅、国家收储压力加大；财政负担严重等一系列问题。为此，国家启动粮食去库存和粮食收储体制改革，这必将对粮食市场以及粮食信贷政策产生重大影响。

**1. 粮食收储政策调整的窗口期已来临**

从2014年对新疆棉花和东北大豆实行目标价格改革开始，粮食收储政策调整的序幕已经拉开。2015年国家退出了油菜籽政策收储，实行国家财政定额补贴下的市场化收购；大幅降低了国家临储玉米收购价格，从严掌握粮食收购质量标准；小麦、稻谷最低收购价格虽然维持2014年不变，但改变了只涨不跌的定价模式，对外发出了强烈的信号，政策性粮食收储已收紧价格上行区间。根据中央1号文件精神，按照分品种施策、渐进式推进的原则，对主要粮食品种收储制度的改革将逐步实施。粮食收储制度改革的方向是充分发挥市场机制的作用，由市场形成价格，并通过价外补贴的方式保障农民收益。粮食价格由市场供需决定，在供大于求的市场格局下，粮食价格将步入下行区间，防控市场风险将成为粮食信贷工作的主要任务。

**2. 粮油加工企业去产能进程加快**

我国经过30多年的改革开放，已经由短缺经济发展到过剩经济时代，社会物质条件已经非常丰富。随着我国经济由高速增长转化为中高速增长这一新常态的出现，我国粮食加工企业面临去产能问题，粮油加工行业洗牌和整合势在必行。在这个过程中，一些企业将会发展壮大，而另一些企业的关停、倒闭、破产不可避免，这将对银行现有客户，尤其是中小企业的生存带来严重考验。如何对现有客户结构进行调整以及在未来如何选择新客户，将成为粮食信贷工作的重点和难点。

**3. 粮食流通市场化竞争的序幕已经拉开**

随着国家粮食收储制度改革的推进，国家将逐步退出或减少政策性粮食收储，粮食流通市场将回归市场化收购为主导的格局。当前，国内一些有实力的粮食企业已经开始进行市场布局，东北地区已经初步形成了中储粮、中粮、中纺、中航国际和象屿集团五大粮商聚集的局面，华北地区也呈现出大型粮商和地方性粮食企业开疆拓土、布局定点的趋势。粮食市场化必定会带来收购主体的多元化，必将给市场带来活力，同时，粮食企业也将接受市场的洗礼和考验，特别是当前粮食市场又面临着国家储备去库存和进口低成本粮食的双重挤压，这些都将对粮食经营者带来重大挑战，也将对习惯了连续多年服务于政策性粮食收储的农发行粮食信贷工作带来挑战。

## （二）信贷政策

面对 2015 年严峻复杂的粮食市场形势，农发行进一步明确了粮食信贷工作要坚持在不“打白条”的前提下防控风险的指导思想，深化客户结构调整，强化风险防控措施，确保了粮食信贷业务的健康发展。归纳起来，出台的信贷政策主要有以下几个方面：

### 1. 进一步明确粮食信贷业务的指导思想和发展战略

农发行总行进一步明确了粮食信贷业务的指导思想和发展战略。要求继续坚持在不“打白条”的前提下防控风险的指导思想和“多收粮、收好粮、防风险”的总体要求不动摇，确保粮食收购资金供应和管理不出大的问题。一是全力做好政策性粮食收购信贷工作，及时足额保障国家托市收购和地方储备粮增储的资金需要，确保国家粮食调控政策的有效落实。二是积极支持优质客户参与市场性收购，择优支持有效益的龙头加工企业入市收购，择优支持有稳定销售渠道、有购销合同的贸易企业入市收购，稳定和提高开户企业粮食收购市场份额，确保支持收购不出大的问题。同时，明确不把贷款规模的增长作为业务发展战略，防止出现为追求贷款规模的增长而脱离粮食购销发放贷款的现象。三是对待自营性业务按照有利于解决粮食收购问题、有利于发挥示范带动作用、有利于带动非信贷资产业务发展的原则，选择“五好”客户予以支持，做到成效明显、风险可控。

### 2. 强化“双结零”管理，加快粮食促销收贷

农发行进一步明确了粮棉油收购贷款“双结零”标准，明确了企业库存销售进度的监测指标要求，明确了粮棉油收购贷款延期“双结零”的条件，督促粮食经营企业及时销售粮食。特别是在国家调整玉米收储政策和玉米价格下行趋势明显的情况下，为防止玉米收购贷款出现区域性风险，及时下发通知督促企业加快玉米销售，指导河北、山东等非预案区玉米主产省市场性玉米收购贷款及时促销收贷，以防止价格大幅下跌带来的市场风险。

### 3. 积极支持粮食仓储设施贷款

为贯彻落实国家“粮安工程”战略部署，农发行及时调整粮食仓储设施贷款政策，对列入各级政府粮食仓储设施建设名录并落实财政补贴的建仓项目，都可视为符合《中国农业发展银行仓储设施贷款管理办法》（农发银发［2014］124 号）中关于“借款人为完成政府宏观调控任务申请粮食仓储设施贷款”的要求，按照政府调控类建仓贷款办理，不再对企业的信用等级提出要求，降低了贷款准入门槛。同时，对于财政补贴不能覆盖的贷款本息部分，在企业有效资产应抵尽抵的前提下，要求必须做好贷款担保，有效控制风险敞口，防范信贷风险。

### 4. 积极支持粮食企业加工经营

为认真落实银监会流动资金贷款无还本续贷政策，积极帮扶实体经济企业渡过难关，农发行及时转发《中国银监会关于进一步落实小微企业金融服务监管政策的通知》，明确两类企业可以通过发放新贷款结清已有贷款的方式，继续使用贷款资金：一是依法合规经营，生产经营基本正常，具有财务可持续能力，能够主动配合农发行贷款监管的企业；二是地方政府或银监部门为化解区域性金融风险，要求金融部门通过重组、续贷、展期等方式实施救助的企业。同时明确，通过无还本续贷方式办理的续贷业务，风险缓释措施不能降低，不能扩大风险敞口。

### 5. 进一步完善风险管控措施

一是强化政策性贷款风险管控。中央储备粮轮换贷款只能发放给中储

粮直属企业，轮换贷款额度必须在中储粮分公司确定的轮换计划和轮换额度内；地方储备粮贷款要在地方政府明确粮权和落实各项财政补贴的前提下发放。从严控制地方调控贷款和地方储备轮换贷款的发放。二是严格控制新客户准入。新准入的客户要符合“五好”标准，新发放（含续贷）的产业化龙头企业贷款，须具备合法、有效的地市级（含）以上农业产业化龙头企业资格。三是强化贷后监管。切实落实粮食收购资金封闭运行管理的各项措施，落实贷后监管责任。利用信息科技手段，在粮食主产区推广信贷远程视频监控系统，实现实时在线监控，提高监管效率和监管水平。

## （三）实施效果

### 1. 确保了粮食收购资金供应

2015 年，全年累计投放粮油收购贷款 5 738 亿元，支持企业收购粮油 5 428 亿斤，同比分别增加 527 亿元和 590 亿斤；农发行开户企业粮食收购量分别占全国粮食产量和全社会收购量的 43% 和 67%，同比分别提高 2. 17 和 2. 35 个百分点。其中，全年累计投放政策性粮油收购贷款 4 851 亿元，收购粮油 4 082 亿斤，占全部粮油贷款投放金额和数量的比重分别是 85% 和 75%；全年累计发放市场性粮食收购贷款 847 亿元，收购粮食 1 316 亿斤。全力保障了粮油收购平稳有序运行，确保粮油收购没有出现大的问题，较好地履行了政策性银行的职能作用。

### 2. 确保了国家粮食调控政策有效落实

全年累计发放最低收购价和临储托市收购贷款 4 455 亿元，同比多发放 1 131 亿元，增幅为 34%；支持企业收购粮食 3 649 亿斤，同比多收 1 116 亿斤，增幅为 44%，保障了国家政策性收购资金及时足额供应。同时，积极支持地方储备增储，全年累计发放地方储备粮贷款 639 亿元，同比增加 71 亿元，增幅为 11%，确保了地方储备增储计划的落实。

### 3. 缓解了库存紧张状况

一是积极支持政策性粮食促销压库。农发行积极配合有关部门加大对政策性粮食的拍卖力度，全年累计投放政策性粮食4 851亿斤，成交370亿斤，收回国家粮油调控贷款694亿元，缓解了主产区的仓容压力。二是对市场性收购贷款按照“双结零”管理要求及时促销收贷。截至2015年底，全年收回政策指导性收购贷款812亿元，贷款收回率为97%，特别是玉米促销收贷效果显著，避免了因市场风险集中爆发带来的贷款大规模损失。三是支持政策性粮食跨省移库，累计发放跨省移库费用贷款28亿元，支持企业移库粮食254亿斤，有效缓解了主产区仓容紧张压力。四是积极支持企业仓储设施以及物流节点建设，2015年发放粮油仓储设施贷款13亿元，支持仓储设施项目39个，有效实施了国家“粮安工程”战略。

### 4. 有效管控了信贷风险

一是客户结构进一步优化。截至2015年末，全行93%的粮油类贷款客户信用等级在A－级（含）以上，其中，AA－级（含）以上客户占比54%，占全部粮油贷款余额的87%，余额占比比年初提高了2个百分点。二是政策性贷款占比较大。2015年，农发行粮油政策性贷款余额占全部粮油类贷款余额的97%，其中，国家和地方储备及调控贷款余额占全部粮油类贷款的80%，贷款资产质量较高。三是贷款风险得到有效控制。2015年末粮油类贷款不良贷款率虽然比年初增加0.16个百分点，但不良贷款主要集中在少数省份，贷款风险仍然整体可控。

### 5. 服务水平进一步提高

2015年，农发行在对中储粮公司开通银企直联的基础上，对中粮、中航国际等大型粮食企业也开通了银企直联系统，并且在收购旺季延长结算服务时间到晚8点，确保企业能够及时将售粮款支付给农民。同时，将系统升级作为常态化工作，不断为企业提供便捷的结算服务。

（中国农业发展银行　　朱远洋　李楠）

# 第五部分

## 2015 年中国
## 粮食市场体系建设

# 一、粮食批发市场发展状况与展望

【内容提要】

2015年是“十二五”规划收官之年，国内粮食生产实现创历史的“十二连增”，粮食收购迈上新台阶。随着国内外粮食价差持续拉大、粮食生产成本大幅提高，国家粮食安全面临新的挑战。在新形势下，国家加大对粮食批发市场建设的政策和资金扶持力度，全国粮食统一竞价交易系统实现平台整合、并网运行，宏观调控的精准性、有效性显著增强。一年来，各地粮食行政管理部门在全面完成“十二五”粮食市场体系规划任务的同时，抓紧编制粮食行业“十三五”规划，进一步完善粮食批发市场体系建设。成品粮市场继续发挥城市“米袋子”作用；商流市场继续发挥保供稳价的主渠道作用。各类市场在做好主业的同时，不断开拓创新，既取得了可喜的成绩，也面临巨大的难题。2016年是“十三五”规划开局之年，也是粮食行业落实“四个全面”战略布局、保障国家粮食安全、推进粮食经济持续健康发展大有作为的一年。国家将进一步加大政策扶持力度，加强粮食批发市场建设，完善市场功能，充分发挥粮食批发市场在保障国家粮食宏观调控、促进粮食市场流通、保障城市粮食供应和价格稳定方面的重要作用。

## （一）粮食批发市场发展外部环境

### 1. 粮食生产创历史性“十二连增”

2015年世界经济增速放缓，反映出全球经济复苏之路崎岖艰辛。全球谷物产量与2014年基本持平，国际粮食价格总体保持弱势运行。在中央一系列强农惠农政策支持下，我国粮食生产实现“十二连增”，粮食总产量达到62 143.5万吨，比2014年增加1 440.8万吨，增长2.4%，创造了中国乃至世界粮食史上的奇迹，为确保国家粮食安全奠定了坚实的物质基础。

### 2. 粮食安全面临新的挑战

当前，我国粮食安全形势总体是好的，但也必须清醒认识到我国粮食安全面临一些新情况新问题。一是粮食价格的“天花板”问题。国内粮食价格受国家托市政策的支撑始终处于高位，而国际市场粮价继续低迷，国内外粮食价差持续拉大，粮食进口增加。二是国内粮食生产成本在大幅度提高，粮食的“地板”在不断上升。三是我国粮食补贴“黄线”问题，中国加入世贸组织时承诺的价格支持、与农产品现期产量等挂钩的直接补贴等对贸易有较大扭曲作用的“黄箱补贴”不得超过产值的8.5%。据统计，中国“三农”财政补贴已经接近这条“黄线”。四是粮食生产环境中的“红灯”开始亮起。由于过度使用耕地发展粮食生产，带来了粮食生态环境的破坏，如农药、化肥的过度使用造成部分耕地污染，质量下降，影响粮食生产健康可持续发展。

### 3. 粮食收购迈上新台阶

面对我国粮食连年丰收、收储矛盾十分突出的新形势，特别是2015年在粮价下行压力加大、主产区仓容缺口巨大、政策调整影响较大的困难条件下，各级粮食部门和相关央企认真落实国家粮食收购政策，适时启动政策性收储，着力强化市场监管，切实规范收购秩序，粮食收购工作平稳有序，有效防止了农民“卖粮难”。“十二五”期间，全国各类粮食企业收购总量连创新高，2015 年高达 8 484 亿斤，同比增加 1 186 亿斤，首次跨上 8 000 亿斤新台阶。近 5 年累计托市收购粮食 8 460 亿斤、油菜籽 1 573 万吨，通过价格托底、优质优价、整晒提等、产后减损等措施带动农民增收 2 510 亿元，有效保护了种粮农民利益，调动了地方政府抓粮积极性。

#### 4. 粮食批发市场建设的政策扶持力度加大

2014 年底国务院下发的国发［2014］69 号文件《关于建立健全粮食安全省长责任制的若干意见》提出：“要增强粮食流通能力，进一步完善粮食交易中心功能，加快联网竞价交易平台建设，推进政策性粮食联网交易，同时培育一批公益性成品粮批发市场。”2015 年的中央 1 号文件《关于加大改革创新力度　加快农业现代化建设的若干意见》中提出：“要创新农产品流通方式，健全交易制度，完善全国农产品流通骨干网络，同时继续开展公益性农产品批发市场建设试点，发展农产品期货交易，开发农产品期货交易新品种。”这些政策的出台对粮食批发市场的发展起到了重要的推动作用，粮食批发交易市场得到长足发展，全国粮食统一竞价交易系统实现平台整合、并网运行，宏观调控的精准性、有效性显著增强。

### （二）加强行业指导，促进粮食批发市场健康有序发展

#### 1. 加强粮食批发市场建设的规划指导

“十二五”时期，国家粮食局加强对粮食市场体系建设的规划指导，认真抓好规划的实施，围绕发展目标，深入各地实地调研，提出指导意见，推动“十二五”市场规划目标任务的全面完成，基本形成了以粮食收购市场和零售市场为基础、批发市场为骨干、粮食期货交易稳步发展，统一开放、竞争有序的现代粮食市场体系，使粮食收购服务体系更加高效规范，粮食零售供应网络更加健全，粮食批发市场体系更加完善，粮食期货交易功能进一步发挥。

“十三五”时期是我国全面建成小康社会的决胜阶段，也是粮食行业落实“四个全面”战略布局、保障国家粮食安全、推进粮食经济持续健康发展大有作为的重要机遇期。国家粮食局在认真总结“十二五”规划实施情况和成效的基础上，及时召开“十三五”规划编制工作座谈会，深入粮食产销区进行调研，征求各地对编制粮食行业“十三五”规划的建议。

**2. 加强粮食批发市场间的横向联系**

2015年10月中国粮食行业协会粮食批发市场分会三届四次理事（扩大）会议在天津召开。国家粮食局、中国粮食行业协会、中国粮食行业协会粮食批发市场分会负责同志及会员单位共计一百余人参加了会议，总结交流了一年来市场改革发展情况，分析了面临的形势和存在的问题，对今后的各项工作进行了具体安排部署。会议还听取了郑州、天津、杭州三家市场分别就商流、物流市场专题调研成果汇报。与会代表建议国家有关部门要高度重视粮食批发市场基础设施建设，在政策、资金等方面给予一定扶持，在税费、租金等方面给予相应减免优惠。同时，要加强对粮食批发市场的顶层设计，推动粮食批发市场间的交流合作，加快“互联网+粮食”电商平台建设，坚持市场化导向，实现多样化经营，促进粮食批发市场健康持续发展。

**3. 建立全国统一粮食竞价交易平台**

为适应经济发展新常态的需要，经过近两年的辛勤奋斗，国家粮食局粮食交易协调中心与各省（市、区）的国家粮食交易中心联网搭建的全国统一粮食竞价交易平台于2016年1月8日正式上线运行。国家粮食局粮食交易协调中心承担中心市场职责，负责组织国家政策性粮食竞价交易，制定政策性粮食交易规则，协调政策性粮食交易和出库，提供交易资金结算服务。安徽粮食批发交易市场、郑州粮食批发市场不再代行中心市场职责，各有关省（区、市）已明确一家粮食批发市场与全国统一竞价交易平台联网，作为国家粮食交易中心的在地交易中心。

## （三）2015 年各类粮食批发市场发展状况

为全面了解全国粮食批发市场整体现状，中国粮食行业协会粮食批发市场分会根据年度工作安排和新形势下批发市场发展的需要，委托郑州粮食批发交易市场、天津粮油批发交易市场、杭州粮油物流中心批发市场分别牵头，根据商流市场、物流市场的特性，结合实际拟定调研课题，采取实地考察、报送资料、问卷调查等多种方式，积极开展调研活动。

**1. 成品粮批发市场**

全国粮食成品粮批发市场承担着城市粮油流通集中分散、价格形成和保障“米袋子”供应的功能，集物流、商流、信息、资金流为一体，是我国粮食流通链上的中心环节。经过多年的发展，形成了以区域性大型成品粮批发市场为龙头、中型成品粮批发市场和城市农产品批发市场粮油交易区为骨干的成品粮流通批发体系。近两年来，部分大型成品粮市场也出现了互联网 + 粮食的产区、销区和集散地市场相结合的经营模式，形成了较为成熟的以市场为导向、企业自主经营、政府适度调节、流通有序、渠道多样的粮食流通网络。

目前，成品粮批发市场发展主要呈现出以下几个特点：一是现货粮食保供比重不断加大，苏州、福州等地成品粮市场业务经营量占到该市粮油批发业务量的 90%，贵阳谷丰市场、湖北宜昌泰丰市场占 80%，沈阳、东莞常平、南京、杭州等地成品粮批发市场均占 60% 以上。二是一批成交额 20 亿元的龙头市场快速崛起，贵阳谷丰等部分市场的年成交额逼近百亿元大关。三是检验检测和信息服务能力增强。随着社会越来越关注食品安全问题，各地成品粮批发市场严把商品质量关，南京下关等地建立了具有一定规模的检验化验室，大部分市场还加入了全国性的粮油信息网，建立了电子化信息管理平台。四是互联网 + 交易模式异军突起，逐步开始从点对点的传统集贸式交易向电子商务线上线下交易变革。

虽然成品粮批发市场发展有目共睹，取得了长足的进步，但也存在一些亟待解决的问题：一是政府对成品粮市场的建设、运行扶持有限，成品粮市场“动态粮库”的作用尚未得到发挥。二是粮食主产区成品粮市场受基础条件、粮食收购模式、经济效益等因素影响，发展相对滞后。三是成品粮市场的功能亟待完善，特别是在有效抵御风险方面存在缺陷。四是硬件设施投入后劲明显不足，大部分市场房屋、设施老化，没有充足资金维修或更新。成品粮批发市场应在争取资金、政策扶持上下功夫，加快推进市场全面升级改造，完善质量监督检测体系建设，积极开拓多元化成品粮市场体系。

**2. 商流粮食批发市场**

商流粮食批发市场主要承担的是国家政策性粮食竞价交易工作。2015 年各商流市场的国家政策性粮食交易业务较 2014 年大幅下降，全年共成交国家政策性粮食 1 824.56 万吨，成交额 473.05 亿元。“十二五”期间，共成交国家政策性粮食 11 274.67 万吨，成交额 2 820.41 亿元，在保障国内粮食供给、全面搞活粮食流通、服务宏观调控大局方面发挥了重要的主渠道作用。

随着市场化改革的不断深入，商流市场已进入重要的发展时期，即深化改革期、加快发展期、转型升级期和功能完善期。就目前商流市场发展状况来看，由于政策市效果显著，各商流市场发展迅猛，逐步形成了较为完善的批发市场体系，但也面临巨大的危机和挑战。一是对政策性粮食的依赖性过强，成交量呈下降趋势。由于国内外粮价、新旧粮价差不断拉大，国家政策性粮食成交率持续走低，直接影响了批发市场的生存发展，部分市场已经几年没有交易。二是地方储备粮油尚未完全进场交易。目前在全国 27 家市场中，只有天津、四川、广东、湖北、浙江等少数几个省份实现省、市、县三级储备粮的轮换、采购、销售全部进场交易。三是基础设施建设不足，科技投入有限。除郑州、安徽、天津等大型市场基础设施较为完善、科技投入有保证外，其他市场基本都存在基础设施陈旧落后、硬件设备超期服役等问题，信息化建设与现在蓬勃发展的电子商务还存在较大差距。四是交易出库难问题时有发生。在实际交割过程中，有的存储库点漫天要价，故意刁难出库；有的对库存粮食掺杂使假，增加买方成本；有的保管不当，造成粮食质量与销售清单不符。这些行为牵制了批发市场大量精力，一定程度上限制了市场的健康发展。

作为商流市场，国家政策性粮食竞价交易是批发市场的主营业务，也是首要任务。在做好国家政策性粮食交易的同时，各批发市场也需要积极探索、创新发展。

（1）要积极拓展地方储备粮入场交易业务。随着地方储备规模不断增大，商流市场要积极争取和引导地方储备粮进入市场交易。通过市场公开交易既可以完全保证地方储备粮轮换过程的透明、规范，又可以实现国家利益最大化，同时可以促进粮食批发市场稳定发展，真正实现多赢局面。目前安徽省粮食局、财政厅为规范地方储备的轮换，联合出台了《地方储备粮油轮换实行公开竞价交易的通知》，进一步明确了地方储备粮油轮换必须通过批发市场来进行。现在，安徽的省级储备粮已全部入场交易，市、县级储备粮绝大多数进入省级市场交易。这样既规范了交易行为，又有效规避了风险，对批发市场的稳定发展也起到了重要的促进作用。

（2）积极开展市场间交流、培训。商流市场间要做好相互间的交流协作，相互学习、借鉴好的经验做法，真正实现信息和资源互补，增强市场间的合力。要进一步拓宽交流协作的渠道，积极组织开展各种业务学习、系统培训、总结交流等活动，推动观念创新、机制创新，促进市场可持续发展。

（3）强化商流市场与电子商务的有机融合。随着我国商品流通电子商务的不断兴起，粮食网上交易在国家政策性粮食交易的推动下已经越来越成熟，但这仅仅是电子商务的一个方面，在广度和深度上还有很大文章可做。2015 年的中央 1 号文件就提出“加快农产品市场体系转型升级，健全交易制度，支持涉农电子商务平台建设”。目前有不少成品粮市场正在积极推进电子商务平台建设。如北京盛华宏林大力推出的“盛华宏林购”、苏州市场倾心打造的“良粮网”以及南京下关市场通过微信平台创新营销等，这些都是在充分利用“互联网 +”新技术，逐步实现农副产品从传统交易模式向电子商务线上线下交易方式的转变。商流市场和物流市场间需要进一步加强合作，做到优势互补、资源共享。充分利用现有软硬件设施，建立网络营销平台，面向广大消费者销售农副产品，充分发挥其降低交易成本、增加交易机会、提高企业效益的作用，进一步推动电子商务的应用，更好地适应新形势发展的需要。

## （四）2016 年粮食批发市场展望

2016 年是“十三五”规划的开局之年，也是粮食行业落实“四个全面”战略布局、保障国家粮食安全、推进粮食经济持续健康发展大有作为的一年。粮食批发市场面临巨大的机遇和挑战，在保障国家粮食供给、稳定国内市场价格等方面将发挥更加重要的作用。

### 1. 国家有关政策将促进粮食批发市场加快发展

2016 年中央 1 号文件明确指出要“加强农产品流通设施和市场建设。健全统一开放、布局合理、竞争有序的现代农产品市场体系”，“加快农产品批发市场升级改造，完善流通骨干网络”，“推动公益性农产品市场建设”。这些都给粮食批发市场的发展指明了方向。2016 年，各类粮食批发市场将创新发展，加快市场的升级改造，全面提升市场功能，不断推动公益性农产品市场建设，继续在保证国内粮食供给、稳定粮食市场价格方面发挥重要作用。

### 2. 全国统一粮食竞价交易平台将发挥积极作用

全国统一粮食竞价交易平台于 2016 年 1 月 8 日正式上线运行，国家粮食局粮食交易协调中心作为中心市场联网全国 26 家省级批发市场，共同肩负起保证国内粮食供给、稳定粮食价格的重任，更好地为国家粮食宏观调控服务。全国统一粮食竞价交易平台的运行将使得国家政策性粮食竞价交易更加规范、透明，有利于进一步提高交易效率、规范交易行为，确保国家财政资金安全。

### 3. 粮食批发市场建设投入将进一步加大

国家有关部门和地方政府将认真贯彻落实中央 1 号文件精神，进一步加大对批发市场的政策和资金支持力度，特别是对物流市场的基础设施建设、土地租金、物流运输等方面将给予更有针对性的扶持和优惠措施。国家将大力推进公益性农产品市场的建设，加大对公益性农产品市场的投入力度，培育一批公益性农产品市场，更好地发挥城市“米袋子”供应作用。

（国家粮食局调控司　　姚秀敏）

# 二、粮食期货市场发展状况与展望

【内容提要】

2015年国内外粮食期、现货市场均发生了翻天覆地的变化，大部分粮食期、现货价格持续下滑，引起了市场的广泛关注。

从2015年粮食期货市场的发展状况来看，期、现结合的“交易商”模式正在形成，很多涉粮企业凭借对现货市场十分熟悉的优势，利用在产业链上下游均有合作伙伴的便利条件，使用期货市场工具，很好地完成了对价格波动的风险规避操作，对企业原材料采购、成品库存管理、产品销售、订单保值等进行了相应的期货市场操作，为粮食期货市场服务实体企业，特别是服务中小微和涉农企业等进行了积极探索。

2016年，国内外政治、经济环境将发生更为复杂的变化，局部政治与经济形势不稳会对全球商品价格尤其是粮食期、现货价格产生重大影响，涉粮企业参与期货交易和利用期货市场工具的需求可能更加强烈。

美联储加息虽然已尘埃落定，但其对全球经济状态的影响却是长期的。从国际市场来看，虽然美国经济恢复较为稳定，但全球主要经济体的经济状态存在较大差异，美元升值预期进一步强化将令全球大宗商品的价格、股市、汇市出现大幅动荡。

面对国内“三高”的粮食市场格局，已实施多年的粮食收储政策出现了大范围调整，对国内粮食流通格局、价格涨跌机制等造成了冲击，2016年政策调整的作用会集中释放。

从国内最新出台的很多农业政策来看，农业生产方式、农业种植结构、价格形成机制等均正在频繁调整。其中，“十三五”规划发出了一定程度上适当调整粮食产量的信号。2016 年的全国粮食流通工作会议强调，积极稳妥推进玉米收储制度改革，继续执行并完善稻谷、小麦最低收购价政策；中央农村工作会议提出要着力加强农业供给侧结构性改革。更值得关注的是 2016 年中央 1 号文件提出，坚持市场化取向和保护农民利益并重，采取“分品种施策、渐进式推进”的办法，推进“粮改”，当前国内粮食市场的“政策市”将被打破，各市场主体的活力有望真正释放，粮食期货市场的作用将进一步得到发挥。

## （一）2015 年粮食期货市场运行状况

### 1. 2015 年粮食期货价格受市场供需失衡影响与资本抛售等打压跌至历史低位区

2015 年，国内经济环境较差，市场供需失衡，资本抛售以及托市收购政策调整等使得绝大部分粮食期货价格出现了“飞流直下三千尺”的走势。

2015 年，国内外经济增速持续下滑，如接近年底时，国内 GDP 增长速度已降至 6.9%，各项经济指标均不尽如人意。在经济增速下滑的状态下，市场对粮食尤其是对大宗粮食品种的需求是下降的，市场疲态持续出现，小麦、玉米、稻谷、大豆及其下游产品价格难有好的表现。

国际市场方面，以原油为代表的商品价格狂跌不止，截至 2016 年 2 月上旬，纽约原油 3 月合约期价跌到 26.05 美元/桶，和前几年的高位 140 美元/桶左右相比，跌幅惊人。受国际原油价格持续重挫的影响，玉米、大豆、菜油、糖料等农产品的生物能源属性基本消失，并追随国际原油价格一路走低。

国内粮食市场方面，高产量、高库存量、高进口量的“三高”现象十分突出。有关部门陆续出台了各项政策和措施对粮食市场进行调控，其中对市场影响较大的是粮食收储政策的调整，如下调东北三省一区 2015 年产玉米临储收购价的信息公布以后，国内玉米、小麦等粮食价格立即出现“断崖式”下跌，河南、山东等地玉米收购价直接从 2 100 元/吨左右跌到 1 600 元/吨附近，个别地区 2015 年产玉米收购价跌至 1 440 元/吨。

粮食期货市场外部经济环境的巨变，全球主要经济体经济状况的改变与市场角色的转换，粮食市场供求关系的质变，资本投入与操作粮食期货交易的方法和方式的调整，以及国内农业政策的变动等，为粮食期货市场提供了丰富的炒作题材，也让市场风险与机遇并存，并为 2015 年粮食期货市场的活跃打下了基础。

2015 年国内外粮食期货市场交易十分活跃，国内部分粮食品种如玉米、玉米淀粉的成交量出现了大幅增长。由于粮食现货市场复杂多变，价格波动频繁，很多涉粮企业参与了期货交易，并主动利用期货市场工具为企业的生产经营服务。

目前，在粮食期货市场已初步形成了一些比较可行的业务模式。例如，通过仓单质押、仓单返售等方式解决企业资金匮乏难题；通过“基差贸易” + “点价中心”的业务模式，帮助中小企业降低原材料库存压力与资金成本，开拓新的贸易渠道；利用“二次点价”、“复制期权”等手段提供“保底价订单农业服务”，缓解农民“卖粮难、卖价低”难题；与保险机构进行合作，通过“保险 + 期货”的方式，解决农业保险的风险对冲问题，探索为粮食目标价格管理提供风险管理方案；通过设计开发场外期权、互换等衍生产品，针对实体企业的个性化需求，提供库存管理和风险对冲工具（见表 5 - 2 - 1）。

**2. 2015 年主要粮食期货品种市场表现**

（1）小麦。2015 年国内普通小麦期、现货价格全年表现低迷，优质强筋小麦期、现货价格则走势较强，市场成交较为活跃。2015 年国内外小麦市场的联动性不强，但进口的普通饲用小麦数量较大，对国产普通小麦的需求形成冲击。2015 年小麦下游需求不旺，面粉等行业整体亏损的格局没有改变。2015 年小麦托市收购政策没有大的变化。市场具体情况如下：

第一，2015 年国内普通小麦现货价格基本上呈现震荡下行态势，其中上半年下行速度较快，下半年主要在近年来的底部区域震荡整理，一年中也有偶发因素所引起的市场价格短期内剧烈波动的行情，如 10 月上旬，

表 5－2－1　**2015 年郑州商品交易所、大连商品交易所交易情况表**　单位：手，亿元

| 交易所名称 | 品种名称 | 2015 年累计成交总量 | 2014 年累计成交总量 | 2015 年累计成交总额 | 2014 年累计成交总额 |
|---|---|---|---|---|---|
| 郑州商品交易所 | 早灿稻 | 3 545 | 332 485 | 1.75 | 154.05 |
| | 菜籽油 | 7 775 243 | 13 894 567 | 4 537.73 | 9 349.88 |
| | 油菜籽 | 44179 | 17 219 | 16.72 | 8.37 |
| | 菜籽粕 | 261 486 104 | 303 514 400 | 55 808.38 | 77 837.15 |
| | 普通小麦 | 1 175 | 1 203 | 1.46 | 1.54 |
| | 强筋小麦 | 457 594 | 1 025 486 | 252.92 | 561.60 |
| | 粳稻 | 99 | 8 855 | 0.06 | 5.53 |
| | 晚灿稻 | 1 059 | 52 116 | 0.59 | 29.50 |
| | 总　额 | 269 768 998 | 318 846 331 | 60 619.58 | 87 947.61 |
| 大连商品交易所 | 黄豆 | 18 810 903 | 27 197 413 | 7 722.09 | 12 216.11 |
| | 玉米 | 42 090 235 | 9 329 939 | 8 276.01 | 2 214.74 |
| | 玉米淀粉 | 27 053 680 | 71 958 | 5 835.30 | 19.87 |
| | 豆粕 | 289 496 780 | 204 988 746 | 76 963.61 | 66 563.18 |
| | 豆油 | 92 504 264 | 64 082 631 | 51 831.06 | 41 410.53 |
| | 总　额 | 469 955 862 | 305 670 687 | 150 628.07 | 122 424.44 |
| 全国期货市场交易总额 | | 739 724 060 | 624 517 018 | 211 247.65 | 210 372.05 |

说明：

（1）本表根据郑州商品交易所、大连商品交易所提供数据计算。

（2）表中数据均为单边计算。

（3）表中数据均不含期转现数据。

在有关部门公布了玉米降价收储的消息之后，小麦现货价格出现“断崖式”下跌，主产区小麦市场主流成交价下滑了 200 元/吨。与此同时，普通小麦期货交易较为清淡，主要是当前很多普通小麦的经营主体还是十分偏爱“面对面”的交易模式。

第二，2015 年国内优质强筋小麦现货价格依然保持高位运行态势，但和 2014 年相比，2015 年国产优质强筋小麦质量较差，很多产区的优质强筋小麦的稳定时间、湿面筋等内在指标不及往年。2015 年郑州商品交易所修改了优质强筋小麦的交割标准，对入库交割的优质强筋小麦品种纯

度加强了管理，大大减少了可用于交割的优质强筋小麦数量，优质强筋小麦期货价格出现了回升，部分合约期货价格临近交割时一度涨到3 200元/吨。

第三，制粉行业进入“大鱼吃小鱼”的洗牌阶段。近几年，国内制粉行业一直处在全行业亏损的困境中。分析导致制粉全行业亏损的原因可以发现，托市收购引导形成的麦强面弱格局一直存在，制粉企业生产成本居高不下。国内制粉行业近年来盲目扩张，产能严重过剩，当前全行业已进入“大鱼吃小鱼”的行业洗牌阶段，除了几个大型制粉企业和专用粉生产企业开机率较高并略有利润外，大部分中小型制粉企业经营困难。

穷则思变，持续多年的制粉全行业亏损让一些制粉企业开始改变经营思路，除了提高面粉生产的机械化程度、大力降低人工成本外，很多企业不再追求销量的增加，转而关注面粉质量的提升、产品多样化的供给等。更引人注意的是，很多制粉企业追随市场消费变化的潮流，加大了专用粉的生产与营销；一些制粉企业还利用期货市场进行融资和企业经营管理，并取得了较好的效益。

第四，国内小麦市场需求开始“升级换代”。近年来，国内小麦需求的不确定性增大。首先是传统需求减弱。由于我国人口老龄化加速和副食消费增加，导致口粮需求自高位回落。其次是饲用需求基本消失。如由于玉米等饲料原料价格重挫，加上进口谷物及副产品的挤占，国产小麦及其副产品的饲用需求大幅下调。最后是收购需求下滑。2015年，河南、江苏等9个主产区各类粮食企业收购新产小麦6 631万吨，比上年同期减少732万吨。

虽然市场需求端的变化多集中在传统需求量的变化上，但一些新的变化还是值得市场重视的。其中，市场对优质强筋小麦的需求逐年增加表现明显，这是市场需求“升级换代”的一个信号。笔者在调研中发现，在国内面粉市场中，民用粉的销量不增反降，专用粉的销量则不断增加。这使得国内小麦市场的需求端出现分化，主要表现为普麦需求弱、优麦需求强。

第五，普通小麦与优质强筋小麦价格出现分化。当前河南地区大部分制粉企业优质强筋小麦（新麦26与师栾02－1等品种）进厂价为2 880～3 000元/吨，国标二级以上普通小麦进厂价为2 400元/吨，两者的价差为480～600元/吨。

第六，强麦期市参与者数量与活跃度提高。2015 年 8 月下旬至今，郑州强麦一直呈现成交量、持仓量稳步增长和期价稳步走高的态势。其中，强麦主力 1 605 合约的持仓量从 500 手左右增长到了 6 万手左右，市场参与者数量与市场活跃度双双提高。

从郑州强麦期价走势分析，强麦期价涨跌与现货市场优质强筋小麦的走势高度一致，较好地反映了现货市场供给趋紧、制粉行业发展方向转变等市场因素对价格的影响，为小麦产区广大农民和农业组织提供了种植趋向信息。一些制粉企业还利用强麦期价稳步上涨的市场信号提前备足了生产原料，避免了价格上涨所带来的成本增加风险。特别值得市场关注的是，郑州强麦树起了国内小麦市场优质优价的大旗，这将促进我国小麦种植结构合理调整，将为小麦市场供给侧改革打下基础（见图 5－2－1）。

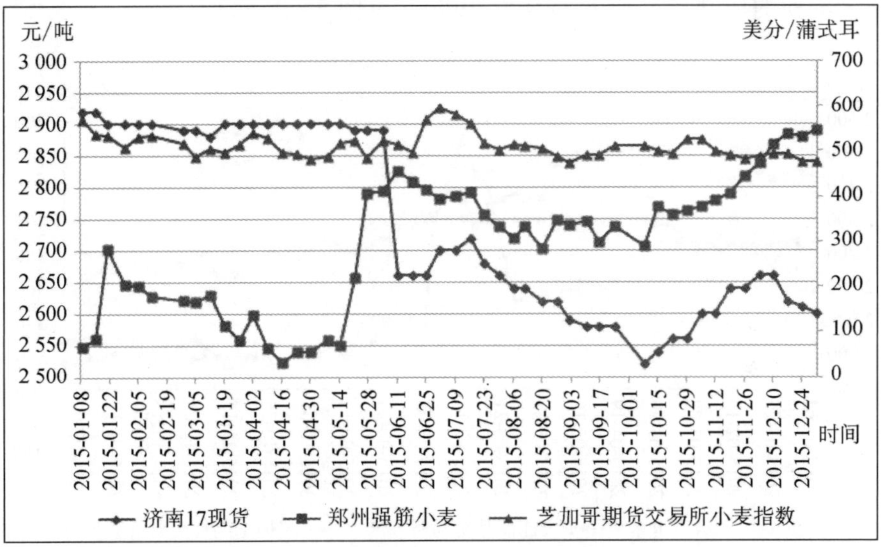


**图 5－2－1　2015 年郑州强麦与芝加哥期货交易所小麦近月结算价、郑州优质小麦出库价走势图**

（2）玉米与玉米淀粉。2015 年国内玉米与玉米淀粉期、现货价格均呈现持续下滑行情，东北三省一区 2015 年产玉米临时收储政策公布以后，市场出现了突发性重挫，如内地产区玉米农户收购价一度滑到 1 400 元/吨左右。

从当前玉米市场发展态势来看，一是产量、库存量、收购量庞大，对市场形成了较大压力。截至2016年2月上旬，有关部门已在东北三省一区收购2015年产玉米近9 000万吨，再创新高，当前的玉米临储库存已达数亿吨。二是玉米替代品进口量增长迅猛，加上玉米下游需求较弱，玉米市场去库存的任务很重，过程将是漫长的。在2015年我国进口的5 000万吨谷物及其副产品中，大部分是进口玉米、大麦、高粱和酒糟蛋白质饲料，其主要用途是用作饲料原料，对国产玉米销量与价格形成了较大冲击，已挤占了国产玉米的很大一部分市场份额。三是针对玉米的生产、去库存等有关部门制定并公布了很多政策，实施了较多的得力措施，玉米市场正在从“政策市”向“市场市”转化，在这个转化过程中，市场波动较为频繁。四是玉米与玉米淀粉行业越来越多的市场主体参与到了玉米和玉米淀粉的期货交易中，其中2015年大连玉米的成交量增长了351. 13%，玉米淀粉的成交量增长了37 496. 49%（见图5－2－2）。

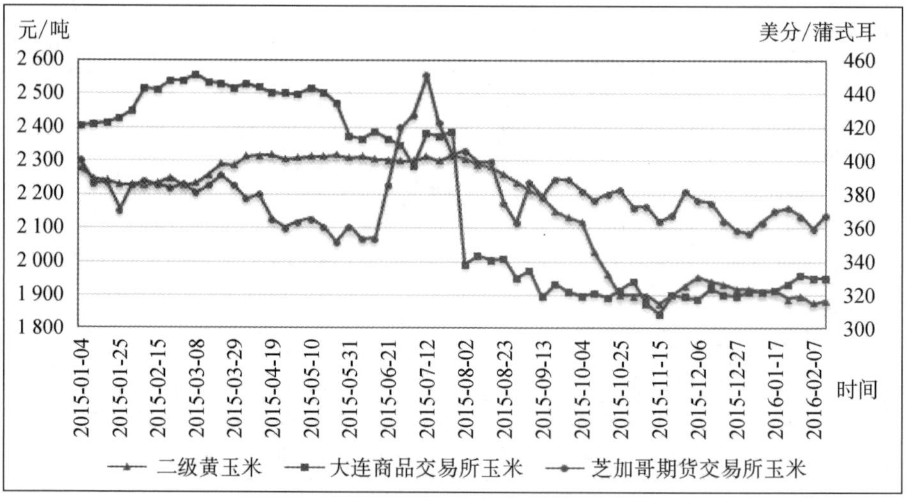


**图5－2－2 2015年大连商品交易所玉米、芝加哥期货交易所玉米期货交易收盘价与二级黄玉米全国均价走势图**

（3）稻谷。2015年国内早籼稻、晚籼稻、粳稻价格整体表现较弱，三个品种的期货市场交易基本停滞，仅部分合约有少量成交。目前，国内稻谷市场仍是“政策市”，产量增、库存大、需求差仍是市场面临的主要问题。与此同时，稻强米弱格局仍然没有改善，进口与走私大米仍对国内市场有冲击。从政策方面来看，2016 年有关部门仍将在稻谷市场实施收储政策，收储价格保持不变（见图 5－2－3）。

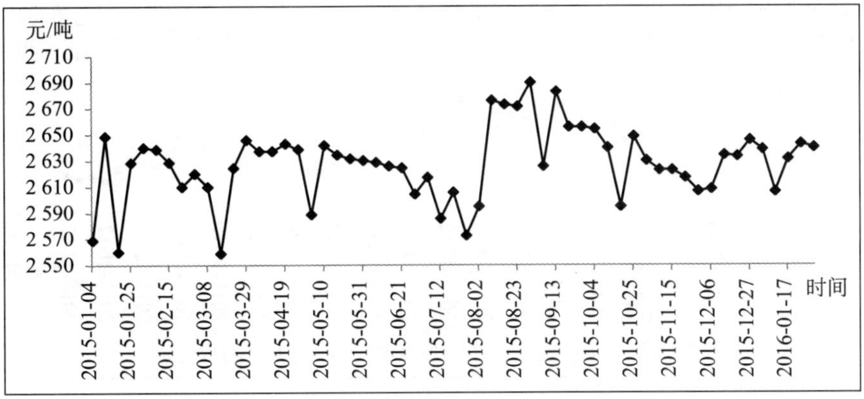


**图 5－2－3　2015 年以来国内三级早籼稻均价走势图**

（4）油脂油料和粕类。2015 年大豆、豆油、油菜籽、菜油等油料、油脂价格与豆粕、菜粕等粕类价格主要呈现持续下跌行情，其中豆粕、菜粕期货价格跌幅较大，两者的价差和往年相比也大幅缩小。从市场影响因素来看，国际市场大豆等油料丰收打压了价格，更为重要的是国际原油价格一路下行削弱了油料与油脂的生物能源属性，并拖累了油料与油脂的价格。2015 年豆油、豆粕、菜粕期货市场交易十分活跃，很多产业链的实体企业参与了市场交易。与国内粮食供应大量过剩相比，国内食用植物油料油脂供应基本依靠进口来满足。我国海关等部门公布的信息显示，2015 年我国进口大豆量再创新高，总量在 8 000 万吨以上。此外，我国还大量进口了豆油、菜油、棕榈油、菜粕、豆粕等植物油料下游产品。

近年来我国各地农民不断调减油料作物种植面积，很多地区农民基本上不再种植油菜、大豆、芝麻等农作物，取而代之的是小麦、稻谷和玉米。一些地区如河南信阳、湖北、湖南部分丘陵山区的农民宁愿土地撂荒也不种油菜。

目前，我国油料与油脂、植物蛋白粕类的价格与国际市场的联动性很强，国内市场基本没有话语权（见图 5－2－4）。

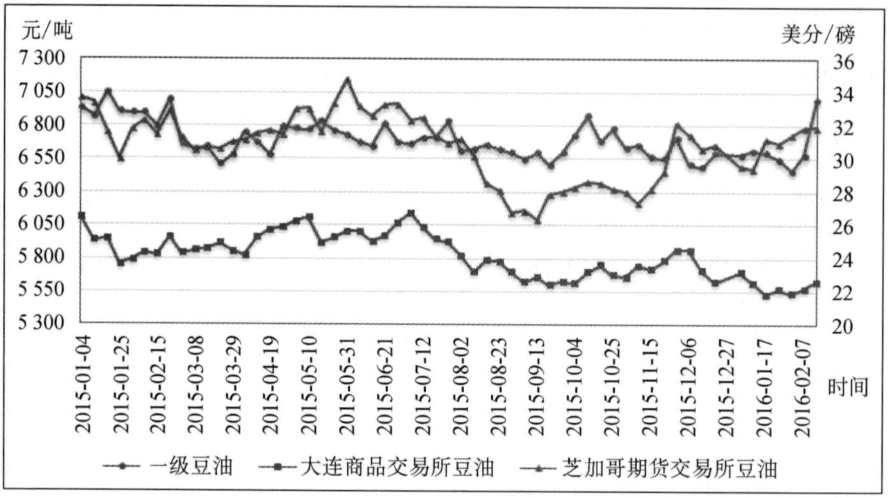


**图5-2-4 2015年国内一级豆油现货价、大连商品交易所豆油与芝加哥期货交易所豆油期价走势图**

## （二）2016年粮食期货市场发展展望

2016年粮食期货市场的外部经济环境将更加复杂多变，全球经济尤其是我国经济增长态势能否恢复稳定将对粮食期货市场价格形成重要影响，同时美联储加息的步子如何迈、国际原油价格能否触底反弹等也会让期、现货粮食价格的波动较为频繁。更值得市场关注的是，2016年我国农业及粮食行业政策处在集中调整期，农业和粮食领域所进行的供给侧改革等会对粮食的生产、供应、流通、价格形成产生长期和深远的影响，粮食市场的政策性特征会进一步减弱，市场化程度会提高，预计2016年国内粮食期货市场将更加活跃。

**1. 粮食期货市场外部经济大环境不太平静**

2015年12月17日美联储宣布加息25个基点至0.25%～0.50%。这是美联储9年多以来首次加息，自2008年底金融危机以来一直奉行的超低近零利率政策结束，标志着美国经济完全进入健康增长的新时期。虽然美联储加息的决策完全符合市场主流预期，此前市场对此所进行的两年左右时间的炒作也消化了其大部分影响力，但这并不意味着全球粮食期货市场的外部经济大环境就此风平浪静。

2015 年 12 月 18 日美国国会批准解除长达 40 年原油出口禁令，这又会对粮食期货市场特别是油脂市场产生重要影响，豆油等商品期货价格将面临新的压力，价格波动也会扩大。

目前，全球主要经济体为了经济增长出台了各项政策与措施，这会对今后各经济体与全球经济变动趋势产生深远影响，粮食期货市场也会深受这些政策与措施的影响。

从国际市场来看，一是全球经济复苏不及预期。虽然美国经济恢复较为稳定，并进入了加息周期，但世界银行、货币基金组织等国际机构仍不是十分看好全球经济增长的预期，美元升值预期进一步强化将令全球大宗商品的价格、股市、汇市出现大幅动荡。二是我国与欧洲等国家和地区仍在不断降息，全球主要经济体的经济状态存在较大差异，如果这些经济体经济增长呈现长期低水平波动，那么将导致全球贸易流量下降，市场对粮食的需求能力减弱。三是日本、印度等国的经济政策时有调整，会刺激粮食价格频繁波动，

从国内因素来看，我国经济增长放缓是一个大的前提，在这个大前提下，粮食价格更多的时候不会出现大幅上涨，维持低位平稳运行的可能性更大。当前国内经济仍处在结构调整的关键阶段，传统产业不仅去库存，也在去产能。尽管在下行压力大的形势下，稳增长等政策力度将进一步强化，货币政策很大程度上会松动并逐渐走向宽松，但专业人士认为，GDP 低速增长已常态化，粮食工业需求减少，货币宽松政策短期内难见成效。与此同时，如果国际原油等商品价格进一步重挫，全球粮食价格的联动性将加强，廉价进口粮食数量会增加，并会对国内粮食市场形成较大的冲击力。从当前的主要进口品种与数量分析，油料油脂价格已完全由国际市场主导，每年 8 000 多万吨的大豆进口量以及飞速增长的豆油、豆粕、油菜籽、菜油、玉米、高粱、大麦等进口量将令国内对这些粮食品种的定价权与主动权进一步弱化，国内粮食价格追随国际市场波动的特征将更加明显。

## 2. 我国农业和粮食政策调整进入高峰期

外部经济环境毕竟不是决定粮食价格涨跌的主要因素，决定粮食期货价格长期走势的内因仍是市场供求关系。

目前，国内粮食市场存在的高产量、高收购量、高库存量市场格局尤其引人关注，今后这些问题如何解决以及农业政策如何调整等，将会对粮食价格形成较大影响。

现阶段，国内外稻谷、大豆、玉米、小麦、豆粕等主要粮油品种期、现货价格均受到了供应过剩的打压，大豆、玉米、小麦等粮油品种期货价格重挫。更引人注意的是，由于我国粮油价格高于国际市场很多，导致我国粮油进口数量庞大，这一方面加剧了国内销售的难度，增加了市场供应，加大了库存量，冲击了价格，另一方面使得国内农业产业发展困难，并引起了有关部门对农业产业发展的重视，我国针对农业方面的政策出现了重大调整，这将引起粮油期货市场参与者机构等的变化。

从最新出台的很多农业和粮食调控政策来看，农业生产方式、农业种植结构、价格形成机制等均要进行调整。

“十三五”规划提出，要实行轮作休耕的试点，实行“藏粮于地、藏粮于技”的战略，这实际上一定程度上发出了适当调整粮食产量的信号。中央农村工作领导小组副组长、办公室主任陈锡文指出，进口大麦、高粱、酒糟蛋白质饲料、木薯等替代玉米，使得国内玉米的销售受到冲击，出现滞销积压，这是我国粮食市场当前面临的突出问题。对我国而言，需要考虑的问题是采取何种措施调节国内的粮食价格，以抑制玉米替代品进口的任意增长。

2014年国内启动了东北和内蒙古大豆、新疆棉花目标价格补贴试点，2015年有关部门在总结目标价格改革试点经验的基础上，提出继续执行稻谷、小麦最低收购价政策，同时对玉米等非口粮农产品市场政策做出了调整。从2015年新产玉米上市起，虽然有关部门仍在东北地区实施了临时收购政策，但却大幅下调了玉米收购价，一度引起国内玉米期、现货价格“断崖式”下跌，并触动了农民的种粮收益等问题。此外，自2015年新产油菜籽上市开始，有关部门决定取消了油菜籽的临储收购，产区油菜籽收购价与2014年上市时的价格相比下跌近2 000元/吨，政策调整对价格的影响由此可见。

**3. 粮食价格的金融属性需要重视**

全球经济高速增长时期，粮食价格的金融属性表现得比较强烈，大量资金进入粮食期货市场，推高了一个又一个粮食品种价格，并让价格与价值发生了较大背离。目前，虽然在经济大环境不景气的情况下全球粮食市场价格在更大程度上由自身的供求关系所决定，但资金对粮食价格的影响依然不容忽视，粮食价格的金融属性并没有完全消失，只是表现得更为低调而已。由于资金紧张，很多粮食产业链上的企业生存困难，粮食价格表面上来看是需求不足造成的，实现上是资金供应不足导致的。值得市场关注的是，当前很多投资机构把粮食产品作为宏观对冲对象，他们一方面大量投资股市等市场，另一方面大量在粮食期货市场抛空，粮食期货市场存在很多的“打产能、打暴利”等新现象。

2016 年对于资本市场仍将是一个动荡不安的年份，诸如美联储加息、我国降息与降准的事件会时有发生，粮食市场价格的金融属性可能会表现得强一些。

**4. 粮食期货市场将得到长远发展**

随着国内粮食期货市场上市品种的产业化、系统化，参与的涉粮企业越来越多，以及粮食期货市场的价格引导作用等越来越明显，粮食期货市场的发展获得了市场的认可与支持，估计 2016 年会有更多的涉粮企业参与粮食期货市场的交易。

部分行业人士认为，为了提高粮食市场的市场化程度，需要大力发展粮食期货交易，而这又需要政府和各行业的管理部门简政放权，市场的事情让市场去解决。目前，一些行业管理部门已经取消了不允许国营企业等参与期货交易的“行规”，一些部门开始鼓励粮食企业利用期货市场规避经营风险，更多粮食产业链上的企业愿意使用期货工具来为企业的生产经营服务。在农业产业客户参与期货交易比较积极的情况下，粮食期货市场容量会得到扩大，市场形成的价格更具有代表性，对国内粮食产业发展的指导性也更强，灵活的粮食市场机制将会形成。

目前，经过 20 多年的发展以后，国内粮食期货市场已上市的油菜籽、菜油、菜粕和大豆、豆油、豆粕，以及玉米、玉米淀粉等粮食及其加工品种形成了较为完整的产业链，这些品种产业链上的生产、流通、贸易企业均已大规模参与到期货市场中来，并有效地利用期货工具为企业经营提供了风险控制保证。在小麦、食糖、棉花、大豆、豆粕等期货市场，很多大中型企业表现活跃，而随着农业生产领域新型合作组织的出现等，粮食期货市场长期稳定发展的基础更加扎实。此外，有关机构正筹备尿素等农业生产资料的期货品种上市，未来国内粮食期货市场的产品体系会更加完善，交易规模会再上一个新台阶，市场投资机会也会增加很多。

（河南期货日报传媒有限公司　　陈邦华　乔林生）

# 三、粮食电子商务发展状况及展望

【内容提要】

无所不在的网络汇同无所不在的计算、数据和知识，一起推进了无所不在的创新以及数字向智能并进一步向智慧的演进，并推动了“互联网+”的演进与发展。“互联网+”作为一种新的经济形态代表，正成为国民经济的一大新引擎，且预示着这个新经济时代背景下必将产生许多新的商业模式。目前各行各业都在探索将互联网作为引擎推动行业的发展创新，以智能化、精准化、定制化为主要标志的农业3.0时代已经到来，中国粮食行业正在发生翻天覆地的变化。

2015年“互联网+”行动计划的提出，为粮食行业创造出新的生态，助推粮食产业的新升级；粮食电子商务平台蓬勃发展，大型国企、粮食批发市场、粮食企业等积极参与电子商务的建设和发展；政策性粮食网上交易仍然是国家宏观调控的重要手段，有力地保障了国家的粮食安全；粮食行业网络融资实现零的突破，为粮食企业的发展注入新的活力；传统的供销合作社开始拥抱互联网，成为推动农村电子商务发展的中坚力量；着眼整条产业链的云农场模式颠覆和改变了传统的农业思路，开启了智慧农业的新篇章。

2016年，国家进一步对托市粮收购进行改革，各级粮食批发市场将加快市场化步伐；在政策的扶持下，农村电商蓝海市场即将爆发；互联网技术、移动电商在粮食行业的深度应用将引领粮食行业的新变革；粮食众筹不断创新，积极探索粮食产销合作的新模式。

## （一）2015 年粮食行业电子商务发展现状

### 1. “互联网 +” 助推粮食产业新升级

2015 年，李克强总理在政府工作报告中首次提出制订“互联网 +”行动计划，“推动移动互联网、云计算、大数据、物联网等与现代制造业结合，促进电子商务、工业互联网和互联网金融（ITFIN）健康发展，引导互联网企业拓展国际市场”。“互联网 +”通过利用互联网的平台、信息通信技术，把互联网和包括传统行业在内的各行各业结合起来，在粮食领域创造了新的生态。

2015 年我国“三农”正处于一个新的转型时期，面对“让农业更强、农民更富、农村更美”的改革发展任务，仍然存在着发展基础不牢、现代化水平有待提升、粮食安全机制不健全等短板和不足。物联网、大数据等先进信息技术进入传统粮食行业，为粮食产业转型带来了契机，通过播种、栽培、收储、加工、销售等环节倒逼“精细农业”，让粮食全产业链产生化学效应。通过精细农业、物联网、云服务、大数据分析等来实现粮食生产技术、农业规模化、粮食质量安全以及产品价值实现等问题的改造，大幅推动了智慧农业的进程。粮食企业和粮食生产合作社及种粮大户也顺应大势，纷纷拥抱互联网，不仅及时地获取了生产经营信息及价格行情，而且优化了供应链，降低了生产经营成本，以获取最大效益。

### 2. 粮食电子商务平台蓬勃发展

随着粮食流通体制改革的不断深入和市场化进程的加快，积极参与电子商务的建设和发展已成为粮食行业无法回避的选择。2015 年，粮食电子商务平台蓬勃发展：大型国企发力建设粮食电子商务平台，引领变化；各地粮食批发市场在积极利用电子交易手段开展地方粮油购销交易活动的同时，不断创新交易模式，进行差异化经营；粮食企业通过建立自营电子商务平台或依托第三方电子商务平台在网络上销售自己的产品，最大化整合资源。

2015 年 9 月 16 日由中储粮物流有限公司与中华粮网共同打造的中储粮电子商务平台正式上线运营。截至 2015 年底，平台已实现东北三省一区和主销区玉米上线交易，下一步将逐渐拓展其他品种上线交易，并将覆盖范围拓展至全国，着力打造成为国内一流的社会化、开放式电子商务平台。2015 年 11 月 23 日，粮达网上线运营，上线的原粮品种包括玉米、小麦、稻谷、大豆、棕榈油、大麦、高粱等。粮达网是中粮集团和招商局集团两大央企重塑农粮贸易新模式、努力打造粮食电商生态圈的积极尝试。郑州粮食批发市场自 2012 年开展场际交易以来，经过 3 年发展，参与场际交易会员数量快速增长，交易量逐年攀升，各签约市场结合当地实际不断开发引导新品种进场交易，交易品种涉及小麦、玉米、稻谷、面粉、糠粕、食用油等 12 大类、51 个小类品种，交易品种日趋多样化。2015 年 4 月 15 日，恒大粮油产品分别在自营平台恒优米 App、恒优米官方商城以及京东商城、天猫、我买网等五大电商平台全面上线，构建起了传统渠道、商超渠道与电子渠道的立体化的恒大粮油销售体系。

### 3. 政策性粮食网上交易情况

实施最低收购价政策，通过网上集中竞价的交易模式将政策性粮油投放市场，仍然是目前我国粮食宏观调控的重要手段。近年来，由于我国粮食生产成本上升快、竞争力下降，政府定价、政府收购造成粮食价格无法反映市场供求、产供销割裂、品种品质不适应市场需求等情况，导致在近些年经济下行的情况下，政府财政难以负荷。

2015 年政策性小麦收购出现了粮食市场需求低迷、政策收购仓容紧张、部分地区粮食质量下降等复杂情况。由于小麦市场价格弱势运行，政策性小麦销售价格高于市场价格，导致政策麦库存高企难销，国家政策性小麦拍卖成交量持续低迷。截至 2015 年末，政策性小麦总成交量仅为 600 多万吨，不及 2014 年成交总量的一半。庞大的政策麦库存增加了国内小麦市场的整体供应压力，限制了麦价的上行空间（见图 5 -3 -1）。

### 4. 粮食行业网络融资零的突破

互联网金融模式的出现打破了以传统商业银行贷款为主的融资方式，为粮食企业的发展提供了新的资金来源。2015 年，中华粮网创新互联网

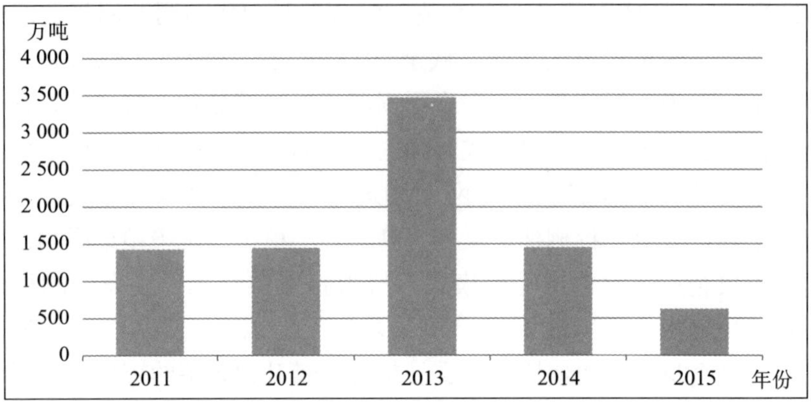


数据来源：中华粮网。

**图5－3－1　2011—2015年国家政策性小麦成交情况**

融资模式，与建设银行和监管公司联手推出网络银行业务，完成了粮食行业第一笔网络融资贷款服务，授信总额度3 000万元，首次投放金额500万元。网络银行业务实现了粮食企业融资贷款全流程网上操作，切实解决了新常态下中小粮食加工企业、贸易企业贷款难、融资难的老问题，解开了制约中小企业发展的桎梏。粮食贷是国内首家P2C模式农业互联网金融借贷平台，平台坐拥北大仓潜力无限的粮食大市场，利用互联网技术，开启网贷平台与金融仓储合作新模式，是普惠金融创新精神的具体实践，实现了粮食互联网金融的创新。

粮食行业网络金融为粮食企业尤其是中小型粮食企业发展注入了活力，但由于我国的互联网金融整体是在相对宽松的监管环境中发展起来的，使其在炙手可热的同时，也产生了风险控制能力不强、相关法律规范缺失、监管体系不健全、征信体系不完善等一系列问题，直接影响着互联网金融能否为粮食企业发展提供长期、稳定的金融服务。

**5. 供销合作社成为推动农村电子商务发展的中坚力量**

近年来，随着电子商务的迅猛发展，消费潜力巨大的农村已经成为电商竞相角逐的主战场，电子商务对传统商业模式的冲击日益凸显。2015年，《中共中央　国务院关于深化供销合作社综合改革的决定》为供销社加快发展电子商务、构建具有自身特色的电商平台指明了方向。各地发展农村电子商务，根据千差万别的农村市场、多种多样的农民需求以及当地优势，因地制宜，坚持创新，积极探索符合自身的运营模式。

2015 年 11 月 5 日，全国供销合作社电子商务平台“供销 e 家”正式上线，这标志着具有供销合作社特色的知名电子商务综合平台将成为引领农村电子商务发展的国家队。截至 2015 年 12 月底，供销 e 家 B2C 商城总销售额达到 6 100 万元，商品种类达 1.9 万种，其中农产品 1.7 万种，占比约为 90%。义乌市社供销集团借助青岩刘“网店第一村”的影响力，于 2015 年 4 月在青岩刘开设了农产品网货中心，展销义乌及国内部分省市的优质、绿色农产品。依托青岩刘网货中心，供销集团在淘宝、阿里巴巴、微商城等第三方电商平台开设网店，建立“展销实体 + 网店”的线上线下良性互动平台，有效拓展了本地农产品的辐射范围。

#### 6. 云农场模式开启智慧农业新篇章

传统的粮食产业链从交易层面看，上游集中在农资贸易环节，中游集中在加工环节，下游集中在粮食贸易环节，物流、金融则贯穿整条产业链。随着互联网技术在粮食行业的不断渗透，粮食电商不再局限于扎堆产业链下游，开始把目光投向上游农资交易环节，将服务对象锁定农业生产者。

2015 年 3 月，联想控股与云农场签订战略投资协议。云农场旗下拥有 18 家子公司，通过搭建集农资电商、农产品电商、农村物流、农技服务及农村金融等领域为一体的平台，建立以村站和测土配肥站模式为基础的标准化电商服务体系，提供测土配肥、农技通、云农宝、乡间货等特色增值服务，形成了农业产前、产中、产后全方位的现代农业服务生态圈。这种着眼整条产业链的“云农场模式”颠覆和改变了传统的农业思路，为智慧农业的发展摸索出了新的发展方向。

### （二）2016 年粮食行业电子商务发展展望

#### 1. 粮食行业走向市场化

2016 年中央 1 号文件提出，要坚持市场化改革取向和保护农民利益并重，采取“分品种施策、渐进式推进”的办法，完善农产品市场调控制度，并正式提出对主粮玉米的改革。玉米的改革将会起到引路作用，如果能够成功，那么小麦、口粮稻谷的托市收购改革进程也将推进，改革托市收购将成为盘活中国粮食以及农产品市场的关键。

2016 年全国粮食统一竞价交易平台上线运行，国家政策性粮油竞价交易将交由该平台统一组织。全国粮食统一竞价交易平台的建立将在进一步优化粮食流通，帮助粮食行政管理部门实施更加精准科学高效的市场调控，营造更加公开、公平、公正的市场交易环境方面发挥积极的作用。

粮食批发市场是粮食市场中的重要一环，2016 年随着国家对粮食行业市场化的进一步推进，各级粮食批发市场都应尽快地改革，积极开展市场化交易。通过加强地域之间的联系、拓展交易品种等方式，发展社会化粮食电子商务。同时，应抓住政府的国家级顶层战略“一带一路”带来的机遇，利用好“一带一路”带来的国内外两个市场，推动我国粮食市场与世界粮食市场的融合。

**2. 农村电商将成一片蓝海**

在当前经济进入新常态的背景下，农村经济发展正面临前所未有的新挑战。2016 年中央 1 号文件再次将“农村现代化”写入标题，这已经是连续第三年。文中指出，要强化现代农业科技创新推广体系建设，大力推进“互联网 +”现代农业，应用物联网、云计算、大数据、移动互联等现代信息技术，推动农业全产业链改造升级。半年前，商务部的《“互联网 + 流通”行动计划》将电子商务进农村确定为第一大目标。中央针对一个较为细分的涉农领域如此连续地抛出扶持意见和政策，显示了当前政府对现阶段大力发展农村电商的决心和思路。

2016 年农村电子商务将成为一片蓝海，国家在改善农村电商发展环境、农村电商人才培养、加大农村电商政策扶持等方面下大功夫，电商巨头斥巨资投入农村电商，抢占农村电商入口。县域电子商务建设将更着力于立足本地资源优势，发展特色产业，通过合理区域布局，提高产品品质，优化品种结构，培育龙头企业，以特色产业引领电商发展。

### 3. 互联网技术在粮食行业的进一步应用

随着互联网的不断普及和互联网技术的不断发展，传统的粮食流通模式通过物联网技术、大数据技术、商业智能技术等得以改造。传统的粮油贸易市场将逐渐升级为智能化粮油贸易市场，引领线下粮油产品的电子商务发展。如通过智能电子标签，规范市场价格；通过手机、智能卡等消费，为交易带来更为安全便捷的体验；粮油市场更是可以通过电子平台，对交易量、价格等形成数据累积。

物联网、二维码等技术在粮食行业的应用，为我国粮油食品安全与科学监管提供了有力保障。通过建立粮食追溯云平台，将粮食从选种、种植到加工、包装、销售等全过程的信息录入、传递和汇总到平台，并生成相关信息的二维码作为粮油产品的“身份证”，实现粮食从田间到餐桌全过程监督。

### 4. 移动电商引领粮食电商发展潮流

移动互联网因其传播速度快、适用度高等优点，现如今已逐渐替代 PC 端，开始引导潮流，主导市场。随着粮食行业对移动互联网为代表的新技术的认知程度不断提高，利用移动信息化手段开展各项市场活动的需求不断高涨，粮食行业移动电子商务的前景被普遍看好。相比传统的电子商务而言，移动电子商务的优点在于其及时性，可以随时随地不受限制地在移动端进行操作。移动电子商务的终端一般为个人使用，认证方便，私密性较高，资金安全也较有保证，支付更加方便快捷。粮食行业移动电商的建设不应再局限于提供一个简单的资讯平台，而是要建设一个粮食行业的移动端生态圈，不仅为粮食贸易服务，更应为自粮食生产到粮食收储、加工、终端销售的全粮食产业链服务。粮食行业从业者可以通过粮食电商 APP 在各个产业链各取所需，同时还可以通过移动电商平台进行沟通、社交，彼此形成业务支撑和良性循环。未来，参与移动电商平台建设，发展粮食移动电商，培育线上交易市场，拓展盈利空间，将成为粮食企业谋求更大发展的战略选择。

**5. 粮食众筹为粮食行业寻找新的利润增长点**

近几年，作为热度飙升的互联网金融的一个分支，众筹对很多人来说已不再陌生。根据订单决定生产，消除过多中间环节的损耗，粮食众筹正在试图给传统的粮食产业链环节重新排序。粮食众筹通过“农户+公司+消费者”的新型发展模式，以及大众化、低门槛的特点，形成了完整的产销链和经济生态圈，不仅给消费者带来实惠，而且降低了农户的风险，保障了农户和企业的收益。粮食众筹的发展在经历了解决农民土地里的粮食怎么卖的问题之后，未来将更着力于解决如何让消费者深度参与进来。通过互联网金融企业、粮食众筹平台和相关服务中介，消费者将成为粮食生产的合伙人，实现 F2F（Farm to Family）的新生活方式，让参与感成为消费者在粮食众筹模式中的附加价值。粮食众筹还应与粮食电子商务结合好，建立起更完备的物流体系，为客户带来更好的配送服务，通过粮食众筹客户端，配合粮食移动电子商务，让粮食电商、粮食众筹更灵活。

传统的粮食行业在互联网的渗透下走向了现代化、生态化、智能化，未来在“互联网+”的大背景下，粮食电子商务将更加深入到粮食生产、流通、消费等全产业链的各个环节，不断引领粮食行业前行。

（中华粮网　　傅宏）

# 第六部分

## 中国粮食市场资料

# 一、统计数据汇编

表 6－1－1　　全国粮食作物播种面积、粮食总产量

| 年　份 | 粮食作物播种面积（万公顷） | 粮食总产量（万吨） | | | | |
|---|---|---|---|---|---|---|
| | | | 谷　物 | | | |
| | | | | 稻　谷 | 小　麦 | 玉　米 |
| 1978 | 12 058.7 | 30 476.5 | | 13 693.0 | 5 384.0 | 5 594.5 |
| 1980 | 11 723.4 | 32 055.5 | | 13 990.5 | 5 520.5 | 6 260.0 |
| 1985 | 10 884.5 | 37 910.8 | | 16 856.9 | 8 580.5 | 6 382.6 |
| 1990 | 11 346.6 | 44 624.0 | | 18 933.1 | 9 822.9 | 9 681.9 |
| 1991 | 11 231.4 | 43 529.0 | 39 566.3 | 18 381.3 | 9 595.3 | 9 877.3 |
| 1992 | 11 056.0 | 44 265.8 | 40 169.6 | 18 622.2 | 10 158.7 | 9 538.3 |
| 1993 | 11 050.9 | 45 648.8 | 40 517.4 | 17 751.4 | 10 639.0 | 10 270.4 |
| 1994 | 10 854.4 | 44 510.1 | 39 389.1 | 17 593.3 | 9 929.7 | 9 927.5 |
| 1995 | 11 006.0 | 46 661.8 | 41 611.6 | 18 522.6 | 10 220.7 | 11 198.6 |
| 1996 | 11 254.8 | 50 453.5 | 45 127.1 | 19 510.3 | 11 056.9 | 12 747.1 |
| 1997 | 11 291.2 | 49 417.1 | 44 349.3 | 20 073.5 | 12 328.9 | 10 430.9 |
| 1998 | 11 378.7 | 51 229.5 | 45 624.7 | 19 871.3 | 10 972.6 | 13 295.4 |
| 1999 | 11 316.1 | 50 838.6 | 45 304.1 | 19 848.7 | 11 388.0 | 12 808.6 |
| 2000 | 10 846.3 | 46 217.5 | 40 522.4 | 18 790.8 | 9 963.6 | 10 600.0 |
| 2001 | 10 608.0 | 45 263.7 | 39 648.2 | 17 758.0 | 9 387.3 | 11 408.8 |
| 2002 | 10 389.1 | 45 705.8 | 39 798.7 | 17 453.9 | 9 029.0 | 12 130.8 |
| 2003 | 9 941.0 | 43 069.5 | 37 428.7 | 16 065.6 | 8 648.8 | 11 583.0 |
| 2004 | 10 160.6 | 46 946.9 | 41 157.2 | 17 908.8 | 9 195.2 | 13 028.7 |
| 2005 | 10 427.8 | 48 402.2 | 42 776.0 | 18 058.8 | 9 744.5 | 13 936.5 |
| 2006 | 10 495.8 | 49 804.2 | 45 099.2 | 18 171.8 | 10 846.6 | 15 160.3 |
| 2007 | 10 563.8 | 50 160.3 | 45 632.4 | 18 603.4 | 10 929.8 | 15 230.0 |
| 2008 | 10 679.3 | 52 870.9 | 47 847.4 | 19 189.6 | 11 246.4 | 16 591.4 |
| 2009 | 10 898.6 | 53 082.1 | 48 156.3 | 19 510.3 | 11 511.5 | 16 397.4 |
| 2010 | 10 987.6 | 54 647.7 | 49 637.1 | 19 576.1 | 11 518.1 | 17 724.5 |
| 2011 | 11 057.3 | 57 120.8 | 51 939.4 | 20 100.1 | 11 740.1 | 19 278.1 |
| 2012 | 11 120.5 | 58 958.0 | 53 934.7 | 20 423.6 | 12 102.4 | 20 561.4 |
| 2013 | 11 195.6 | 60 193.8 | 55 269.2 | 20 361.2 | 12 192.6 | 21 848.9 |
| 2014 | 11 272.3 | 60 702.6 | 55 740.7 | 20 650.7 | 12 620.8 | 21 564.6 |
| 2015 | 11 334.0 | 62 144.0 | 57 225.0 | 20 825.0 | 13 019.0 | 22 458.0 |

资料来源：国家统计局：《中国统计年鉴》，中国统计出版社出版；国家统计局网站。

表 6－1－2　　　　全国油脂、油料播种面积与产量

| 年份 | 精制食用植物油总产量（万吨） | 油料播种面积（万公顷） | 油料总产量（万吨） | 花　生 | 油菜籽 | 芝　麻 |
|---|---|---|---|---|---|---|
| 1978 | | 622.2 | 521.8 | 237.7 | 186.8 | 32.2 |
| 1980 | | 792.8 | 769.1 | 360.0 | 238.4 | 25.9 |
| 1985 | | 1 180.0 | 1 578.4 | 666.4 | 560.7 | 69.1 |
| 1990 | 544.1 | 1 090.0 | 1 613.2 | 636.8 | 695.8 | 46.9 |
| 1991 | 644.3 | 1 153.0 | 1 638.3 | 630.3 | 743.6 | 43.5 |
| 1992 | 660.7 | 1 148.9 | 1 641.2 | 595.3 | 765.3 | 51.6 |
| 1993 | 965.4 | 1 114.2 | 1 803.9 | 842.1 | 693.9 | 56.3 |
| 1994 | 723.0 | 1 208.1 | 1 989.6 | 968.2 | 749.2 | 54.8 |
| 1995 | 1 144.5 | 1 310.1 | 2 250.3 | 1 023.5 | 977.7 | 58.3 |
| 1996 | 946.5 | 1 255.6 | 2 210.6 | 1 013.8 | 920.1 | 57.5 |
| 1997 | 893.7 | 1 238.1 | 2 157.4 | 964.8 | 957.8 | 56.6 |
| 1998 | 602.5 | 1 291.9 | 2 313.9 | 1 188.6 | 830.0 | 65.6 |
| 1999 | 733.8 | 1 390.6 | 2 601.2 | 1 263.9 | 1 013.2 | 74.3 |
| 2000 | 835.3 | 1 540.0 | 2 954.8 | 1 443.7 | 1 138.1 | 81.1 |
| 2001 | 1 383.2 | 1 463.1 | 2 864.9 | 1 441.6 | 1 133.1 | 80.4 |
| 2002 | 1 531.2 | 1 476.6 | 2 897.2 | 1 481.8 | 1 055.2 | 89.5 |
| 2003 | 1 584.3 | 1 499.0 | 2 811.0 | 1 342.0 | 1 142.0 | 59.3 |
| 2004 | 1 682.6 | 1 443.1 | 3 065.9 | 1 434.2 | 1 318.2 | 70.4 |
| 2005 | 2 071.0 | 1 431.8 | 3 077.1 | 1 434.2 | 1 305.2 | 62.5 |
| 2006 | 2 335.2 | 1 173.8 | 2 640.3 | 1 288.7 | 1 096.6 | 66.2 |
| 2007 | 2 637.0 | 1 131.6 | 2 568.7 | 1 302.7 | 1 057.3 | 55.7 |
| 2008 | 2 805.1 | 1 282.5 | 2 952.8 | 1 428.6 | 1 210.2 | 58.6 |
| 2009 | 3 433.4 | 1 365.4 | 3 154.3 | 1 470.8 | 1 365.7 | 62.2 |
| 2010 | 3 878.5 | 1 389.0 | 3 230.1 | 1 564.4 | 1 308.2 | 58.7 |
| 2011 | 4 331.8 | 1 385.5 | 3 306.8 | 1 604.6 | 1 342.6 | 60.5 |
| 2012 | 5 172.97 | 1 393.0 | 3 436.8 | 1 669.2 | 1 400.7 | 63.9 |
| 2013 | 5 590.55 | 1 402.3 | 3 517.0 | 1 697.2 | 1 445.8 | 62.3 |
| 2014 | 6 534.10 | 1 404.3 | 3 507.4 | 1 648.2 | 1 477.2 | 63.0 |
| 2015 | | 1 406.0 | 3 547.0 | | | |

资料来源：国家统计局：《中国统计年鉴》、《中国统计摘要》，中国统计出版社出版；国家统计局网站。

表 6－1－3　　2015 年我国主要农产品产量及其增长速度　　单位：万吨

| 产品名称 | 产　量 | 比上年增长（%） |
|---|---|---|
| 粮　食 | 62 144 | 2.4 |
| 夏　粮 | 14 112 | 3.3 |
| 早　稻 | 3 369 | －0.9 |
| 秋　粮 | 44 662 | 2.3 |
| 油　料 | 3 547 | 1.1 |
| 棉　花 | 561 | －9.3 |
| 糖　料 | 12 529 | －6.2 |
| 茶　叶 | 224 | 6.9 |

资料来源：国家统计局：《2015 年国民经济和社会发展统计公报》。

表 6－1－4　　我国谷物、油料进口数量　　单位：千吨

| 年份 | 2002 | 2003 | 2004 | 2005 | 2006 | 2007 | 2008 | 2009 | 2010 | 2011 | 2012 | 2013 | 2014 | 2015 |
|---|---|---|---|---|---|---|---|---|---|---|---|---|---|---|
| 小　麦 | 604.57 | 424.18 | 7 233.15 | 3 510.13 | 584.09 | 83.42 | 31.87 | 893.71 | 1 218.72 | 1 248.82 | 3 688.62 | 5 507.05 | 2 971.39 | 2 972.74 |
| 大　米 | 236.19 | 257.00 | 761.46 | 514.18 | 718.99 | 470.53 | 295.57 | 337.54 | 366.17 | 578.38 | 2 344.62 | 2 244.32 | 2 556.55 | 3 349.98 |
| 玉　米 | | 0.12 | 2.32 | 3.90 | 65.13 | 35.12 | 49.07 | 83.47 | 1 572.14 | 1 752.74 | 5 207.38 | 3 264.88 | 2 598.04 | 4 730.04 |
| 大　麦 | 1 907.14 | 1 362.72 | 1 707.21 | 2 179.21 | 2 140.59 | 913.43 | 1 076.26 | 1 738.49 | 2 367.16 | 1 775.52 | 2 527.65 | 2 335.28 | 5 413.47 | 10 731.27 |
| 大　豆 | 11 315.22 | 20 741.11 | 20 229.92 | 26 590.23 | 28 269.88 | 30 821.43 | 37 435.89 | 42 551.65 | 54 796.82 | 52 639.55 | 58 383.82 | 63 375.15 | 71 398.98 | 81 740.34 |
| 豆　油 | 870.27 | 1 884.36 | 2 516.51 | 1 694.33 | 1 542.64 | 2 822.91 | 2 585.67 | 2 391.22 | 1 340.91 | 1 143.19 | 1 826.11 | 1 157.59 | 1 135.47 | 817.88 |
| 豆　粕 | 0.69 | 1.79 | 55.45 | 202.56 | 674.18 | 104.91 | 220.30 | 132.83 | 187.74 | 224.25 | 45.42 | 16.68 | 22.60 | 59.68 |
| 棕榈油 | 2 220.66 | 3 324.81 | 3 856.57 | 4 330.14 | 5 081.92 | 5 095.13 | 5 282.33 | 6 441.28 | 5 696.11 | 5 912.23 | 6 341.16 | 5 979.07 | 5 323.89 | 5 909.66 |
| 油菜籽 | 618.17 | 166.71 | 424.01 | 296.24 | 738.00 | 833.10 | 1 302.46 | 3 285.85 | 1 599.85 | 1 262.27 | 2 929.59 | 3 662.41 | 5 081.04 | 4 469.66 |
| 菜籽油 | 77.83 | 151.58 | 352.93 | 177.56 | 44.00 | 374.78 | 269.79 | 467.53 | 985.32 | 550.90 | 1 175.82 | 1 526.83 | 809.96 | 815.06 |

资料来源：国家粮油信息中心。

表 6－1－5　　我国谷物、油料出口数量　　单位：千吨

| 年份 | 2002 | 2003 | 2004 | 2005 | 2006 | 2007 | 2008 | 2009 | 2010 | 2011 | 2012 | 2013 | 2014 | 2015 |
|---|---|---|---|---|---|---|---|---|---|---|---|---|---|---|
| 小　麦 | 687.62 | 2 237.48 | 783.93 | 260.26 | 1 114.08 | 2 336.62 | 125.95 | 8.40 | 0.00 | 39.79 | 0.00 | 2.52 | 0.96 | 5.30 |
| 玉　米 | 11 673.25 | 16 389.45 | 2 317.86 | 8 610.84 | 3 070.40 | 4 913.60 | 252.32 | 129.03 | 127.16 | 136.00 | 257.26 | 77.63 | 20.01 | 11.07 |
| 大　米 | 1 965.37 | 2 588.88 | 881.92 | 657.33 | 1 221.18 | 1 304.52 | 946.72 | 760.76 | 596.19 | 515.50 | 279.09 | 478.40 | 419.07 | 285.94 |
| 大　豆 | 280.00 | 270.00 | 330.00 | 400.00 | 380.00 | 460.00 | 470.00 | 350.00 | 163.60 | 208.26 | 320.10 | 208.97 | 207.07 | 133.60 |
| 花生及花生仁 | 520.00 | 490.00 | 400.00 | 450.00 | 320.00 | 290.00 | 230.00 | 240.00 | 190.0 | 170.0 | 150.0 | 130.0 | 138.2 | |
| 豆　粕 | 1 013.16 | 770.62 | 656.46 | 552.95 | 381.54 | 850.06 | 534.89 | 1 123.21 | 1 016.01 | 406.32 | 1 232.67 | 1 070.11 | 2 090.95 | 1 695.71 |
| 菜籽粕 | 259.87 | 182.26 | 124.90 | 84.93 | 48.52 | 93.72 | 49.84 | 335.01 | 56.31 | 9.96 | 73.60 | 72.99 | 36.56 | 10.94 |

资料来源：国家统计局：《中国统计年鉴》，中国统计出版社出版；国家粮油信息中心。

**表6-1-6　　　全国居民消费价格指数（上年=100）**

| 年份 | 全国居民消费价格指数 | | |
|---|---|---|---|
| | | 粮食 | 油脂 |
| 1993 | 114.7 | | |
| 1994 | 124.1 | 150.7 | 161.3 |
| 1995 | 117.1 | 136.8 | 116.0 |
| 1996 | 108.3 | 106.5 | 92.1 |
| 1997 | 102.8 | 91.1 | 101.5 |
| 1998 | 99.2 | 96.9 | 100.0 |
| 1999 | 98.6 | 96.9 | 94.5 |
| 2000 | 100.4 | 88.6 | 86.8 |
| 2001 | 100.7 | 99.3 | 91.7 |
| 2002 | 99.2 | 98.3 | 98.7 |
| 2003 | 101.2 | 102.3 | 112.6 |
| 2004 | 103.9 | 126.4 | 118.2 |
| 2005 | 101.8 | 101.4 | 94.3 |
| 2006 | 101.5 | 102.7 | 98.6 |
| 2007 | 104.8 | 106.3 | 126.7 |
| 2008 | 105.9 | 107.0 | 125.4 |
| 2009 | 99.3 | 105.6 | 81.7 |
| 2010 | 103.3 | 111.8 | 103.8 |
| 2011 | 105.4 | 112.2 | 113.4 |
| 2012 | 102.6 | 114.0 | 115.1 |
| 2013 | 102.6 | 104.6 | 100.3 |
| 2014 | 102.0 | 103.1 | 95.1 |
| 2015 | 101.4 | 102.0 | |

资料来源：国家统计局：《中国统计年鉴》，中国统计出版社出版；《2015年国民经济和社会发展统计公报》。

**表 6－1－7**　　**2015 年全国主要粮油批发市场价格指数**（月度综合指数）

| 月　份 | 1 | 2 | 3 | 4 | 5 | 6 | 7 | 8 | 9 | 10 | 11 | 12 |
|---|---|---|---|---|---|---|---|---|---|---|---|---|
| 粮食类 | 229.13 | 229.25 | 229.59 | 231.31 | 230.23 | 227.54 | 226.81 | 225.08 | 221.57 | 214.20 | 211.54 | 213.78 |
| 食油类 | 118.36 | 117.94 | 117.50 | 116.68 | 116.17 | 115.32 | 115.74 | 114.20 | 112.39 | 112.10 | 109.15 | 108.39 |
| 粮油综合类 | 224.51 | 224.61 | 224.91 | 226.53 | 225.48 | 222.86 | 222.18 | 220.46 | 217.02 | 209.95 | 207.27 | 209.38 |

资料来源：中华粮网。

基期：1994 年 6 月 =100。

**表 6－1－8**　　**全国主要粮油批发市场价格指数**（年度综合指数）

| 年　份 | 2000 | 2001 | 2002 | 2003 | 2004 | 2005 | 2006 | 2007 | 2008 | 2009 | 2010 | 2011 | 2012 | 2013 | 2014 | 2015 |
|---|---|---|---|---|---|---|---|---|---|---|---|---|---|---|---|---|
| 粮食类 | 89.24 | 95.87 | 90.65 | 97.47 | 131.29 | 125.37 | 127.17 | 141.74 | 151.72 | 159.45 | 176.42 | 200.19 | 219.17 | 226.46 | 231.27 | 224.47 |
| 食油类 | 74.86 | 65.46 | 68.57 | 87.80 | 96.19 | 82.06 | 81.63 | 117.76 | 159.81 | 114.56 | 123.63 | 147.82 | 146.69 | 141.73 | 124.36 | 114.66 |
| 粮油综合类 | 88.64 | 94.60 | 89.73 | 97.07 | 129.83 | 123.57 | 125.27 | 140.74 | 152.06 | 157.57 | 174.21 | 198.00 | 216.15 | 222.94 | 226.81 | 219.89 |

资料来源：中华粮网。

说明：1994 年 6 月 =100。

**表6-1-9　　2015年全国主要粮油批发市场年度平均交易价格**

单位：元/吨

| 品　　种 | 等　　级 | 本期平均价 | 上期平均价 | 本期与上期比（%） |
|---|---|---|---|---|
| 白小麦（普通） | 三 | 2 398.86 | 2 496.54 | -3.91% |
| 黄玉米 | 二 | 2 188.67 | 2 329.81 | -6.05% |
| 大豆（油脂业） | 三 | 4 288.77 | 4 618.55 | -7.14% |
| 豆粕 | 二 | 2 986.78 | 3 711.84 | -19.53% |
| 花生仁 | 二 | 8 995.59 | 7 597.64 | 18.40% |
| 早粳米 | 标一 | 4 609.77 | 4 615.77 | -0.12% |
| 早籼米 | 标一 | 3 828.08 | 3 854.64 | -0.68% |
| 晚籼米 | 标一 | 4 170.87 | 4 137.23 | 0.82% |
| 白小麦（优质） | 西农979 | 2 698.67 | 2 692.48 | 0.23% |

资料来源：中华粮网。

说明：以上价格均为卖方火车板交货价格，包装另计。

**表6-1-10　　2009—2015年粮食批发市场交易国家政策粮油情况**

单位：万吨，元/吨

| 品种 | 2009年 | | 2010年 | | 2011年 | | 2012年 | | 2013年 | | 2014年 | | 2015年 | |
|---|---|---|---|---|---|---|---|---|---|---|---|---|---|---|
| | 成交量 | 成交均价 | 成交量 | 成交均价 | 成交量 | 成交均价 | 成交量 | 成交均价 | 成交量 | 成交均价 | 成交量 | 成交均价 | 成交量 | 成交均价 |
| 小　麦 | 3 980.00 | 1 807 | 4 006.00 | 1 873 | 1 427.00 | 1 906 | 1 447.00 | 2 144 | 3 467.97 | 2 320 | 2 008.95 | 2 364 | 759.54 | 2 525 |
| 超标小麦 | | | | | 161.00 | 1 810 | 4.31 | 1 856 | | | | | 76.09 | 1 747 |
| 稻　谷 | 924.00 | 2 116 | 1 338.00 | 2 026 | 790.00 | 2 017 | 24.45 | 2 397 | | | 98.70 | 3 020 | 536.14 | 2 981 |
| 粳　稻 | 852.00 | 2 126 | 331.00 | 2 270 | 21.00 | 2 465 | 6.37 | 2 983 | | | 98.70 | 3 020 | | |
| 早籼稻 | 3.00 | 1 955 | 189.00 | 1 910 | 206.00 | 1 948 | | | | | | | | |
| 中晚籼稻 | 69.00 | 1 997 | 818.00 | 1 955 | 563.00 | 2 026 | 18.08 | 2 190 | | | | | | |
| 玉　米 | 1 632.00 | 1 622 | 2 745.00 | 1 774 | 360.00 | 1 895 | | | | | 2 965.02 | 2 259 | 586.79 | 2 299 |
| 大　豆 | 14.00 | 3 764 | | | 1.60 | 3 959 | 375.83 | 4 255 | 242.93 | 4 024 | 248.13 | 4 145 | | |
| 食用油 | | | 50.00 | 9 854 | 90.00 | 9 453 | | | 0.66 | 10 256 | | | 23.47 | 5 675 |

资料来源：郑州粮食批发市场、安徽粮食批发市场。

**表 6－1－11　　2015 年全国期货市场交易情况**

| 交易所名称 | 品种名称 | 2015 年累计成交总量（手） | 2014 年同期成交总量（手） | 2015 年累计成交总额（亿元） | 2014 年同期成交总额（亿元） |
|---|---|---|---|---|---|
| 上海期货交易所 | 铜 | 88 318 558 | 70 510 306 | 175 913.80 | 168 728.76 |
| | 铝 | 22 900 691 | 13 926 276 | 12 741.35 | 9 628.45 |
| | 锌 | 45 237 435 | 40 429 347 | 32 178.85 | 33 285.68 |
| | 铅 | 1 310 106 | 1 457 822 | 845.40 | 1 036.43 |
| | 锡 | 515 789 | — | 562.37 | — |
| | 镍 | 63 590 118 | — | 52 047.12 | — |
| | 黄金 | 25 317 200 | 23 865 406 | 59 919.53 | 59 913.14 |
| | 白银 | 144 786 451 | 193 487 650 | 76 151.47 | 115 091.49 |
| | 天然橡胶 | 83 067 547 | 88 631 586 | 102 448.18 | 127 785.03 |
| | 燃料油 | 3 875 | 1 469 | 5.75 | 2.48 |
| | 石油沥青 | 32 397 823 | 650 169 | 7 358.81 | 276.86 |
| | 螺纹钢 | 541 035 860 | 408 078 103 | 114 949.40 | 116 204.03 |
| | 线材 | 327 | 665 | 0.08 | 0.22 |
| | 热轧卷板 | 2 012 366 | 1 255 424 | 430.52 | 400.68 |
| | 总　额 | 1 050 494 146 | 842 294 223 | 635 552.63 | 632 353.25 |
| 郑州商品交易所 | 棉花 | 22 612 511 | 31 781 857 | 14 349.44 | 21 897.11 |
| | 早籼稻 | 3 545 | 332 485 | 1.75 | 154.05 |
| | 甲醇 | 314 747 394 | 24 614 677 | 69 470.49 | 17 146.68 |
| | 菜籽油 | 7 775 243 | 13 894 567 | 4 537.73 | 9 349.88 |
| | 油菜籽 | 44 179 | 17 219 | 16.72 | 8.37 |
| | 菜籽粕 | 261 486 104 | 303 514 400 | 55 808.38 | 77 837.15 |
| | 白糖 | 187 306 805 | 97 723 498 | 100 611.77 | 45 900.91 |
| | PTA | 231 498 305 | 117 839 489 | 55 657.68 | 36 491.93 |
| | 普麦 | 1 175 | 1 203 | 1.46 | 1.54 |
| | 强麦 | 457 594 | 1 025 486 | 252.92 | 561.60 |
| | 玻璃 | 41 548 298 | 78 725 425 | 7 419.24 | 16 845.52 |
| | 动力煤 TC | 1 670 862 | 5 645 895 | 1 353.39 | 5 832.36 |
| | 动力煤 ZC | 980 710 | — | 294.80 | — |
| | 粳稻 | 99 | 8 855 | 0.06 | 5.53 |
| | 晚籼稻 | 1 059 | 52 116 | 0.59 | 29.50 |
| | 硅铁 | 39 406 | 767 619 | 7.62 | 221.23 |
| | 锰硅 | 50 439 | 361 462 | 10.68 | 115.97 |
| | 总　额 | 1 070 223 728 | 676 306 253 | 309 794.68 | 232 399.30 |

续表

| 交易所名称 | 品种名称 | 2015 年累计成交总量（手） | 2014 年同期成交总量（手） | 2015 年累计成交总额（亿元） | 2014 年同期成交总额（亿元） |
|---|---|---|---|---|---|
| 大连商品交易所 | 黄大豆一号 | 18 810 903 | 27 197 413 | 7 722. 09 | 12 216. 11 |
| | 黄大豆二号 | 4 936 | 6 952 | 1. 50 | 2. 56 |
| | 胶合板 | 182 704 | 17 760 375 | 103. 73 | 12 059. 32 |
| | 玉米 | 42 090 235 | 9 329 939 | 8 276. 01 | 2 214. 74 |
| | 玉米淀粉 | 27 053 680 | 71 958 | 5 835. 30 | 19. 87 |
| | 纤维板 | 68 271 | 15 354 378 | 20. 08 | 4 875. 85 |
| | 铁矿石 | 259 572 085 | 96 359 128 | 98 963. 68 | 60 505. 43 |
| | 焦炭 | 15 662 329 | 63 688 294 | 13 162. 74 | 75 275. 41 |
| | 鸡蛋 | 14 718 738 | 35 188 187 | 5 936. 40 | 16 897. 95 |
| | 焦煤 | 15 706 560 | 57 605 436 | 5 932. 84 | 28 559. 13 |
| | LLDPE | 119 856 998 | 71 754 393 | 52 741. 03 | 36 992. 52 |
| | 豆粕 | 289 496 780 | 204 988 746 | 76 963. 61 | 66 563. 18 |
| | 棕榈油 | 111 515 010 | 79 996 388 | 52 496. 48 | 44 783. 15 |
| | 聚丙烯 | 107 513 311 | 24 781 150 | 38 965. 30 | 12 138. 02 |
| | 聚氯乙烯 | 1 566 571 | 1 471 673 | 407. 88 | 430. 52 |
| | 豆油 | 92 504 264 | 64 082 631 | 51 831. 06 | 41 410. 53 |
| | 总　额 | 1 116 323 375 | 769 637 041 | 419 359. 74 | 414 944. 31 |
| 中国金融期货交易所 | 10 年期国债期货 | 1 683 921 | — | 16 511. 76 | — |
| | 沪深 300 股指期货 | 277 101 989 | 216 658 274 | 3 419 065. 91 | 1 631 384. 56 |
| | 5 年期国债期货 | 4 403 572 | 922 871 | 43 594. 99 | 8 785. 17 |
| | 上证 50 股指期货 | 35 483 920 | — | 306 922. 81 | — |
| | 中证 500 股指期货 | 22 195 929 | — | 391 509. 24 | — |
| | 总　额 | 340 869 331 | 217 581 145 | 4 177 604. 71 | 1 640 169. 73 |
| 全国期货市场交易总额 | | 3 577 910 580 | 2 505 818 662 | 5 542 311. 75 | 2 919 866. 59 |

资料来源：中国期货业协会。

**表 6－1－12　　芝加哥期货交易所农产品期货交易量情况**

单位：张

| 品种＼年份 | 2004 | 2005 | 2006 | 2007 | 2008 | 2009 | 2010 | 2011 | 2012 | 2013 | 2014 | 2015 |
|---|---|---|---|---|---|---|---|---|---|---|---|---|
| 小麦期货合约 | 7 955 155 | 10 114 098 | 16 224 871 | 19 582 706 | 19 011 928 | 17 677 547 | 23 090 255 | 24 283 331 | 27 379 403 | 24 993 158 | 31 722 024 | 38 460 544 |
| 小麦小型期货合约 | 31 044 | 32 295 | 67 637 | 79 282 | 70 971 | 61 355 | 91 560 | 149 102 | 95 600 | 125 944 | 101 124 | 82 987 |
| 玉米期货合约 | 24 038 233 | 27 965 057 | 47 239 893 | 54 520 152 | 59 957 118 | 50 948 804 | 69 841 420 | 79 004 801 | 73 184 337 | 64 322 600 | 69 437 304 | 83 094 271 |
| 玉米小型期货合约 | 86 771 | 102 292 | 162 545 | 156 210 | 219 562 | 203 474 | 237 394 | 363 832 | 267 428 | 206 491 | 172 411 | 132 596 |
| 燕麦期货合约 | 416 448 | 351 539 | 427 315 | 432 741 | 441 588 | 314 305 | 344 587 | 349 316 | 279 570 | 254 958 | 200 531 | 194 575 |
| 大豆期货合约 | 18 846 021 | 20 216 137 | 22 647 785 | 31 726 316 | 36 373 096 | 35 758 855 | 36 933 960 | 45 143 755 | 52 041 615 | 46 721 081 | 49 169 361 | 54 095 051 |
| 大豆小型期货合约 | 362 829 | 459 313 | 581 047 | 540 940 | 475 231 | 466 367 | 412 732 | 394 119 | 359 324 | 299 308 | 316 771 | 229 208 |
| 豆粕期货合约 | 8 569 243 | 8 324 616 | 9 350 043 | 12 213 315 | 13 354 174 | 12 880 767 | 14 052 845 | 16 920 194 | 18 187 433 | 20 237 181 | 20 637 382 | 24 315 276 |
| 豆油期货合约 | 7 593 314 | 7 676 130 | 9 488 524 | 13 170 864 | 16 928 361 | 17 132 082 | 20 791 164 | 24 156 509 | 27 627 590 | 23 805 912 | 23 769 391 | 28 897 275 |
| 稻谷期货合约 | 168 165 | 228 502 | 321 330 | 358 905 | 362 565 | 277 065 | 448 724 | 555 854 | 388 936 | 280 048 | 225 694 | 316 315 |

资料来源：芝加哥期货交易所。

说明：小麦、玉米、燕麦、大豆期货合约单位为5 000 蒲式耳，小型小麦、玉米、大豆期货合约单位为1 000 蒲式耳，其中，小麦、大豆1 蒲式耳约等于0.0272 吨，玉米1 蒲式耳约等于0.0254 吨，燕麦1 蒲式耳约等于0.0172 吨；豆粕期货合约单位为100 短吨（约90.72 吨）；豆油期货合约单位为60 000 磅（约2.72 吨）；稻谷期货合约单位为2 000 英担（约101.6 吨）。

**表6-1-13　　美国农业部世界谷物统计与预测　　单位：百万吨**

| 品　种 | 分　类 | 2010/2011年度 | 2011/2012年度 | 2012/2013年度 | 2013/2014年度 | 2014/2015年度（预估） | 2015/2016年度（预测） |
|---|---|---|---|---|---|---|---|
| 小麦 | 产量 | 652.0 | 697.3 | 658.3 | 715.4 | 725.9 | 735.8 |
| | 消费 | 654.0 | 688.9 | 686.9 | 690.8 | 699.8 | 709.5 |
| | 期末库存 | 197.9 | 199.0 | 177.0 | 194.0 | 214.5 | 238.9 |
| | 贸易量 | 133.7 | 153.8 | 147.1 | 165.9 | 164.4 | 163.1 |
| 大米 | 产量 | 449.1 | 465.8 | 472.5 | 478.4 | 478.1 | 469.5 |
| | 消费 | 443.6 | 456.5 | 466.1 | 478.2 | 478.9 | 481.7 |
| | 期末库存 | 98.7 | 104.4 | 110.5 | 107.4 | 103.5 | 89.3 |
| | 贸易量 | 36.2 | 39.1 | 39.5 | 43.4 | 42.5 | 41.6 |
| 全部粗粮 | 产量 | 1 099.4 | 1 151.3 | 1 136.2 | 1 281.0 | 1 297.5 | 1 264.3 |
| | 消费 | 1 130.2 | 1 133.6 | 1 140.8 | 1 225.2 | 1 251.0 | 1 266.5 |
| | 期末库存 | 165.8 | 165.4 | 163.5 | 211.2 | 242.0 | 245.2 |
| | 贸易量 | 116.2 | 133.4 | 132.2 | 164.6 | 173.2 | 170.1 |
| 全部谷物（包括大米） | 产量 | 2 200.5 | 2 314.4 | 2 266.9 | 2 474.8 | 2 501.5 | 2 469.6 |
| | 消费 | 2 227.8 | 2 279.0 | 2 293.8 | 2 394.2 | 2 429.7 | 2 457.8 |
| | 期末库存 | 462.4 | 468.8 | 451.1 | 512.6 | 560.0 | 573.3 |
| | 贸易量 | 286.1 | 326.4 | 318.9 | 370.4 | 377.1 | 374.8 |

资料来源：美国农业部。

说明：

（1）贸易数据为7月/6月，其他为各国市场年度数据的加总。

（2）贸易量的统计不包括欧盟内部贸易，包括前苏联各加盟共和国间的贸易。

# 二、2015年中国粮食市场大事记

## 1月

**7日**，农业部发出文件，我国将启动马铃薯主粮化战略，把马铃薯作为我国第四大主粮，加工成馒头、面条、米粉等主食。主粮化战略实施后，马铃薯产业风生水起，以马铃薯为原料的蛋糕、杏仁酥等产品琳琅满目，有的企业开始筹建马铃薯面条和石磨面粉生产线。马铃薯作为粮食安全的一个重要补充，有助于新形势下国家粮食安全战略的顺利实施。

**8—9日**，全国粮食流通会议在北京召开。会议要求，2015年粮食流通工作重点要守住四条底线，狠抓改革攻坚，依法加强监管，提升三个能力，统筹三大建设。一要坚决守住粮食总量安全、质量安全、农民增收、市场稳定等四条底线，进一步增强忧患意识，确保饭碗牢牢端在自己手上。二要从理顺中央政府与地方政府关系、全面落实粮食安全省长责任制入手，创新宏观调控思路和方式，进一步全面深化粮食流通领域各项改革。三要进一步推进粮食法制建设，依法加强对地方落实储备规模、粮食仓储设施和粮食收储企业的监管，着力推进依法治粮。四要大力加强粮食流通能力建设，提升粮食收储能力、科技支撑能力和粮食加工转化能力。五要持续深入转变职能、转变作风，统筹融合党务、业务、队伍建设。

**13日**，国务院办公厅印发《关于加快木本油料产业发展的意见》（以下简称《意见》），部署加快木本油料产业发展，大力增加健康优质食用植物油供给，切实维护国家粮油安全。《意见》提出到2020年建成800个油茶、核桃、油用牡丹等木本油料重点县，木本油料树种种植面积从现有的1.2亿亩发展到2亿亩，产出木本食用油150万吨左右。

**22日**，国务院印发《关于建立健全粮食安全省长责任制的若干意见》（以下简称《意见》），从粮食生产、流通、消费等环节进一步明确了各省级人民政府在维护国家粮食安全方面的事权与责任，对建立健全粮食安全省长责任制做出全面部署。《意见》指出，粮食安全是实现经济发展、社会稳定和国家安全的重要基础。随着国内粮食生产实现“十一连增”，一些地方存在放松粮食生产、忽视粮食流通、过度依靠中央的现象，自觉承担维护国家粮食安全责任有待进一步加强。为加快构建国家粮食安全保障体系，确保谷物基本自给、口粮绝对安全，把饭碗牢牢端在自己手上，必须建立健全粮食安全省长责任制。《意见》的出台，把粮食安全“负责制”调整为粮食安全省长“责任制”，实现了理顺粮食流通管理体制的新突破，为全面深化粮食流通改革、全面推进依法治粮奠定了重要的制度基础。

国务院办公厅印发《关于引导农村产权流转交易市场健康发展的意见》（以下简称《意见》）。《意见》指出，引导农村产权流转交易市场健康发展，事关农村改革发展稳定大局，有利于保障农民和农村集体经济组织的财产权益，有利于提高农村要素资源配置和利用效率，有利于加快推进农业现代化。要坚持公益性为主、公开公正规范、因地制宜、稳步推进的基本原则，以坚持和完善农村基本经营制度为前提，以保障农民和农村集体经济组织的财产权益为根本，以规范流转交易行为和完善服务功能为重点，扎实做好农村产权流转交易市场建设工作。

## 2 月

**1 日**，2015 年中央 1 号文件发布，粮食安全首当其冲。文件表示，经济步入新常态之后，如何在“双重挤压”下创新农业支持保护政策、加快现代农业发展方式、提高农业竞争力成为我国农业发展的破局关键。要加强对粮食主产省和主产县的政策倾斜，不断增强粮食生产能力、提升粮食收储能力、提高农产品质量安全、不断完善农产品价格形成机制成为聚焦粮食行业的亮点。

**5 日**，国务院公布 2015 年稻谷主产区最低收购价政策。2015 年生产的早籼稻（三等，下同）、中晚籼稻和粳稻最低收购价格分别为 135 元/50 千克、138 元/50 千克和 155 元/50 千克，保持 2014 年水平不变。

**28 日**，农业部、最高人民法院、最高人民检察院、工业和信息化部、公安部、工商总局、质检总局、供销合作总社八部门联合召开 2015 年全国农资打假专项治理行动电视电话会议，动员各地、各部门迅速行动起来，深入开展农资打假专项治理行动，保障春耕生产，维护农民权益，为农业稳粮增收保驾护航。2015 年农资打假和监管工作要坚持问题导向、依法行政、打防结合、标本兼治，进一步加大农资监管力度，严厉打击违法违规行为，健全完善长效监管机制，努力营造公平竞争的市场环境和安全放心的消费环境。

## 3 月

**18—19 日**，全国粮食质量安全监管工作会议在贵阳召开。会议肯定了 2014 年的粮食质量安全工作，并指出 2015 年是全面推进依法治粮的开局之年，是继续贯彻实施国家粮食安全战略、深入推进粮食流通改革转型和创新发展的关键之年，也是全面深化实施粮食安全省长责任制的开篇之年。各级粮食行政管理部门要积极作为，主动适应经济发展新常态，坚决守住三个重点环节，全力推进三个体系建设，着力提升三个能力，大力推动粮食质量安全工作迈上新台阶。

国家粮食局在云南昆明召开全国粮食调控与统计工作会议。会议强调，2015 年粮食调控与统计工作要以落实粮食安全省长责任制为核心，以全国粮食流通工作会议的部署为重点，突出抓好“五个并举”，着力提升“五个能力”。坚持政策性收购与市场化收购并举，提升为农服务能力；调销腾库与应急保障并举，提升粮食市场供应能力；优化中央储备与强化地方储备并举，提升储备调控能力；夯实基础与优化创新并举，提升统计信息服务能力；立足当前与着眼长远并举，提升形势分析和政策研究能力，努力推动粮食调控和统计工作再上新台阶。

**22 日**，农业部发布消息，决定在部分具备条件的县（市、区）开展土地经营权入股发展农业产业化经营试点，试点范围包括黑鲁浙渝 4 省（市）自选的县级行政区和 3 个农村改革试验区。根据农业部的要求，试点工作由省级农业产业化主管部门牵头负责，会同农村改革试验区工作主管部门，组织各试点县（市、区）的农业部门具体实施。试点内容包括探索多元化的载体（股份组织）、股份组织的运行机制和政府部门的政策创设。可以是农民以土地经营权直接入股企业，或者先入股到合作社、合作社再入股企业；也可以是农民以土地经营权、企业和个人以其他要素入股到合作社等，让资本、土地、劳动、技术等各种要素优化配置，实现一、二、三产业融合发展。通过试点，挖掘和培育一批以土地经营权入股发展农业产业化经营的龙头企业、合作社。

## 4月

**2—3日**，国家粮食局在福建省福州市召开全国粮食流通监督检查工作会议。会议指出，做好今年的粮食流通监督检查工作责任十分重大。各地一定要结合本地实际，坚持改革方向和问题导向，厉行法治，统筹兼顾，突出重点，继续提升监管效能，着力抓好政策性粮食收购和销售出库检查、粮食库存检查工作，加快库存粮食识别代码在粮食库存监管中的运用，加快推进粮食经营者信用体系建设，加强监督检查组织体系和依法管粮能力建设，全面完成好今年各项工作任务。

**9—10日**，国家粮食局在北京召开全国粮食系统军粮供应工作会议。会议要求，2015年军粮供应工作要认真贯彻落实全国粮食流通工作会议部署，紧贴部队现代后勤建设新要求，适应加快推进粮食流通能力现代化新形势，加强军粮供应全产业链管理，切实提高军粮供应工作水平；加强军供网点危仓老库的维修改造，切实提高军粮供应保障能力；加强军粮供应法规制度建设，切实提高规范化管理水平；加强军粮供应队伍建设，切实提高服务能力和水平。要以提升军粮保障能力为重点，把保障平台做大、把保障载体做强、把保障体系做优，加快推动军粮供应军民融合深度发展，持续开创军粮供应工作新局面。

**12日**，国务院办公厅印发《关于同意中国农业发展银行改革实施总体方案的批复》。文件指出，中国农业发展银行改革要坚持以政策性业务为主体，通过对政策性业务和自营性业务实施分账管理、分类核算，明确责任和风险补偿机制，确立以资本充足率为核心的约束机制，建立规范的治理结构和决策机制，把中国农业发展银行建设成为具备可持续发展能力的农业政策性银行。

**17日**，辽宁、吉林两省曝出个别粮库在政策性粮食收储和销售出库过程中“以陈粮顶新粮，恶意套取价差和国家补贴”事件。

**18日**，国家粮食局派出核查工作组赶赴辽宁铁岭开原、吉林松原前郭等地开展实地核查，现场督办，即刻封存涉案粮食，依法控制关键涉案人员，查清问题真相，严肃追究有关企业和人员的责任。同时还对东北三省一区国家政策性粮食收储和销售出库过程中的买陈抵新、先收后转、低收高转等各种“转圈粮”问题进行了严查。国家粮食局的快速反应，说明我国在粮食收购、存储等领域打击违法违纪行为的高压态势。

**28日**，黑龙江对俄农业协会对外称，中俄（滨海边疆区）现代农业产业合作区成为中国首个国家级境外农业产业园区，成为中俄农业合作最大的平台。该园区于2004年开始投资建设，目前已发展成为集种植、养殖、加工于一体的中俄最大农业合作项目。该园区由黑龙江省东宁华信集团投建，中国商务部、财政部联合签发了《境外经济贸易合作区确认函》。截至目前，合作区拥有耕地面积6.8万公顷，设有14个种植区。截至2014年末，已完成投资1.2亿美元。

**30日**，天津市整合农垦集团、二商集团、粮油集团、立达集团等四大集团，组建天津食品集团有限公司。重组后，天津食品集团在食品供应保障、提升名优品牌的市场影响力、扩大供应区域和服务范围、保障居民饮食安全等方面的能力进一步增强；为建设成品牌优、效益好、百姓放心的国有大食品产业龙头集团奠定了基础。

## 5月

**1日**，李经谋先生主编的第11卷中国粮食市场发展报告——《2015中国粮食市场发展报告》由中国财政经济出版社出版。

**7日**，上海市国资委发布光明食品集团与上海良友集团联合重组的通知，光明与良友联合重组拉开帷幕。光明食品集团与良友集团的联合重组，产生了“1+1>2”效应，无论在体量还是板块覆盖方面，都增加了与中粮集团正面竞争的资本。企业并购重组是搞活企业、盘活资产、提升竞争力的重要途径。

**16日**，由国家粮食局、教育部、中国科协、全国妇联联合举办的“2015年粮食科技活动周”在京启动，5月16—24日在全国各地同步开展。本次活动以“爱粮节粮，健康消费——粮食科普进家庭进学校”为主题，目的是普及粮食安全科学知识、提高全民节粮意识、推广科学储粮技术。

**19日**，国家粮食局在江苏南京召开全国夏季粮油收购工作会议。会议要求各级粮食行政管理部门要把做好夏粮收购作为当前粮食流通工作的中心任务，切实抓好各项政策措施的落实。一是要及早做好收购仓容、资金、器材、人员培训等各项准备工作。二是要严格执行国家粮食收购政策，认真组织好收购，及时掌握收购进度，加强政策执行情况的监督检查。三是要做好收购信息服务，引导各类企业积极搞好市场化收购。四是要积极采取措施，努力提高收购服务质量和水平。同时，各地要抓住新粮上市的有利时机，抓紧落实地方储备增储规模。

**22日**，财政部、农业部下发《关于调整完善农业三项补贴政策的指导意见》，决定从2015年起调整完善农作物良种补贴、综合直补和粮食直补等农业三项补贴政策（简称“农业三项补贴”），将“农业三项补贴”合并为“农业支持保护补贴”，目标调整为支持耕地地力保护和粮食适度规模经营。其目标为有两个：一是支持耕地地力保护；二是支持粮食适度规模经营。其中，支持耕地地力保护就是原来所说的“农业三项补贴”。

**25日**，国家粮食局下发《关于深化粮食科技体制改革和加快创新体系建设的指导意见》（以下简称《意见》），提出粮食科技体制机制改革要取得新突破，紧扣行业发展，使粮食科技创新更加聚焦国家目标、重大任务和行业需求。《意见》指出，各级粮食科研机构和广大粮食企业要落实粮食科技工作的基本定位要求，把保障和支撑国家粮食安全作为粮食科技工作天大的责任和崇高的使命，着力解决粮食行业创新发展最急需、最重要、最关键的科技难题。各级粮食行政管理部门要从保障国家粮食安全的战略高度和粮食流通事业科学发展的全局角度，深刻认识粮食科技体制改革和粮食行业创新发展的重要性和紧迫性，切实增强推进粮食科技体制改革、抓好粮食科技创新工作的责任感、使命感。

**27日**，指导我国农业可持续发展的纲领性文件《全国农业可持续发展规划（2015—2030年）》对外发布。根据规划，全国农业将被划分为优化发展区、适度发展区和保护发展区等三大区域，国家将因地制宜、梯次推进、分类施策。其中，优化发展区主要包括东北区、黄淮海区、长江中下游区和华南区。这是我国大宗农产品主产区，农业生产条件好、潜力大，应坚持生产优先、兼顾生态、种养结合原则，在确保粮食等主要农产品综合生产能力稳步提高的前提下，实现生产稳定发展、资源永续利用、生态环境友好。适度发展区包括西北及长城沿线区和西南区，这一区域农业生产特色鲜明，但水土配置错位、资源环境承载力有限，应坚持保护与发展并重，适度挖掘潜力、集约节约、有序利用。保护发展区包括青藏区和海洋渔业区，在生态保护与建设方面具有特殊重要的战略地位，应坚持保护优先、限制开发，适度发展生态产业和特色产业，促进生态系统良性循环。规划提出，到2020年农业科技进步贡献率达到60%以上，到2030年全国基本实现农业废弃物趋零排放。

河南省第十二届人民代表大会常务委员会第14次会议通过了《河南省高标准粮田保护条例》，这是全国第一部高标准粮田保护的地方法规，并将于10月1日起开始施行。高标准粮田建设是河南省委、省政府贯彻落实“三大国家战略”、加快国家粮食生产核心区建设、保障国家粮食安全的战略举措，其目的就是为了实现保粮田面积、保粮食产量、保农民收益的“三保”目标。

**6月**

**15日**，国家发改委、国家粮食局、财政部等三部门印发《粮食收储供应安全保障工程建设规划（2015—2020年）》（以下简称《规划》），这是粮食流通基础设施建设方面的第一个国家级专项规划。要求全面提升粮食收储供应安全保障能力，守住“种粮卖得出、吃粮买得到”粮食流通工作底线，保持粮食供求基本平衡和价格基本稳定，促进粮食增产、农民增收和粮食流通现代化，确保国家粮食安全。作为今后一个时期我国粮食流通基础设施建设的重要依据，《规划》为我国改善粮食流通设施条件、保证粮食收储供应、增强粮食宏观调控能力、保障军需民食提供了政策参考和制度保障。

**17日**，由中国农业科学院农业环境与可持续发展研究所牵头组织的国家“华北地区节水保粮”协同创新项目在石家庄启动。该项目针对华北地区水资源严重短缺、降水不能满足现行的种植制度，地下水超采严重、水资源浪费等问题，以减少地下水开采为导向，以水资源可持续利用为目标，以提高水资源利用率和作物水分生产力为核心，以主要作物高效用水和区域整体解决方案为主线，组织京津冀鲁豫等五地的55家农业科研院所联合攻关，为政府部门决策提供科学依据，为水资源高效利用提供技术支撑，为区域农业高效用水提供可落地、可复制、可推广的技术模式，促进华北地区农业可持续发展。

**18日**，国家粮食局等部门印发《关于做好2015年油菜籽收购工作的通知》，决定自2015年起取消油菜籽临时收储政策，由地方政府负责组织各类企业进行油菜籽收购，中央财政将对油菜籽主要产区适当予以补贴，并通过对产油大县奖励政策继续支持各地发展油料产业。至此，大豆、棉花、油菜籽三种油料作物的临时收储政策全部取消，价格改革进一步向前推进。

**22日**，国务院印发《关于开展第三次全国农业普查的通知》，决定于2016年开展第三次全国农业普查，其目的是查清、查实我国农业、农村、农民基本情况，全面掌握农业现代化进程、社会主义新农村建设和农民生活新变化，为党中央、国务院科学制定“三农”政策提供全面扎实可靠的决策依据。普查的主要内容包括：农业从业者基本情况，农业土地利用与流转情况，农业生产与结构情况，新型农业经营主体与农业规模化、产业化发展情况，新农村建设情况，农村人居环境与农民生活方式变化情况等。普查的标准时点为2016年12月31日，时期资料为2016年度资料。

## 7月

**1日**，中国农业发展银行面向企业客户成功发行首单理财产品。本期理财产品发行规模5亿元人民币，期限为1年，保本浮动收益型，预期收益率4.2%。农发行理财产品的成功发行，进一步完善了政策性金融服务功能，健全了市场化定价金融产品体系，提升了服务“三农”和实体经济的能力。

新颁布的《中华人民共和国国家安全法》把粮食安全纳入国家安全问题的范畴。这是我国第一次将粮食安全纳入国家安全体系，粮食安全被置于金融安全之后，凸显粮食安全在国家安全治理中的重要性。

**15日**，国家统计局河南调查总队发布了2015年夏粮产量数据。今年河南省夏粮总产量达到702.36亿斤，比上年增产34.56亿斤，增幅为5.2%，河南夏粮实现了连续13年增产，也是自2007年以来河南夏粮增产幅度最大的年份。

**21日**，一艘装载着24 750吨玉米酒糟粕的巴拿马籍货轮顺利抵达莆田秀屿港口，这是莆田口岸首次进口玉米酒糟粕。这批作为饲料用途的玉米酒糟粕顺利入境，标志着莆田乃至闽东饲料加工企业从此有了自己原料进口的“黄金通道”。

**29 日**，第九届世界马铃薯大会在北京市延庆区隆重举行。本届大会首次实现了“四会合一”，即世界马铃薯大会、中国国际薯业博览会、中国马铃薯大会、马铃薯主食产品及产业开发国际研讨会同期举行。来自 37 个国家的 3 000 余名马铃薯领域的学术精英、产业精英和政府代表参加会议。大会以科技交流、商业合作、展示展览为主题，旨在通过技术交流和经贸合作促进全球马铃薯产业发展。

## 8 月

**4 日**，农业部公布了 103 个国家农产品质量安全县和 4 个国家农产品质量安全市创建试点单位名单以及配套的管理办法。这批创建试点单位以“菜篮子”产品主产县为主，涵盖全国 31 个省（区、市）和新疆生产建设兵团。农业部开展国家农产品质量安全县创建活动的总体思路是：以“菜篮子”产品主产县为重点，“产”、“管”并举，推动各地落实属地管理责任，探索建立有效的监管模式，以点带面，整体提升农产品质量安全监管能力和水平。在创建内容上，主要围绕投入品监管、标准化生产、打击违法违规行为、监管体系建设、制度机制创新等八个方面开展，突出了责任落实、全程监管、能力提升和社会共治。

**6—7 日**，全国退耕还林还草工作现场经验交流会在贵州毕节市召开。会议透露，中央政府已累计在 25 个省（区、市）投入 4 056. 6 亿元用于第一轮退耕还林工程建设，共完成退耕地造林 1. 39 亿亩、配套荒山荒地造林和封山育林 3. 09 亿亩，涉及 3 200 万户农户、1. 24 亿农民。第一轮退耕还林工程区森林覆盖率平均提高 3 个多百分点，林木保存率达 99%，水土流失和风沙危害明显减轻；退耕户通过基本口粮田建设和集中力量精耕细作，提高了粮食单产，较好地解决了吃饭问题。

**7 日**，国务院办公厅印发《关于加快转变农业发展方式的意见》（以下简称《意见》），这是国家层面首个系统部署转变农业发展方式工作的重要文件。《意见》指出，转变农业发展方式是一项系统工程、长期战略，必须坚持把增强粮食生产能力作为首要前提，把提高质量效益作为主攻方向，把促进可持续发展作为重要内容，把推进改革创新作为根本动力，把尊重农民主体地位作为基本遵循，力争到 2020 年转变农业发展方式取得积极进展，农业内生活力进一步激发，农业综合生产能力稳步提升，农业资源利用和生态环境保护水平不断提高，农民收入持续增加，为全面建成小康社会提供重要支撑。到 2030 年，转变农业发展方式取得显著成效，农业质量和效益明显提升，竞争力显著增强。

**22 日**，泸州口岸迎来首批 500 吨柬埔寨大米。泸州进境粮食指定口岸运营以来，凭借其巨大物流成本优势，已成为四川乃至西部粮食进口主要港口。2015 年以来，泸州口岸进口粮食包括大麦、高粱、大米三个品种，共计 30 批，15 000 余吨。

**24 日**，国务院印发《关于开展农村承包土地的经营权和农民住房财产权抵押贷款试点的指导意见》（以下简称《意见》）。《意见》明确，开展农村承包土地的经营权和农民住房财产权抵押贷款试点要坚持依法有序、自主自愿、稳妥推进、风险可控的原则，按照所有权、承包权、经营权三权分置和经营权流转有关要求，以落实农村土地的用益物权、赋予农民更多财产权利为出发点，深化农村金融改革创新，稳妥有序开展“两权”抵押贷款业务，有效盘活农村资源、资金、资产，增加农业生产中长期和规模化经营的资金投入，为稳步推进农村土地制度改革提供经验和模式，促进农民增收致富和农业现代化加快发展。

**28 日**，作为江西唯一对外开放的水运口岸，九江城西港码头顺利通过国家质检总局进口粮食考核组考核验收，标志着九江口岸获得了进口粮食“绿卡”，结束了江西不能直接进口粮食的历史。

## 9 月

**2 日**，农业部发布公告，要求 41 个农作物品种即日停产，并在一年后停止推广，“两优 0293”名列其中。农业部种子管理局品种管理处认为该品种被认为有重大缺陷，因而停止推广。10 年前，“两优 0293”通过农业部的评审，成为“国审稻”，并长期被种子生产企业冠以“超级稻”的称谓。

**7 日**，财政部公布数据，2015 年中央财政已安排农业综合开发资金 235.65 亿元用于高标准农田项目，预计可建设高标准农田 2 777.45 万亩，亩均新增粮食生产能力 100 千克以上。国家农发办多措并举，创新驱动，确保高标准农田建设取得更好成效。一是突出重点，因地制宜开展项目建设；二是加大投入，进一步提升亩均投资标准；三是简政放权，加大新型农业经营主体支持力度；四是创新机制，撬动金融资本投入高标准农田建设。

**9日**，中国农科院中国水稻研究所超级稻种质创新团队与中国科学院遗传与发育生物研究所等单位合作，从浙江地方大粒品种“宝大粒”中成功分离并克隆了一个能够显著提高超级稻产量的重要基因GS2。相关研究成果在线发表在最新一期的国际知名刊物《分子植物》杂志上。

**17日**，国家相关部门出台2015年玉米临储相关通知，玉米收储价格调低至1元/斤。

**18日**，国家粮食局在黑龙江省哈尔滨市召开全国秋粮收购工作会议，分析研判秋粮收购形势，安排部署收购工作。会议强调，各地要把秋粮收购作为当前粮食流通工作的重中之重抓实抓好，确保收购工作平稳有序进行。要扎实做好仓容、资金、物资和人员培训、政策宣传等各项准备工作。要严格执行最低收购价和临时收储政策，认真按照粮食安全省长责任制的要求，抓好质量超标粮食的收购，同时积极鼓励和引导企业开展市场化收购，防止发生农民“卖粮难”。要进一步强化市场监管工作，督促企业严格执行“五要五不准”收购守则，严厉查处各种违法违规和违反政策的行为，坚决防止给农民“打白条”现象的发生，切实维护收购市场秩序。要利用新粮上市的有利时机，抓紧落实新增地方储备，确保增储任务按期完成。要认真抓好安全储粮和安全生产工作，防止发生坏粮事故，坚决杜绝重大安全事故发生。

**22日**，农业部、发改委、商务部联合印发《推进农业电子商务发展行动计划》（以下简称《计划》），以推进以农产品和农业生产资料为主要内容的农业电子商务快速健康发展。《计划》明确了未来3年的总体目标，到2018年，农业电子商务基础设施条件明显改善，制度体系和政策环境基本健全，培育出一批具有重要影响力的农业电子商务企业和品牌等。

## 10月

**10日**，为保护农民利益，防止“谷贱伤农”，2016年国家继续在小麦主产区实行最低收购价政策。综合考虑粮食生产成本、市场供求、国内外市场价格和粮食产业发展等各方面因素，经国务院批准，2016 年生产的小麦（三等）最低收购价为 118 元/50 千克，保持 2015 年水平不变，以稳定粮食生产，促进粮食产业健康发展。

**13 日**，习近平主持召开中央全面深化改革领导小组第 17 次会议，强调鼓励基层改革创新、大胆探索，推动改革落地生根造福群众。会议审议通过了《关于进一步推进农垦改革发展的意见》等文件，指出，我国农垦是在特定历史条件下为承担国家使命而建立的。推进农垦改革发展，要坚持社会主义市场经济改革方向，坚持政企分开、社企分开，以保障国家粮食安全和重要农产品有效供给为核心，以推进垦区集团化、农场企业化改革为主线，依靠创新驱动，加快转变经济发展方式，推进资源资产整合、产业优化升级，建设现代农业的大基地、大企业、大产业，全面增强内生动力、发展活力、整体实力，发挥现代农业建设的骨干引领作用。要加强党对农垦工作的组织领导，加强农垦资产管理，防止国有资产流失。要按照统筹兼顾、标本兼治、上下联动、点面结合的原则稳步推进。

**16 日**，河南省政府与农业部在北京签署共同推进河南省转变农业发展方式合作备忘录。河南省省长谢伏瞻、农业部部长韩长赋出席省部合作座谈会并签字。

**18 日**，中储粮东北综合产业基地项目开工仪式在盘锦港港区内举行。该项目是中储粮总公司迄今投资规模最大、设备工艺最先进、配套功能最齐全，以仓储为主，集仓储、物流、加工于一体的大型粮油综合项目。主要建设内容包括 128 万吨粮油储备仓、100 万吨粮食物流仓、4 条共 4 400 米铁路专用线、两个 7 万吨级粮油专用泊位等。项目分两期建设，一期项目的物流和仓储部分计划于 2017 年 10 月投产，油脂加工部分计划于 2018 年 5 月投产。该项目整体建成投产后，将借助盘锦港便捷高效的铁路、公路、海路货物集疏运条件和装卸能力，成为中储粮系统乃至全国最大的以粮油仓储为主的现代化综合产业基地，同时为盘锦港的发展带来新活力，有力拉动盘锦港吞吐量的显著增长，促进区域经济的发展。

**23 日**，大连北良港码头靠泊的“中粮 1 轮”汽笛一声长鸣，卸船设备在门机的带动下探入船舱，随着吸粮器高速运转，来自南美的 7 万吨大豆源源不断地被传送带送进岸上的库房中。这标志着中粮集团、中国海运粮食班轮航线正式启动。

## 11月

**2日**，中共中央办公厅、国务院办公厅印发了《深化农村改革综合性实施方案》。文件指出，农村改革是全面深化改革的重要内容。当前，我国经济发展进入新常态，新型工业化、信息化、城镇化、农业现代化持续推进，农村经济社会深刻变革，农村改革涉及的利益关系更加复杂、目标更加多元、影响因素更加多样、任务也更加艰巨。农村改革综合性强，靠单兵突进难以奏效，必须树立系统性思维，做好整体谋划和顶层设计，找准牵一发而动全身的“牛鼻子”和主要矛盾，进一步提高农村改革决策的科学性。要从总体上把握好农村改革的方向，提出深化农村改革的总目标、大原则、基本任务、重要路径，从全局上更好地指导和协调农村各项改革，加强各项改革之间的衔接配套，最大限度释放改革的综合效应。

农业部公布了《农业部关于“镰刀弯”地区玉米结构调整的指导意见》，提出力争到2020年“镰刀弯”地区玉米种植面积稳定在1亿亩，比目前减少5 000万亩以上。推进“镰刀弯”地区玉米结构调整是在保障谷物基本自给的前提下，促进玉米生产持续稳定发展的有效途径。

**3日**，《中共中央关于制定国民经济和社会发展第十三个五年规划的建议》发布，首次建议在部分地区实施耕地轮作休耕制度，以缓解水源严重透支及土地资源面临的压力。开展土地轮作休耕试点，使辛劳了数千年的土地得以休息，对于恢复地力、调节粮食供求平衡、确保粮食安全等具有十分重要的作用，同时也是“藏粮于地、藏粮于技”得以实施的前提和保证。

国务院办公厅印发《粮食安全省长责任制考核办法》（以下简称《考核办法》）。考核的主要内容包括：确保粮食可持续生产能力不断增强，保护种粮积极性，落实地方粮食储备，保障粮食市场供应和价格基本稳定，加强耕地污染防治，落实农业、粮食等相关行政主管部门的职责任务等六个方面。《考核办法》不但明确了各项责任，还加强了对省长监督考核的力度。对因不履行职责、存在重大工作失误等造成严重影响的，依法依纪追究相关责任人的责任。

**9日**，国务院办公厅印发《关于促进农村电子商务加快发展的指导意见》（以下简称《意见》），全面部署指导农村电子商务健康快速发展。《意见》指出，农村电子商务是转变农业发展方式的重要手段，是精准扶贫的重要载体。通过大众创业、万众创新，发挥市场机制作用，加快农村电子商务发展，把实体店与电商有机结合，使实体经济与互联网产生叠加效应，对于促消费、扩内需，推动农业升级、农村发展、农民增收具有重要意义。《意见》强调，按照全面建成小康社会目标和新型工业化、信息化、城镇化、农业现代化同步发展的要求，深化农村流通体制改革，创新农村商业模式，培育和壮大农村电子商务市场主体，加强基础设施建设，完善政策环境。到2020年，初步建成统一开放、竞争有序、诚信守法、安全可靠、绿色环保的农村电子商务市场体系。

**10日**，第十三届中国国际农产品交易会在福建福州市落下帷幕。本届农交会现场贸易额达到490亿元，现场零售额达到3.53亿元，均超上届水平。

**11日**，国务院总理李克强主持召开国务院常务会议，确定稳定粮食生产、增加种粮收入的措施，保障粮食安全和农民利益；部署以消费升级促进产业升级，培育形成新供给、新动力，扩大内需。会议指出，我国粮食连年增产，今年再获丰收，有力支撑了经济社会发展和民生改善，但也存在库存大幅增加、价格下降等问题。当前正值秋收冬种，要多措并举，切实保护农民利益和种粮积极性。

**18日**，“2015中国中部（湖南）农业博览会”在长沙隆重开幕，本届大会参展的国家级、省级龙头企业达300多家，国内有30多个省市参会参展。西班牙、越南、俄罗斯等国以及中国宝岛台湾也带来了各自颇具特色的地方产品。

由中国粮食行业协会、广东省粮食行业协会、东莞市人民政府共同主办的“把握新常态 适应新发展”全国粮食行业改革创新座谈会在广东省东莞召开。全国政协委员、中国粮食行业协会会长聂振邦同志作了重要讲话，国务院发展研究中心农村经济部叶兴庆部长作了题为“十三五时期农产品托市改革总体思路”的主旨演讲。国家粮食局信息中心王晓辉副主任、中国粮食行业协会专家委员会委员刘笑然、深圳粮食集团董事长祝俊明、暨南大学管理学院教授陈海权等分别就“粮食托市改革的现状与未来趋势”、“东北粮食形势分析”、“新常态下深化粮食企业改革的方向”、“互联网 + 食品粮食” 等进行多角度专题发言。

**23 日**，中粮试水“互联网 +”，粮达网上线启动。这是由中粮集团和招商局集团注资 3 亿元携手打造的粮食电子交易平台。借助粮达网金融服务进行玉米采购，流动资金周转次数可从传统的 3 ~ 4 次/年加速到 8 ~ 10 次/年。目前，粮达网已经上线的原粮有玉米、小麦、稻谷、大豆、棕榈油、大麦、高粱等。

## 12 月

**2 日**，山西省粮食局、中国粮食行业协会和中华粮网在太原共同主办“2015 山西粮食（玉米、小杂粮）产销衔接会”。会议以“互利、共赢、合作、发展”为主题，旨在实现山西与兄弟省份交流合作、优势互补、互利共赢的目标。本次会议主要取得四方面成果：合作发展，创新和深化了山西与兄弟省（区、市）的产销衔接机制；展示形象，促进山西省优势粮食资源产业化、品牌化发展；互利共赢，粮食产销衔接签约成果丰硕；研判形势，达成了抢抓战略机遇、落实粮食安全责任的重要共识。

**3 日**，中粮集团总裁于旭波与泰国商业部外贸厅厅长在曼谷签署了 100 万吨泰国大米进口合同。大米是泰国重要的农产品和贸易产品，在泰国经济和中泰双边经贸合作中的地位举足轻重。适量增加进口泰国大米，用于调剂中国大米的品种结构，可以满足消费者的差异化需求。通过承担进口泰国大米的任务，中粮集团有力推动和配合了中泰“高铁换大米”项目和我国政府“一带一路”倡议的落实，促进了中泰双边经贸关系的深化和发展。

**7 日**，中国首个转基因玉米种子产品将进入世界顶尖农业科技公司的本土主场美国。北京奥瑞金种业股份有限公司宣布将试水美国市场。美国市场一直以来被转基因巨头孟山都等企业把持，这是中国企业进入这一高技术产业的又一突破。

**8 日**，国家统计局发布的数据显示，2015 年，全国粮食总产量 62 143.5 万吨（12 428.7 亿斤），比 2014 年增加 1 440.8 万吨（288.2 亿斤），增长 2.4%，迎来了粮食的“十二连增”。在国内经济下行压力较大、国际粮价可能反弹等背景下，今年我国粮食再获丰收，对经济社会的平稳运行意义重大。

农业部部长韩长赋主持召开部常务会，传达学习中央扶贫开发工作会议精神，研究农业部贯彻落实意见，原则通过《农业部关于推进农业农村大数据发展的实施意见》。韩长赋指出，各级农业部门要认真学习贯彻习近平总书记、李克强总理重要讲话和《中共中央 国务院关于打赢脱贫攻坚战的决定》精神，从战略和全局的高度，充分认识脱贫攻坚对全面建成小康社会、巩固党的执政基础的重大意义，进一步增强做好扶贫开发工作的责任感、使命感和紧迫感。

**13日**，郑州经济技术开发区与大连良运集团签署《郑州进境粮食指定口岸合作框架协议》，携手共建郑州进境粮食指定口岸。为做实粮食口岸项目，提前完成通道测试，大连良运集团与河南保税物流中心平台公司按照“小批量、多品种、多方向、多方式”原则，开展进境粮食口岸业务测试。

**23日**，中粮集团与来宝集团达成一致协议，中粮集团旗下的中粮国际有限公司以7.5亿美元收购来宝集团所持有的中粮来宝农业49%的股权。交易完成后，中粮国际将持有中粮来宝农业100%的股权，同时，中粮来宝农业将更名为“中粮农业”。

大连商品交易所发布通知，对《大连商品交易所指定交割仓库管理办法》和《大连商品交易所交割细则》进行修改，允许玉米期货的指定交割仓库设立延伸库区。首批试点的指定交割仓库为营口港，其延伸库区拟选择分别位于辽宁省铁岭市和吉林省德惠市的辽宁益海嘉里地尔乐斯淀粉科技有限公司和德惠金信粮油收储有限公司。

**24—25日**，中央农村工作会议在北京召开。会议指出，“十三五”是全面建成农村小康社会的决胜期、巩固农业农村好形势的关键期、农业发展方式的转型期、提升农业竞争力的爬坡期、全面深化农村改革的攻坚期、推进城乡一体化的深化期。我国已经进入传统农业向现代农业加快转变的关键时期。“十三五”农业农村经济工作要牢固树立五大发展理念：围绕“一个目标”，就是农业现代化取得明显进展；坚持“一条主线”，就是加快转变农业发展方式；突出“一个中心”，就是促进农民持续较快增收；努力实现“六个全面提升”，即全面提升粮食等重要农产品供给保障水平、多种形式适度规模经营的引领水平、农业技术装备水平、农业生产经营效益水平、农产品质量安全水平、农业可持续发展水平。会议要求，必须以改革创新精神加强农业系统自身建设。要转变发展理念，树立“创新强农”、“协调惠农”、“绿色兴农”、“开放助农”和“共享富农”理念。要转变工作职能，继续简政放权，规范制约用权，加强政策创设、体系建设和法治建设。要转变工作方式，优化决策方式、管理方式和投入方式。要转变工作作风，大兴敢于担当、狠抓落实和清正廉洁之风。

**26日**，农业部副部长陈晓华在“2015—2016中国经济年会”上表示，要实现农业现代化的目标，“十三五”时期需加快转变农业发展方式，做到“六个全面提升”：一是要全面提升粮食等重要农产品的供给水平，“不必再追求连年数量的增长”，而要把重点放在巩固和提升产能上，实施“藏粮于地”和“藏粮于技”的战略；二是全面提升农业技术装备水平，首先抓科技创新，抓物质技术装备、农机装备的水平提升；三是全面提升多种形式适度规模经营的引领水平，核心是提高农业的集约化程度和组织化程度；四是要全面提升农产品质量安全水平；五是要全面提升农业的经营效益水平；六是要全面提升农业的可持续发展水平。

全国种植业结构调整工作会议召开，我国5年内拟调减玉米种植面积5 000万亩。农业部副部长余欣荣介绍，重点是调减东北冷凉区、北方农牧交错区、西北风沙干旱区及西南石漠化区等“镰刀弯”地区的玉米种植面积。到2020年，调减5 000万亩，其中2016年力争调减1 000万亩。调减出的耕地将根据市场需求和农牧发展需要，因地制宜地发展青贮玉米、饲草、杂粮杂豆等作物。余欣荣还介绍，“2016年我国将启动实施耕地轮作休耕制度试点。要鼓励轮作，谨慎休耕。休耕要限定在地下水漏斗区、重金属污染区和生态严重退化地区开展试点，休耕不能减少耕地、不能搞‘非农化’、不能削弱生产能力，禁止弃耕、严禁废耕，确保国家急用时产得出、供得上。”

**28日**，由九三集团承办的油脂行业最具权威性和专业性的“全国大豆系列标准制修订暨大豆产业发展研讨会”在哈尔滨举行，150余位来自全国油脂行业的顶级专家、大豆行业系列标准起草人、科研院所专家、大专院校教授及企业代表齐聚大豆之乡黑龙江，共同研究制修订“十三五”期间的13项大豆系列国家标准。

农业部优质农产品开发服务中心正式发布《2015 年度全国名特优新农产品目录》，包括粮油、蔬菜、果品、茶叶及其他 5 大类 741 个产品和 1 000 家生产单位。该目录产品来源广泛，产品类别齐全，优势区域特色显著，知名品牌众多，90%通过了无公害农产品、绿色食品、有机食品或良好农业规范（GAP）认证，有健全和有效的运行质量管理体系和质量追溯制度，还有一定数量的产品通过了地理标志注册、登记、保护。

# 三、2015年中国粮食经济重要论著索引

## （一）2015年中国粮食经济重要论文索引

### 1月

1. 陈凡、蒋传谊、呙俊超：《新常态下粮食经济发展的压力与机遇》，《中国粮食经济》。

2. 尚强民：《粮食流通流域的五大挑战》，《中国粮食经济》。

3. 卢彦超：《充分发挥河南省粮食主产区的作用》，《中国粮食经济》。

4. 聂英：《中国粮食安全的耕地贡献分析》，《经济学家》。

5. 付争艳、王瑞彬、唐华仓：《基于转基因视角下的粮食安全文献综述》，《农业经济》。

6. 曾福生：《建立农地流转保障粮食安全的激励与约束机制》，《农业经济问题》。

7. 丁声俊：《以价值法则引领农业粮食新常态》，《价格理论与实践》。

8. 张红宇、张海阳、李伟毅、李冠佑：《中国特色农业现代化：目标定位与改革创新》，《中国农村经济》。

9. 王梅：《经济新常态下的国内玉米市场》，《中国粮食经济》。

10. 陈晓华：《正确认识和把握国家粮食安全新战略——在中国农业经济学会年会上的致辞》，《农业经济问题》。

11. 陶泽良、陈卫洪：《粮食生产安全视域下的耕地资源保护与利用发展对策》，《世界农业》。

12. 石秀华：《从大豆风波看中国的食用植物油产业安全》，《理论月

刊》。

13. 王铮、吴凤羽：《中国粮食进口量逼近红线原因分析及定量测算》，《农业经济》。

14. 冯璐、武功文、张焱、吴春梅：《粮食作物生产结构与农户粮食消费的演变》，《华南农业大学学报（社会科学版）》。

15. 沈家山：《适应新常态 构建新优势 以粮食收储现代化服务民生新改善》，《中国粮食经济》。

16. 顾莉丽：《中国粮食主产区经济发展水平的区域差异评价》，《中国农机化学报》。

17. 马木炎：《发挥市场决定性作用 推进粮食价格支持政策改革》，《中国粮食经济》。

18. 张秀青：《临储价格刚性上浮结束 玉米产业回归市场可期》，《中国粮食经济》。

19. 郑红明：《粮食市场十年牛市行情或将终结》，《中国粮食经济》。

20. 张雄化：《水资源利用效率与虚拟水国际贸易关系分析——基于粮食安全的视角》，《云南社会科学》。

21. 郭亮：《世界粮食安全现状及粮食供求展望》，《世界农业》。

## 2月

1. 王洋、余志刚：《中国粮食市场的供需结构、趋势及政策需求分析——基于 ARIMA - GRNN 模型的预测》，《中国农学通报》。

2. 张书冬：《抓住时代机遇引领粮食发展》，《粮食问题研究》。

3. 黄守坤：《国内外农产品价格传导路径》，《技术经济》。

4. 金梅、刘洋、张华昌、陶诚：《粮食安全与粮食储备制度的发展演变》，《粮油仓储科技通讯》。

5. 孙宏岭、韩国山：《我国粮食安全的主要指标与保障途径研究》，《粮食科技与经济》。

6. 朱远洋：《我国经济发展新常态下的粮食信贷问题》，《农业发展与金融》。

7. 姚成胜、滕毅、黄琳：《中国粮食安全评价指标体系构建及实证分析》，《农业工程学报》。

8. 武舜臣、王静、树成军、殷冉：《中国粮食生产区位差异与产需格局变动分析——基于1978—2012年粮食生产的泰尔指数分解》，《湖南农业大学学报（社会科学版）》。

9. 化贯军：《农村人口转移对我国粮食安全的影响及对策》，《江苏经贸职业技术学院学报》。

10. 胡冰川、肖卫东：《方式转变、永续发展与国家粮食安全——中国国外农业经济研究会学术研讨会综述》，《改革》。

11. 王佳宁、李国祥、秦中春、蒋和平、周应恒、程国强：《中央"1号文件"背景的国家粮食安全改革传媒发行人、编辑总监王佳宁深度对话五位农经学者》，《改革》。

12. 符亮：《人民币汇率变动对我国粮食出口影响的实证研究》，《现代经济信息》。

13. 高鸣、宋洪远：《生产率视角下的中国粮食经济增长要素分析》，《中国人口科学》。

14. 刘成玉、周国辉：《强化流通安全 挖掘粮食安全保障潜力》，《粮食问题研究》。

15. 郭钦：《扎实推进放心粮油工程 保障群众舌尖上的安全》，《粮食问题研究》。

16. 张兴、张炜：《节粮型畜牧业发展一定有益于粮食安全吗？——基于省域面板数据的实证分析》，《生态经济》。

17. 宋扬：《我国粮食经济及其政策研究》，《商场现代化》。

18. 高峰：《守住我国粮食安全的底线》，《学习月刊》。

19. 方言：《认真落实粮食政策 确保国家粮食安全》，《宏观经济管理》。

20. 黎明：《中国粮食安全政策改革：由中央下放粮食产区自主经营权》，《农学学报》。

21. 辛毅、李宁、温铁军：《我国应对国际粮食市场"金融化"的对策研究》，《价格理论与实践》。

22. 詹琳、蒋和平：《粮食目标价格制度改革的困局与突破》，《农业经济问题》。

23. 袁玲、吴晗、李虹：《依靠科技创新保障粮食安全》，《农业与技术》。

**3 月**

1. 常蕊：《抓好农业生产 确保粮食安全》，《农业机械》。

2. 谢俊：《加强粮食企业文化建设 努力创建星级粮库》，《中国粮食经济》。

3. 宋洪远：《新形势下更需关注粮食安全问题》，《农业工作通讯》。

4. 杜志雄、王永春、张梅林：《我国粮食生产困境及解决思路》，《中国党政干部论坛》。

5. 毛学峰、刘靖、朱信凯：《中国粮食结构与粮食安全：基于粮食流通贸易的视角》，《管理世界》。

6. 赵学彬、王炳旭：《论粮食安全中的政府行为》，《河南师范大学学报（哲学社会科学版）》。

7. 彭道宾：《中部地区的粮殇与出路——谈中部地区保障粮食安全的代价与补偿机制》，《中国统计》。

8. 滕红、吕怒江、谌思：《新常态下重庆粮食供需及安全评价分析》，《中国统计》。

9. 翁鸣：《美国推行 TPP 的战略目的和主要特征——基于农产品贸易的视角》，《国际经济合作》。

10. 黄禹：《旱涝灾害对我国粮食生产影响分析》，《中国农业信息》。

11. 刘春阳、霍灵光：《吉林省吉林市粮食安全预警研究》，《农业展望》。

12. 杨惠、王凤兰：《基于耕地压力指数的粮食安全研究——以云南省为例》，《云南农业科技》。

13. 任正晓：《深刻认识新常态 准确把握新形势 扎实做好粮食流通工作》，《中国经贸导刊》。

14. 辛毅、刘力华、李宁：《原粮收购价格与成品粮销售价格关系的实证研究——基于城市居民应对粮价上涨承受力的视角》，《价格理论与实践》。

15. 苗作华、黄志平、陈勇、曾向阳：《基于粮食安全策略的耕地需求量预测》，《江苏农业科学》。

16. 胡文海:《中部地区粮食生产比较优势分析与基地建设》,《地理科学》。

17. 苏远新、刘文中、眭达明:《保障国家粮食安全是一个永恒课题——江西省粮食主销区赣州市保障粮食安全调查》,《中国粮食经济》。

18. 张利国、陈苏:《中国人均粮食占有量时空演变及驱动因素》,《经济地理》。

## 4 月

1. 李可:《用作为诠释担当 以担当开创未来——〈国务院关于建立健全粮食安全省长责任制的若干意见〉出台的前前后后》,《中国粮食经济》。

2. 刘松:《确保粮食安全责任在流通领域落到实处》,《中国粮食经济》。

3. 谢佩军:《粮食安全影响因素分析》,《安徽农业科学》。

4. 李立清、江维国:《农民专业合作社"失真"问题研究:基于粮食安全视角》,《中州学刊》。

5. 贾彬良、宋长水、王紫艳、侯立功:《浅谈转变生产方式,促进粮食安全》,《山西农经》。

6. 卢彦超:《我国口粮安全战略分析与对策》,《河南工业大学学报(社会科学版)》。

7. 苏敏智:《基于人口发展的粮食安全与耕地保障机制探析》,《农业经济》。

8. 徐晓冬:《鄂尔多斯市粮食局:服务"三农三牧"保障粮食安全》,《中国粮食经济》。

9. 李晓俐:《确立新的粮食安全观》,《黑龙江粮食》。

10. 马林静、王雅鹏、吴娟:《中国粮食生产技术效率的空间非均衡与收敛性分析》,《农业技术经济》。

11. 王孟伦:《粮食存"银行"安全又增值——对河北省圣康"粮食银行"的调查与思考》,《中国粮食经济》。

12. 李方旺:《充分利用国际市场资源增强粮食安全》,《黑龙江粮食》。

13. 黄超：《加强粮食市场监管 规范粮食流通秩序——广东廉江粮食部门粮食行政执法工作纪实》，《中国粮食经济》。

14. 丁声俊：《守土有责 任重如山——让粮食安全省长责任制落地生根》，《中国粮食经济》。

15. 吴昊、李育冬：《基于状态空间模型的气候变化与中国粮食安全动态关系研究》，《中国农业资源与区划》。

16. 李旭：《浅析粮食安全生产的时代重要性》，《南方农业》。

17. 蔡保忠、曾福生：《粮食生产对经济发展的影响及利益补偿途径分析——基于我国13个粮食主产区2002—2012年数据的实证研究》，《粮食科技与经济》。

18. 李亮科、马骥：《粮食规模化经营中的土地细碎及其对规模经济的制约分析——基于我国7个小麦主产省的农户调研数据》，《科技与经济》。

## 5月

1. 邹美因、胡岳岷：《农民问题：中国粮食安全的根本问题》，《西部论坛》。

2. 廖春林：《粮食经济发展已进入新常态》，《中国粮食经济》。

3. 聂雷、郭忠兴、汪险生、何如海：《我国主要粮食作物生产重心演变分析》，《农业现代化研究》。

4. 杨建利、靳文学：《粮食主产区利益补偿机制研究》，《农村经济》。

5. 张静伟：《中国粮食进口风险影响因素研究》，《价格月刊》。

6. 李光泗、马学琳：《粮食市场开放对我国粮食生产影响的实证研究——基于大豆和大米数据的VaR模型分析》，《南京财经大学学报》。

7. 李首涵、何秀荣、杨树果：《中国粮食生产比较效益低吗?》，《中国农村经济》。

8. 邓磊：《城镇化、粮食价格传导体系重构与粮食安全管理关系研究》，《价格理论与实践》。

9. 夏益国、宫春生：《粮食安全视阈下农业适度规模经营与新型职业农民——耦合机制、国际经验与启示》，《农业经济问题》。

10. 张雨薇：《关于我国粮食进口国际定价权的思考》，《价格月刊》。

11. 刘超、朱满德：《我国粮食价格支持政策：实施效果与当前挑战》，《价格月刊》。

12. 钟真、孔祥智：《经济新常态下的中国农业政策转型》，《教学与研究》。

13. 聂雷、郭忠兴、汪险生、何如海：《我国主要粮食作物生产重心演变分析》，《农业现代化研究》。

14. 李轩：《重构中国粮食安全的认知维度、监测指标及治理体系》，《国际安全研究》。

15. 马浩峰：《我国城市化进程对粮食产量影响的综合分析》，《商》。

16. 刘晓峰、孟军：《粮食主产区生猪产业发展与粮食安全竞协机理研究——基于黑龙江省实证分析》，《中国农学通报》。

17. 吴建寨、徐克、王盛威、张建华：《新形势下保障中国粮食安全的思考》，《农业展望》。

18. 晏莹、龙方：《美日韩粮食安全保障资源国际配置的经验》，《世界农业》。

19. 卫荣、宋莉莉、王秀东：《法国粮食安全政策对中国的启示》，《世界农业》。

20. 张颖、徐阳华：《中国国家粮食安全战略演进及前瞻》，《国际安全研究》。

## 6月

1. 丁声俊：《决不可放松粮食安全这根“弦”》，《中国粮食经济》。

2. 尚强民：《从社会经济发展角度认识粮食问题》，《中国粮食经济》。

3. 于桐、宋继华：《基于城镇化战略视角下土地流转与粮食安全问题研究》，《科技创新导报》。

4. 王彦：《保障我国粮食安全的目标体系及其治理机制》，《求实》。

5. 蔡文香、卢万合、冯婧、吴妍、杨学坤：《中国粮食安全脆弱性评价与政策建议》，《中国人口·资源与环境》。

6. 蔡晓黎：《河南省城镇化发展对粮食安全的影响研究》，《河南农业》。

7. 王雅鹏、马林静：《农村劳动力转移对粮食安全的影响》，《中国党政干部论坛》。

8. 刘松：《粮食部门要争做粮食安全的拓荒牛》，《中国粮食经济》。

9. 李维刚、徐晓婧：《城镇化进程中土地流转与粮食安全问题研究》，《中国管理信息化》。

10. 王大为、郑风田：《新形势下中国粮食安全的现状、挑战与对策——第五届中国经济安全论坛综述》，《河南工业大学学报（社会科学版）》。

11. 丁华、杨耀旭：《河南省粮食产量影响因素的实证分析——基于多元线性回归计量经济模型》，《粮食科技与经济》。

12. 张维理、徐爱国、张认连、冀宏杰：《中国耕地保育技术创新不足已危及粮食安全与环境安全》，《中国农业科技》。

13. 裴东鑫、张冬平：《土地流转背景下促进河南粮食稳产的思考》，《宏观经济管理》。

14. 马述忠、叶宏亮、任婉婉：《基于国内外耕地资源有效供给的中国粮食安全问题研究》，《农业经济问题》。

15. 王锐、刘春雨：《开放框架下中国粮食价格波动的影响因素分析》，《河南农业大学学报》。

16. 陈波、陈翔：《拷问粮食安全》，《浙江人大》。

17. 王沛栋：《新常态下河南粮食生产保障国家粮食安全的路径探析》，《河南工业大学学报（社会科学版）》。

18. 王国庆、金君良、鲍振鑫、刘翠善、严小林：《气候变化对华北粮食主产区水资源的影响及适应对策》，《中国生态农业学报》。

19. 周兴明：《维修改造“危仓老库”夯实粮食安全基础——江苏省扬州市粮食“危仓老库”维修改造工作纪实》，《中国粮食经济》。

## 7月

1. 王向辉：《新阶段中国粮食安全问题探讨——“中国粮食安全专题研讨会”综述》，《中国农村经济》。

2. 陈刚：《修复“危仓老库”保障粮食安全》，《中国粮食经济》。

3. 杨万江：《中国粮食安全：进步、转型与政策方向》，《湖州师范学院学报》。

4. 谢春凌：《新型城镇化背景下我国粮食安全战略探讨》，《农村经济》。

5. 陈宇峰、田珊：《定价主导权争夺下的中国粮食安全》，《经济研究参考》。

6. 王端好、彭华：《快速城镇化背景下的泛粮食安全研究》，《轻工科技》。

7. 苏珊珊：《世界粮食贸易视角下的中国粮食安全问题研究》，《区域经济评论》。

8. 尚强民：《粮食市场变化辨析》，《中国粮食经济》。

9. 王立祥：《近65年我国粮食生产能力提升及发展预期》，《西北农林科技大学学报（社会科学版）》。

10. 王倩、余劲：《农地流转对粮食生产投入产出的冲击效应》，《西北农林科技大学学报（社会科学版）》。

11. 李晓俐：《中国粮食安全的多重制约因素》，《黑龙江粮食》。

12. 廖富洲、廖婧怡、杨程：《耕地流转中的“非粮化”问题及对策研究》，《学习论坛》。

13. 蔡瑞林、陈万明、朱雪春：《成本收益：耕地流转非粮化的内因与破解关键》，《农村经济》。

14. 周桂林：《山区粮食产、销、存的现状与发展对策——对湖北省秭归县2015年度农户存粮情况的调查》，《中国粮食经济》。

15. 向涛、綦勇：《粮食安全与农业面源污染——以农地禀赋对化肥投入强度的影响为例的实证研究》，《财经研究》。

16. 赵丽平、王雅鹏、何可：《城镇化、农村人力资本与粮食生产技术效率——基于环境规制视角的面板数据分析》，《农业现代化研究》。

## 8月

1. 李文锋：《新常态下对陕西省粮食安全的再认识》，《中国粮食经济》。

2. 许高峰：《新常态下实现“粮食银行”的科学发展》，《中国粮食经济》。

3. 王瑞元：《我国粮食生产、加工简况及发展趋势》，《粮食加工》。

4. 陈光军：《我国民族地区粮食安全问题及对策研究》，《改革与战略》。

5. 蒋和平、丁声俊、蒋黎：《论开创中国特色粮食安全道路》，《价格理论与实践》。

6. 孙林、庞冠琪、王健：《国际粮食价格对粮食主产国实施出口限制的影响——损失规避视角》，《中国农村经济》。

7. 杨中柱：《新常态下转型创新助力我国粮食产业发展》，《上海商学院学报》。

8. 曹军军、李建龙、陈奕兆、谢天宁、孙政国：《快速城镇化模式下苏南中小城市粮食安全绿色健康综合评价体系构建研究》，《天津农业科学》。

9. 王为萍、赵姚阳：《流转农地“非粮化”利用研究》，《陕西农业科学》。

10. 刘颖、江松颖：《粮食价格形成、波动与价格支持政策的国内外研究进展》，《财经理论研究》。

11. 冯磊：《撒哈拉以南非洲地区粮食安全问题研究——基于经济发展的视角》，《商》。

12. 吴小芳：《新形势下主产区粮食安全的思考》，《中国粮食经济》。

13. 李光泗、曹宝明、马学琳：《中国粮食市场开放与国际粮食价格波动——基于粮食价格波动溢出效应的分析》，《中国农村经济》。

14. 王晶、杨宏恩、张志明、田晓燕：《工业化与粮食产量的关系研究：兼论粮食核心区推进工业化的依据》，《管理评论》。

15. 徐振伟、王旭隆：《俄罗斯农业生产与粮食安全评析》，《欧亚经济》。

## 9月

1. 孙晓明：《搭建粮食质量安全监管载体 确保问题粮食可追溯可召回》，《中国粮食经济》。

2. 李援亚：《“粮食银行”的风险规避与制度优化》，《农业经济》。

3. 丁声俊：《应对粮食高成本新常态》，《黑龙江粮食》。

4. 李桂军：《多措并举 确保粮食质量安全》，《中国粮食经济》。

5. 张宗毅、杜志雄：《土地流转一定会导致“非粮化”吗？——基于全国1740个种植业家庭农场监测数据的实证分析》，《经济学动态》。

6. 杨中柱：《新常态下创新我国粮食安全保障机制》，《江西科技学院学报》。

7. 池芳春：《普通粮农的粮食安全保障试析》，《山西农业科学》。

8. 刘俊：《贯彻粮食安全省长责任制要注重“三个优化”》，《中国粮食经济》。

9. 杨中柱：《新常态下我国粮食安全问题研究》，《农业科学研究》。

10. 齐皓天、程国强：《构建“五位一体”的社会治理体系 保障粮食质量安全》，《中国粮食经济》。

11. 魏晓卓、金丽馥、吴君民：《为什么应将“农民增收”同“粮食安全”一样也上升为国家战略？——“粮食财政直接补贴”战略目标的视角》，《中国软科学》。

12. 雍自生：《浅议粮食收购资格核查与行政许可年审（检）的关系》，《中国粮食经济》。

13. 刘松：《粮食质量安全重在让条块监管责任有机融合》，《中国粮食经济》。

## 10 月

1. 王学辉：《顺应经济发展形势发展粮食规模化经营》，《现代农业》。

2. 陈锋正、刘新平、刘向晖：《经济发展新常态下城镇化与粮食生产问题分析》，《农业经济》。

3. 郭晓东、蔡荣：《中国粮食安全态势的转变与应对》，《粮食科技与经济》。

4. 武舜臣、王静、顾智鹏：《粮食安全预警指标体系研究述评》，《农业经济》。

5. 程名望、刘雅娟、黄甜甜：《我国粮食主产区农村劳动力外流对粮食供给安全的影响》，《商业研究》。

6. 杨中柱:《新常态下国家粮食安全问题研究》,《黑龙江粮食》。

7. 朱智敏:《中国粮食价格波动特征研究——基于 ARCH 类模型》,《中国物价》。

8. 靳亚亚、赵凯、肖桂春:《陕西省耕地保护经济补偿分区研究:基于粮食安全与生态安全双重视角》,《中国土地科学》。

9. 余文远:《农业劳动力外流与粮食安全问题的研究——以四川省农村为例》,《四川职业技术学院学报》。

10. 汤丹:《基于粮食安全的我国粮食价格波动成因分解研究》,《统计与决策》。

11. 陈晨:《粮食安全概念的演变及重要意义》,《学理论》。

12. 蔡棕宇:《经济新常态下的粮食储备安全性与协调性探讨》,《品牌》。

13. 赵杨:《中国粮食稳产增产的路径选择》,《学习与探索》。

14. 贾龙:《明确中国经济新常态特征 整体提升粮食加工行业水平》,《吉林农业》。

15. 李保全、苏磊、路燕、李茜茜、田云峰:《新常态下增强河南省粮食生产能力的对策》,《农业科技管理》。

16. 任正晓:《解决好吃饭问题始终是治国理政的头等大事——深入学习贯彻习近平总书记关于粮食安全的重要论述》,《中国粮食经济》。

## 11 月

1. 谢智勇、孙瑞:《学习国家粮食安全新战略的思考》,《中国粮食经济》。

2. 沈贵银:《怎么看待中国的粮食安全问题》,《中国粮食经济》。

3. 朱信凯、夏薇:《论新常态下的粮食安全:中国粮食真的过剩了吗?》,《华中农业大学学报(社会科学版)》。

4. 王雅鹏:《国际粮价异动、金融化与中国粮食保障战略——评〈国际粮价波动下中国粮食安全实证研究〉一书》,《经济管理》。

5. 罗海平、宋炎:《基于偏离份额法的我国粮食主产区农业产值结构与增长效益研究:1980—2012 年》,《经济经纬》。

6. 岳国君:《燃料乙醇:消纳"问题粮食"保障粮食安全》,《中国战略新兴产业》。

7. 阮晓东：《智慧粮仓确保粮食仓储安全》，《新经济导刊》。

8. 孙国军：《基于耕地压力指数的敦煌市粮食安全状况研究》，《西北师范大学学报（自然科学版）》。

9. 黄光荣、陈宗杰、雷斌、眭达明：《江西省宜春市保障粮食安全的调查》，《中国粮食经济》。

10. 陈沫：《黑龙江省粮食主产区利益补偿机制研究》，《农场经济管理》。

11. 俞婷婷：《金融因素对江苏省粮食价格影响研究——基于 VEC 模型分析》，《沈阳师范大学学报（社会科学版）》。

12. 任晓芳、高齐圣：《基于双重预警的粮食生产安全预警研究》，《中国管理信息化》。

13. 尚强民：《新常态下调整中的粮食市场》，《中国粮食经济》。

14. 赵新浩：《粮食主产区农村土地流转调查与分析》，《学习论坛》。

15. 张如祖、周静：《新形势下构建浙江粮食安全保障体系对策研究》，《中国粮食经济》。

## 12 月

1. 姚蔚：《中国农业补贴的经济分析》，《中国经济报告》。

2. 蒋和平、朱福守：《我国粮食储备管理现状和政策建议》，《中国农业科技导报》。

3. 丁声俊：《复杂形势下务必坚守粮食战略定力——兼谈正确把握粮食“走出去”和“适度进口”方针》，《价格理论与实践》。

4. 陈会玲、罗伟、马彦：《印度粮食储备安全制度的绩效分析》，《世界农业》。

5. 田甜、李隆玲、武拉平：《新形势下中国粮食安全问题及与其他粮食主产国的比较——基于世界粮食安全指标（GFSI）分析》，《世界农业》。

6. 段禄峰：《中国粮食安全保障机制研究》，《世界农业》。

7. 王佳莹、郭天宝、闫雪：《中美财政支农政策的国际比较》，《世界农业》。

8. 姜群鸥、程雨薇、薛筱婵等:《基于联立方程组的东北区粮食生产力和耕地变化影响要素分析》,《农业工程学报》。

9. 王艺、刘民培:《海南粮食自给率影响因素研究》,《广东农业科学》。

10. 石秀华:《我国粮食安全和农业可持续发展的风险研究》,《武汉科技大学学报(社会科学版)》。

11. 矫江、项洪涛、王立志:《黑龙江省粮食单产大幅度提高的原因分析》,《中国农学通报》。

12. 周士跃:《基于国际贸易传导路径的国际粮价对中国粮价的影响探析》,《价格月刊》。

13. 苏航:《国内外粮食价差导致我国粮食进口激增的解决途径》,《价格月刊》。

14. 吕辛:《城镇化背景下农户储粮意愿及影响因素研究——基于江苏中部地区农村的调查》,《重庆交通大学学报(社会科学版)》。

15. 陈玉珠、周宏:《三大玉米主产区农户种植优势的比较分析——基于种植净收益因素贡献率视角》,《湖南农业大学学报(社会科学版)》。

16. 刘合光、王静怡、陈珏颖:《金砖国家建立FTA对五国农业的可能影响及中国对策》,《农业经济问题》。

17. 李明:《全球化视野中的中国粮食安全》,《新经济导刊》。

18. 郑红明:《保持定力 坚定不移贯彻落实国家粮食安全新战略》,《中国粮食经济》。

19. 于旭波:《粮食安全:要开放,更要自强》,《中国经济报告》。

20. 尚强民:《玉米价格的昨天、今天和明天》,《中国粮食经济》。

21. 王梅:《临储玉米价格首次下调释放出哪些讯号》,《中国粮食经济》。

22. 刘松:《确保粮食安全省长责任考核细则落地生根》,《中国粮食经济》。

23. 曹前程、汪淼:《江苏省粮食主销区秋粮收购形势及对策建议——以江苏省太仓市为例》,《中国粮食经济》。

24. 吴思:《粮食安全新战略——2015中国粮食与食品安全战略峰会综述》,《中国经济报告》。

25. 马玉荣、李大巍、王艺璇：《粮食安全的全球治理——访联合国粮农组织驻中国、朝鲜及蒙古国代表伯希·米西卡》，《中国经济报告》。

## （二）2015 年中国粮食经济重要著作索引

1. 闵九康：《土壤生物修复工程——粮食安全之保护伞》，中国农业科学技术出版社 2015 年 1 月版。

2. 傅雪柳、朱定真、唐健：《气候变化与粮食安全》，中国农业科学技术出版社 2015 年 1 月版。

3. 孔祥智、毛飞、伍振军：《土地流转与新型农业经营主体培育》，中国农业出版社 2015 年 1 月版。

4. 孙东升、李慧、梁仕莹：《汇率改革对中国农业政策的经济影响研究》，中国农业科学技术出版社 2015 年 1 月版。

5. 王薇薇：《中国粮食流通市场主体利益协调研究》，中国社会科学出版社 2015 年 1 月版。

6. 祁华清：《国际粮价波动下中国粮食安全实证研究》，经济日报出版社 2015 年 1 月版。

7. 李孟刚、郑新立：《国家粮食安全保障体系研究》，社会科学文献出版社 2015 年 1 月版。

8. 曹国庆：《农村土地流转的探索与实践》，江西人民出版社 2015 年 2 月版。

9. 蒋和平、张忠明、蒋黎等：《粮食主产区利益补偿机制研究》，经济科学出版社 2015 年 2 月版。

10. 张宁、杨正周、阳军：《上海合作组织农业合作与中国粮食安全》，社会科学文献出版社 2015 年 3 月版。

11. 杨建利：《完善我国粮食直补政策研究》，科学出版社 2015 年 3 月版。

12. 李禄胜：《中国“三农”问题研究——以宁夏为例》，经济科学出版社 2015 年 3 月版。

13. 吴海峰：《河南蓝皮书：河南农业农村发展报告（2015）——推

进现代农业大省建设》，社会科学文献出版社 2015 年 4 月版。

14. 汤惠民：《“三农”情缘》，中国农业科学技术出版社 2015 年 5 月版。

15. 杨团：《综合农协——中国“三农”改革突破口》，中国社会科学出版社 2015 年 5 月版。

16. 多瑞斯·科恩编，黄佳、邹涛译：《粮食金融——迈向农业和农村金融新范式》，中国金融出版社 2015 年 5 月版。

17. 李经谋：《中国粮食市场发展报告 2015》，中国财政经济出版社 2015 年 5 月版。

18. 王兆华：《山东省种植制度与粮食安全研究》，中国农业出版社 2015 年 5 月版。

19. 马述忠：《中国粮食安全与全球粮食定价权——基于全球产业链视角的分析》，浙江大学出版社 2015 年 5 月版。

20. 巴忠谈、糜振玉：《中国粮食安全（第十二届中国国家安全论坛文集)》，时事出版社 2015 年 6 月版。

21. 王瑞元：《现代粮食工业发展》，科学出版社 2015 年 6 月版。

22. 吕火明、李晓、吕新业：《粮食安全、科技创新与现代农业（中国农业技术经济学会 2014 年学术研讨会论文集)》，中国农业科学技术出版社 2015 年 6 月版。

23. 李利英：《粮食经济问题》，中国农业出版社 2015 年 6 月版。

24. 宋亚平：《“三农”中国》，第 24 辑，崇文书局 2015 年 7 月版。

25. 娄耀辉：《中国粮食安全与法律评述》，新华出版社 2015 年 8 月版。

26. 李国祥：《中国粮食安全评论》，第 1 卷，金城出版社 2015 年 8 月版。

27. 曾志华：《粮食安全监管制度研究》，中国社会科学出版社 2015 年 8 月版。

28. 韦本辉：《中国粉垄助力粮食和环境安全》，中国农业出版社 2015 年 9 月版。

29. 吕修涛：《粮食绿色增产增效技术模式》，中国农业出版社 2015 年 9 月版。

30. 王晓华：《粮食流通信息化与物联网》，化学工业出版社 2015 年 9

月版。

31. 祁慧博、陆文聪、李元龙：《全球化背景下中国粮食供求区域均衡与政策研究》，中国农业出版社 2015 年 9 月版。

32. 汪迪棣、郑可心、朱莉：《我国粮食价格波动分析》，四川大学出版社 2015 年 9 月版。

33. 李海东：《新时期中国“三农”问题的发展及对策研究》，哈尔滨工程大学出版社 2015 年 10 月版。

34. 肖春阳：《国有粮食企业改革和发展》，经济管理出版社 2015 年 10 月版。

35. 何明、高巍、潘迪：《互联网 + 智慧粮食：粮食流通信息化建设白皮书》，东南大学出版社 2015 年 10 月版。

36. 曹宝明、夏伯锦：《长三角粮食发展报告 2015——长三角地区的粮食安全》，经济管理出版社 2015 年 10 月版。

37. 黄英：《农村土地流转法律问题研究》，中国政法大学出版社 2015 年 10 月版。

38. 胡超：《中国—东盟农产品市场一体化研究》，北京理工大学出版社 2015 年 10 月版。

39. 黄彬红、周洁红：《农产品食品质量安全治理：以追溯体系建设为切入点》，浙江大学出版社 2015 年 11 月版。

40. 宋莉莉：《我国农民收入增长及区域差异比较研究：以苏、豫、川三省为例》，经济科学出版社 2015 年 11 月版。

41. 胡振华：《“三位一体”农协机制研究：基于新农村建设组织路径的农合体系创新》，北京大学出版社 2015 年 11 月版。

42. 叶兴庆：《农村经济调查与研究（第 1 部）》，中国发展出版社 2015 年 11 月版。

43. 威廉·恩道尔：《粮食危机》，（增订版），中国民主法制出版社 2015 年 12 月版。

44. 马洪伟、鲁小亚等：《转型与治理：河南现代农业与新型城镇化发展评价》，社会科学文献出版社 2015 年 12 月版。

45. 刘慧等：《农产品目标价格改革试点进展情况研究》，中国农业出版社 2015 年 12 月版。

# 四、小麦、稻米、玉米、大豆价格走势图

说明：黑色线为郑州粮食批发市场三等白小麦旬平均价（火车板交货价）；灰色曲线为郑州商品交易所普麦近交割月合约的旬平均价。

**图 6－4－1　1991—2015 年郑州粮食批发市场小麦价格历史走势图**

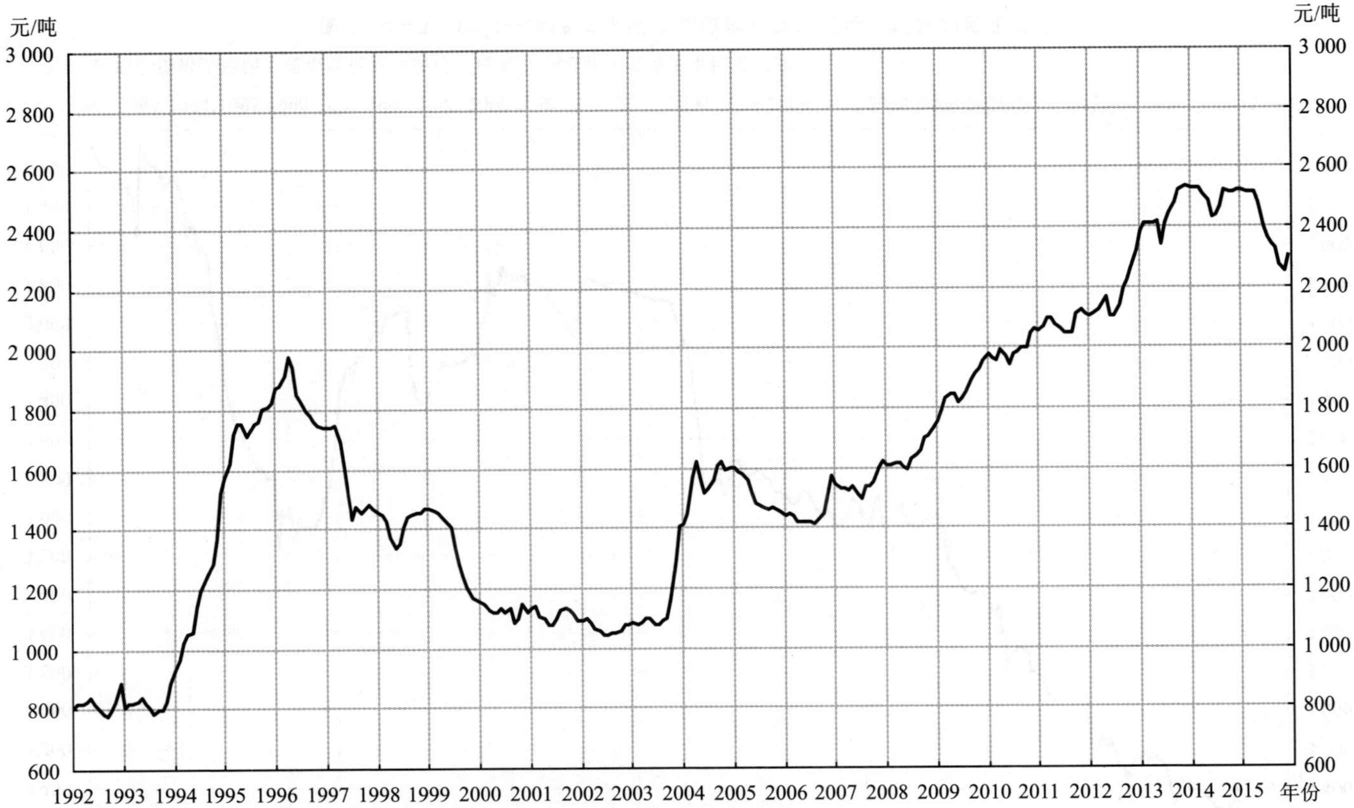


说明：价格为全国主要粮食批发市场三级硬冬白小麦月平均价（当地火车板交货价）。

**图 6－4－2　1992—2015 年全国主要粮食批发市场三级白麦均价走势图**

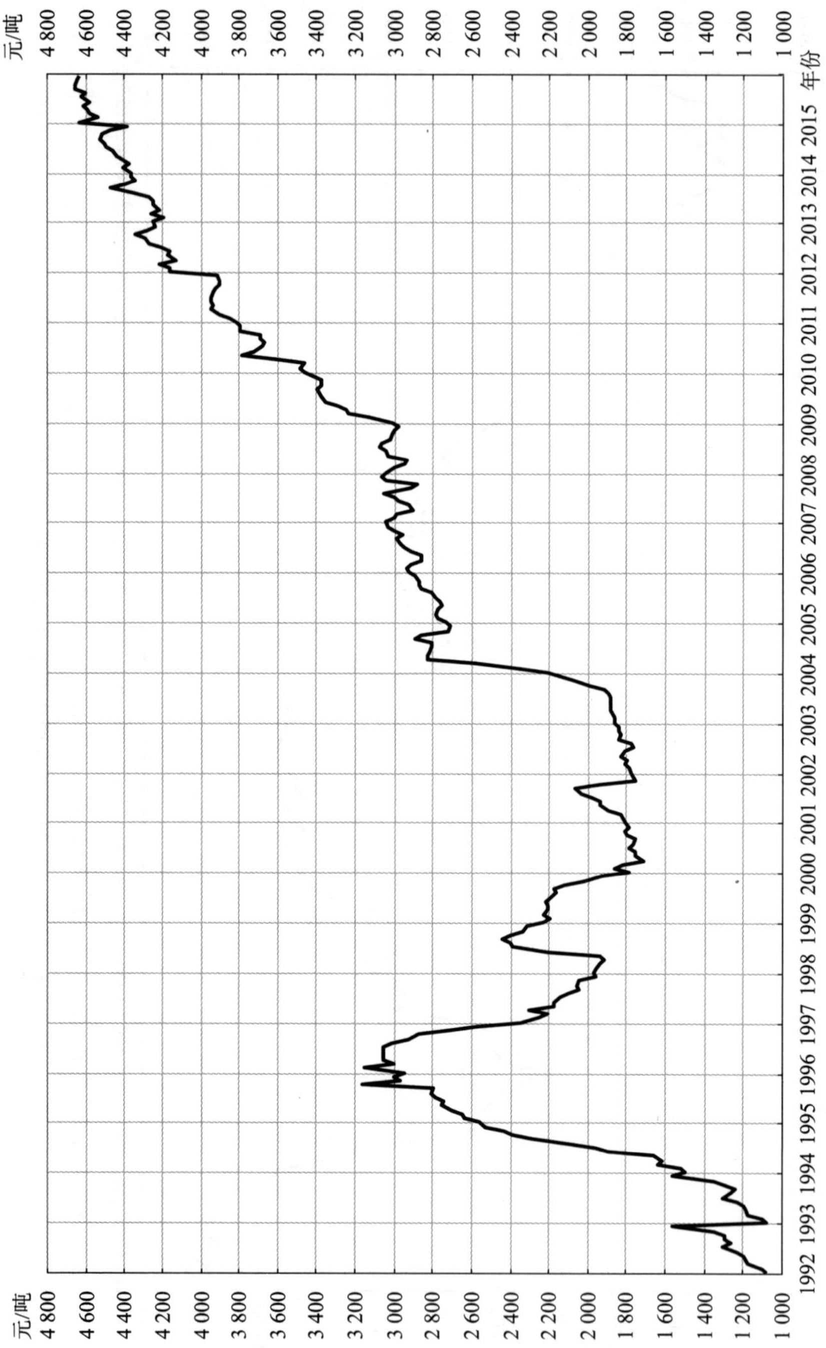


说明：价格为全国主要粮食批发市场标一粳米月平均价（当地火车板交货价）。

**图 6－4－3 1992—2015 年全国主要粮食批发市场标一粳米均价走势图**

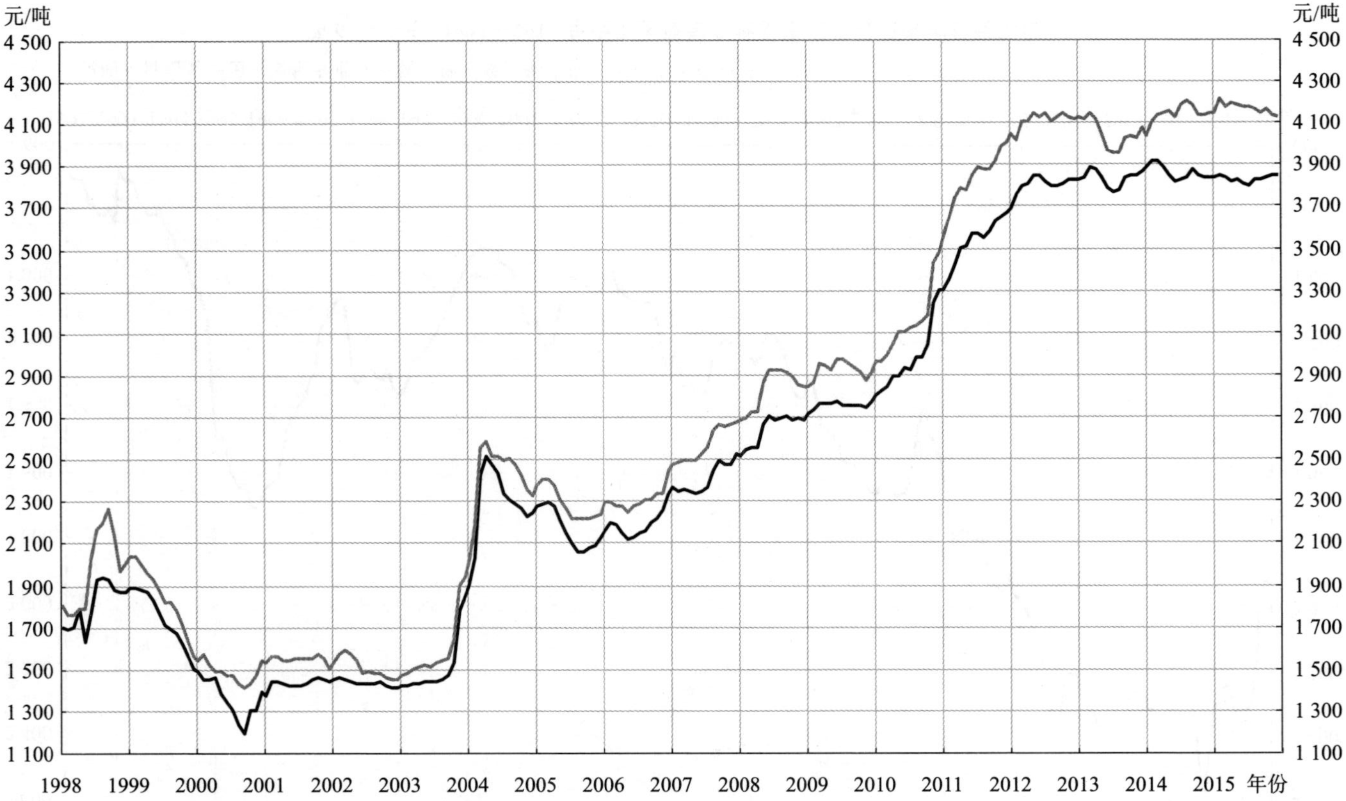


说明：价格为全国主要粮食批发市场标一早籼米（黑色曲线）、晚籼米（灰色曲线）月平均价（当地火车板交货价）。

**图 6－4－4　1998—2015 年全国主要粮食批发市场标一早籼、晚籼均价走势图**

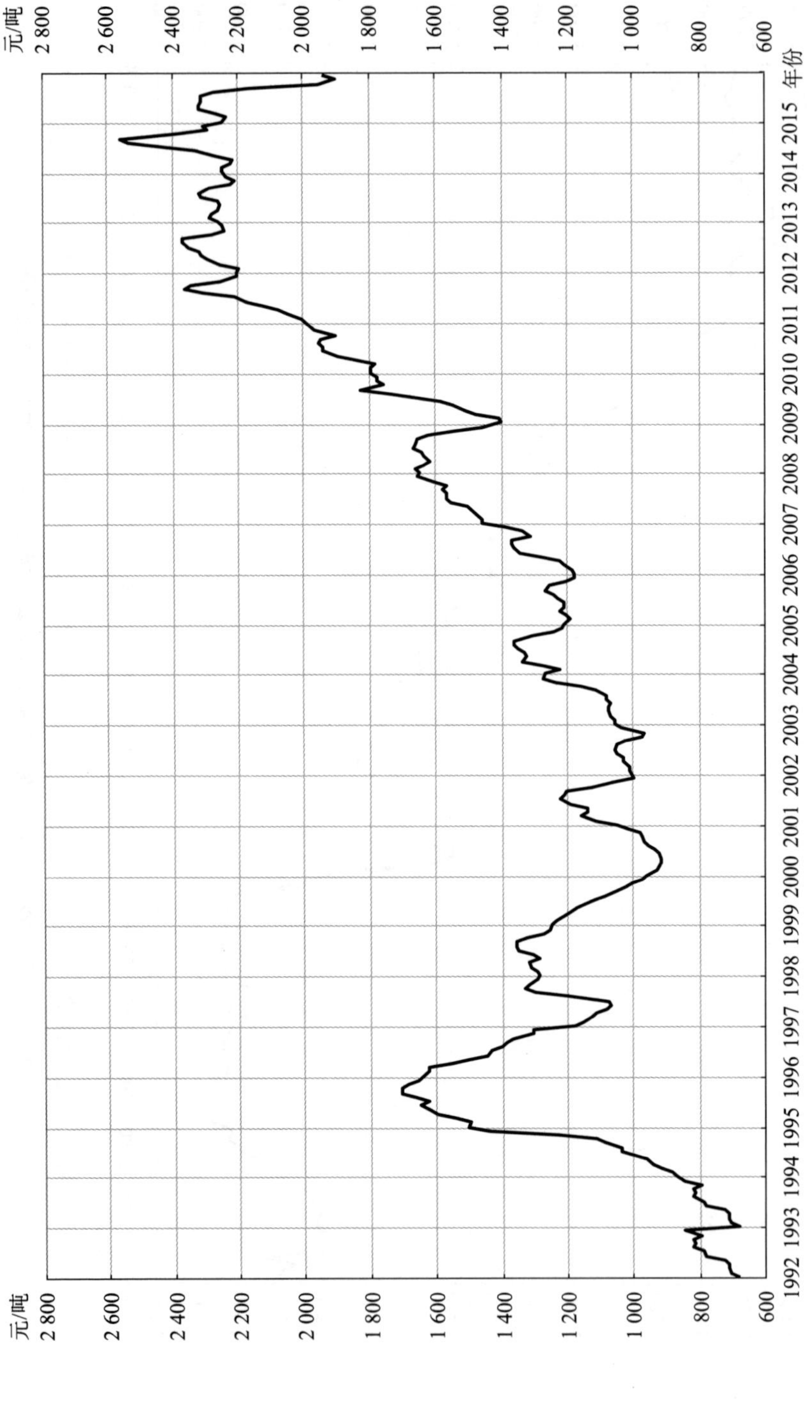


说明：价格为全国主要粮食批发市场二级玉米月平均价（当地火车板交货价）。

**图 6－4－5　1992—2015 年全国主要粮食批发市场二级玉米均价走势图**

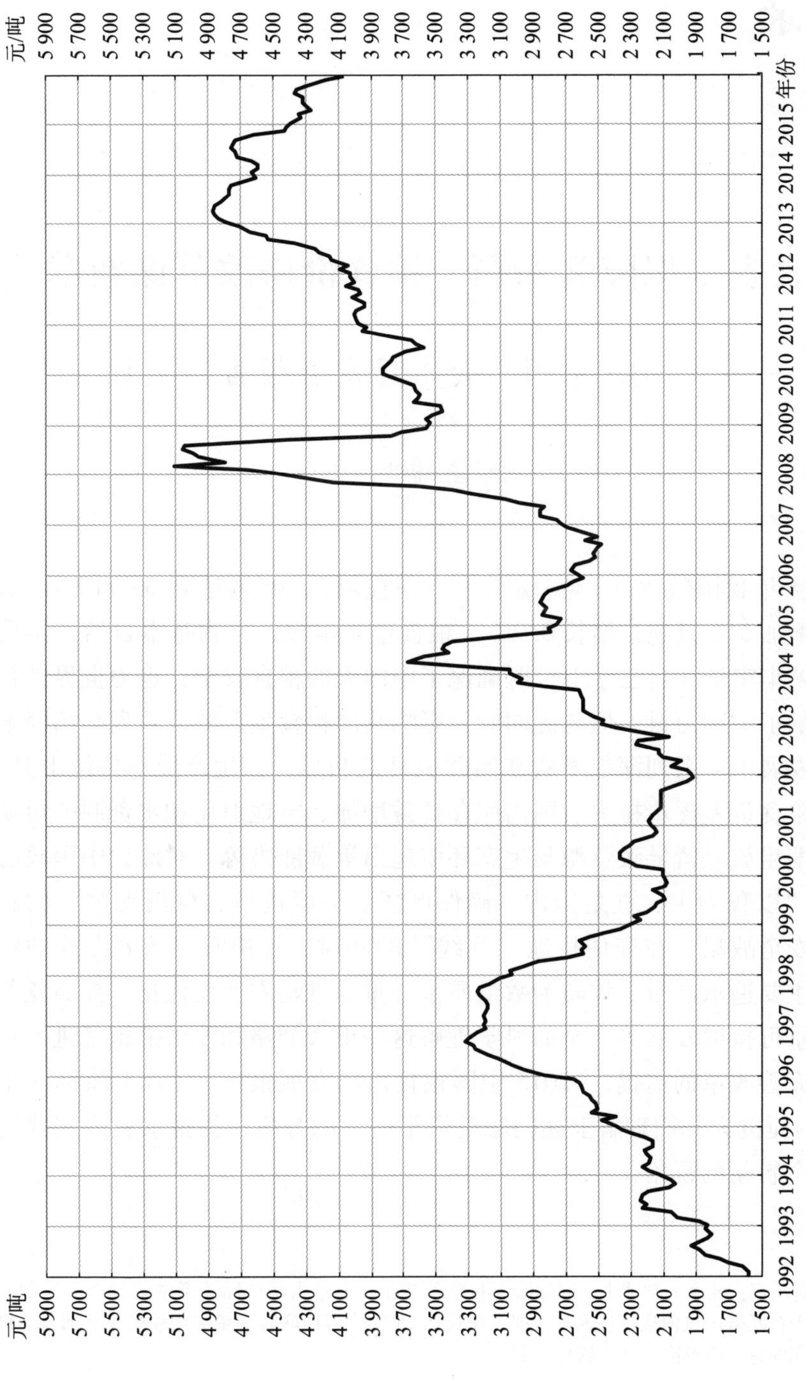


说明：价格为全国主要粮食批发市场三级大豆月平均价（当地火车板交货价）。

**图 6-4-6　1992—2015 年全国主要粮食批发市场三级大豆均价走势图**

# 附　录

## 粮食安全保障著新篇　粮食价格改革谋新章

### ——《2015 中国粮食市场发展报告》简评

何昌垂[1]

2014 年我国粮食生产实现了“十一连增”，产量达到 60 710 万吨，比上年增加 516 万吨，增长 0.9%。粮食连年丰收，谷物基本自给，实现了把饭碗牢牢端在自己手上，既确保了中国人的粮食安全，也为世界粮食安全贡献了中国力量。但与此同时，影响我国粮食生产的一系列制约因素和农业发展中一系列深层矛盾和问题也日益凸显，如生产成本持续上升、国内外粮食价差逐步拉大、国内库存日益增加、土地退化和水资源的短缺以及长期粗放经营导致资源与生态环境超出承载能力等。对此，中国政府提出了“以我为主、立足国内、确保产能、适度进口、科技支撑”的新的粮食安全战略，在守住耕地“红线”的同时，加快农业发展方式的转变，从主要追求产量尽快转为数量质量并重、推动农业现代化、提高竞争力、注重可持续发展等。全面科学理解这些重大战略和改革措施是进一步推进和完善改革的前提，《2015 中国粮食市场发展报告》（以下简称《报告》）的面世为我们理解上述问题提供了科学的分析，为推动良好实践提供了一个崭新的视角。

---

① 何昌垂：北京大学博士，国际欧亚科学院院士。北京大学国际关系学院教授（兼职）。何昌垂博士在联合国机构从事技术和管理工作长达 25 年，历任联合国粮农组织处长、司长、助理总干事和副总干事等高级技术管理职务。

第一，《报告》序言“开弓没有回头箭”紧扣时代脉搏，主题突出，言简意赅。

在《中国粮食市场发展报告》系列丛书中，由李经谋主编执笔的序言向来是点睛之笔。2015 年“开弓没有回头箭”的序言聚焦粮食目标价格改革，在鸟瞰评述了 2014 年的全球经济形势后，针对国内实施多年的粮食最低收购价政策，提醒在取得成就的同时应开始注意愈发明显的负面效应，主张改革势在必行。作者以我国对东北的大豆以及新疆的棉花陆续启动的目标价格改革近一年的实践及其预期效果为例，指出存在诸多亟需解决的问题，但基本属于操作层面的，是可以解决的，既然迈出了第一步，就应该勇敢地走下去，“开弓没有回头箭”。序言阐述了目标价格制度的基本内涵，提出再不能把粮食增产、农民增收以及粮食安全寄托在不断提高粮食价格上，并结合发达国家的目标价格政策对完善我国的目标价格改革提出了相应的对策建议，包括主张应从提高对目标价格认知度、合理确定目标价格适用的品种范围、加快农村经济体制改革、完善目标价格改革的配套政策、健全目标价格体系、将目标价格改革纳入法制轨道等方面完善我国的目标价格改革，具有较强的可操作性。作为中国现代粮食市场的奠基者之一，作者不仅对我国的托市收购政策的利弊具有深切地认知，更有为推进目标价格改革振臂高呼之势，体现了一个老粮食人的洞见力和社会责任感。

第二，撰稿团队具有较强的权威性，《报告》实用性和学术性兼蓄。

经过多年的编撰出版工作，《报告》的撰稿人队伍日益壮大，汇聚了来自政府主管部门和知名企业的管理者、大学及科研机构的知名专家学者。可以看出，他们理论素养深厚，视野广阔，长期关注国内外粮食领域动态，或直接活跃在粮食市场第一线。他们注意理论联系实际，所论所述不但基于经验，更依赖数据和数据分析，结论客观，观点深刻，政策建议明确，具有较强的学术性和实用性。

第三，《报告》结构完整，逻辑合理，内容丰富。

《报告》紧紧围绕粮食市场这一主题进行顶层设计，谋篇布局。从中国粮食市场到世界粮食状况；从主要粮食品种形势分析到粮食政策法规；从粮食批发市场、粮食期货市场到粮食电子商务市场；从粮食领域的热点、焦点问题的深度分析到各种统计资料、数据以及相关信息的详实汇总等，涵盖广泛，内容十分丰富。《报告》为人们在国际大框架下认识中国粮食市场提供了独特的视野、厚实的基底和综合的平台。

《报告》的每个部分各具特色。

第一部分，中国及世界粮食市场概述。《报告》首先对中国及世界粮食市场从总体上进行描述，世界粮食市场主要从粮食生产、消费、贸易、库存以及价格等角度对 2014 年的变化进行详尽描述和分析；中国粮食市场对 2014 年我国粮食市场新动向进行了全面梳理和总结，着重分析了临储政策变化及目标价格政策的实施、调控与市场运行、粮价变化及进口状况等。一书在手，读者可一览中国及世界粮食市场概况及最新变化。通过中国和世界粮食市场的比较，能够从宏观角度了解中国粮食市场在全球粮食市场的份额及地位。把中国的饭碗放在世界粮食安全的大盘中考量，从而对中国粮食安全问题有一个更清醒的认识，同时也便于国外读者参考比较。

第二部分，主要粮食品种分析。本部分对我国主要粮油品种的生产、消费、进出口、政策变化、2014 年行情走势以及 2015 年行情展望等作了系统分析，主要覆盖小麦、稻米、玉米、大豆及豆油、油菜籽及菜籽油、花生及花生油等品种。这些来自市场最前沿的品种分析报告，以官方正式公布的数据及作者的实地调研为依据，分析视角独到、实在，能够为政府的宏观调控、粮油企业及农民的生产经营提供决策依据。本部分的品种分析在其他类似的发展报告中较少见到，堪称本书的一大亮点。

第三部分，中国粮食市场体系发展状况。本部分对我国 2014 年粮食批发市场、粮食期货市场及粮食电子商务发展状况展开分析。从粮食批发市场看，2014 年，面对国内粮食生产“十一连增”、国内外粮价剪刀差持续拉大、大量国外低价粮食进口的新苗头及其冲击，分析了如何加强粮食宏观调控，加大对粮食批发市场建设发展的政策和资金扶持力度，充分发挥其在保供稳价方面的重要载体作用以及保障粮食市场稳定的职能。在具体业务方面，商流批发市场政策性业务放量增长，贸易粮场际间交易量稳步提高；成品粮市场积极做好粮油销售工作，交易量继续保持增长态势。各类市场在做好粮油批发主营业务的同时，大力拓展经营范围，加强市场基础设施建设，提升质量安全管理水平，市场的建设和发展都取得了可喜的成绩。从粮食期货市场看，2014 年，期货市场传导国家宏观调控成效明显，促进国家产业政策实现的导向作用日益突出，期货新业务模式已经成为助推农业产业化经营发展的利器。同时，期货市场在粮食生产、流通、贸易和需求等领域发挥着重要作用。从粮食电子商务看，2014 年，政策性粮食交易通过电子商务的方式更好地发挥了宏观调控作用，各地粮食批发市场不断创新粮食交易形式服务企业，粮食企业电子商务发展呈现百花齐放的局面，不仅金融企业依托平台满足了粮食电子商务发展需求，“科技兴农”在电子商务 C2B 模式中更是得到了初步的发展。

第四部分，政策法规分析。本部分深入诠释了大豆目标价格政策及试点运行状况、2014 年中央 1 号文件、粮食信贷政策与管理等方面的内容。令人可喜的是，本部分并没有照搬政策法规的内容，而是从政策出台背景、主要内容及实施效果等方面来进行诠释。该部分的作者均是相关部门的权威人士，有些甚至是政策的制定或实施者，他们的功力可见一斑，其分析与结论具有明显的说服力。

第五部分，专题研究。该部分对 2014 年中国粮食市场热点、焦点问题进行深度剖析。《报告》就粮食安全、目标价格改革、国际合作等公众广泛关注的问题展开专题研究，进行理论上的分析和总结，极大地增强了《报告》内容的理论性和厚重感。

第六部分，主要参考资料。主要包括近年来中国粮食市场统计数据、2014 年中国粮食市场大事记、2014 年中国粮食经济重要论著索引以及主要粮食品种的价格走势图等。该部分是全书的一个有益和必要的补充，为读者使用本书提供了诸多便利。值得一提的是，作为“郑州价格”重要组成部分的主要粮食价格走势资料，尤其是小麦价格走势图，是郑州粮食批发市场多年积累的结晶并为其所独有。

第四，《报告》的专题研究学术色彩浓厚，涌现了诸多创新性观点，是本书的另一大亮点。

2015 年《报告》围绕粮食和农业发展问题，遴选了粮食安全、目标价格改革、国际经验借鉴和国际合作、粮食价格与粮食贸易、产业发展等热点焦点问题，共 12 篇文章，分别从粮食生产、贸易、补贴、价格等方面对我国粮食市场进行了全方位的深入剖析，形成了一批极具参考价值的研究成果。

粮食安全是国家安全的一个重要组成部分，是一个永恒的主题，在国际、国内一直是社会各界的关注焦点。2015 年的专题报告聚焦我国粮食安全新战略和粮食安全保障程度。作者详细解读了粮食安全新战略的重大意义，认为粮食安全新战略有多方面新的内涵和发展。让市场的正确信号配置农业资源、决定粮食生产能力，发挥政府的宏观调控作用，是实现国家粮食安全的正确路径；适当增加粮食进口，加快农业走出去步伐，充分利用国内、国外两种资源、两个市场，是保障国家粮食安全的必由之路。关于我国粮食生产能力和粮食安全保障程度，作者认为按照国内粮食总产量与中国居民口粮和饲料粮消费量保障要求估算，2020 年，中国粮食生产能力要达到 7 亿吨。从中国目前的粮食安全保障政策及其资源条件看，届时中国将具备 7 亿吨的粮食生产能力。因此，中国的粮食安全是有保障的。不过，也应当清醒地看到中国耕地和水资源的压力和进一步提高中国粮食生产的环境生态代价。

目标价格改革是 2014 年粮食领域中的热点问题，专题报告中几位作者均对此问题进行了探讨。对于目标价格改革，作者普遍认为建立目标价格制度是农产品领域市场化改革的必然选择，具有重要的意义。经过近一年的试点，目标价格改革在完善农产品价格形成机制等方面取得了初步成效，但在改革目标选择、补贴依据确定、基础数据健全、风险化解体系等方面还面临很多难题。因此，目标价格改革必须坚持“试点先行、稳健推进、组织实施、健全法规、依法行政”。此外，还对我国建立目标价格保险问题进行了深入探讨，提出了一些值得借鉴的观点和政策建议。

关于粮食和农业发展中的国际经验借鉴和国际合作问题，作者主要分析了美国农业补贴的改革走向和日本农业发展过程中农业公司迅速崛起的新动向。通过剖析发达国家农业发展的新动向及政策走向，能够为我国的粮食及农业发展提供一些有价值的启示。在我国粮食安全新战略中，利用国际市场被提到了重要位置，国际合作问题日益受到重视。作者具体分析了亚太地区粮食安全及加强合作的问题，认为亚太地区各经济体粮食安全挑战和机遇并存，事关区域发展与稳定和平，需要各方协调合作，共同应对。

随着城市化发展，人们收入水平的提高及消费结构的改变，近年来，饲料养殖业的发展颇受关注。《报告》专门遴选了一篇中国饲料养殖业的专题报告，作者认为从中长期看，饲料行业由总量发展转向结构性升级将是未来相当长一段时期的主导趋势，差异化的发展模式将进一步分化现存的饲料企业，没有竞争优势的企业将退出市场，优势企业市场份额将得到提升。

此外，《报告》还讨论了粮食价格以及粮食贸易等问题，提出了一些有针对性的政策建议。

诚然，由于《报告》的编写是由一个多学科的团队执行，且作者背景各异、写作风格不同，所用数据来源也不相同，因此各自独立成篇汇总之后会出现文风脉络差异，甚至个别地方运用数据参考点不一致的情况。但综合来看，《2015 中国粮食市场发展报告》是一部难得的优秀著作，对于从事粮食安全的政策制定和规划者、企业管理者以及国内、国际从事粮食安全研究的人员都有极好的参考价值，值得细细品读。

# 主要参考资料

1. 聂振邦：《世界主要国家粮食概况》，中国物价出版社2003年版。

2. 国家粮食局课题组：《中国粮食批发市场发展研究报告》，经济管理出版社2004年版。

3. 李经谋：《2003中国粮食市场发展报告》，中国财政经济出版社2003年版。

4. 李经谋：《2004中国粮食市场发展报告》，中国经济出版社2004年版。

5. 李经谋：《2005中国粮食市场发展报告》，中国财政经济出版社2005年版。

6. 李经谋：《2006中国粮食市场发展报告》，中国财政经济出版社2006年版。

7. 李经谋：《2007中国粮食市场发展报告》，中国财政经济出版社2007年版。

8. 李经谋：《2008中国粮食市场发展报告》，中国财政经济出版社2008年版。

9. 李经谋：《2009中国粮食市场发展报告》，中国财政经济出版社2009年版。

10. 李经谋：《2010中国粮食市场发展报告》，中国财政经济出版社2010年版。

11. 李经谋：《2011中国粮食市场发展报告》，中国财政经济出版社2011年版。

12. 李经谋：《2012中国粮食市场发展报告》，中国财政经济出版社2012年版。

13. 李经谋：《2013 中国粮食市场发展报告》，中国财政经济出版社 2013 年版。

14. 李经谋：《2014 中国粮食市场发展报告》，中国财政经济出版社 2014 年版。

15. 李经谋：《2015 中国粮食市场发展报告》，中国财政经济出版社 2015 年版。

16. 任正晓：《农业与粮食热点问题研究》，中国经济出版社 2006 年版。

17. 邓亦武：《粮食宏观调控论》，经济管理出版社 2004 年版。

18. 黄汉权、蓝海涛：《中国粮食综合生产能力研究》，中国计划出版社 2007 年版。

19. ［美］威廉·恩道尔：《粮食危机》，知识产权出版社 2008 年版。

20. 张晓涛、王扬：《大国粮食问题：中国粮食政策演变与食品安全监管》，经济管理出版社 2009 年版。

21. ［英］拉查·帕特尔：《粮食战争》，东方出版社 2008 年版。

22. 唐风：《粮食新战争》，中国商业出版社 2008 年版。

23. 农业部课题组：《现代农业发展战略研究》，中国农业出版社 2008 年版。

24. 聂振邦：《现代粮食流通产业发展战略研究》，经济管理出版社 2008 年版。

25. 马晓河、蓝海涛：《中国粮食综合生产能力与粮食安全》，经济科学出版社 2008 年版。

26. 聂振邦：《2008 中国粮食发展报告》，经济管理出版社 2008 年版。

27. 聂振邦：《2009 中国粮食发展报告》，经济管理出版社 2009 年版。

28. 聂振邦：《2010 中国粮食发展报告》，经济管理出版社 2010 年版。

29. 聂振邦：《2011 中国粮食发展报告》，经济管理出版社 2011 年版。

30. 聂振邦：《2012 中国粮食发展报告》，经济管理出版社 2012

年版。

31. 国家粮食局：《2013中国粮食发展报告》，经济管理出版社2013年版。

32. 国家粮食局：《2014中国粮食发展报告》，经济管理出版社2014年版。

33. 国家粮食局：《2015中国粮食发展报告》，经济管理出版社2015年版。

34. 中华人民共和国农业部：《2008中国农业发展报告》，中国农业出版社2008年版。

35. 中华人民共和国农业部：《2009中国农业发展报告》，中国农业出版社2009年版。

36. 中华人民共和国农业部：《2010中国农业发展报告》，中国农业出版社2010年版。

37. 中华人民共和国农业部：《2011中国农业发展报告》，中国农业出版社2011年版。

38. 中华人民共和国农业部：《2012中国农业发展报告》，中国农业出版社2012年版。

39. 中华人民共和国农业部：《2013中国农业发展报告》，中国农业出版社2013年版。

40. 中华人民共和国农业部：《2014中国农业发展报告》，中国农业出版社2014年版。

41. 中华人民共和国农业部：《2015中国农业发展报告》，中国农业出版社2015年版。

42. 张冬平、魏仲生：《粮食安全与主产区农民增收问题》，中国农业出版社2006年版。

43. 尹成杰：《粮安天下——全球粮食危机与中国粮食安全》，中国经济出版社2009年版。

44. 刘斌、张兆刚、霍功：《中国“三农”问题报告》，中国发展出版社2004年版。

45. 丁声俊、杨振海：《粮食——新阶段及对策》，中国商业出版社2002年版。

46. 肖春阳、熊本国：《国有粮食企业改革》，经济管理出版社 2005 年版。

47. 游宏炳：《温饱之后的中国粮食安全研究》，中国言实出版社 2009 年版。

48. 柯炳生：《入世以来中国农业发展与新一轮谈判》，中国农业出版社 2005 年版。

49. 林毅夫：《制度、技术与中国农业发展》，上海人民出版社 2008 年版。

50. 郭宏宝：《中国财政农业补贴：政策效果与机制设计》，西南财经大学出版社 2009 年版。

51. 国家发展和改革委员会、国家粮食局：《全国粮食现代物流规划（征求意见稿）》，2005 年 4 月。

52. 肖国安、王文涛、朱有志、唐之享：《中国粮食安全报告：预警与风险化解》，红旗出版社 2009 年版。

53. 洪涛：《中国粮食市场化大趋势经济》，经济管理出版社 2004 年版。

54. 鲁靖：《粮食经济中的和谐——中国粮食市场与政府宏观政策的耦合》，东南大学出版社 2006 年版。

55. 何蒲明：《粮食安全与农产品期货市场发展研究》，中国农业出版社 2009 年版。

56. 蓝海涛、王为农：《中国中长期粮食安全重大问题》，中国计划出版社 2008 年版。

57. 刘颖：《基于国际粮荒背景下的中国粮食流通研究》，中国农业出版社 2008 年版。

58. 程国强：《中国农业补贴制度设计与政策选择》，中国发展出版社 2011 年版。

59. 丁声俊、王耀鹏等：《反饥饿反贫困》，中国农业出版社 2012 年版。

60. 丁声俊：《中国有能力养活中国》，中国农业出版社 2014 年版。

61. 国家统计局：历年《中国统计年鉴》，中国统计出版社出版。

62. 国家统计局农村社会经济调查总队：历年《中国农村统计年鉴》，

中国统计出版社出版。

63.《2015中国财政年鉴》，中国财政杂志社2015年版。

64.《粮油市场报》，2015年有关各期。

65.《期货日报》，2015年有关各期。

66.《中国粮食经济》，2015年有关各期。

67.《调研世界》，2015年有关各期。

68.《农业经济问题》，2015年有关各期。

69.《粮食经济研究》，2015年有关各期。

70.《中国农村经济》，2015年有关各期。

71. 中华人民共和国国家统计局：《中华人民共和国2008年国民经济和社会发展统计公报》。

72. 中华人民共和国国家统计局：《中华人民共和国2009年国民经济和社会发展统计公报》。

73. 中华人民共和国国家统计局：《中华人民共和国2010年国民经济和社会发展统计公报》。

74. 中华人民共和国国家统计局：《中华人民共和国2011年国民经济和社会发展统计公报》。

75. 中华人民共和国国家统计局：《中华人民共和国2012年国民经济和社会发展统计公报》。

76. 中华人民共和国国家统计局：《中华人民共和国2013年国民经济和社会发展统计公报》。

77. 中华人民共和国国家统计局：《中华人民共和国2014年国民经济和社会发展统计公报》。

78. 中华人民共和国国家统计局：《中华人民共和国2015年国民经济和社会发展统计公报》。

79. 新华网：《中共中央 国务院关于促进农民增加收入若干政策的意见》（2004年中央1号文件）。

80. 新华网：《中共中央 国务院关于进一步加强农村工作 提高农业综合生产能力若干政策的意见》（2005年中央1号文件）。

81. 新华网：《中共中央 国务院关于推进社会主义新农村建设的若干意见》（2006年中央1号文件）。

82. 新华网:《中共中央 国务院关于积极发展现代农业 扎实推进社会主义新农村建设的若干意见》(2007 年中央 1 号文件)。

83. 新华网:《中共中央 国务院关于切实加强农业基础建设 进一步促进农业发展农民增收的若干意见》(2008 年中央 1 号文件)。

84. 新华网:《中共中央 国务院关于促进农业稳定发展 农民持续增收的若干意见》(2009 年中央 1 号文件)。

85. 新华网:《中共中央 国务院关于加大统筹城乡发展力度 进一步夯实农业农村发展基础的若干意见》(2010 年中央 1 号文件)。

86. 新华网:《中共中央 国务院关于加快水利改革发展的决定》(2011 年中央 1 号文件)。

87. 新华网:《中共中央 国务院关于加快推进农业科技创新 持续增强农产品供给保障能力的若干意见》(2012 年中央 1 号文件)。

88. 新华网:《中共中央 国务院关于加快发展现代农业 进一步增强农村发展活力的若干意见》(2013 年中央 1 号文件)。

89. 新华网:《中共中央 国务院关于关于全面深化农村改革 加快推进农业现代化的若干意见》(2014 年中央 1 号文件)。

90. 新华网:《关于加大改革创新力度 加快农业现代化建设的若干意见》(2015 年中央 1 号文件)。

91. 新华网:《关于落实发展新理念 加快农业现代化 实现全面小康目标的若干意见》(2016 年中央 1 号文件)。

92. 新华网:《国务院关于完善粮食流通体制改革政策措施的意见》(国发[2006] 16 号)。

93. 新华网:《中共中央关于完善社会主义市场经济体制若干问题的决定》, 2003 年 10 月。

94. 新华网:《中共中央关于制定“十二五”规划的建议》, 2010 年 10 月。

95. 新华网:《中华人民共和国国民经济和社会发展第十二个五年规划纲要》, 2011 年 3 月。

96. 新华网:《中共中央关于全面深化改革若干重大问题的决定》, 2013 年 11 月。

97. 郑州粮食批发市场:《中国粮油市场月度分析报告》, 2015 年各期。

98. 郑州粮食批发市场：《2015中国粮油市场年度分析报告》，2015年1月。

99. 国家发展和改革委员会网站：http：//www. sdpc. gov. cn/。

100. 财政部网站：http：//www. mof. gov. cn/。

101. 国家粮食局网站：http：//www. chinagrain. gov. cn/。

102. 中国农业信息网：http：//www. agri. gov. cn/。

103. 国家统计局网站：http：//www. stats. gov. cn/。

104. 国土资源部网站：http：//www. mlr. gov. cn/。

105. 中国海关网站：http：//www. customs. gov. cn/。

106. 新华网：http：//www. xinhuanet. com/。

107. 中华粮网：http：//www. cngrain. com/。

# 后　记

经过编撰队伍的精心组织和紧张工作，《2016中国粮食市场发展报告》（第14卷）终于如期与广大读者见面了。在此，向多年来支持《中国粮食市场发展报告》编撰和出版工作的领导、专家、学者及社会各界人士表示由衷的感谢！

过去的2015年必将成为中国粮食史上具有纪念意义的一年。这一年，我国经济增长速度明显放缓，经济进入新常态，财政收入增速放缓，供给侧改革的思路愈发清晰；这一年，我国粮食产量“十二连增”，以玉米为代表的谷物库存和以大豆为代表的油料进口均创下历史新高，粮食产量、库存量以及进口量“三量齐增”的现象愈演愈烈，国内不同粮食品种严重过剩和短缺并存。种种现象表明，现有粮食价格形成机制和补贴制度已难以为继，新一轮粮改的倒逼机制已经形成。

2016年，中国粮食市场化改革进程料将提速。《2016中国粮食市场发展报告》延续历年《中国粮食市场发展报告》的年度性、专业性、民间性、国际性特色，邀请业内外权威专家、学者解析2015年粮食市场热点、焦点问题，力求完整地再现年度粮食市场运行情况，并对2016年粮食市场进行展望。

《2016中国粮食市场发展报告》（第14卷），按照写作内容的先后顺序，作者分别为：

第一部分：一、杨京，二、刘桂才；第二部分：一、申洪源，二、胡锋，三、冯利臣，四、刘兆福，五、陈艳军，六、张修志；第三部分：一、程国强，二、叶兴庆，三、李国祥，四、丁声俊，五、杨光焰，六、黄汉权、蓝海涛、王为农、涂圣伟、张义博、卞靖，七、韩继志，八、洪涛，九、蒋和平、詹琳，十、顾善松、车进，十一、亢霞，十二、史振厚、杨京；第四部分：一、潘文博，二、张顺喜，三、方言，四、朱远洋、李楠；第五部分：一、姚秀敏，二、陈邦华、乔林生，三、傅宏；第六部分：一、邱烈金，二、史振厚，三、杨京，四、陈艳军；附录：何昌垂。

本书在出版过程中得到了众多专家、学者及相关单位的大力支持和帮助。国家发改委经济贸易司刘小南副司长对“中国粮食市场”一节提出了修改意见，《粮油市场报》承担了该书的总纂工作，南京财经大学朱行研究员翻译了序言和目录，中国财政经济出版社刘瑞思、樊闽编审精心编校，正是由于他（她）们的鼎力相助，使得报告的质量不断提升，影响不断扩大。在此，对所有支持和帮助我们的同志致以诚挚的谢意。

编　者
2016年5月

**图书在版编目（CIP）数据**

2016中国粮食市场发展报告／李经谋主编．—北京：中国财政经济出版社，2016.5

ISBN 978-7-5095-6740-1

Ⅰ.①2…　Ⅱ.①李…　Ⅲ.①粮食市场-研究报告-中国-2016
Ⅳ.①F724.721

中国版本图书馆CIP数据核字（2016）第111581号

责任编辑：刘瑞思　　　　责任校对：刘　靖
封面设计：汪俊宇

中国财政经济出版社出版

**URL**：http：//www.cfeph.cn

E-mail：cfeph@cfeph.cn



社址：北京市海淀区阜成路甲28号　邮政编码：100142

发行处电话：88190406　财经书店电话：64033436

北京富生印刷厂印刷　各地新华书店经销

787×1092毫米　16开　24印张　356 000字

2016年5月第1版　2016年5月北京第1次印刷

定价：52.00元

ISBN 978-7-5095-6740-1/F·5422

（图书出现印装问题，本社负责调换）

本社质量投诉电话：010-88190744